A–Z OF MODERN EUROPE SINCE 1789

Students will find this a lucid and reliable source of essential information.
Patricia Clavin, Keele University

A–Z of Modern Europe since 1789 is a succinct guide to the major issues and personalities of the past 200 years of European history. It is thoroughly cross-referenced and will surely prove indispensable.
Ruth Henig, University of Lancaster

A–Z of Modern Europe since 1789 is a comprehensive historical dictionary which defines modern Europe through its important events and people. It includes entries on:

- key people from Napoleon Bonaparte to Hitler
- key political, military, diplomatic and economic events
- influential political movements and ideologies

A–Z of Modern Europe since 1789 offers accessible and concise accounts of over 400 subjects. The book is cross-referenced and thus provides associated links and connections, while the appendix contains essential extra information on European monarchies. The book also contains six helpful maps of the continent's geopolitical organisation.

A–Z of Modern Europe since 1789 is a valuable companion for school and undergraduate students of history and politics, and is a source of ready information for anyone interested in Europe's past and present. It is intended to complement *A–Z of Modern Britain* by John Plowright.

Martin Polley is a senior lecturer in history at King Alfred's College, Winchester, and author of *Moving the Goalposts: A History of Sport and Society since 1945* (Routledge, 1998).

A–Z OF MODERN EUROPE SINCE 1789

Martin Polley

London and New York

First published 2000
by Routledge
11 New Fetter Lane, London EC4P 4EE

Simultaneously published in the USA and Canada
by Routledge
29 West 35th Street, New York, NY 10001

Routledge is an imprint of the Taylor & Francis Group

Typeset in Times by Taylor & Francis Books Ltd
Printed and bound in Great Britain by Biddles Ltd,
Guildford and King's Lynn

British Library Cataloguing in Publication Data
A catalogue record for this book is available from the British Library.

Library of Congress Cataloging in Publication Data
Polley, Martin, 1965–
A–Z of modern Europe since 1789 / Martin Polley.
Includes bibliographical references and index.
1. Europe–History–1789–1900–Dictionaries.
2. Europe–History–20th century–Dictionaries.
I. Title

D299.P64 2000
940.2–dc21 00-027724

ISBN 0–415–18597–1 (hb)
ISBN 0–415–18598–X (pb)

for Victor Bennett

Contents

Maps

Acknowledgements

I am grateful to the staff of the following institutions and organisations for the help they have provided during my work on this book: Martial Rose Library, King Alfred's College, Winchester; Hampshire County Library Service; the Associated Examining Board; Edexcel; the Northern Examinations and Assessment Board; the Northern Ireland Council for the Curriculum; OCR; the Scottish Examination Board; and the Welsh Joint Education Committee. My colleagues in the School of Humanities and Heritage Studies at King Alfred's College have provided me with a supportive environment in which to work, and the students who have taken my modern European history modules have contributed to my enhanced understanding and enjoyment of this period.

Heather McCallum, Victoria Peters, and Emma DeVita provided excellent editorial guidance and support. Thanks also go to Chris Aldous for his generous technical assistance, and to Rachel Martin for her hospitality during the latter stages of the writing. Patricia Clavin of Keele University and David Grace of Beaufort Community School, Gloucester, read the manuscript and made many useful suggestions and comments, for which I am grateful. Any errors that appear in the book are my own.

Finally, thanks to Catherine and James for everything: 'It's time to hold your loved ones while the chains are loosed and the world runs wild.'

Martin Polley
Winchester
November 1999

Introduction

This book is designed to provide you with accessible reference information on the major issues and personalities in continental European political history since the French Revolution. It also covers military history and, as appropriate, social and economic issues. As such, it aims to provide you with basic factual coverage of the most significant themes and events covered by its timespan and geographical remit, which excludes the British Isles: these will be covered by another book in Routledge's *A–Z* series.

Norman Davies began his monumental *Europe: A History* with the folowing words: 'History can be written at any magnification. One can write the history of the universe on a single page, or the life-cycle of the mayfly in forty volumes. The history of Europe, too, can be written at any degree of magnification' (Davies 1996: 1). Remember this when using this book: to cover the French Revolution in under 1,000 words, or Hitler in under 500, has involved a very narrow focus, and selections have been made. However, if you use this quick reference guide in conjunction with textbooks and monographs, it will provide you with a good introduction to each individual subject; while cross-references, indicated by small caps, will allow you to build on the information given in each entry. An appendix provides details of the major European monarchies of the period.

Looking back over two centuries of European history from the late twentieth century, there are two important points about perspective that you should keep in mind when using this book.

The first point is that apparent certainties implicit in our idea of the nation state are far from stable. We need to remember that 'Germany' emerged only in the 1860s and 1870s; that the former Soviet republics, such as Belarus and Ukraine, have regained independence only in the 1990s. This phenomenon is nowhere better illustrated than in international sport, where the range of entries to the Olympic Games or football's European Championships through history show the fluctuating existences of nations as units. Try to remember this aspect of geopolitical organisation when using this book, as it can keep you from treating 'Italy' or 'Russia', for example, anachronistically as single units over time.

The second point to appreciate is historiographical. The end of the Cold War has helped historians to appreciate a variety of new perspectives on the past. Some of these are very obvious: having witnessed the collapse of communism in the USSR, we now have a different view of the Russian Revolution and all that came after it than our predecessors enjoyed; while having access to previously restricted primary sources, we now know more than they did about a whole range of issues, such as Stalinism and the Final Solution. Beyond this important development, our late twentieth-century perspective, influenced by the end of the Cold War and the growth of both federalism and regionalism, can give us a greater appreciation of the diversity of events that can be hidden under inherited and orthodox titles. The best example of this as it relates to this book is, perhaps, the Russian Civil War, which we are now far more likely to see as more imperial and international than the purely domestic traditional title would suggest. For this reason I have used the phrase 'umbrella term' in some of the entries. By keeping an open mind on how we name events, we can also gain a greater understanding of how some of the titles we use uncritically were invented by historians. The two most obvious examples of this phenomenon from this book are the First International and the First World War: but many others exist. When using the convenient labels that we have inherited, and which I have used here because of their familiarity, make sure you think about how those labels came to be applied.

Note on names

For ease of use, I have employed the following conventions for individuals' names: modern European forms for non-royals; and English forms for monarchs (for example, Francis Joseph rather than Franz Joseph; Catherine II rather than Ekaterina II). Where an individual is best known under one name, but has used another name for a significant part of their career, I have entered them under their best known name, but included a name-only entry under the other name: for example, Kemal Atatürk's entry is under that name in 'A', but readers searching 'M' for Mustafa Kemal will find a name-only entry there which will refer them to the Atatürk entry. Where an individual changed their name early on in their career, and was widely known under an adopted or assumed name, then there is no separate entry: so, for example, there is no 'Ulyanov' entry for Lenin, or 'Frahm' entry for Willy Brandt. However, in these cases the individual's name at birth has been included in parentheses as part of the entry heading: for example: **Brandt, Willy** (Karl Frahm). For place names, I have generally applied those in common use at the time of the events under discussion (for example, Laibach not Ljubljana in the entry on the Congress of Laibach; and Stalingrad not Volgograd for the entry on the battle of Stalingrad). Such usage does not reflect any personal views on political and ideological debates over the naming of places.

Further reading

This book is introductory, and you need to use it alongside more detailed books. It would take another book of the same size to provide even an introductory bibliography that covered all of the countries and issues included here. As this is beyond my remit, I recommend the following texts, and encourage you to follow up your reading on specific topics by using these books' bibliographies and notes. Some of them cover more than just the post-1789 period, some cover less; but together, they will provide you with a thorough overview.

Blanning, T. C. W. (ed.) (1996) *The Oxford Illustrated History of Modern Europe*, Oxford: Oxford University Press.

Briggs, Asa and Clavin, Patricia (1997) *Modern Europe 1789–1989*, Harlow: Longman.

Davies, Norman (1996) *Europe: A History*, Oxford: Oxford University Press.

Gildea, Robert (1987) *Barricades and Borders: Europe 1800–1914*, Oxford: Oxford University Press.

Hayes, Paul (ed.) (1992) *Themes in Modern European History, 1890–1945*, London: Routledge.

Laqueur, Walter (1992) *Europe in Our Time: A History 1945–1992*, Harmondsworth: Penguin.

Lee, Stephen (1982) *Aspects of European History 1789–1980*, London: Routledge.

Pilbeam, Pamela (ed.) (1995) *Themes in Modern European History, 1780–1830*, London: Routledge.

Thomson, David (1966) *Europe since Napoleon*, revised edn, Harmondsworth: Penguin.

Waller, Bruce (ed.) (1990) *Themes in Modern European History, 1830–1890*, London: Routledge.

It is also essential for you to use this book in conjunction with a historical atlas so you can follow the territorial changes covered. I recommend the following, both of which cover far more than continental Europe since the French Revolution, and thus put the period's shifts in wider contexts:

Boyd, Andrew (1998) *An Atlas of World Affairs*, 10th edn, London: Routledge.

The Times Atlas of European History, 2nd edn, London: Times Books (1998).

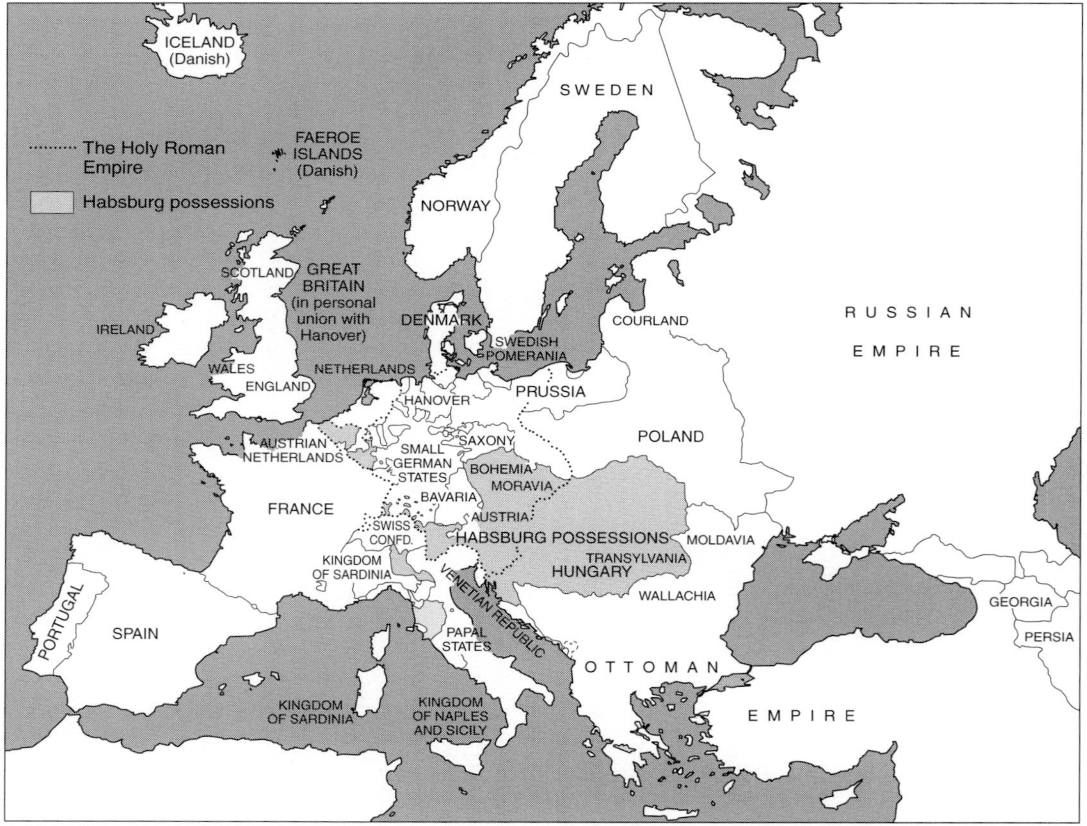

Map 1 Europe in 1789
Source: *The Times Atlas of European History*, London: Times Books, 1998

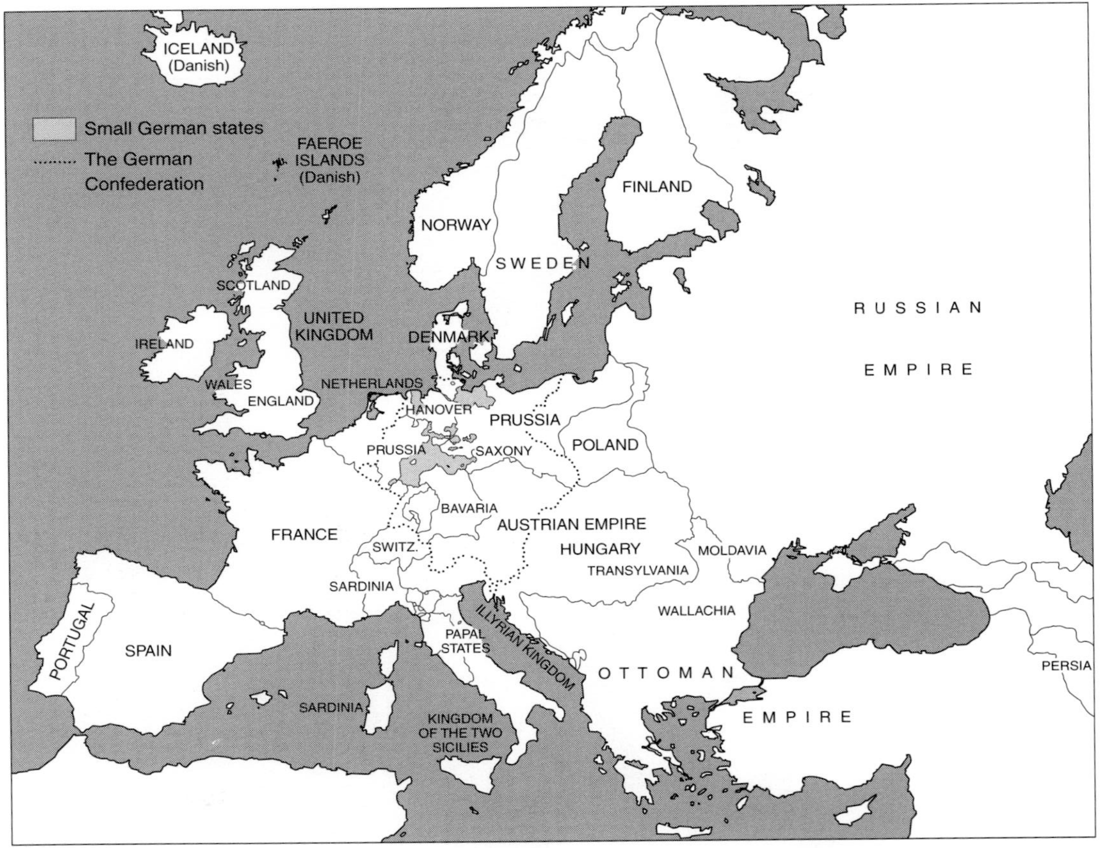

Map 2 Europe in 1815
Source: *The Times Atlas of European History*, London: Times Books, 1998

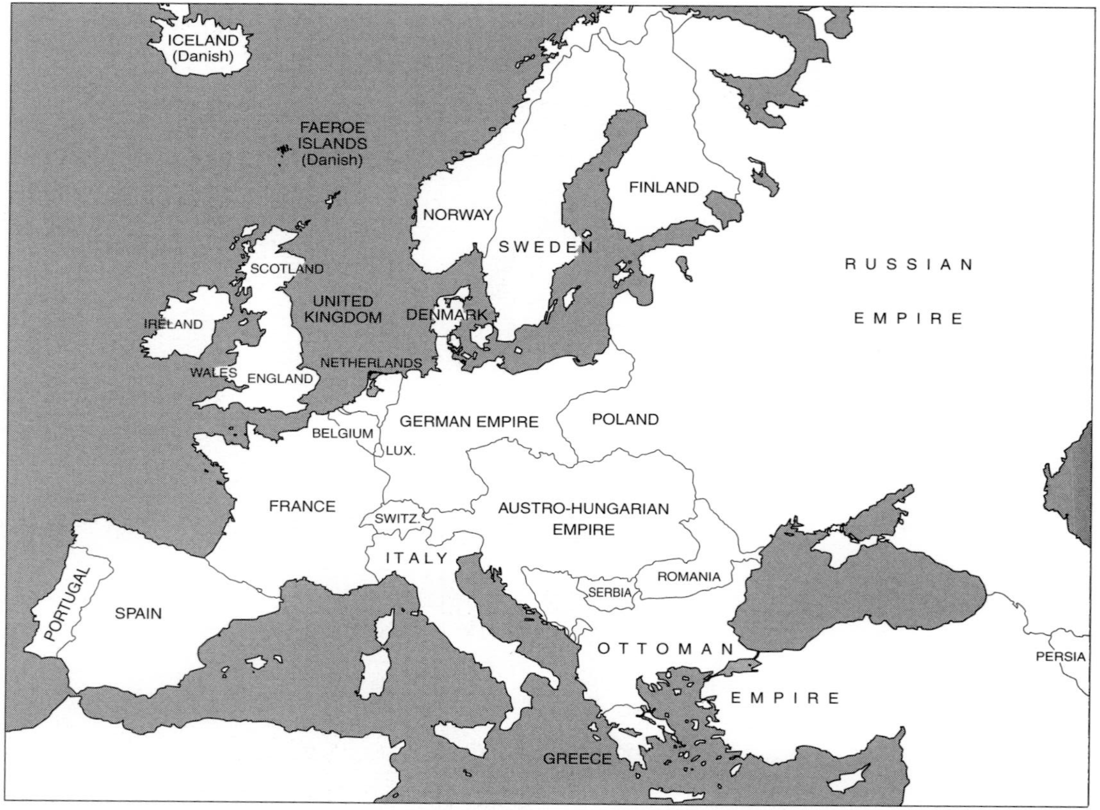

Map 3 Europe in 1871
Source: *The Times Atlas of European History*, London: Times Books, 1998

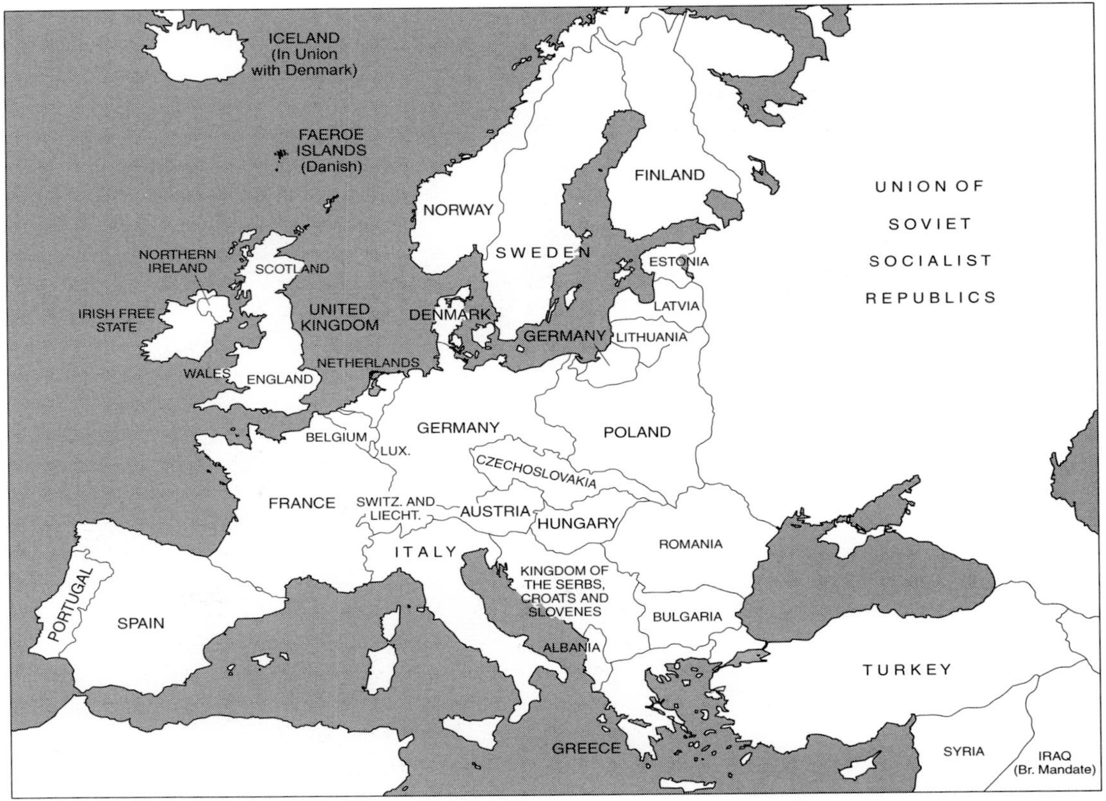

Map 4 Europe in 1925
Source: *The Times Atlas of European History*, London: Times Books, 1998

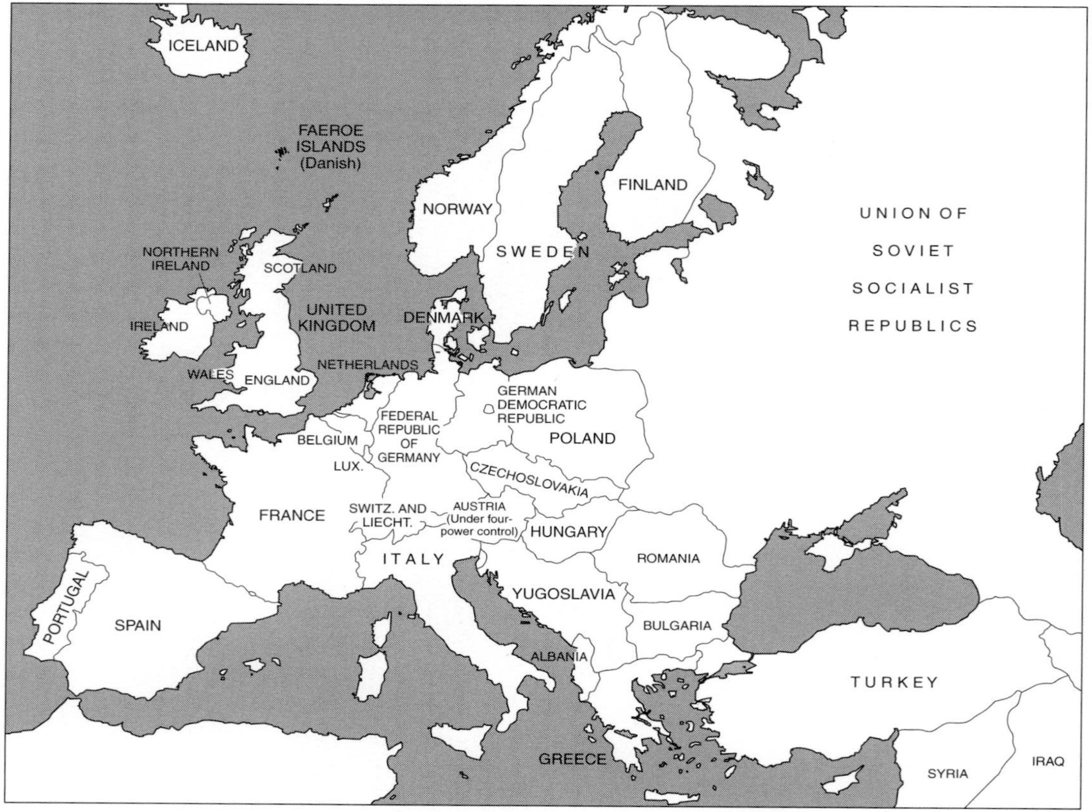

Map 5 Europe in 1949
Source: *The Times Atlas of European History*, London: Times Books, 1998

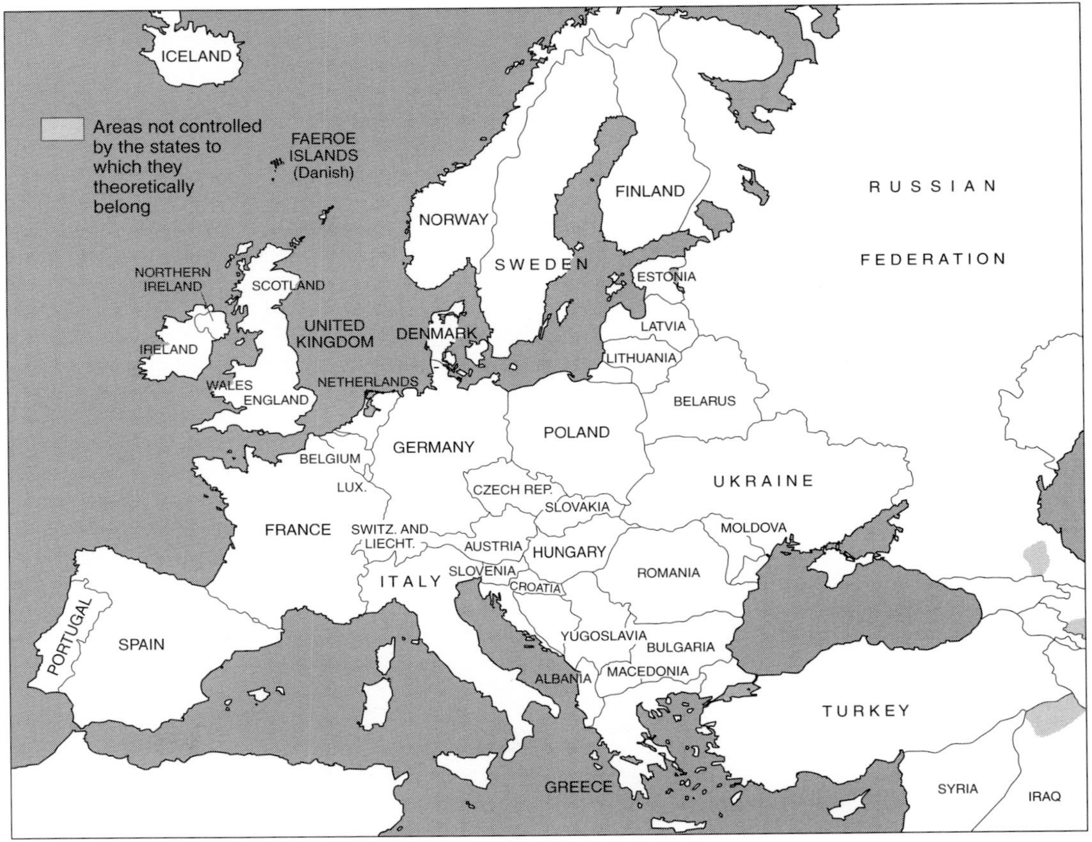

Map 6 Europe in 1997
Source: *The Times Atlas of European History*, London: Times Books, 1998

A

Abyssinian War *see* ITALO-ABYSSINIAN WAR.

Acerbo law Italian electoral law, passed in 1923. Under the law, any party gaining one quarter of the vote, and more votes than any of its rivals, would automatically receive two thirds of the seats in the Assembly. While it was presented by MUSSOLINI as a way of halting the series of weak coalition governments, and was supported by the Liberals on those terms, the law helped to strengthen the Fascist government in its early stages. *See also* FASCISM.

Action Française French political movement. *Action Française* was founded by the poet and journalist Charles Maurras in 1899 in the wake of the DREYFUS AFFAIR as an anti-republican and anti-semitic (*see* ANTI-SEMITISM) movement which promoted NATIONALISM, militarism, and a restoration of the monarchy. From 1908, Maurras edited *L'Action Française* as a daily newspaper. The movement had some middle-class appeal, but was never populist and never gained much influence in parliament. In the inter-war period, it moved close to FASCISM, and it was proscribed in 1936, although the newspaper continued publication. The movement re-emerged during the SECOND WORLD WAR, giving its support to the VICHY government and promoting collaboration with the German occupation. The movement and its newspaper were banned in 1944 after the allied victory in France (*see* NORMANDY CAMPAIGN), and Maurras was given a life term of imprisonment.

Adenauer, Konrad (1876–1967) German politician. A lawyer from Cologne, Adenauer first rose to prominence as the city's Centre party mayor in 1917. He achieved higher office in 1920 when he became President of the Prussian State Council. He lost both positions in 1933 when the Nazis removed him, and was imprisoned twice during the THIRD REICH. He re-entered politics after the SECOND WORLD WAR with US backing, and helped to form a new party, the Christian Democratic Union (CDU). He was influential in the framing of the Basic Law in 1948, and was elected as the first Chancellor of the Federal Republic of Germany (FRG) in 1949, a position he retained in elections in 1953, 1957, and 1961. From 1951 to 1955, he also served as Foreign Minister. Adenauer played a significant role in the FRG's rehabilitation after 1945: his achievements here included the promotion of Franco-German relations, the entry of the FRG to NATO in 1955 and to the EUROPEAN ECONOMIC COMMUNITY in 1957, and the 1952 Restitution Agreement with Israel. *See* FINAL SOLUTION.

Adrianople, treaty of (September 1829) Peace treaty between Russia and the OTTOMAN EMPIRE that ended the conflict that had started in 1828 as part of the GREEK WAR OF INDEPENDENCE. The treaty established Greece as an autonomous state; Russia gained navigation rights to the Black Sea Straits; Moldavia and Wallachia were established as autonomous states under Russian protection; and the Ottoman empire ceded territories in Armenia, Georgia, and on the Danube to Russia.

Aix-la-Chappelle, Congress of (September–November 1818) First of the post-1815 meetings under the CONGRESS SYSTEM. The Congress was called to deal primarily with France and wind up the work of the conference of ambassadors which had managed the occupation (*see* PARIS, TREATY OF 1815). The Congress agreed to end the occupation in November 1818, as the French government had repaid the indemnity set at Paris, and France was duly admitted to the Congress System on an equal footing to the QUADRUPLE ALLIANCE powers, thereby creating the Quintuple Alliance. In addition, ALEXANDER I proposed the formation of a common army, and called for the Alliance to give military support to any monarch facing a revolution: he was mainly thinking of the Spanish colonial revolts, but was also attempting to set the Alliance up as a conservative enforcer. These moves were resisted by Viscount Castlereagh, the UK's representative, and by METTERNICH. Aix-la-Chappelle also saw the secret renewal of the Quadruple Alliance on its original lines as a defender of the treaty of Paris of 1815.

Alexander I (1777–1825) ROMANOV Tsar of Russia, 1801–25. Alexander I succeeded his murdered father, Paul, in 1801. Having had a relatively liberal education, he began his reign with the promise of some significant reforms: and, under the influence of his adviser Count Speranski, he introduced some limited modernisation to Russian society and politics. This included the establishment of state schools and some new universities, some initiatives for local and regional representation, and the limitation of both censorship and torture. However, the impact of these changes was limited, and in the latter part of his reign he became far more repressive. This reaction was seen most clearly with the establishment of the military colonies. Alexander's foreign policy involved a number of territorial gains, including Finland, Bessarabia and parts of the Caucasus, and he was a leading figure in the diplomatic and military aspects of the NAPOLEONIC WARS and their aftermath in the CONGRESS SYSTEM, and in the HOLY ALLIANCE with Prussia and Austria from 1815. His death in 1825 gave rise to a succession crisis, and provided the opportunity for some Russian liberals to stage the DECEMBRIST CONSPIRACY. He was succeeded by his brother, NICHOLAS I.

Alexander II (1818–81) ROMANOV Tsar of Russia, 1855–81. Alexander II succeeded his father NICHOLAS I during the CRIMEAN WAR. His reputation as a reforming monarch was earned through his attempts to modernise Russian politics and society after this military defeat. In the 1860s and 1870s, he oversaw a number of reforms, including, most famously, the limited EMANCIPATION OF THE SERFS in 1861. Other steps included reform of central and local government, the establishment of a legal code, expansion of the education system, the introduction of conscription, and the encouragement of industrialisation. Liberal reforms were also introduced in Finland and the Kingdom of Poland, although the POLISH REVOLUTION of 1863 led to a more repressive rule (*see also* IMPERIALISM). Russia's main foreign successes under Alexander II were in central Asia and in the Balkans, including a number of moves designed to increase the Russian empire and its influence, and to reduce the influence of Turkey (*see* RUSSO-TURKISH WAR). In this process, PANSLAVISM played a part. The later years of his reign saw a number of tensions emerge as Russia's new industrial cities grew rapidly and the emancipation of the serfs created problems in the agricultural economy. In this context, a number of oppositional movements grew on the left and the right, and Alexander followed a more repressive line. This began to change in 1880 as a way of diluting the opposition, and by early 1881 he accepted the idea of a constitution. However, he was assassinated by members of the People's Will, a populist group, before this could be followed through (*see* POPULISM). He was succeeded by his son, ALEXANDER III.

Alexander III (1845–94) ROMANOV Tsar of Russia, 1881–94. Alexander III succeeded his assassinated father ALEXANDER II, and much of his reign was characterised by a reaction to the limited LIBERALISM that his father had overseen. Influenced by conservative advisers, he immediately introduced a range of repressive measures designed to limit the opportunities for oppositional views to be discussed. These included greater censorship, state control of the universities, and increased police powers. He also reduced the rights of the non-Russian nationalities within the empire through Russification policies in language, law and administration, and promoted ANTI-SEMITISM (*see also* IMPERIALISM). His economic policies encouraged industrialisation and urban growth but failed to prevent agricultural decline, despite some efforts to improve peasants' income through reducing the redemption repayments established by his father's EMANCIPATION OF THE SERFS. This broadly repressive regime provided the context for the growth of a significant underground opposition, which became more evident during his son NICHOLAS II's reign from 1894 to 1917 (*see* RUSSIAN REVOLUTION 1905, RUSSIAN REVOLUTIONS 1917). Under Alexander, and in response to changes in German policy, Russia moved closer to France, culminating in the formation of the FRANCO-RUSSIAN ALLIANCE in 1894 for mutual support in case of war with Germany. He was succeeded by his son, NICHOLAS II.

Alfonso XIII (1886–1941) King of Spain, 1886–1931. Alfonso XIII succeeded his father Alfonso XII posthumously, with his mother, Archduchess Maria Cristina, ruling as regent until 1902. He was unable to maintain the role of constitutional monarch established by his father, preferring instead to by-pass parliament and work by intrigue with military figures. His reign saw frequent expressions of discontent, particularly over Spanish IMPERIALISM, and he survived five assassination attempts. He was implicated in the military coup of 1923 that brought PRIMO DE RIVERA to power, and he worked with the dictator until the latter's resignation in 1930. Alfonso XIII left Spain in 1931 after republican victories in local elections, but refused to abdicate. His departure heralded the establishment of the Second Republic. He lived in exile in Italy, and carried on working with monarchist politicians and soldiers throughout the 1930s. However, he was not called back to Spain when the Republic was defeated by nationalist rebels in the SPANISH CIVIL WAR. He abdicated in favour of his son, Don Juan, in 1940, and died in Rome the following year.

Alma, battle of (September 1854) *see* CRIMEAN WAR.

Altenkirchen, battle of (September 1796) *see* FRENCH REVOLUTIONARY WARS.

Amiens, treaty of (March 1802) Peace treaty between France and the UK during the NAPOLEONIC WARS. The treaty brought peace between the two countries, following on from the withdrawal of Russia from the Coalition and the French defeat of Austria (*see* treaty of LUNÉVILLE). By the treaty, the UK was allowed to keep its colonial acquisitions of Ceylon and Trinidad, but returned other colonies to France, the Netherlands, and Spain (*see also* IMPERIALISM). France withdrew its forces from the Papal States and Naples, and returned territory to Portugal and Turkey, while the Ionian islands were established as a republic and Malta was returned to the Knights of St John. The treaty thus settled a number of territorial issues that had been contested by the British and the French during the latter stages of the FRENCH REVOLUTIONARY WARS as well as the early stages of the Napoleonic Wars, although it was seen by both sides as a temporary respite from fighting rather than a solution. The treaty collapsed in 1803.

anarchism Umbrella term for a number of strands of political ideology which share common ground in the notion that government and authority are undesirable, and obstruct human development. The concept developed during the seventeenth century as a way of describing the belief that people could live well without leaders, but became more focused on some of the ideas of individual liberty that were disseminated during and after the FRENCH REVOLUTION. From the mid-nineteenth century, anarchism developed into various forms. One form, based on the idea that people could organise on small, local scales, without any need for authority, was developed in France by PROUDHON: this shared some features with LIBERALISM, and later fed into SYNDICALISM. Another form had more in common with COMMUNISM and SOCIALISM, developed in the Russian tradition by BAKUNIN. It was marginalised by mainstream communist thought after Bakunin split with MARX and the FIRST INTERNATIONAL in 1872 over the role of political parties. The Russian tradition was also focused on the more utopian ideas of Peter Kropotkin and Lev Tolstoy. From the 1870s, a number of revolutionary organisations committed to political violence represented another form of anarchism: and the publicity created by high-profile anarchist assassinations, such as those of President Sadi Carnot of France in 1894, and King Umberto of Italy in 1900, forged a popular link between anarchism and terrorism. Anarchists in France, Italy and Spain developed the most formal identities, particularly around the time of the FIRST WORLD WAR and its aftermath, with trade union links adding to their significance. In Spain, anarchists joined one of the coalition governments of the SPANISH CIVIL WAR period. However, the USSR's hard line against deviation ensured that the anarchist tradition became marginalised on the left. On the right, anarchism has shared some common ground with CONSERVATISM, particularly on the issue of individual liberty, although mainstream European conservatism has rejected this. Anarchism enjoyed something of a revival in some radical student and intellectual circles in the 1960s and 1970s, with some violent revolutionary groups, such as the Red Army Faction, basing their terrorist activities on anarchist ideas.

Andrássy, Julius (1823–90) Hungarian and Austro-Hungarian politician. A trained lawyer, Andrássy was elected to the Hungarian Diet in 1847, where he supported KOSSUTH and the Hungarian nationalist movement in the 1848 revolution (*see* REVOLUTIONS OF 1848). After the revolution's failure, he lived in exile, and was condemned to death in his absence. He returned to Hungary after an amnesty in 1857, and re-entered politics. He was influential in the establishment of the *Ausgleich* of 1867, and was appointed as the first Hungarian Prime Minister that year, a post he held until 1871. Through this post, and through his role as Foreign Minister for Austria-Hungary from 1871 until 1879, he consistently worked for the promotion of Hungarian influence and identity, and for the limitation of Russian influence in the Balkans (*see* PANSLAVISM). He played a leading role at the BERLIN CONGRESS in 1878, helping to secure Bosnia-Herzogovina from Russia, and helped to establish the DUAL ALLIANCE with Germany in 1879 on grounds favourable to Austria-Hungary. He resigned in 1879.

Andropov, Yuri (1914–84) Soviet politician. Andropov joined the Communist party in 1939, and fought as a partisan in the SECOND WORLD WAR (*see also* RESISTANCE). He advanced within the party after the war, gaining his first major role in 1957 when KHRUSHCHEV appointed him Soviet Ambassador to Hungary, a position he held until 1962. Here, and in his role of coordinating the USSR's relations with other communist countries, he helped to enforce Soviet centrality (*see also* COLD WAR, IMPERIALISM). He headed the KGB from 1967 until 1982. On BREZHNEV's death in 1982, Andropov became effective ruler of the USSR, his position confirmed in 1983 with his appointment as Chairman of the Supreme Soviet. During his brief time in office, he began to address the inefficiencies that were becoming apparent in the USSR's polity and economy, although he died in office before achieving much. This process was taken up more fully by GORBACHEV.

Anglo-German Naval Agreement (June 1935) Bilateral agreement between Germany and the UK on the relative sizes of their naval forces. Germany was allowed to develop a navy 35 per cent the size of the Royal Navy, and to have parity in its submarine fleet. The agreement effectively recognised the redundancy of the relevant arms limitation clauses of the treaty of VERSAILLES, and caused a rift in the STRESA FRONT. For Germany, the agreement was negotiated through the RIBBENTROP Bureau rather than the Foreign Office, and was thus an example of the Nazi government's practice of by-passing official state channels.

Anglo-Russian Entente *see* TRIPLE ENTENTE.

Anschluss (German: 'union') The idea and practice of political union between Austria and Germany. With its roots in the common language and some shared history, the mid-nineteenth century idea of an *Anschluss* for a 'greater Germany' became viable when the HABSBURG empire collapsed in 1918, at the end of the FIRST WORLD WAR. However, such a union was specifically barred by the treaties of VERSAILLES and ST GERMAIN. It remained an attractive option to many Austrians and Germans in the following years, and was one of the Nazi party's declared aims (*see* NAZISM). In 1931, the two countries' governments tried unsuccessfully to establish a customs union: this was blocked by opposition from France and the LITTLE ENTENTE. In 1934, the German government attempted to achieve a union through an Austrian Nazi coup in Vienna. This failed, despite the murder of the Austrian Chancellor DOLLFUSS, when the Italian government threatened to intervene on Austria's behalf. In 1937, MUSSOLINI changed his anti-*Anschluss* policy: and the following year, Germany successfully managed the *Anschluss.* After pressure from Berlin to admit Nazis to his government, Chancellor Kurt von Schuschnigg resigned, and Arthur Seyss-Inquart, the Austrian Nazi leader, duly invited the Germans into Austria to maintain order. This peaceful invasion took place in March 1938: and while the subsequent plebiscite results of 99.75 per cent in favour of *Anschluss* were dubious, the union was welcomed by many Austrians. It provided Germany with economic, manpower, and strategic advantages, weakened Czechoslovakia, and effectively destroyed the LITTLE ENTENTE. *See also* APPEASEMENT.

Anti-Comintern Pact *see* AXIS.

anti-semitism Racial and political ideology based on antipathy towards Jews. Jews had historically been persecuted and discriminated against in most European countries with Christian establishments before the nineteenth century, a tradition justified variously on religious, cultural and economic grounds. In the late nineteenth century, influenced by NATIONALISM and by developments in science (especially those on evolution associated with Darwin), more rationalised forms of anti-semitism emerged, particularly in France, Germany and Russia. Under this, Jews were defined in predominantly racial terms – that is, 'blood' rather than culture or religion was seen as their defining characteristic – and were accused of diluting and corrupting non-Jewish races. The emergence of these ideas was strongly linked both to economic depression, in which the Jews were blamed as scapegoats, and to the growing belief after ITALIAN UNIFICATION and GERMAN UNIFICATION that the nation state was the ideal form of political organisation: as there was no Jewish nation state, Jews were easy to characterise as alien.

Under such influences, anti-semitism was influential in many parts of Europe in the late nineteenth century. In the Russian empire, for example, officially backed pogroms against Jewish communities killed thousands and forced millions to migrate. In France, the DREYFUS AFFAIR demonstrated that many in the political, military, and religious establishments had anti-semitic beliefs; while predominantly anti-semitic organisations were active throughout the HABSBURG empire and in Germany. ZIONISM emerged as a reaction to this development. There was a striking revival of anti-semitism in Germany after the FIRST WORLD WAR, when older traditions of scapegoating in a time of crisis were merged with allegedly scientific views in a number of political parties' agendas, particularly that of NAZISM. Anti-semitism became a key feature of the THIRD REICH, involving legislative persecution (*see* NUREMBERG LAWS), economic sanctions, and, during the FINAL SOLUTION, mass murder; while in some of the areas occupied by Germany, notably Poland, Lithuania and France, local traditions of anti-semitism were evident in native collaboration. Anti-semitism as government policy survived the SECOND WORLD WAR in the USSR, where discrimination was consistently evident from the early 1950s onwards, although elsewhere it became essentially a fringe ideology. However, its attraction to the neo-nazi and fascist organisations that emerged in many countries from the 1970s onwards, in which it became blended with a wider racism against colonial migrants, gave it a higher profile.

anti-socialist laws (1878) German legislation designed to limit socialist politics. BISMARCK's antipathy towards SOCIALISM was exacerbated by the formation in 1875 of the Social Democratic party (SPD) in Germany. On similar lines to the *Kulturkampf*, which was based in part on the notion that Catholics could not be loyal both to Germany and the church, the government denounced socialism for its internationalist tendencies. In 1877, the SPD gained twelve seats in the parliamentary election. In this context, Bismarck attempted to link an assassination attempt on WILLIAM I with the socialists by using the moment to introduce anti-socialist legislation in May 1878. This failed due to the lack of liberal support: but after a second assassination attempt, Bismarck reacted by dissolving the parliament and calling for new elections. The SPD still won nine seats, but with a decline in liberal support the new law against socialist groups came into force in October 1878. The Exceptional Law banned socialist meetings, publications, and fund-raising, proscribed socialist trade unions, and created new police powers for the deportation of suspected socialists, but it did not affect socialists' electoral rights. Despite the state's subsequent promotion of conservative welfarism from 1881, seen, for example, in the introduction of medical and accident insurance for workers and their families, socialism did not die out in Germany: and when parliament allowed the law to lapse in 1890, the SPD re-emerged as a significant party.

Antonescu, Ion (1882–1946) Romanian soldier and politician. Antonescu served in the FIRST WORLD WAR, and remained in the army afterwards, serving as Military Attaché to Rome and London, and as Chief of Staff from 1934. He was strongly associated with the IRON GUARD, and was briefly imprisoned in 1938 for his activities. However, he was quickly rehabilitated on release, and served as CAROL II's Minister of War from 1938. In 1940, Carol appointed Antonescu as Prime Minister with dictatorial powers, a position he used as the base for a full military dictatorship under the title of *Conducator*. A pro-Nazi, he took Romania into the war against the USSR in 1941 (*see* BARBAROSSA, SECOND WORLD WAR). As the war turned against Germany, Antonescu's position became difficult, and he was deposed by Michael I in 1944 as the Red Army invaded Romania and the new government changed sides. Antonescu was tried for war crimes, and executed in 1946.

Anzio landings (January 1944) *see* ITALIAN CAMPAIGN.

appeasement Label used to describe the policies of the French and British governments towards Germany, Italy and Japan in the 1930s, although its basic principles were established in international relations after the FIRST WORLD WAR. Based on the notion that disputes could be settled by negotiation and compromise rather than war, appeasement came to be discredited when the SECOND WORLD WAR broke out. Although the British and French governments of the inter-war period had different interests and agendas in relation to continental Europe, there was significant feeling in both countries that the settlements arising out of the PARIS PEACE CONFERENCE may have created new problems (particularly territorial) that should be settled peacefully. Moreover, the costs of rearming in readiness for future conflicts, the problems posed by imperial commitments (*see* IMPERIALISM), and popular anti-war feelings after 1918, added to the view that negotiation could be preferable to conflict. This view can also be seen in some of the key assumptions underpinning the LEAGUE OF NATIONS.

In relation to Italy, appeasement was seen most clearly in 1935 when France and the UK failed to oppose Italy's invasion of Abyssinia (*see* ITALO-ABYSSINIAN WAR), and when Italian involvement in the SPANISH CIVIL WAR was not resisted or punished. In relation to Germany (*see* THIRD REICH), in which revision of the treaty of VERSAILLES was a key feature of NAZISM, appeasement was evident in the 1935 ANGLO-GERMAN NAVAL AGREEMENT, by acceptance of rearmament beyond the Versailles limits, and, in 1936, by France and the UK's acceptance of the remilitarisation of the RHINELAND. From this stage, rearmament and strategic planning in both France and the UK suggest that appeasement could be seen as a time-buying policy until Germany could be met militarily. Major acts of appeasement that followed this included the lack of opposition to the 1938 *ANSCHLUSS*, and the negotiated settlement of the Sudeten crisis in the MUNICH AGREEMENT of 1938. From March 1939, when Germany invaded the rest of Czechoslovakia, French and British policy shifted more obviously away from appeasement, with both governments guaranteeing Poland: although even after the German invasion of Poland in September 1939, the British government sought a negotiated settlement before declaring war.

The apparent failure of appeasement in this period, for which it is frequently presented in purely negative terms as a policy of weakness, informed some aspects of international relations in the post-SECOND WORLD WAR period.

Aragon offensive (February 1939) *see* SPANISH CIVIL WAR.

Arcola, battle of (November 1796) *see* FRENCH REVOLUTIONARY WARS.

Ardennes campaign (December 1944) *see* NORTH-WEST EUROPE CAMPAIGN; SECOND WORLD WAR.

Arnhem, battle of (September 1944) *see* NORTH-WEST EUROPE CAMPAIGN.

Asiago, battle of (June 1916) *see* FIRST WORLD WAR.

Atatürk, Kemal (Mustafa Kemal) (1881–1938) Turkish soldier and politician. Kemal was involved in the YOUNG TURKS' rebellion of 1908, and served in the OTTOMAN EMPIRE's army in the ITALO-TURKISH WAR of 1912, the BALKAN WARS of 1912–13, and the FIRST WORLD WAR of 1914–18. At the end of the war, he began a national resistance movement to Greek and allied intervention, which focused around removing the Greeks from western Turkey and overturning the treaty of SÈVRES. This included the establishment of a provisional republican government in Anatolia, which Kemal led to victory in the GREEK-TURKISH WAR of 1921–22. His success here, which included the signing of the treaty of LAUSANNE in 1923, provided the foundation for his republican constitution for Turkey. Kemal became the republic's President for life, a position he held as an autocrat in what remained essentially a one-party state. His main remit was to modernise Turkey, a process which included the disestablishment of Islam, the introduction of western forms in various cultural spheres, and central planning on Soviet lines to establish an industrial sector. He took the name 'Atatürk', meaning 'Father of the Turks', in 1934. He died in office in 1938.

Atlantic, battle of the (1939–45) *see* SECOND WORLD WAR.

Auerstadt, battle of (October 1806) *see* NAPOLEONIC WARS.

Ausgleich 1867 'compromise' agreement on the structure of the HABSBURG empire. In 1865, the Austrian government of Emperor FRANCIS JOSEPH began negotiations with prominent Magyar politicians, led by ANDRÁSSY, over the relationship between Austria and Hungary within the Habsburg empire. The need for a compromise, based on the growing strength of the Magyars, became more pressing during the negotiations after defeat in the AUSTRO-PRUSSIAN WAR of June and July 1866. In February 1867, the *Ausgleich* was signed. It gave Austria and Hungary equal status, and established national legislatures and executives for each country. They were to share a defence and foreign policy, and were to raise money for military purposes jointly. The Habsburg monarch became the Emperor of Austria and the King of Hungary, with the title 'the Dual Monarchy' coming into usage for the area. The *Ausgleich* also involved a commercial union, to be renewed every ten years. Although the *Ausgleich* was seen as a triumph of Hungarian nationalism, it was essentially a narrow deal between two dominant nationalities: the Germans and the Magyars. Other national and ethnic groups in both countries and the rest of the Habsburg empire were marginalised culturally, politically, economically and linguistically (*see also* IMPERIALISM). The deal lasted until the end of the FIRST WORLD WAR, and while it provided the Habsburg monarchy with some stability in the short-term after its losses in the processes of ITALIAN UNIFICATION and GERMAN UNIFICATION, it failed to address the nationality issue within the empire, and contributed to the rise of PANSLAVISM.

Austerlitz, battle of (December 1805) Battle between France and a joint Austro-Russian army in the NAPOLEONIC WARS, sometimes known as the battle of the Three Emperors. After taking Vienna in November 1805, NAPOLEON marched north to fight the combined Austrian and Russian force in order to end the war in central Europe before the winter set in. After concealing some of his troops, Napoleon contacted the Austro-Russian army near Austerlitz and asked for an armistice. The Austro-Russian army moved in to attack the French rear, but as they passed by the French flank, Napoleon attacked and split the force, inflicting heavy losses. The Austrians and Russians began to retreat to Austerlitz under artillery fire from the French, who then cut off their retreat to Olmütz. The numerically superior Austro-Russian force suffered approximately 16,000 casualties and lost 11,000 men as prisoners, compared to 8,500 French losses. Austria sued for peace the next day (*see* PRESSBURG, TREATY OF), while the Russians immediately drew back to the Russian frontier. The battle was one of Napoleon's most successful, and it proved decisive in destroying the Third Coalition and keeping Prussia out of the war.

Austrian State Treaty (May 1955) Multilateral treaty on Austria, signed in Vienna in May 1955. The treaty, signed by representatives of the four post-SECOND WORLD WAR occupying powers (France, the UK, the USA, the USSR), re-established Austria as an independent republic for the first time since the *ANSCHLUSS* of 1938. The treaty restored Austria's pre-*Anschluss* frontiers, thus reaffirming the treaty of TRIANON, and committed the new republic to remaining out of any military alliances. It also prohibited any future *Anschluss* and any restoration of the HABSBURG monarchy. In return, the four powers agreed to end their occupation by October 1955. The treaty was welcomed for ending the occupation of Austria without the kind of geopolitical divisions that had taken place in Germany, and for allowing Vienna to return to a unified status after the withdrawal of the four allied powers, unlike Berlin. However, the potential thawing of COLD WAR relations that this treaty signified was diminished by the simultaneous creation of the WARSAW PACT, which continued the Soviet military presence in eastern Europe. For Austria, the treaty formed the basis of the second republic.

Austro-Piedmontese War (1848–49) War, in two stages, between the HABSBURG empire and the Kingdom of Piedmont-Sardinia and Italian nationalist groups. In late March 1848, after Habsburg troops had been driven out of Milan and Venice (*see* REVOLUTIONS OF 1848), King Charles Albert of Piedmont-Sardinia declared war on the Habsburg empire. Although this was primarily driven by Piedmontese anti-Habsburg interests, for which the revolutions provided an opportunity, a number of Italian nationalist interest groups attached themselves to the war, thus giving it the flavour of a liberal national rising (*see* ITALIAN UNIFICATION). The Habsburgs responded by sending an army under RADETZKY, which captured Vicenza in June 1848, and the Piedmontese forces were beaten at Custozza in late July. When help from revolutionary France failed to appear, Charles Albert agreed to an armistice, under which the Habsburg forces reoccupied Lombardy. In March 1849, after fresh revolutionary activity in Hungary and some parts of the Italian states, Charles Albert broke the armistice and attacked the Habsburg army. The Habsburgs regained control at the battle of Novara in late March. Charles Albert abdicated in favour of his son, VICTOR EMMANUEL II, who sued for peace. Under the treaty of August 1849, Piedmont-Sardinia had to pay an indemnity, but was not deprived of any territory. However, the Habsburg empire ensured its right to intervene in a number of the Italian states in which it had interests. Overall, the war showed that even Piedmont-Sardinia, the strongest of the Italian states, was unable to dent Habsburg hegemony in the Italian states without the backing of other countries.

Austro-Prussian War (1866) War between Austria and Prussia and Italy, also known as the Six Weeks War. After the Austro-Prussian victory over Denmark in the SCHLESWIG WAR of 1864, tensions between the two most powerful German states were exacerbated. Prussia, under BISMARCK and WILLIAM I, was pressing for greater leadership within the German states, which challenged Austria's historical dominance. These tensions came to a head in June 1866 when Bismarck suggested that the GERMAN CONFEDERATION should be dismantled, a direct threat to Austria's influence, and that Prussia should gain control of Schleswig and Holstein. Bismarck had strengthened Prussia's position before taking this step by ensuring French neutrality and Italian involvement: the former was kept out of the conflict by the suggestion of territorial gains in the Rhine, while the latter was brought in through the promise of Venetia if Austria was defeated.

War started on 14 June 1866. Prussia quickly conquered Hanover, Hesse-Cassel and Saxony, which effectively removed Austria's major allies from the war. Austria started well, beating the Italians at Custozza in late June, but then lost the battle of SADOWA in Bohemia to Prussia on 3 July. The Austrian commander, Ludwig von Benedek, had advised Emperor FRANCIS JOSEPH to sue for peace before any conflict in Bohemia, but his view was overturned. The smaller southern German states continued to fight against Prussia during July, but this was relatively ineffectual. The war was settled by the treaty of PRAGUE of 23 August 1866.

As well as confirming Prussia's position as the most dominant German state, the war weakened Austria's standing within the German states. It made Austria more vulnerable to challenges within the HABSBURG empire, which led to the *AUSGLEICH* with Hungary in 1867. The war also helped the process of ITALIAN UNIFICATION through the award of Venetia to Italy by the treaty of Vienna in October 1866.

Aventine secession Incident in Italian politics, taking its name from an episode in classical Roman history. In June 1924, in protest over the murder of Giacomo Matteotti (*see* MATTEOTTI AFFAIR), a majority of opposition deputies left the parliament. King VICTOR EMMANUEL III refused to act on their demands to curb the Fascists' tactics, and MUSSOLINI reacted by annulling the deputies' seats and passing anti-opposition legislation. The protesters thus failed to limit Mussolini's growing dictatorship, and presented the Fascist government with a pretext to act against parliamentary opposition.

Axis Term used from November 1936 to describe Germany and Italy's relationship, which later extended to cover the alliance system of the SECOND WORLD WAR involving Germany, Hungary, Italy, Japan, Romania and Slovakia. Relations between Italy and Germany improved in the autumn of 1936 in the face of the two governments' hostility towards the republic in Spain (*see* SPANISH CIVIL WAR), and in the light of German assurances that it would not attempt an *ANSCHLUSS*. In October 1936, CIANO and HITLER concluded a treaty of cooperation, which MUSSOLINI subsequently described as an 'axis' between Rome and Berlin. Germany and Japan's mutual condemnation of the THIRD INTERNATIONAL, the Anti-Comintern Pact of November 1936, brought Japan into this relationship. The relationship was formalised by the 'Pact of steel', Germany and Italy's bipartite mutual defence alliance signed in May 1939, and furthered by Japan's mutual defence treaty with Germany and Italy in September 1940.

Azaña, Manuel (1880–1940) Spanish politician. A civil servant and successful writer with a legal training, Azaña became active in party politics in the mid-1920s when he helped to form Republican Action. He became the Minister of War for the Second Republic on ALFONSO XIII's departure in 1931. Subsequently Prime Minister, a post he held until 1933, his modernising agenda was evident in both posts, exemplified by his army reforms, his limitations of Church authority, and in his backing for Catalan autonomy. He was imprisoned in 1934 for his apparent implication in the general strike in Barcelona. In February 1936, he became Prime Minister again after the POPULAR FRONT's election victory, becoming President in May. However, tensions within the Popular Front and the worsening crises in Spain formed the context for the nationalist rising which began the SPANISH CIVIL WAR that summer. Azaña remained in office, attempting to keep the republican parties together, and he attempted to establish a negotiated peace in 1938. He left Spain for France, and resigned the presidency, in February 1939, shortly after the fall of Barcelona. He died in exile the following year.

B

Badoglio, Pietro (1871–1956) Italian soldier and politician. After serving in Africa and the FIRST WORLD WAR, Badoglio became Chief of Staff in 1919, and MUSSOLINI's Chief of General Staff in 1925. After a period as Governor of Libya, he returned to active service in the ITALO-ABYSSINIAN WAR in 1935. However, he unsuccessfully opposed Italian involvement in the SPANISH CIVIL WAR and the SECOND WORLD WAR. He led the abortive invasion of Greece in 1940, and resigned after it. When Mussolini was deposed in July 1943 (*see* ITALIAN CAMPAIGN), Badoglio was appointed Prime Minister. He negotiated peace with the allies in September 1943, and led the Italian declaration of war against Germany in October 1943. He resigned this post in June 1944 when it became clear that some of the partisan groups (*see* RESISTANCE) would not work with him.

Bakunin, Mikhail (1814–76) Russian political theorist. A career soldier from a noble family background, Bakunin left the Russian army over the treatment of the Poles. Through his writing and journalism, he became involved in revolutionary politics, and was active in Paris, Prague and Dresden during the REVOLUTIONS OF 1848. He was imprisoned for his role in the Dresden risings, and was extradited to Russia and exiled to Siberia. After his escape in 1861, he lived in western Europe. He joined the International Working Men's Association (IWMA) (*see* FIRST INTERNATIONAL) in 1868, but diverged from the predominant theories of MARX and ENGELS: in particular, Bakunin argued against the need for political parties in a revolutionary situation, and called for workers to take direct action and run post-revolutionary societies through workers' associations (*see* ANARCHISM). Although Bakunin and his supporters were expelled from the IWMA for their anarchist views in 1872, the ideas he developed were influential on Russian nihilism and on SYNDICALISM. He died in Switzerland in 1876.

Balaclava, battle of (October 1854) *see* CRIMEAN WAR.

Balkan rebellions (1875–78) Series of nationalist and panslav revolts in OTTOMAN territory, 1875–76 (*see* NATIONALISM, PANSLAVISM). With long-term ethnic and religious differences creating tensions, rebellions broke out in many parts of the European Ottoman empire. The rebels were variously pressing for greater religious and political freedoms. The rebellions started in Herzogovina in July 1875, spreading to Macedonia and Bosnia by December, and to Bulgaria in 1876. The rebellions took on a Europe-wide significance, as foreign interests in the fate of the Ottoman empire gave Austria-Hungary, Russia and other powers a stake. This became more crucial in mid-1876, when the Ottoman massacres of Bulgarian Orthodox Christians were publicised abroad, and when Serbia and Montenegro declared war on the Ottoman empire in support of the risings. Serbia's calls for Russian intervention in August 1876, combined with the condemnation of the Ottoman tactics being expressed in many countries, led to an international conference in Constantinople in December 1876. Here, Sultan Abdul Hamid II promoted a reformist line as a concession to the visiting powers. Peace was made between the Ottoman empire and Serbia in March 1877. However, the issues raised by the rebellions were not satisfactorily resolved, and, in April 1877, Russia used the crisis as an opportunity to declare war on Turkey. *See* RUSSO-TURKISH WAR.

Balkan Wars (1912–13) Two conflicts in the Balkan region. In 1912, at a time when the OTTOMAN EMPIRE was involved in the ITALO-TURKISH WAR, Bulgaria, Greece, Montenegro and Serbia formed the Balkan League, with Russian support. In October, the League attacked the Ottoman empire, quickly defeating its forces in Europe and pushing the Turks out of their European possessions bar the area around Constantinople. The war attracted the attention of other European powers: Austria-Hungary threatened to intervene and mobilised against Serbia; while Russia threatened to defend the League if war came. Representatives of the major powers created the treaty of LONDON in May 1913, which was designed to end the war and to impose a territorial settlement. While this worked in the short term, the settlement was unstable, particularly due to Serbia's lack of access to the Adriatic, and due to the creation of Albania. In June 1913, a second war broke out when Bulgaria, dissatisfied with the division of Macedonia at London, attacked its former partners Greece and Serbia. However, their response, plus Ottoman and Romanian intervention, led to Bulgaria's defeat. The war was settled by the treaty of BUCHAREST in August 1913.

Taken together, the Balkan wars strengthened Serbia's position in the region, considerably weakened Turkey, exacerbated a number of long-running territorial disputes, and demonstrated that major powers were prepared to mobilise and act over Balkan conflicts. *See also* FIRST WORLD WAR.

Barbarossa Codename for the German military campaign of the SECOND WORLD WAR against the USSR, launched in June 1941. Despite the NAZI-SOVIET PACT of 1939, HITLER and the German military planned for an invasion of the USSR from December 1940, when the invasion was set for May 1941. It was finally launched on 22 June 1941, and proved to be a turning point in the war. With support from Finland and Romania, the Germans staged a huge invasion along a front of almost 2,000 miles, using over 3,000,000 troops (75 per cent of the entire German army at the time). The campaign began with *BLITZKRIEG* tactics: air attacks destroyed large parts of the Soviet air force and other strategic targets, and were followed by fast, penetrating ground attacks which enveloped Red Army units and cut them off from supplies and retreat routes. This was extremely successful to begin with on all three of the German attack lines: to Leningrad in the north; to Moscow in the centre; and through Ukraine towards the Caucasus in the south. The regular army was followed by SS *Einsatzgruppen* (special action groups), who carried out massacres of civilians, particularly Jews (*see* FINAL SOLUTION), political commissars from the Red Army, and others. However, despite its early successes, the northern and central attacks did not capture their target cities by December 1941. The southern attack was more successful, gaining the vital economic resources of the Ukraine for Germany. This limited success was not enough: the planning assumptions behind Barbarossa had been based upon a quick victory that would cause the destruction of the Soviet government, and would allow the invading army to be replaced by an occupation before the winter weather conditions hindered movements. It also required limited action on Germany's other fronts. By December 1941, not only had the weather turned against the invaders, but Germany had declared war on the USA, and the British were gaining ground in north Africa. Moreover, the Soviets were able to call on huge reserves of manpower specifically trained in winter conditions for which the Germans had not planned; while Soviet tanks and artillery proved to be successful, and military production increased under STALIN's planning system (*see* FIVE YEAR PLANS). By November 1942, the southern branch's attack on STALINGRAD began to be repulsed. After losing there in January 1943, and at KURSK in July, the German invasion turned into a retreat.

Basic treaty (December 1972) Bilateral mutual recognition between the Federal Republic of Germany (FRG) and the German Democratic Republic (GDR). Under BRANDT, the FRG pursued a friendly policy towards the GDR (*see OSTPOLITIK*), leading to the signature of the Basic treaty in December 1972. By the treaty, each country recognised the other's independence, and agreed to treat each other as normal neighbours. Despite some objections from parties in both countries, the treaty was ratified, and set up an improvement in relations that allowed, for example, former East Germans in the FRG to visit their relatives in the GDR, and facilitated better transport links across the border. However, neither country abandoned its aspirations for a reunified Germany. The Basic treaty provided the legal framework for inter-German relations until GERMAN REUNIFICATION in 1990.

Basle, treaties of (1795) Three treaties of the FRENCH REVOLUTIONARY WARS. After French successes in Holland, Piedmont and Spain, a number of the states with which it was fighting made peace in the spring and early summer of 1795. The treaties were signed at Basle. In April, France signed the first treaty with Prussia, which gave France territory on the west bank of the Rhine and left Prussia neutral in France's continued war against Austria. France also agreed to view the north German states as neutral. The second treaty, signed in May, made peace with Holland, and re-established the Netherlands as the Batavian Republic, a French dependency. The third treaty was made with Spain in July. By this, France returned to Spain the territory it had conquered, but gained half of the island of San Domingo. As well as the territorial gains, the treaties demonstrated that the Coalition against France was at an end, and allowed France to concentrate its efforts against just two enemies, Austria and Great Britain.

Bastille, storming of (July 1789) *see* FRENCH REVOLUTION.

Bautzen, battle of (May 1813) *see* NAPOLEONIC WARS.

Beck, Josef (1894–1944) Polish politician. Beck became PILSUDSKI's Foreign Minister in 1932, pursuing a policy over the next seven years that was designed to minimise Poland's chances of being invaded. To this end, he played key roles in establishing non-aggression pacts with the USSR in 1932 and with Germany in 1934. From the mid-1930s, he attempted to encourage western action against German expansion, notably over Germany's reoccupation of the RHINELAND in 1936. He represented Poland at the Munich conference of September 1938 (*see* APPEASEMENT, MUNICH AGREEMENT), by which Poland gained some territory from Czechoslovakia. In March 1939, he was involved in getting France and the UK to guarantee Polish integrity. This was supplemented by the Anglo-Polish pact for mutual assistance, signed in London in August 1939 two days after the NAZI-SOVIET PACT had effectively left Poland open to German and Soviet intervention. When Germany invaded western Poland in September 1939, Beck fled to Romania, where he was interned. He died there in 1944.

Benelux Union Customs union between Belgium, Luxembourg and the Netherlands, signed in 1948. Building on early monetary and customs unions between Belgium and Luxembourg, the union was agreed in principle by the three countries' governments-in-exile in London in 1944. The union was established in January 1948, providing common tariffs and internal freedom of trade between the member states. It gained the status of a regional union under the 1957 treaty of ROME. In November 1960, the three countries enhanced the original customs union by establishing an economic union, which included free movement of labour and capital. As well as the economic advantages accruing to the member countries, the union improved these relatively small countries' standing in Europe.

Beneš, Eduard (1884–1948) Czechoslovakian politician. A professional academic from a peasant background, Beneš was a supporter of Czechoslovak independence from Austria-Hungary before the FIRST WORLD WAR. From 1914, he worked in Paris with Tómas MASARYK and the Czechoslovak National Council, a group that effectively became the first government of independent Czechoslovakia from 1918. Given the foreign affairs brief, he was the main Czechoslovak delegate to the PARIS PEACE CONFERENCE, and Foreign Minister from 1918 until 1935. He was active in promoting the LITTLE ENTENTE, the LEAGUE OF NATIONS, and Franco-Czechoslovak relations, the latter embodied in the 1924 treaty. He was Prime Minister from 1921 until 1922, and President of the League of Nations Assembly in 1935. He succeeded Masaryk as President of Czechoslovakia in 1935, a position he resigned after the MUNICH AGREEMENT of September 1938 (*see also* APPEASEMENT). In 1939, he helped to establish and lead the Czechoslovak government-in-exile in Paris, moving to London in 1940. In 1945, he went to Moscow, and re-entered

Czechoslovakia with General Ludvik Svoboda's Soviet-backed army. He formally regained the presidency in 1946, but resigned in 1948 in the wake of the communist take-over when he refused to sign the new constitution. He died the same year.

Beria, Lavrenti (1899–1953) Soviet politician. Beria became a BOLSHEVIK in 1917 while still a student, and became director of the secret police, the Cheka, in Georgia in 1921. In 1931, he became First Secretary of the Georgian Communist party. His career in central politics developed in 1934, when STALIN appointed him to the Central Committee of the Communist party. Viewed as an ally by Stalin, he was given a major role in 1938 when Stalin appointed him Commissar for Internal Affairs, from where he ran the secret police (now renamed the NKVD) and the prison camp system, establishing himself as a brutal and feared enforcer of the Soviet police state. He deputised for Stalin during the SECOND WORLD WAR, and helped the communist parties of a number of eastern European countries to establish their internal security systems in the early years of the COLD WAR. Viewed by many as a potential successor to Stalin, he was arrested during the intrigues that followed Stalin's death in 1953, and secretly executed.

Berlin blockade Incident in the early COLD WAR. In June 1948, the differences of approach to Germany's post-war position from the USSR and the western allies reached a crisis point over the French, US and British attempt to introduce the new West German currency into their zones of Berlin. As Berlin lay well within the territory that became the German Democratic Republic (GDR), the USSR responded by closing the city's western zones off to land and water transport in an attempt to force the western powers to abandon it. In order to maintain their presence, the US and the UK organised an airlift of foodstuffs and fuel, which lasted from June 1948 until May 1949, when the USSR backed down after eleven months. The incident demonstrated the deterioration of relations between the wartime allies, and both sides' insistence on maintaining a presence in Berlin.

Berlin Congress (1878) International conference on the Balkans, held in Berlin in June and July 1878. The treaty of SAN STEFANO, which ended the RUSSO-TURKISH WAR of 1877–78, was unacceptable to Austria-Hungary, the UK and others with Balkan interests, due to its creation of a large Bulgaria which would provide Russia with access to the Aegean Sea (*see also* STRAITS CONVENTION). Threats of war over the treaty forced Russia to renegotiate, with BISMARCK hosting the resultant Congress. Attended by delegates from Austria-Hungary, France, Germany, Italy, the OTTOMAN EMPIRE, Russia and the UK, the Congress demonstrated the widespread acceptance of the Ottoman empire's decline.

The act of the Congress, which replaced the treaty of San Stefano, covered a number of Balkan issues. Bulgaria's autonomy was confirmed, but its territory was reduced: it lost Macedonia and its Aegean coast. Eastern Roumelia was given limited independence, while Montenegro, Romania and Serbia had their independence confirmed. Russia was allowed to keep some of its territorial gains from San Stefano, notably those in the Caucasus and Bessarabia, while Austria-Hungary gained Bosnia and Herzegovina as protectorates, which it had been promised by Russia before the war. Other countries also gained: the UK received Cyprus from the Ottoman empire, while Tunisia was recognised as a French sphere of influence, and Albania as an Italian one. The Congress thus averted a major European war, although it alienated Russia, destroyed the *DREIKAISERBUND*, and set up nationalist and territorial issues in the Balkans that were subsequently to reemerge in the early twentieth century. *See* BALKAN WARS, FIRST WORLD WAR.

Berlin Wall Fortified structure around West Berlin, 1961–89. In August 1961, the German Democratic Republic's (GDR) government responded to the heavy flow of migration through the zonal crossing points in Berlin by closing the majority of the crossing points, and constructing an armed barrier of wire and cement around the western sector of the city. This soon became a heavily fortified, permanent structure that was widely seen as symbolic of the divisions in COLD WAR Europe. In its twenty-eight year history, over 100 people were killed in their attempts to cross the wall. In 1989, as East Germans began again to emigrate in large numbers through other routes, the government re-opened the crossings and suspended visa requirements. Parts of the wall were demolished spontaneously by the crowds that celebrated this relaxation, and the rest was officially demolished (*see* REVOLUTIONS OF 1989–91, GERMAN REUNIFICATION). The removal of the wall became a popular symbol of the end of the Cold War.

Bernadotte, Folke (1895–1948) Swedish diplomat. The nephew of King Gustavus V of Sweden, Bernadotte served in the Swedish army before switching his attention to diplomacy and humanitarian issues through the work of the Red Cross. He was involved in organising prisoner-of-war exchanges during the FIRST WORLD WAR, and remained involved with the Red Cross when the war ended. During the SECOND WORLD WAR he organised prisoner exchanges, and also helped to organise the rescue of approximately 30,000 people from Nazi concentration camps. In early 1945, HIMMLER used Bernadotte as a contact in an unsuccessful bid to establish peace negotiations with the British and American governments. Bernadotte became President of the Swedish Red Cross in 1946. In 1948, he was appointed as UNITED NATIONS negotiator in Palestine, where he was killed in a terrorist attack.

Bernstein, Eduard (1850–1932) German politician and political theorist. Bernstein joined the Social Democratic Workers' party in 1872, but was forced abroad by BISMARCK'S ANTI-SOCIALIST LAWS. He edited the party's newspaper from Zurich and London, and became an established figure in the émigré left of the period, associated with ENGELS and others. Under Fabian influences, he created an evolutionary social democratic model for left-wing parties, one that rejected Marxist revolutionary tactics in favour of evolution towards socialism through existing political systems. Although this revisionism was rejected by the party, his writings remained influential. He returned to Germany in 1901, and served as a deputy from 1902 to 1906, and again from 1912 to 1918. He opposed the FIRST WORLD WAR, and briefly joined the anti-war Independent Social Democratic party. He rejoined the Social Democratic party in 1918, and supported the constitution of the WEIMAR REPUBLIC. His final spell as a deputy was from 1920 to 1928.

Bethmann Hollweg, Theobald von (1856–1921) German politician. From a civil service background, Bethmann Hollweg emerged into national politics through provincial and state politics in Prussia, where he was Minister of the Interior from 1905 to 1907. He held the interior portfolio for Germany from 1907 until 1909, when he succeeded BÜLOW as Chancellor. He was involved in building up the German army in the years before the First World War, although he did attempt to limit naval growth as he did not wish to alienate the UK. In 1914, believing that a localised war was inevitable, he committed Germany to support Austria-Hungary's war against Serbia (*see* FIRST WORLD WAR). His miscalculation over Russian and British reactions weakened his position in the wartime government, although he was able to limit the use of U-boats until January 1917, rightly recognising that the destruction of shipping would bring the USA into the war. He retired in 1917 after the two leading military figures, HINDENBURG and LUDENDORFF, threatened to resign their posts.

Bidault, Georges (1899–1983) French politician. Bidault came to prominence through the RESISTANCE movement during the SECOND WORLD WAR, particularly through his leadership of the National Resistance Council from 1943. At the end of the German occupation in 1944, he was a founder member of the Popular Republican Movement. He held the roles of Foreign Minister (1944–6, 1947–8, and 1953–4) and Prime Minister (1946, 1949–50 and 1958) in the post-war caretaker government and in the Fourth Republic. Here, he was influential in promoting a broadly pro-European line, and in building relations with the Federal Republic of Germany. From 1959 he diverged from DE

GAULLE's policy on the Algerian War of Independence, and became involved in both the Union for French Algeria and the controversial Secret Army Organisation (*see* IMPERIALISM). Accused of treason, he left France in 1963, and stayed in exile until 1968, when the warrant for his arrest was withdrawn.

Bismarck, Otto von (1815–98) Prussian and German politician. A conservative and royalist from a Prussian Junker family, Bismarck entered politics in 1847 as a member of the Prussian Diet. From 1851 until 1859, he represented Prussia at the German Diet in Frankfurt, where he developed the view that Prussia and Austria were rivals for the role of dominant German state. After a brief diplomatic career as Prussian Ambassador to St Petersburg in 1859 and Paris in 1862, Bismarck was appointed Minister-President of Prussia in September 1862, a time of constitutional crisis. He reformed the army, dissolved the Diet, and established a strong government. It was from this position that he initiated policies which helped to secure Prussian domination of the German states. GERMAN UNIFICATION under Prussian leadership was gained during the 1860s and early 1870s through a series of wars and alliances, in which Bismarck played a leading role. Bismarck became Imperial Chancellor of the newly unified Germany in 1871. His domestic policies maintained a strong central governmental style, with opposing groups, including Catholics and socialists, often marginalised (*see* ANTI-SOCIALIST LAWS, *KULTURKAMPF*). Despite some welfare provision and universal suffrage, democracy was not given a chance to flourish. Bismarck's foreign policy focused on maintaining the new balance of power in post-1870 Europe, and on isolating France. These aims were pursued through the *DREIKAISERBUND* and the TRIPLE ALLIANCE, and through Bismarck's leading role in the 1878 BERLIN CONGRESS. Bismarck resigned and retired from public life in 1890 over policy differences with the new Emperor, WILLIAM II.

Black Redistribution *see* POPULISM.

Blanc, Louis (1811–82) French politician and political theorist. Blanc worked as a journalist and writer in the 1830s and 1840s, writing a history of the French Revolution and influential works on economics and politics. He was involved in the campaigns against LOUIS-PHILIPPE in 1847, and was a member of the provisional government established in 1848 after the King's fall (*see* REVOLUTIONS OF 1848). Blanc worked on a number of employment and industrial schemes, including the Luxemburg Commission and the National Workshops programme. He left France for England after the June Days of 1848, and remained in exile until 1871. He was elected to the THIRD REPUBLIC's National Assembly in 1871, and to the Chamber of Deputies in 1876. His writings were influential on the development of SOCIALISM.

Blitzkrieg (German: 'lightning war') Military strategy used by Germany in some of the early campaigns of the SECOND WORLD WAR. The idea of rapid, localised attacks developed towards the end of the FIRST WORLD WAR, although the full potential of the *Blitzkrieg* was not realised until fast tanks and armoured vehicles, and powerful air support, could be linked. The technique was used in the invasion of Poland in September 1939, where aerial bombardment was quickly followed by ground attacks on small areas by fast armoured units. Once the small front was broken, the units (with further air support) were able to spread out behind the Polish lines. Western Poland was defeated in under three weeks. The technique was also used very effectively in the German invasion of the Low Countries and France in the spring of 1940: apart from the escape of allied troops from Dunkirk, Belgium, the Netherlands, Luxembourg and France were conquered in just six weeks.

Blood Purge *see* NIGHT OF THE LONG KNIVES.

Bloody Sunday (January 1905) *see* RUSSIAN REVOLUTION 1905.

Blum, Léon (1872–1950) French politician. A civil servant, journalist and critic, Blum joined the Socialist party in 1899. He became the party's Secretary in 1916, and was elected to the Chamber of Deputies in 1919. Blum was influential in the party's moderation after the FIRST WORLD WAR: for example, he led the majority in their rejection of THIRD INTERNATIONAL membership in 1920, while a minority split to form the Communist party. He became the party's leader in 1925, and France's first socialist Prime Minister in June 1936 in the POPULAR FRONT coalition. After introducing some welfare and industrial reforms, this government split over the SPANISH CIVIL WAR: Blum favoured non-intervention. The government fell in June 1937. Blum returned to the premiership briefly in March 1938 at the head of the second Popular Front government. When France fell in 1940 (*see* SECOND WORLD WAR), he was arrested by the VICHY authorities. Their attempt to try him in 1942 for his role in France's military failure was unsuccessful. When the Germans occupied Vichy France, Blum – who was Jewish – was taken to Germany and interned. He was released in May 1945. In 1946, he helped to negotiate a loan for France from the USA, before returning as Prime Minister of the caretaker government from December 1946 until his retirement in January 1947. He was one of the architects of the constitution for the Fourth Republic, introduced in 1947.

Bolsheviks Russian political party. The Bolsheviks, a name taken from the Russian term for 'majority', emerged in 1903 as one of the main factions in the Russian Social Democratic Workers party. The faction won a vote at their London congress over control of *Iskra*, the party's paper, with the losing faction becoming known as MENSHEVIKS (from 'minority'), who subsequently won votes on other matters. Between 1903 and 1912 the two wings co-existed: but in 1912 LENIN, the leading Bolshevik, established an independent party structure for the Bolsheviks. The Bolsheviks stressed the need for peasant involvement in any revolution in Russia, and so developed agrarian policies and propaganda, and also viewed the ideal party structure as one based on a small group of dedicated activists who could influence events in decisive ways. The Bolsheviks gained ground in the immediate aftermath of the February revolution (*see* RUSSIAN REVOLUTIONS 1917) by developing links with the soviets (workers' councils). In October, the Bolsheviks planned and executed the coup that overthrew the provisional government, and thereafter managed the All-Russian Congress of Soviets in order to gain total control. The party renamed itself as the Communist party in 1918, although the name 'Bolshevik' remained in use until 1952.

Bonaparte, Napoleon *see* NAPOLEON BONAPARTE.

Boris III (1894–1943) King of Bulgaria, 1918–43. The eldest son of Ferdinand I, Boris commanded the unsuccessful Bulgarian army in Macedonia during the FIRST WORLD WAR. He succeeded to the throne when his father abdicated in the aftermath of the war. He worked alongside a number of prime ministers during the 1920s and early 1930s, but emerged as dictator in his own right in 1935. Boris III established links with both HITLER and MUSSOLINI. In March 1941, he signed the Tripartite Pact, gaining territory in Macedonia and Thrace from Yugoslavia and Greece respectively. However, he limited Bulgaria's military commitment to the SECOND WORLD WAR by refusing to send troops to support BARBAROSSA in June 1941, and by failing to act on the declaration of war against the UK in December 1941. He also worked to protect Bulgarian Jews from deportation during the FINAL SOLUTION. He died shortly after refusing to change these policies, although rumours that he was murdered have never been proven.

Borodino, battle of (September 1812) *see* NAPOLEONIC WARS.

Bosnian crisis (1908–9) International crisis caused by Austria-Hungary's annexation of Bosnia and Herzegovina, October 1908–March 1909. Austria-Hungary had occupied the OTTOMAN territories of Bosnia and Herzegovina since 1878 (*see* BERLIN CONGRESS). In October 1908, the HABSBURG Foreign Minister Alois von Aehrenthal counselled the annexation of these territories. This was in the context of the YOUNG TURKS movement in the Ottoman empire, which was calling for a removal of foreign influences; but it also offered the Habsburg government a chance to demonstrate its power and to expand the empire in the Balkans at a time when Russia was unlikely to offer much resistance, due to its recent defeat by Japan. Despite having been promised gains in the Straits in return for recognition of the annexation, Russia objected, as did Serbia and the Ottoman empire. It was seen as a contravention of the act of the Berlin Congress, and was read by some in Serbia as a step towards further Austrian IMPERIALISM in the Balkans. The UK also objected to the annexation, while Germany supported it. In January 1909, Russia and Serbia were both threatened by Austria-Hungary and Germany that their continued non-recognition of the annexation could lead to war. They accordingly backed down in March 1909. However, the crisis demonstrated that the Balkans were once again becoming a contested area in continental politics, while the annexation itself fed into the growth of NATIONALISM and anti-Habsburg opinion in Bosnia, Herzegovina and Serbia.

Boulanger affair French political crisis of 1888–89. In 1886, the popular progressive General Georges Boulanger became Minister of War in France's coalition government. The following year, he was removed from office as the government began to fear that, with his popularity and army contacts, he might stage a military coup. When he was also dismissed from the army in 1888, Boulanger and his followers began successfully to contest by-elections under the banner of the National Republican party, with a promise to reform the THIRD REPUBLIC's constitution. He was supported mainly by right-wing politicians, including monarchists and Bonapartists, but he also gained some popular support as a potential alternative to the Republic itself. However, he did not attempt the coup that the government feared. In May 1889, the government attempted to remove this threat by preparing to prosecute Boulanger with a dubious treason charge. Boulanger left France, and committed suicide in Brussels in 1891. Although the 'Boulangist' movement did not long survive him, it served, along with the DREYFUS AFFAIR and other scandals, to show up the tensions and frailties of the Third Republic.

Boulanger, Georges *see* BOULANGER AFFAIR.

Brandt, Willy (Karl Frahm) (1913–92) German and West German politician. A member of the Social Democratic party (SPD) from 1930, Frahm left Germany in 1933 on the Nazi accession to power (*see* THIRD REICH), and lived in Norway until 1940, where he gained citizenship and took on the name of 'Brandt'. When Norway fell to Germany in the SECOND WORLD WAR, he moved to Sweden, working from there for the German RESISTANCE. He returned to Germany in 1945, and rejoined the SPD in 1947. He was elected to the Federal Republic of Germany's (FRG) parliament in 1949, and to Berlin's city assembly in 1950. He was President of the Parliament from 1955 to 1957, and Mayor of West Berlin from 1957 until 1966. He offered skilful leadership to the city during the BERLIN WALL crisis of 1961. Chairman of the SPD from 1964, he joined President Kurt Kiesinger's coalition in 1966 as Foreign Minister. In 1969, he formed the SPD/Free Democrat coalition government, serving as Chancellor until 1974. He was instrumental in refocusing the FRG's external relations by promoting *OSTPOLITIK*, for which he won the 1971 Nobel Peace Prize. Brandt resigned as Chancellor in 1974 after a spying scandal. He remained active in party politics, and, from 1977 until 1989, chaired the UNITED NATIONS North–South Commission on international economic development.

Brest-Litovsk, treaty of (March 1918) Peace treaty between Russia and Germany and Austria-Hungary that ended Russian involvement in the FIRST WORLD WAR. In October 1917, as part of the Russian Revolution (*see* RUSSIAN REVOLUTIONS 1917), the Bolsheviks promulgated their decree for peace, arranged a cease-fire in December 1917, and started talks at Brest-Litovsk. The Russian delegation, under TROTSKY, attempted to delay the negotiations, hoping that Germany and Austria-Hungary would experience their own revolutions: but in response, Germany broke the cease-fire in February

1918. The treaty was duly signed in early March, a day after the German occupation of Kiev. Russia's disadvantages and the Bolsheviks' desire for peace meant that the terms of the treaty were harsh on Russia. Estonia, Finland, Georgia and Ukraine were made independent, while Lithuania and Poland were taken from Russia but controlled by Germany and Austria-Hungary. Russia thus lost approximately half of its European territory, along with significant agricultural and industrial areas (*see* IMPERIALISM). The treaty caused splits within the Russian government, and helped to inspire some of the conflicts that developed into the RUSSIAN CIVIL WAR, notably the conflict over the Ukraine and the intervention of France and the UK. In November 1918 the treaty was formally denounced by the Bolsheviks, and was annulled by the allies on Germany and Austria-Hungary's surrenders. However, most of the territorial losses stood, although Ukraine was regained during the course of the Civil War, while Polish involvement in that conflict led to a renegotiation of the Russo-Polish border. *See* treaty of RIGA.

Bretton Woods Conference (July 1944) International conference on trade, finance and credit, held at Bretton Woods, New Hampshire. As part of the development of the culture and structure of the UNITED NATIONS, and as a response to the international DEPRESSION of the late 1920s and 1930s, President Franklin Roosevelt of the USA hosted the Bretton Woods Conference. Representatives of forty-four nations' governments attended. The conference developed an outline structure for post-SECOND WORLD WAR international trade and finance based on two organisations, both of which became UN agencies: the International Bank for Reconstruction and Development (later the World Bank), which would lend money to individual countries to help finance development work; and the International Monetary Fund, which individual countries could use for short-term loans to cover trade deficits and to help soothe currency crises. Both were to be based on reserves provided by member countries. Due to its economic strength, the USA became the major contributor, and the US dollar replaced the GOLD STANDARD as the currency against which exchange would be gauged. The two organisations were set up after the war.

Brezhnev, Leonid (1906–82) Soviet politician. Born in the Ukraine and trained in engineering, Brezhnev worked for the Communist party from 1938, and served in the Red Army during the SECOND WORLD WAR. His early post-war posts in local and regional party roles paved the way to his elevation to national politics under STALIN and KHRUSHCHEV, and he joined the party's Central Committee in 1952. In 1957 he joined the POLITBURO, and became President of the Praesidium in 1960. In 1964, after Khrushchev's retirement, Brezhnev became the party's First Secretary, a post he held until his death in 1982. As the USSR's leader, he oversaw some limited domestic reforms which eased some of the restrictions of his two predecessors' terms: for example, the government became more tolerant of religion, and some minor individual liberties were introduced. Internationally, Brezhnev was involved in some efforts to dilute COLD WAR tensions, including arms limitation negotiations and the Helsinki conference (*see* CONFERENCE ON SECURITY AND COOPERATION IN EUROPE). However, he also initiated a number of moves which contributed to a worsening international situation. In August 1968, for example, he authorised the WARSAW PACT's invasion of Czechoslovakia (*see* PRAGUE SPRING), a move justified by the 'Brezhnev doctrine' which stressed communist countries' duties to act to protect COMMUNISM in other states. In 1979 Brezhnev led the USSR's military intervention in Afghanistan (*see also* IMPERIALISM). Overall, his term of office saw a weakening of the Soviet economy mixed with a rise in political expectations, a mood which was exploited by subsequent reformist Soviet politicians, notably GORBACHEV. Brezhnev died in office in November 1982. He was succeeded by ANDROPOV.

Briand, Aristide (1862–1932) French politician. Briand was active in the Socialist party from 1894, and was elected to the Chamber of Deputies in 1902. He took up his first ministerial post in 1906 when the Radical coalition appointed him as Minister of Public Instruction and Worship, an appointment that led to his expulsion from the Socialist party (*see* SECOND INTERNATIONAL). His main achievement in this post was the disestablishment of the Catholic church. He was Prime Minister from 1909 until 1911, and again in 1913 and from 1915 to 1917. He was one of the most prominent French politicians of the post-FIRST WORLD WAR period, holding office as Prime Minister from 1921 to 1922, 1925 to 1926, and in 1929, as well as the Foreign Ministry from 1925 until 1932. In this period, he worked for disarmament, Franco-German conciliation, and collective security. He was an architect of the LOCARNO agreement of 1925, for which he shared the Nobel Peace Prize with STRESEMANN, and of the KELLOGG-BRIAND PACT of 1928. He also made plans for a federal Union of European States. His work in this area was to provide important precedents for Franco-German reconciliation and western European cooperation after the SECOND WORLD WAR. He lost the presidential election of 1931, and retired and died the following year.

Britain, battle of (June–September 1940) *see* SECOND WORLD WAR.

Brumaire French coup of 9 November 1799 which brought NAPOLEON to power, taking its name from the month in the REPUBLICAN CALENDAR. The coup was largely engineered by SIEYÈS. It replaced the Directory system that had been in place since November 1795 with the Consulate. This system was less democratic than the Directory, giving extensive executive power to Napoleon as First Consul. *See also* FRENCH REVOLUTION.

Brüning, Heinrich (1885–1970) German politician. After serving throughout the FIRST WORLD WAR, gaining an Iron Cross in 1918, Brüning entered national politics in 1924 as a Centre party deputy, and was appointed Chancellor in 1930 thanks to his knowledge of economics (*see* WEIMAR REPUBLIC). Lacking a majority in the Reichstag, particularly after the 1930 election, Brüning worked closely with President HINDENBURG to secure legislation by decree. He introduced various radical measures in an attempt to lessen the impact of the DEPRESSION on Germany, including deflation, tax rises, and retrenchment in government spending, while also attempting to break down the VERSAILLES settlement by stressing Germany's economic instability to the allies. He banned the Nazi party's paramilitary organisations in April 1932, and encouraged Hindenburg to stand for re-election to the presidency in 1932 as an attempt to limit HITLER's advances. He lost Hindenburg's support in 1932 after attempting to resettle unemployed workers on bankrupt Junkers' estates as a public works scheme. He left Germany in 1934, and settled in the USA.

Brusilov offensive (June–August 1916) Russian campaign of the FIRST WORLD WAR. In June 1916, four Russian armies under General Alexei Brusilov launched an attack on the Austro-Hungarian lines. As well as aiming to gain ground for Russia, the offensive aimed to help the allies on the western and southern fronts by forcing the Germans to move troops and resources to the east. The offensive was successful at first, with the Russians taking 250,000 prisoners, routing the Fourth Austrian army, gaining up to 12,000 square miles of territory, and persuading Romania to declare war on the central powers. It also managed to divert German forces from the west, thus helping the French and British efforts in the long-running battles of VERDUN and the SOMME, and some Austro-Hungarian forces were moved east from the southern front. However, Russia lost approximately 1,000,000 men in the offensive, which ended in August when supplies failed.

Brussels, treaty of (March 1948) Mutual defence and economic cooperation treaty between Belgium, France, Luxembourg, the Netherlands and the UK, signed in March 1948. Building on the BENELUX UNION and the Anglo-French alliance of the treaty of DUNKIRK, the treaty of Brussels involved all signatories in pledging to aid any other signatory if it was invaded or attacked by a third party. This was aimed at both Germany and the USSR, and was to be binding for fifty years. The treaty also included clauses on social and economic cooperation, and it established a permanent organisation with specialised committees. Politically, the treaty helped to convince the USA to remain involved in European military issues after the SECOND WORLD WAR, as it showed that the leading western democracies were initiating greater cooperation in this sphere. It thus served as something of a model for NATO. In 1954, the treaty of Brussels was revised in order to turn the organisation into the WESTERN EUROPEAN UNION, involving the Federal Republic of Germany and Italy, a sign that the organisation had become predominantly anticommunist in focus.

Bucharest, treaty of (May 1812) *see* RUSSO-TURKISH WAR.

Bucharest, treaty of (August 1913) Peace treaty that ended the second of the BALKAN WARS, between Greece, Montenegro, the OTTOMAN EMPIRE, Romania and Serbia on one side, and Bulgaria on the other. Bulgaria lost most of its gains from the first Balkan War, formalised in the treaty of LONDON of May 1913. Part of eastern Thrace went to the Ottoman empire, some of Bulgaria's Macedonian gains were ceded to Greece and Serbia, and southern Dobruja went to Romania.

Bukharin, Nikolai (1888–1938) Soviet politician and political theorist. Born in Moscow, Bukharin joined the BOLSHEVIKS in 1906, and became a leading figure in their Moscow group by 1908. He was arrested and exiled to Siberia in 1911, but escaped and spent the next six years in various parts of Europe and the USA. During this period, he developed relationships with LENIN, STALIN and TROTSKY, and became a prominent writer on COMMUNISM. He returned to Russia in 1917, and played a leading role in the Bolsheviks' actions in Moscow during the October Revolution (*see* RUSSIAN REVOLUTIONS 1917). He supported Stalin in the leadership struggles after Lenin's death, joined the POLITBURO in 1924 and chaired the THIRD INTERNATIONAL from 1925. A supporter of NEW ECONOMIC POLICY, he lost Stalin's backing in 1929 when the latter introduced collectivisation: labelled as a 'right deviationist', Bukharin lost his place on the Politburo. He briefly regained influence in the mid-1930s, editing *Izvestia* from 1934 and helping to draft the USSR's 1936 constitution. However, he was targeted by Stalin's 1937 purge of the old Bolsheviks, and was executed after a show trial in 1938 (*see* YEZHOVSHCHINA). In 1988, the USSR's Supreme Court rehabilitated him.

Bulganin, Nikolai (1895–1975) Soviet politician. Having served in the FIRST WORLD WAR, Bulganin joined the BOLSHEVIKS in 1917. He worked for the secret police (Cheka) from 1918 to 1922. He rose to greater prominence in the 1930s as Chairman of the Moscow Soviet from 1931 to 1937, and played a role in organising the defence of the city during the SECOND WORLD WAR. He was appointed Deputy Minister of Defence in 1944, and succeeded to the ministerial post in 1947. In 1949 he became Deputy Prime Minister, and served as Vice-Premier to MALENKOV after STALIN's death. In 1955 he became Premier, ostensibly sharing power with KHRUSHCHEV, although the latter quickly emerged as the effective leader. Khrushchev removed Bulganin from office in 1958 due to his links with Malenkov. He worked in a relatively minor banking role until his retirement in 1960.

Bülow, Bernhard von (1849–1929) German politician. Bülow served in the FRANCO-PRUSSIAN WAR before entering the diplomatic service, a career that led him to be Germany's Ambassador to Rome in 1894. In 1897 WILLIAM II appointed Bülow as Secretary of State for Foreign Affairs, and in 1900 he became Chancellor. His main initiatives came in foreign affairs, where he promoted German naval and imperial expansion, although these were not generally successful. For example, he dismissed the possibility of an Anglo-German alliance in 1900, and alienated France in 1906 over the MOROCCAN CRISIS. He also over-committed Germany to supporting Austria-Hungary's actions during the BOSNIAN CRISIS of 1908, thus setting a precedent for 1914 and alienating Russia. The fragmentary nature of his support in the Reichstag was exposed in 1908 when his proposed tax increases were rejected, and he was dismissed in 1909 after losing William II's support. His final public role came in 1914, when he was re-appointed to the Rome Embassy with the main aim of keeping Italy apart from the TRIPLE ENTENTE powers. He was unsuccessful in this (*see* LONDON, TREATY OF 1915), and left the post in 1915.

C

Cambrai, battle of (November 1917) *see* FIRST WORLD WAR.

Campo Formio, treaty of (October 1797) Peace treaty between France and the HABSBURG empire during the FRENCH REVOLUTIONARY WARS. In April 1797, the Habsburg empire made an armistice with France after NAPOLEON's successful campaigns in the Italian states. Peace was made at Campo Formio in October after Napoleon's force had advanced into Austria itself. By the treaty, France's conquest of Belgium was recognised, as was its establishment of the Cisalpine Republic in northern Italy. France gained the Ionian Islands, and its western frontiers were recognised. The Habsburg empire kept Venice, part of Venezia, and its Adriatic territories. The treaty also contained secret clauses which gave French recognition to Habsburg claims for Bavaria and Salzburg, in return for the Habsburg evacuation of its defences at Mainz. The treaty was significant in bringing an end to the first main stage of the French Revolutionary Wars, allowing France to concentrate on its war against Great Britain. It also demonstrated Napoleon's rising political power: leading the negotiations without proper reference to the French government, he effectively conducted his own diplomacy.

Caporetto, battle of (October–November 1917) First World War battle between Italy and the central powers. After joining the war against its former TRIPLE ALLIANCE partners by the treaty of LONDON in May 1915, Italy had fought against Austria-Hungary, mainly in north-east Italy and into Austria. In October 1917, the central powers were able to address this front more fully as their commitment to the eastern front diminished (*see* RUSSIAN REVOLUTIONS 1917), and a joint Austro-Hungarian and German force was built up to attack the Italian line. The offensive began on 24 October with an artillery attack being followed by a heavy infantry attack. Caporetto was taken after two days, followed by an Italian retreat back to the Piave river where they were joined by French, British and American troops. The Italians suffered approximately 45,000 deaths and lost 300,000 troops as prisoners, while many also deserted. The consolidation of this force prevented an invasion of Italy: and, despite the long-term humiliation of Caporetto, the force provided the basis of the successful attack on the central powers at the battle of Vittorio Veneto in October 1918.

Caprivi, Georg Leo (1831–99) German politician and soldier. At the end of his military career, Caprivi succeeded BISMARCK as Minister-President of Prussia and Chancellor of Germany in 1890. He initiated a number of changes in policy that became known as the New Course, including backing further INDUSTRIALISATION and commercial developments, and promoting a central European trading area through tariffs and customs agreements. His foreign policy was aimed at improving relations with the UK, in the process of which he pushed Russia closer to France (*see* FRANCO-RUSSIAN ALLIANCE). Caprivi also shifted from the CONSERVATISM of the Bismarck era by dropping the ANTI-SOCIALIST LAWS. These moves helped to alienate both Junkers and the Centre party, and the growth of socialist representation in the Reichstag caused WILLIAM II to lose confidence in Caprivi. He resigned in October 1894.

Carlism Spanish political movement. In 1833, King Ferdinand VII was succeeded by his three-year old daughter Isabella II. This succession was resisted by Ferdinand's brother Charles, who put forward his own claim as the rightful Bourbon heir. His cause, which came to be known as Carlism from his name, was characteristically conservative and Catholic, and it proved attractive to many rural anti-liberals and anti-capitalists, particularly in the

Basque area and in Navarre. He was able to mobilise a military force of roughly 30,000 men against the government in a civil war which lasted from 1833 until 1840. The Carlists conducted this mainly through guerrilla and terrorist tactics, which were met with terrorist tactics from the army. The Carlists took Morella in 1838, but were already over-stretched logistically by that time, particularly as their ambitious march on Madrid failed. A peace was negotiated in August 1839, whereby the Carlists dropped their royal claim, and the movement's leading figures, including Ram-n Cabrera, left Spain.

Carlism re-emerged in 1846 when guerrilla attacks on the Spanish army started again, this time in support of Montemolin, Charles' son, but this failed to gain the full backing of the rebels of the 1830s and was defeated by 1849 (*see also* REVOLUTIONS OF 1848). The movement was clearly splintered by this time, with only some common issues – such as distrust of urban capitalism and Madrid-backed centralism – holding the Carlists together. Carlists were involved in the plots against Isabella that led to her departure from Spain in the SPANISH REVOLUTION of 1868, and in the subsequent civil war. Carlist traditions of anti-LIBERALISM and anti-centralism survived into the twentieth century, and it became politically significant again during the Second Republic of 1931–6, during which time Carlist risings fed into the country's instability. FRANCO subsequently merged remaining Carlist organisations with the *FALANGE.*

Carlsbad Decrees (August 1819) GERMAN CONFEDERATION legislation of 1819. After the murder of the writer and spy August von Kotzebue by a radical student, METTERNICH saw an opportunity to introduce tighter internal security throughout the Confederation, thereby maintaining Austrian leadership and limiting the opportunities for the discussion of alternative politics. Metternich bypassed the Confederation's General Assembly by chairing a meeting of Confederation representatives at Carlsbad in August 1819. The meeting agreed to three decrees, all of which were passed by Frankfurt the following month. They allowed for greater state control over student politics; for the widespread censorship of the press and literature in general; and for the establishment of a commission at Mainz dedicated to identifying and closing down revolutionary societies throughout the Confederation. These ideas fed into the subsequent constitutional reform of the Confederation. The decrees successfully suppressed the open discussion of radicalism, progressivism and NATIONALISM in the German states until the 1840s.

Carnot, Lazare (1753–1823) French soldier and politician. An army officer and military engineer before the FRENCH REVOLUTION of 1789, Carnot entered politics in 1791 when he was elected to the Legislative Assembly. In August 1793 he joined the Committee of Public Safety, taking on the role of military advisor. He was responsible for a number of military reforms that helped France's efforts in the FRENCH REVOLUTIONARY WARS, including conscription, regimental restructuring, and state control of munitions production. He also continued to take an active military role, leading the French counterattack on the invading armies of 1793. He was a member of the Directory from its foundation in 1795, but fell during the Fructidor coup of 1797, and was exiled. He returned to office as NAPOLEON's Minister of War in 1800, but retired the following year. His final recall came during Napoleon's return from exile in 1814–15, when he served as Minister of the Interior and organised the defence of Antwerp. He was exiled by LOUIS XVIII.

Carol II (1893–1953) King of Romania, 1930–40. The son of King Ferdinand, Carol moved to France after being disinherited in 1925. He returned to Romania in 1930, three years after his father's death, and took the throne from his son, Michael, who was ruling with a regency. He was supported in this move by the Prime Minister, Iuliu Maniu. He maintained the role of a constitutional monarch until 1937, but then moved towards a corporate-style royal dictatorship, influenced by FASCISM, by assuming full political control and closing down political parties in February 1938. Carol's foreign policy was designed to keep Romania out of military commitments, and he aimed to gain HITLER's protection by supplying Germany with oil. However, Hitler refused to provide any support when Romania was faced with territorial demands in the realignments that followed the NAZI-SOVIET PACT of August 1939, and Romania lost significant territories to Bulgaria, Hungary and the USSR. In the face of public criticism over these losses, Carol abdicated in favour of Michael in September 1940, and left Romania. He died in Lisbon in 1953.

Casablanca Conference (January 1943) Inter-allied planning conference of the SECOND WORLD WAR. With allied successes in North Africa, and pressure from the USSR for the western allies to open a second front in Europe to relieve the German pressure, British and American representatives, led by Prime Minister Winston Churchill and President Franklin Roosevelt, met at Casablanca to discuss the next steps of their strategy. The FREE FRENCH, who controlled Morocco, were also represented, a move which stressed the western allies' acceptance of DE GAULLE's group as the French government-in-waiting. Despite major differences over the issue of the second front, particularly on the wisdom of the invasion of northern France for which STALIN was calling, the allies agreed on a number of key issues. They rejected an invasion of France in favour of an invasion of Italy, through Sicily (*see* ITALIAN CAMPAIGN), designed to remove Italy from the war and divert German resources to southern Europe. The USA committed itself to further bombing offensives against Germany, while the UK committed itself to further intervention in the Far East after the defeat of the AXIS in Europe. A final key issue was the declaration that the allies would fight on until Germany and its allies surrendered unconditionally.

Cassino, battle of (January–May 1944) *see* ITALIAN CAMPAIGN.

Catherine II (Princess Sophia of Anhalt-Serbst) (1729–96) Empress of Russia, 1762–96. Born in Stettin, Sophia married the heir to the Russian throne, Peter, in 1745, taking the name 'Ekaterina' on her conversion to the Russian Orthodox faith. She succeeded as Empress in her own right in 1762 after deposing her husband, who then died in captivity. An enthusiast of French and German philosophy, Catherine introduced a number of reforms in administration and education which earned her the reputation of an 'enlightened despot'. Her main achievements came in foreign affairs. Under her rule, Russia gained the Crimea from Turkey in wars of 1768–74 and 1787–92, and annexed Sweden in 1790. Catherine also oversaw Russian gains in Poland, in 1772, and again in the partitions of 1793 and 1795 (*see* POLISH PARTITIONS). She died in 1796, and was succeeded by her son, Paul.

Cavour, Camillo di (1810–61) Piedmontese and Italian politician. Before he entered the Piedmontese government in 1850, Cavour was active in promoting the idea of an Italian nation state, most notably through his work on the journal *Il Risorgimento*. As Minister of Industry from 1850, and Prime Minister from 1852, he played a leading role in the diplomatic and military manoeuvres that led, by the time of his death in June 1861, to the unification of the bulk of the Italian peninsula (*see* ITALIAN UNIFICATION). His most important acts as Prime Minister included gaining the support of France and the UK by backing their efforts in the CRIMEAN WAR in 1855, and the brokering of the Pact of PLOMBIÈRES with NAPOLEON III in 1858. He was out of power between July 1859 and January 1860, due to his resignation over the terms of the treaty of VILLAFRANCA, but his last eighteen months saw him take a leading role in the formal creation of the Kingdom of Italy. His pragmatic backing for GARIBALDI's Sicilian expedition, his work in establishing the first Italian parliament, which met at Turin in 1860, and his successful negotiations to bring Parma, Modena, Tuscany and the Romagna into the union of Piedmont-Sardinia, helped to establish the structure of a unified nation state.

Ceauçescu, Nicolae (1918–89) Romanian politician. Ceauçescu joined the

Communist party in 1936. After the Communist takeover of 1948, he emerged as one of GHEORGHIU-DEJ's supporters, and was promoted to the party's secretariat in 1954. He was Gheorghiu-Dej's deputy leader from 1957 until his death in 1965, when Ceauçescu succeeded as General Secretary of the Party. He became President of the State Council in 1967, a role redefined as national President in 1974. Domestically, Ceauçescu's government was authoritarian, with internal espionage, repression of minorities, and an excessive personality cult. He also practised nepotism: for example, Elena Ceauçescu, his wife, held the office of Deputy Prime Minister. Internationally, Ceauçescu promoted the cause of sovereignty for communist states, a line that led to his criticism of BREZHNEV and to the non-communist states seeing him as an independent: however, he kept Romania within the WARSAW PACT and COMECON. Ceauçescu was highly critical of GORBACHEV's reformist policies from the mid-1980s, and reacted brutally to popular anti-government demonstrations in 1989 that led to a revolution (*see* REVOLUTIONS OF 1989–91). In December 1989 he was arrested when the army leadership turned against the government. After a brief trial, he was executed.

Charles X (1757–1836) King of France, 1824–30. Charles, Comte d'Artois, was LOUIS XVI's youngest brother. He left France soon after the outbreak of the FRENCH REVOLUTION in 1789, and was involved in anti-revolutionary activities from his exile in the Great Britain, including an unsuccessful part in the Vendée revolts of 1795. He returned to France at the restoration. He succeeded his brother LOUIS XVIII in 1824, and quickly established a reactionary style of government that went against much of the post-Napoleonic settlement. For example, aristocratic and religious influences in politics and society were increased, and émigré nobles were compensated for lands lost during the revolution. His reaction was most evident from 1829 when he appointed Prince de Polignac as his Prime Minister; and when the 1830 elections produced a predominantly oppositional parliament, Charles dissolved the Chamber and introduced the St Cloud Ordinances, which included a limitation of the franchise and press censorship. These acts directly provoked the French revolution of 1830 (*see* REVOLUTIONS OF 1830), and Charles was forced to abdicate in favour of his Orleanist cousin, LOUIS-PHILIPPE. Charles died six years later.

Chaumont, treaty of (March 1814) *see* NAPOLEONIC WARS.

Chernenko, Konstantin (1911–85) Soviet politician. Chernenko joined the Communist party in 1930, and worked in both secret police and propaganda posts. He became a colleague of BREZHNEV in the 1950s through their mutual involvement in Moldavan politics, and he was subsequently advanced by Brezhnev, who viewed Chernenko as a possible successor. He joined the party's Central Committee in 1971. He missed out on the succession after Brezhnev's death due to ANDROPOV's advance, but he became Chairman of the Supreme Soviet on Andropov's death in 1984. He was, however, seriously ill, and his brief period as head of state was an ineffective one. He died in office in March 1985, and was succeeded by the more reformist GORBACHEV.

Chetniks Serbian guerrilla forces of various periods. The name was first used by anti-OTTOMAN Serbian nationalists in the late nineteenth and early twentieth centuries, during which time they were involved in guerrilla warfare in Macedonia and elsewhere. Chetniks fought for the Balkan League during the BALKAN WARS of 1912 and 1913, and attacked German troops during the FIRST WORLD WAR. Chetnik groups were revived in Yugoslavia in the early stages of the SECOND WORLD WAR, under Draza Mihailovich. Alongside TITO's communist partisans, they were an effective force in the RESISTANCE to the German and Italian invasion, and received backing from the UK. However, the Chetniks' predominantly Serbian and monarchist ideologies placed them apart from Tito's forces, and the anti-communist acts of some Chetnik groups were effectively acts of collaboration with the occupation. When the war ended, Tito, with Soviet backing, moved to suppress the Chetniks, which led to a brief period of civil war that ended with Mihailovich's execution in March 1946. The Chetnik legacy was revived again by Serbian nationalists in the late 1980s and 1990s during the break-up of Yugoslavia. *See* YUGOSLAVIA, DISSOLUTION.

Ciano, Galeazzo (1903–44) Italian politician. A career diplomat with a legal training, Ciano's political advancement was linked to his 1930 marriage to Edda Mussolini, MUSSOLINI's daughter. After serving as Envoy to China, Ciano returned to Italy and worked for the propaganda department, becoming Minister of Propaganda in 1935. He served as a pilot in the ITALO-ABYSSINIAN WAR, and then returned to office as Foreign Minister in 1936. Despite being involved in the negotiations that established the AXIS, Ciano attempted to follow a policy that would give Italy some freedom of action. He advised Mussolini to stay out of the SECOND WORLD WAR in 1939, and promoted intervention in the Balkans to offset German expansion. His influence declined from June 1940 when Italy joined the war, a decline that was hastened by the unsuccessful Greek campaign of 1940–41. In February 1943, Mussolini appointed Ciano as Ambassador to the Vatican, an effective demotion. Ciano supported Mussolini's deposition in July 1943. Later that year he was arrested in Germany, and returned to Mussolini's Salo government. He was tried for treason, and executed in 1944.

Clemenceau, Georges (1841–1929) French politician. Clemenceau came to prominence in 1870 as the Mayor of Montmartre during the PARIS COMMUNE. He entered national politics in 1876 when, as a Radical, he was elected to the Chamber of Deputies. He lost his seat in 1893 due to his implication in a financial scandal. He returned as a senator in 1902, and became Minister of the Interior and then Prime Minister in 1906. This term of office was characterised by repression of strikes and trade union activities. He spoke out against military failures during the FIRST WORLD WAR, before being appointed as Prime Minister by POINCARÉ in 1917. He provided successful leadership for the final stages of the war, and attempted to promote French interests and a strongly anti-German line as convenor of the PARIS PEACE CONFERENCE of 1919. The perceived leniency of the final settlement damaged his standing, and he left office in 1920 when the new Assembly refused to accept him as president.

Coalition, First *see* FRENCH REVOLUTIONARY WARS.

Coalition, Fourth *see* NAPOLEONIC WARS.

Coalition, Second *see* NAPOLEONIC WARS.

Coalition, Third *see* NAPOLEONIC WARS.

Code Napoleon Codification of civil law in France, March 1804. Various attempts were made during the period of the FRENCH REVOLUTION to rationalise and coordinate France's civil law, which was divided between Roman and customary traditions in the south and north respectively, and was complicated by the decline of church influence after 1789. NAPOLEON forced the issue through during his time as First Consul, and the code was published in March 1804. Some of the liberal ideas of the revolutionary period were consolidated, including the notion of individual equality, and the land reforms of that time were rationalised. Less liberal strands included restrictions on the rights of women and of trade unions. In 1807 the code was renamed as the *Code Napoleon*. It was revised in 1904, and has influenced the civil law codes of a number of countries.

Cold War The name popularly used to describe relations between the USA and its allies and the USSR and its allies from the end of the SECOND WORLD WAR until the early 1990s. The phrase was used in 1947 to stress the non-military conflict that existed between the USA and the USSR. The Cold War had its immediate origins in the Second World War itself, and in the divergent interests of the anti-AXIS allies beyond their desire to force Germany into an unconditional surrender. The different views of STALIN and President Franklin Roosevelt of the USA towards the post-war settlement of eastern Europe were, for example, evident at the TEHRAN CONFERENCE and YALTA CONFERENCE. When Germany was defeated in May 1945, these differences immediately became apparent in the victorious allies' attitudes towards the parts of Europe in which their armies had won. While the USA promoted the establishment of democratic and capitalist systems in western Europe, the USSR promoted communist systems in eastern Europe: despite the obvious ideological clashes involved, which characterised a great deal of Cold War discourse, both policies must also be linked to the two countries' strategic and economic interests.

In Poland, the USSR installed a communist government; while in Germany, the two powers clashed over the management of their occupied zones. This growing division of Europe found a contemporary resonance in British politician Winston Churchill's March 1946 speech in which he described an 'iron curtain' descending across Europe. The Cold War developed dramatically in 1947. In March, in response to the GREEK CIVIL WAR, in which communists were gaining ground, the USA's president, Harry Truman, committed the USA to provide financial and military support to counter communism; while the MARSHALL PLAN of June provided economic aid to help with reconstruction in non-communist countries. By the end of the year, the USA had sent both money and military advisers to Greece. In response, the USSR refused to allow any of the countries in which it had a controlling interest through military presence and communist control from receiving Marshall Aid, and established the COMINFORM to help coordinate communist party activities. The continued division of Europe was hastened in 1948 by a number of events, including a Soviet-backed communist coup in Czechoslovakia (*see* BENEŠ, GOTTWALD, MASARYK) in February, the signing of the BRUSSELS TREATY for mutual defence in March, and the BERLIN BLOCKADE and subsequent airlift. These divisions were formalised in 1949, when COMECON was established in January as a Soviet-dominated trading area for the east, NATO was established in April as a US-led military alliance for the west, and Germany was formally split into two separate states as the Federal Republic of Germany (FRG) and the German Democratic Republic (GDR). The stakes were also raised at this time due to the USSR's development of the atomic bomb. With armed conflict on Cold War lines occurring in Korea from 1950 until 1953, the tensions developed a global dimension.

Despite STALIN's death in March 1953, which some commentators thought would cause a relaxation in the Cold War, tensions continued to build in many areas. The communist suppression of demonstrations in the GDR in June 1953 and in Poland in June 1956, the accession of FRG to NATO in May, and the formation of the WARSAW PACT as the USSR's own military alliance system in May 1955 all showed a further formalisation of Cold War fault lines: the latter example, coming just after the AUSTRIAN STATE TREATY had been seen as a positive sign by the USA, was significant as it maintained a Soviet military presence throughout eastern Europe (*see also* IMPERIALISM). These tensions were exacerbated in late 1956 when the USSR used force against the HUNGARIAN RISING, and by the failure of Adam Rapacki's plan for central Europe as a nuclear-free zone under joint NATO-Warsaw Pact inspections. This phase of the Cold War, with little constructive discussion and much mutually reinforcing propaganda on both sides, peaked in the early 1960s. In Europe, this came over the construction of the BERLIN WALL, which became symbolic of the divisions in Europe; while globally, the crisis that developed out of the USSR's placing of nuclear missiles in Cuba led the USA and the USSR very close to open conflict.

There was some improvement in relations in the 1960s, including treaties in 1963 and 1968 on the limitation of nuclear weapons, but the indirect confrontation of communism that characterised the USA's intervention in Vietnam, and the USSR's suppression of the PRAGUE SPRING in August 1968, maintained the Cold War's high profile. This was clarified by BREZHNEV's claim that communist countries had the right to intervene in other countries where communism was under threat. The 1970s, however, saw some constructive moves to decrease the tensions. In the FRG, BRANDT's *OSTPOLITIK* improved relations between the FRG and the GDR, Poland and the USSR; the Strategic Arms Limitation Talks (SALT) between the USA and the USSR led to treaties in 1972 and 1979; while multinational talks in Helsinki and Geneva from 1973 until 1975 resulted in statements on human rights and security, and in the formation of the CONFERENCE ON SECURITY AND COOPERATION IN EUROPE (CSCE). However, the USSR's invasion of Afghanistan in December 1979, and the use of force and martial law against strikes and demonstrations in Poland in 1980 and 1981 (*see* JARUZELSKI, SOLIDARITY, WALESA), and the west's reactions to these actions (including the boycott of the 1980 Moscow Olympic Games over Afghanistan) maintained clear Cold War divisions. The stationing of nuclear missiles in eastern Europe by the USSR and in the UK by the USA in the early 1980s diluted some of the promise of the Helsinki period. However, an improvement in relations became evident from 1985 under GORBACHEV's leadership in the USSR, not least through his recognition that the USSR's resources were over-committed to defence. This change resulted in the US-Soviet Intermediate Nuclear Forces Treaty of December 1987. Politically, his promotion of *GLASNOST* and *PERESTROIKA* fed into reform movements in much of eastern Europe (*see* REVOLUTIONS OF 1989–91): and while the USSR responded with force in some cases, as in Estonia and Latvia in early 1991, the Brezhnev doctrine was explicitly rejected. In this climate of change, the issues that had maintained the Cold War broadly disappeared. In the aftermath, new tensions developed around such diverse issues as NATIONALISM, the political power struggles in the wake of communist domination, and the development of former communist countries as capitalist markets.

Comecon Abbreviated title of the Council for Mutual Economic Assistance, a Soviet-led trading area for eastern Europe. Comecon was established under STALIN's leadership in January 1949, both as a way to boycott Yugoslavia, and as a response to the MARSHALL PLAN and the ORGANISATION FOR EUROPEAN ECONOMIC COOPERATION (OEEC). Consisting originally of Bulgaria, Czechoslovakia, Hungary, Poland, Romania, and the USSR, the USSR's domination of its strategies ensured that it was effectively a form of Soviet IMPERIALISM. Albania joined later in 1949, as did the German Democratic Republic (GDR) in 1950. From the early 1960s, Comecon attempted to develop an integrated union through coordinated planning, although this was resisted by some member governments due to the limitations that central planning would impose on individual members' economies. Comecon expanded in the 1960s: although Albania left in 1961, Mongolia joined, and Yugoslavia gained associate membership; while Cuba and Vietnam joined in 1972 and 1978 respectively. In 1976, informal talks between Comecon and the EUROPEAN COMMUNITY (EC) began, but few results were achieved until the late 1980s, under GORBACHEV's leadership in the USSR. In 1988, Comecon and the EC formally recognised each other, and signed commercial treaties allowing for greater trade. Comecon broke down during the REVOLUTIONS OF 1989–91, and formally dissolved in the summer of 1991. A number of former Comecon countries quickly established links with the EC with a view to future membership (which the former GDR managed in 1990 through GERMAN REUNIFICATION) through Europe Agreements, including Czechoslovakia, Hungary and Poland in 1991.

Cominform Abbreviation for Communist Information Bureau, an international communist organisation under Soviet leadership (*see* COMMUNISM). In mid-1947, STALIN and MOLOTOV promoted the idea of re-establishing an international organisation through which communist parties in different countries could discuss issues under Soviet guidance, although the revival of the THIRD INTERNATIONAL was rejected. The timing was linked to the announcement of the MARSHALL PLAN, and fitted into the early COLD WAR context. The Cominform was subsequently established at a meeting in Poland in September 1947, attended by delegates from the communist parties of Bulgaria,

Czechoslovakia, France, Italy, Hungary, Poland, Romania, the USSR and Yugoslavia. French and Italian involvement was particularly problematic for the USA, as it was seen as evidence of Soviet influence beyond the areas taken by the Red Army at the end of the SECOND WORLD WAR. In June 1948, as part of the wider clash between Stalin and TITO over Balkan policy, the Yugoslav communist party was expelled. The organisation subsequently served as a channel of communication between communist parties until the early KHRUSHCHEV period in the USSR. In April 1956, Khrushchev dissolved it, both as a bridge-building exercise with Tito, and in order to demonstrate to the USA that the USSR did not plan to infiltrate non-communist countries through front parties.

Comintern *see* THIRD INTERNATIONAL.

communism Political and economic ideology. Communism, as it emerged into mainstream continental political discourse through the writings of MARX and ENGELS in the mid-nineteenth century, had some roots in earlier models of utopian, classless societies, often with Christian connotations. Under Marx and Engels, however, particularly through the *Communist Manifesto* of 1848, communism was reshaped as an ideal, ultimate state of human social development which would come about inevitably as a result of classes struggling over power and resources. It was projected to follow a period of proletarian control, and would be characterised by common ownership of all goods and services, and by an end to state control: in this, it shared some ground with both ANARCHISM and SOCIALISM. It differed from these other ideologies in its emphasis upon economic determinism, with all political change being caused by economic forces. While socialism remained the more significant ideology through the rest of the nineteenth century, the appropriation of the label 'communist' by the BOLSHEVIKS from 1918, and their promotion of Marx as read by LENIN as the ideological foundation of the revolutions of 1917 (*see* RUSSIAN REVOLUTIONS 1917), recast communism: it became closely identified with state economic planning, and a repressive management of political activity. This model influenced communist parties in all parts of Europe, some of which were used in the immediate post-SECOND WORLD WAR period as the basis of Soviet IMPERIALISM (*see* COLD WAR) until the REVOLUTIONS OF 1989–91 destroyed the party's power base in the USSR. Although some communist parties remained active in eastern Europe and elsewhere, these revolutions were widely interpreted as signalling the death of communism. However, the re-emergence of communism in Russia in the mid-1990s, and the survival of non-European communist governments (such as those in China, Cuba and the Democratic People's Republic of Korea), suggest the short-term perspective of such an interpretation.

Compromise of 1867 *see AUSGLEICH.*

Confederation of the Rhine Political organisation of the southern and central German states under French control during the NAPOLEONIC WARS. In 1806, after France's defeat of HABSBURG and Prussian forces at the battle of AUSTERLITZ, NAPOLEON organised a number of the medium-sized central and southern German states into a federal alliance system, thereby destroying the HOLY ROMAN EMPIRE. The Confederation was expanded between 1807 and 1810, finally covering an area from the French border to the Austrian border, and from the Baltic in the north to the Tyrol in the south. The Confederation was forced to comply with the CONTINENTAL SYSTEM of economic warfare against the UK, and member states had to provide troops for Napoleon's campaigns. The Confederation dissolved in 1813: as France's military defeats mounted after the battle of LEIPZIG, so individual states deserted the system.

Conference on Security and Cooperation in Europe (CSCE) International organisation. The CSCE was formed as a result of the Helsinki conference of 1973–75. Originally composed of thirty-five nations, it was established by treaty in August 1975 to act as a forum for the discussion of a wide range of issues – including disarmament, security, human rights, economic and technical cooperation, and the environment – that were of mutual interest to nations from NATO and the WARSAW PACT, as well as to neutral states: as such, its creation was a key event in the détente period of the COLD WAR. The CSCE held irregular but lengthy meetings, at Belgrade in 1977 and 1978, Madrid from 1980 to 1983, Vienna from 1986 to 1989, and an extraordinary meeting for heads of governments took place in Paris in November 1990. This meeting concentrated on the issues raised by the ending of the Cold War and the REVOLUTIONS OF 1989–91: it included the signing of the Conventional Forces in Europe treaty, and the Charter of Paris which set out agendas for post-Cold War developments. The CSCE continued to work on the same common interests, developing closer links with the UNITED NATIONS. In 1994, by which time it had fifty-three states as members, it changed its name to the Organisation for Security and Cooperation in Europe, a change which reflected its altered status and institutional growth.

Congress System Structure for international meetings between the victorious powers of the NAPOLEONIC WARS, 1815–23, with France from 1818. At the end of the Congress of Vienna (*see* VIENNA, CONGRESS OF) in 1815, Austria, Prussia, Russia and the UK (*see* QUADRUPLE ALLIANCE) agreed to meet in congress at intervals to discuss their common concerns. The system, devised mainly by METTERNICH, recognised that the wartime allies had diverse peacetime objectives and interests, but created a forum for the mutual discussion of both general and specific issues. In all, four other congresses were held: at AIX-LA-CHAPPELLE in 1818 (which included France); TROPPAU in 1820; LAIBACH in 1821; and VERONA in 1822. The system increasingly came to be used as a conservative agency working against the development of LIBERALISM and NATIONALISM anywhere in Europe, with increasing pressure from France, the HABSBURG empire, Prussia, and Russia for the powers to intervene in civil wars. The UK's opposition to such moves weakened the Congress System, which effectively dissolved after France invaded Spain in 1823 without the formal backing of the other powers. Despite these failings, the system can be seen as an experiment in international diplomatic cooperation.

conservatism Political and economic ideology. While conservatism has developed most fully as a partisan ideology in the UK, particularly from the mid-nineteenth century onwards in the form of the Conservative party, it also developed in continental Europe. It emerged in the wake of the FRENCH REVOLUTION as an anti-reformist ideology, in which the dramatic changes caused to established and inherited forms of authority – the state, the monarchy, the church – were condemned, and attempts were made to reverse them. Theoretically, this came through in the writings of Joseph de Maistre and others; while practically and politically, it was evident in the anti-revolutionary work of the QUADRUPLE ALLIANCE. However, the growth of LIBERALISM, NATIONALISM and SOCIALISM that was evident by the third quarter of the nineteenth century, and the changes in various countries' economies being caused by INDUSTRIALISATION, encouraged conservatives to develop a more dynamic and progressive ideology which could challenge the growing numbers of alternatives on display. By the end of the century, parties and alliances based on some form of conservatism, often involving landowners, industrialists, peasants, the military and the Church, were active throughout Europe. In the twentieth century, conservatism continued to influence a number of parties, particularly those historically specifically linked to religious denominations, such as the Catholic Centre party in Germany, and Christian Democrat parties in the Federal Republic of Germany and Italy after the SECOND WORLD WAR.

Constantine I (1868–1923) King of Greece, 1913–17, 1920–22. The eldest son of George I, Constantine led the Greek army in the BALKAN WARS of 1912–13 before succeeding to the throne on George's assassination in 1913. He opposed VENIZELOS' pro-allied policy during the FIRST WORLD WAR, a line which led to Anglo-French pressure on Greece in

1917. In June 1917, Constantine abdicated in favour of his son, Alexander; but after Alexander died in 1920, a plebiscite supported Constantine's return to the throne. However, the loss of territory through the GREEK-TURKISH WAR forced him to abdicate again in 1922. He died in Sicily the following year.

Constantine II (born 1940) King of Greece, 1964–73. The son of Paul I, Constantine succeeded to the throne in 1964 at a difficult time in Greek politics caused by the ongoing ENOSIS struggle and by tensions between the military leadership and the constitutional politicians. In April 1967, Constantine supported the anti-parliamentary coup by the GREEK COLONELS; but his change of attitude and attempt to oust the colonels in December 1967 ended in failure. He left Greece for exile in Italy. In 1973 the military government declared Greece a republic, and Constantine's rejection was finalised by an anti-restoration vote in a referendum of December 1974.

Constantinople agreement (March–April 1915) Secret FIRST WORLD WAR treaty between France, Russia and the UK on OTTOMAN territories. In March 1915, the naval part of the Franco-British DARDANELLES CAMPAIGN was called off. In the context of this failure to set up a speedy defeat of the Ottoman empire, and of Russia's early defeats in eastern Prussia (*see* TANNENBERG), France and the UK negotiated a secret agreement with Russia as a way of maintaining Russian interest in the war. The Constantinople agreement recognised British and Russian interests in the Ottoman empire, and provided mutual assurance for control of those areas after the war. The UK had interests in Arabia, Mesopotamia and Syria: in return, Russia was to be allowed to incorporate Constantinople, the Bosphorous, the bulk of European Turkey, and the Dardanelles. The magnitude of the agreement lay in the fact that it went against a long tradition in British policy of limiting Russian interests in the Straits. In 1918, when the BOLSHEVIKS declared themselves free of inherited treaty obligations, they published the Constantinople agreement (*see* RUSSIAN REVOLUTIONS 1917). The embarrassment caused by this helped to confirm the post-war mood for an end to secret diplomacy (*see* FOURTEEN POINTS). It also fed into Turkish republican nationalism and its rejection of British influence. *See* ATATÜRK, GREEK-TURKISH WAR.

Continental System France's economic blockade against the UK during the NAPOLEONIC WARS, lasting from 1806 until 1813. After the battle of Trafalgar of October 1805, NAPOLEON shifted his style of war against the UK to an economic one by introducing the Continental System, first decreed at Berlin in November 1806. By closing French, allied and satellite ports to British trade, the system aimed to disrupt the UK's economy and so force the British government to sue for peace. It was also designed as an internal imperial economic policy to allow French industry and commerce to develop without British competition (*see* IMPERIALISM). The British government responded in January 1807 by imposing duties on all neutral ships trading with continental Europe. The French response to this came in the Milan Decree of December 1807, which ordered all neutral ships to comply with the blockade. The treaty of TILSIT brought Prussia and Russia into the system, while Portugal and Spain were included in 1808, one of the acts which precipitated the Peninsular War.

The blockade worked to a point, as the UK suffered a recession from 1808 until 1811, and it forced the UK into a war with the USA in 1812 over neutral shipping. However, it was difficult to enforce without a greater naval force, and it was undermined in many areas by smuggling and corruption. It was also diluted by official exemption licences which were issued to allow an exit for some French surpluses, including grain and wine, from 1809, while the UK partially offset the blockade's effects by developing its trade links with South America and Asia. Internally, the system did help the development of some French industries, particularly textiles. Russia's abandonment of the blockade from 1810 precipitated Napoleon's Moscow campaign of 1812, and the system collapsed in 1813 in line with France's military reverses.

Corfu incident International crisis of 1923. In August 1923, five Italians working in Corfu on an international mission to establish the Albanian-Greek border were murdered. MUSSOLINI reacted with force by bombarding Corfu and by sending in an invading force. The Italian grounds for this intervention were to gain recompense for the dead men, and also to help protect Albania's interests, although Corfu's location made it strategically worthwhile in its own right. Greece appealed to the LEAGUE OF NATIONS, which found broadly in favour of Italy, and ordered the Greek government to pay compensation. However, Mussolini did not immediately withdraw the Italian forces: this did not occur until late September, after British and French pressure. Although the incident left Corfu in Greek hands, it demonstrated Mussolini's preparedness to use force at this early stage of his government, and helped to boost his domestic popularity. It also showed up the League of Nations' weaknesses, particularly the fact that without an armed force of its own it was unable to remove occupying armies.

Council of Europe International organisation. In May 1949, in the wake of the SECOND WORLD WAR, the Council of Europe was set up by ten governments. It was designed to be a truly European organisation that did not affect the political rights or sovereignty of any member nation, and was thus welcomed by some governments (notably the UK) which were more sceptical of any supranational model. The original members – Belgium, Denmark, France, Ireland, Luxembourg, the Netherlands, Norway, Sweden and the UK – were soon joined by Greece, Iceland and Turkey, and the Council began work in Strasbourg in August 1949. Its two main bodies were a consultative assembly and a committee of ministers: and while both had powers to debate issues and recommend responses to member governments, it was given no executive or legislative power. In 1955, it established the European Court of Human Rights. From the outset, it concentrated on political, social, cultural and humanitarian issues, and emphasised the notion of a common heritage amongst European democracies while encouraging both sectoral and general integration (*see* EUROPEAN COAL AND STEEL COMMUNITY, EUROPEAN COMMUNITY, EUROPEAN ECONOMIC COMMUNITY). The Council has expanded in each decade of its existence, with new members including the Federal Republic of Germany in 1951, Austria in 1956, Switzerland in 1963, Spain in 1976, Hungary in 1990 and Czechoslovakia in 1991: the timing of many of these memberships stresses the Council's role as a promoter of democratic traditions, as does the suspension of Greece during the period of the GREEK COLONELS. By 1996, the Council had forty member states.

Crimean War (1853–56) War between Russia and Turkey, the latter allied with France, the UK and others. In March 1853, NICHOLAS I attempted to claim special protection rights for Orthodox Christians in the OTTOMAN EMPIRE. This came in response to NAPOLEON III's acquisition of similar rights over Ottoman Catholics. The religious and ethnic issues brought longer-term strategic interests in the Balkans to a head, with France, the HABSBURG empire, Prussia, Russia and the UK all showing an interest in the affair. In June 1853 the Turkish government denied Nicholas I the requested rights. Russia invaded the Ottoman territories of Moldavia and Wallachia in October 1853, which led Turkey to declare war. The following month, a Turkish fleet was beaten at Sinope. The fear of Russian success in the Straits led to Franco-British intervention. In January 1854, a combined naval force entered the Black Sea and sailed for Varna, where it met with a land force in April, having jointly declared war on Russia in March and attempted an ineffective campaign in the Baltic. Russia withdrew its troops from Moldavia and Wallachia in August 1854 after Habsburg threats, and had to face an allied landing at Eupatoria in the Crimea in September. The allies were aiming to capture the port of Sevastopol: and after battles at Alma in September, Balaclava in October, and Inkerman in November, they were able to besiege Sevastopol from January 1855. Piedmont-Sardinia joined the alliance that month, and Russian interests changed after Nicholas I's death in March 1855 and the accession of the less belligerent ALEXANDER II. In September 1855, Sevastopol fell. Russia's economic crisis, and its inability to continue the war against the militarily superior allies, furthered its decline, which was underlined in November 1855 when Sweden joined the alliance and threatened to attack Russia in the Baltic. In January 1856 Alexander sued for peace, which was settled at the treaty of PARIS in March 1856. The Crimean War dead totalled approximately 675,000, of whom some 80 per cent died of diseases.

Crystal Night *see KRISTALLNACHT.*

Curzon Line Nominal Polish-Russian frontier. Poland's eastern frontier was left unsettled at the PARIS PEACE CONFERENCE and in the resultant treaties. In December 1919, in the context of growing tension between Poland and Russia, the Curzon Line (named after the British Foreign Secretary, Lord Curzon) was proposed by the British government as a new frontier. It was based in part on the idea of self-determination (*see* FOURTEEN POINTS), taking account of ethnic and religious groups in the disputed areas. Running from Frodno in the north to the Carpathian mountains in the south, the line left majority Ukrainian, Russian and Belorussian areas with predominantly Orthodox populations outside Poland, while Poland retained majority Polish and Catholic areas. However, the plan was not accepted by either the Polish or the Russian governments, and was not applied. A war between Poland and Russia in 1920 (*see* RUSSIAN CIVIL WAR) left Poland in a stronger position, and the treaty of RIGA established the new frontier to the east of the Curzon Line. A frontier based on the Curzon Line was used by the German and Soviet governments in the NAZI-SOVIET PACT of 1939, part of which defined mutual areas on domination in a conquered Poland. The line also formed the basis for the post-1945 Polish frontier with the USSR.

Custozza, battle of (July 1848) *see* AUSTRO-PIEDMONTESE WAR.

Custozza, battle of (June 1866) *see* AUSTRO-PRUSSIAN WAR.

D

D-Day *see* NORMANDY CAMPAIGN.

Daladier, Edouard (1884–1970) French politician. Daladier entered the Chamber of Deputies in 1919 as a Radical. He gained extensive ministerial experience in the 1920s and early 1930s, notably as Minister of War from 1932 to 1934, and was Prime Minister for two short periods in 1933 and 1934. He returned to the War Ministry in 1936, and became Prime Minister again in April 1938. His domestic record of public works was largely overshadowed by his pro-APPEASEMENT foreign policy, which led him to support the MUNICH AGREEMENT of September 1938. He resigned in March 1940, but stayed on as Minister for War until the fall of France in May 1940 (*see* SECOND WORLD WAR). He unsuccessfully attempted to establish an anti-VICHY government-in-exile in North Africa, but was arrested and tried by the Vichy authorities for his part in taking France into the war. He was imprisoned until 1945. He returned to politics after the war, as a member of the National Assembly from 1946 until 1958.

D'Annunzio, Gabriele (1863–1938) Italian writer and politician. A successful novelist and poet, D'Annunzio was a deputy from 1897 to 1900. He favoured Italian expansion in the Balkans, and argued in favour of Italy joining the FIRST WORLD WAR in 1914. When Italy declared war the following year, D'Annunzio volunteered, and served with distinction, particularly in the air force. In September 1919, when the PARIS PEACE CONFERENCE overturned the terms of the treaty of LONDON of 1915, D'Annunzio led a group of volunteers into the Adriatic port of Fiume, which had been awarded to Yugoslavia, and established a city state. This lasted for sixteen months, and was characterised by a style of rule and display later developed by MUSSOLINI's Fascists (*see* FASCISM). D'Annunzio was forced out of Fiume in January 1921 by the Italian government. Despite supporting the Fascists and the MARCH ON ROME, D'Annunzio retired from public life in 1922.

Danton, Georges (1759–94) French politician. A lawyer, Danton entered politics during the FRENCH REVOLUTION through the JACOBIN Club and the Paris Commune in 1791. He encouraged the August 1792 attack of the Tuileries and the deposition of LOUIS XVI, and was also implicated, as Minister of Justice, in the September massacres of 1792. When the TERROR was first instituted, he broadly supported it, and was a member of the Convention and the Committee of Public Safety. However, he later became more moderate, and spoke in the Convention against ROBESPIERRE and the extent of state terrorism. He was arrested in 1794, charged with accepting bribes from foreign governments during the FRENCH REVOLUTIONARY WARS, and executed with many of his supporters in April 1794.

Dardanelles campaign (1915) Allied military operation against the OTTOMAN EMPIRE during the FIRST WORLD WAR. With stalemate established on the western front by the end of 1914, British planners turned their attention to the Balkans. An attack on the Ottoman empire through the Straits was planned as a way of weakening the central powers through opening a third European front, and as a way of allowing the Russian Black Sea fleet to enter the war. The attack started in February with an Anglo-French naval bombardment of Turkish defences in the Straits, followed in March by a combined naval attack on the Straits. This was called off after the loss of four ships, after which troop landings were attempted at Gallipoli. This campaign lasted until January 1916, and ultimately failed for the allies, as the Ottoman forces had been able to prepare for defence, and were armed with German artillery. The allied forces, comprised of Australasian, British and French troops, lost 36,000 men.

Darlan, Jean (1881–1942) French admiral and politician. A successful naval commander in the FIRST WORLD WAR, Darlan was made Commander-in-Chief of the French navy in 1939. After France fell to Germany in May 1940 (*see* SECOND WORLD WAR), Darlan joined the VICHY government, serving at first as Naval Minister. He became more pro-German after the British attack on the French fleet at Mers-el-Kébir in July 1940, and, as Vice-Premier of Vichy from February 1941, entered into discussions with HITLER about military cooperation. Allied successes in north Africa, combined with the German occupation of Vichy France in November 1942, caused Darlan to side with the Allies. He was assassinated by a French royalist in December 1942.

Dawes Plan *see* REPARATIONS, GERMAN.

De Gasperi, Alcide (1881–1954) Italian politician. A native of Trentino, De Gasperi entered the Austrian parliament in 1911 as a representative of a pro-Trentine autonomy party. When Trentino was awarded to Italy by the treaty of ST GERMAIN, he entered Italian national politics with the Popular party, being elected to the Chamber of Deputies. An opponent of FASCISM, he took part in the AVENTINE SECESSION and lost his seat in 1926, before being imprisoned until 1929. He returned to national politics in 1944 as a leading member of the new Christian Democrat party. De Gasperi became Prime Minister in December 1945, and played a leading role in establishing the new republic. An anti-communist, he helped to win US backing for Italy, and ensured Italian involvement in the growth of European integration by taking Italy into NATO, the COUNCIL OF EUROPE and the EUROPEAN COAL AND STEEL COMMUNITY. He resigned in 1953 after a relatively poor electoral performance, and died the following year.

de Gaulle, Charles (1890–1970) French soldier and politician. After serving in the FIRST WORLD WAR, de Gaulle taught and wrote on military theory, and commanded a division in the SECOND WORLD WAR before taking up a ministerial post in the Ministry of Defence in 1940. He left France for London on the German victory of May 1940. From there, with assistance from the British government, he developed into a leading figure in the French government-in-exile based on the

FREE FRENCH organisation and its contacts in the French RESISTANCE. Based in Algiers from 1943, de Gaulle entered Paris in August 1944, and helped to form a provisional government which was recognised by the victorious allies. He served as provisional President for ten weeks from November 1945, but resigned over the limited presidential powers in the new constitution. Under the Fourth Republic, he offered a distant leadership to the right-wing Union of the French People (RPF). As a popular figure who could also work with the military, he returned to prominence in 1958 during the Algerian crisis as Prime Minister of an emergency government. His acceptance of the post was conditional upon the revision of the constitution to include the presidential powers for which he had previously called.

This revision became the basis for the Fifth Republic, and de Gaulle was elected as its first president in 1958, a post he kept until the 1965 election. He initiated decolonisation, despite this losing the support of some sections of the army (*see also* IMPERIALISM). His government was characterised by a number of foreign policy strands, including the promotion of a Franco-German relationship, the courting of eastern European countries, and the development of the EUROPEAN ECONOMIC COMMUNITY (EEC) without British or American involvement. He also developed a French nuclear capability, and took France out of NATO. Although he remained a popular figure in France, his domestic policies were overshadowed by these international concerns, and the lack of investment in education and welfare precipitated riots in Paris in May 1968. He resigned the following year when he lost a constitutional referendum which developed into a general vote of confidence.

Decembrist Conspiracy (1825) Russian coup attempt of 1825. During and after the NAPOLEONIC WARS, a number of members of the Russian nobility and military elites became influenced by western European political ideas. A number of individuals formed secret societies, in some cases based on freemasonry, as fora for the discussion of such issues as economic reform, republicanism, constitutionalism, and the abolition of serfdom. By 1825, groups in both the north and the south of Russia were planning to stage a coup when ALEXANDER I died. The Tsar's unexpected death in early December 1825 (hence 'Decembrists') forced the issue, and in the three-week succession crisis that followed a number of small-scale rebellions were staged. The most significant took place in St Petersburg, where approximately 3,000 troops under conspiratorial officers took to the streets. However, they surrendered when met by loyalist troops, and this rising collapsed. Five leaders were executed, and over 200 exiled in the aftermath as NICHOLAS I came to the throne and consolidated his position. The plot failed because the plotters were diverse and heterogeneous, with no agreed tactics or objectives, and because no attempt was made to turn it into a popular rebellion. In this context, and with a predominantly loyal military, the Tsar was difficult to topple. However, the plot did show that not all members of Russia's elites were content with the country's political structure, and it provided an example of how some of the FRENCH REVOLUTION's ideas were spreading to all parts of Europe.

Delclassé, Théophile (1852–1923) French politician. Delclassé entered the Chamber of Deputies in 1889, and quickly advanced, taking office as Minister of Colonies in 1893 until 1895. From here, he advocated an expansionist line, but also recognised that France would need to compromise with either Germany or the UK. As Foreign Minister from 1898, he promoted friendly relations with the UK that led to the signing of the *ENTENTE CORDIALE* in 1904, and with Italy as a way of weakening the TRIPLE ALLIANCE. He was forced to resign over the MOROCCAN CRISIS in 1905. He served as Naval Minister from 1911 to 1913, again promoting cooperation with the UK, and as Ambassador to St Petersburg from 1913 to 1914. In 1914, Delclassé was reappointed as Foreign Minister, and also as Minister of War. His main success in this period of the FIRST WORLD WAR was the treaty of LONDON of 1915.

Deniken, Anton (1872–1947) Russian soldier. Deniken joined the army at the age of fifteen. He served as a major in the Russo-Japanese War of 1904, and as a staff officer in the FIRST WORLD WAR, achieving the rank of general in February 1917. He was committed to the provisional government that emerged from the February 1917 revolution (*see* RUSSIAN REVOLUTIONS 1917), and commanded the Russian forces on the western and southwestern fronts until the October revolution. He joined with other counter-revolutionaries after the Bolshevik seizure of power, and became the commander of a White Russian army in the RUSSIAN CIVIL WAR. After some successes in the Caucasus and the Ukraine in 1918 and 1919, his force was repelled by the Red Army under TROTSKY, and pushed back into the Caucasus. He escaped from Russia, later living in both France and the USA.

Depression, Great (1929 onwards) Major international economic depression. In the late 1920s, the US economy began to suffer from agricultural over-production and a decline in demand for consumer goods. This fed into a general depression which, in October 1929, became catastrophic when panic trading on the New York investment markets caused the Wall Street Crash. The US depression quickly impacted upon a number of European nations, as so much of the European recovery since the FIRST WORLD WAR had been dependent upon investment and loans from the USA. In 1931, the primary Austrian bank collapsed, causing investors in banks throughout Europe to withdraw their assets; Germany's banks were also temporarily closed in the summer of 1931 to prevent drains on reserves. The sudden disappearance of foreign investment hit agriculture and industry in many countries, particularly Austria and Germany, causing employers to cut their costs through redundancies and closure of factories and workshops. Many countries raised tariffs and other duties, which in turn depressed international trade still further. The USA's moratorium on REPARATIONS, while helping the defeated nations of the FIRST WORLD WAR, hit recipient nations, such as Belgium, Greece and the UK. The impact of the Depression can be seen in unemployment terms: in Germany, for example, unemployment rose to 4,500,000 in July 1931, and to 6,000,000 by 1932, approximately 30 per cent of the workforce; in Poland, by 1936 approximately 6,000,000 people were out of work, roughly 45 per cent of the workforce. The Depression's impact lessened as the 1930s went on, helped by rearmament and the growth of consumer-led economies, but the economic uncertainties it produced in the early 1930s clearly contributed to the rise of right-wing politics in Austria, Germany (*see* NAZISM, THIRD REICH), Greece, Poland and elsewhere (*see* FASCISM). During the SECOND WORLD WAR, planning for a more stable post-war international economic system was based on the assumption that another depression on this scale could be averted. *See* BRETTON WOODS CONFERENCE.

Dimitrov, Georgi (1882–1949) Bulgarian politician. A trade union activist and social democrat, Dimitrov was elected to the Sobranje in 1913. He was imprisoned for his opposition to Bulgaria's involvement in the FIRST WORLD WAR. In 1917 he joined the Communist party. He was involved in the 1923 coup against BORIS III, after which he left Bulgaria, living variously in Moscow, Vienna and Berlin. He was active in the THIRD INTERNATIONAL, running its Bulgarian section from Berlin from 1929. In 1933 he was charged with starting the Reichstag fire, but he used the trial to criticise the Nazis (*see* NAZISM, THIRD REICH) and to defend COMMUNISM. After his acquittal, the German government deported Dimitrov to the USSR. He returned to Bulgaria in 1945 as the head of the provisional government, and, as Prime Minister from 1946, he was influential in framing the new Soviet-style republican constitution. However, he attempted to follow a foreign policy independent of Moscow, seen most obviously in his links with TITO and the 1947 friendship pact with Yugoslavia. He shifted this policy after STALIN's personal intervention. He died in office in July 1949 while visiting Moscow for medical treatment.

Dollfuss, Englebert (1892–1934) Austrian politician. Dollfuss served in the FIRST WORLD WAR before entering politics through the Farmers League and the Christian Social party. He became Minister of Agriculture and Forestry in 1931. His relative success in dealing with the impact of the DEPRESSION launched him to higher office as Chancellor and Foreign Minister in May 1932. He attempted to keep Austria from domination by Germany (*see ANSCHLUSS*) by developing links with Hungary and Italy, and tried to stabilise Austrian politics by closing down extreme parties. This involved an increasingly dictatorial style of rule: he suspended parliament, and outlawed both the Communist and Nazi parties in 1933. In February 1934, Dollfuss provoked and then violently suppressed a socialist rising in Vienna; and in May, he introduced a new fascist-style constitution with dictatorial power for the chancellor and corporate structures for the economy (*see* FASCISM). He was murdered by Austrian Nazis during their unsuccessful *Anschluss* attempt of July 1934.

Döntiz, Karl (1891–1980) German sailor and politician. Dönitz joined the German navy in 1910, and served in the FIRST WORLD WAR, specialising from 1916 in submarines. A prisoner of war in the UK at the end of the war, he rejoined the navy on his return to Germany. Dönitz welcomed the Nazi government (*see* THIRD REICH), and was given resources to develop submarine building and strategy after the ANGLO-GERMAN NAVAL AGREEMENT of 1935. He was promoted to Rear Admiral and Commander-in-Chief of submarines in 1940, carrying the main responsibility for U-boat attacks on allied shipping in the Atlantic. In 1945, HITLER named Dönitz as his successor, with Dönitz taking on the role of Chancellor on 1 May 1945 after Hitler's suicide. He established a predominantly non-Nazi cabinet, and attempted to make a separate peace with the western allies. When this proved unsuccessful, he declared Germany's unconditional surrender. Dönitz was found guilty of war crimes and crimes against peace at the NUREMBERG TRIALS, for which he served a ten-year prison sentence.

Dragashan, battle of (June 1821) *see* GREEK WAR OF INDEPENDENCE.

Dreikaiserbund (Three Emperors' League) (1873) Informal agreement between the emperors of Austria-Hungary, Germany and Russia. In the aftermath of the FRANCO-PRUSSIAN WAR of 1870–71 and the formation of the German empire (*see* GERMAN UNIFICATION), BISMARCK worked with ANDRÁSSY to develop and promote good relations between Austria-Hungary, Germany and Russia. The *Dreikaiserbund*, based on talks between WILLIAM I, ALEXANDER II and FRANCIS JOSEPH, offered an opportunity for this. The League did not involve any concrete commitments: it simply set up a forum for the discussion of issues of mutual interest, and allowed the imperial powers to condemn republicanism. The League declined in 1875 over Russian opposition to Germany's anti-French stance, and effectively collapsed as a result of the treaty of SAN STEFANO in 1878 due to Austria-Hungary's and Russia's different aspirations in the Balkans. In 1881, Bismarck developed a more formal Three Emperors' Alliance between the same powers. By this, each power committed itself to neutrality if any one other partner was involved in a war, and agreed to allow change in the Balkans only through agreements. The alliance, which was renewed in 1884, also formalised Austria-Hungary's and Russia's respective areas of influence in the Balkans, and closed the Black Sea.

Dreyfus affair (1894–1906) French political crisis. In December 1894 Captain Alfred Dreyfus, a Jewish artillery officer serving on the French General Staff, was convicted in a court martial of passing military secrets to the German Embassy in Paris. The evidence against him was extremely weak: but he was sentenced to life on the prison colony of Devil's Island. In 1896, evidence began to emerge that Major Marie-Charles Esterhazy had been the real spy, and that the case against Dreyfus had been based on forgeries made by another officer, Colonel Hubert-Joseph Henry: but this evidence was suppressed. In January 1898, the issue became much more public when the novelist Emile Zola published an open letter, '*J'accuse!*', in CLEMENCEAU's journal *L'Aurore*, which made specific allegations about officers forging evidence and lying. The publicity aroused by this campaign led to the case being re-opened, and to Henry's arrest and suicide. In August 1899 Dreyfus was retried: the court martial confirmed his guilt, but allowed for 'extenuating circumstances', and reduced his sentence to ten years. He was subsequently pardoned by the president, and his innocence was finally recognised by a civil court in 1906.

The anti-Dreyfus campaign reflected the growth of ANTI-SEMITISM in France: Dreyfus was one of the few highly placed Jews in the French military. This campaign was also associated with monarchists, the Catholic Church, and the higher sections of the military establishment. The pro-Dreyfus campaign mobilised republican and socialist opinion, with his backers seeing the conviction of an innocent man as evidence of the power held by the army and the church. As such, it contributed to a rise in anti-clericalism. Overall, the scandal embodied and aggravated some of the THIRD REPUBLIC's weaknesses: and, along with the BOULANGER AFFAIR and other scandals, it served to discredit the establishment.

Dreyfus, Alfred *see* DREYFUS AFFAIR.

Dual Alliance (October 1879) Military treaty between Austria-Hungary and Germany. In the context of worsening relations between Russia and Germany after the BERLIN CONGRESS of 1878, ANDRÁSSY and BISMARCK developed the idea of an alliance as a block against Russian aggression. The secret alliance provided for mutual aid if either partner was attacked by Russia, and for neutrality in the case of an attack by another country. The alliance was designed to be renewed as appropriate, and thus became a key part of both countries' diplomacy until 1918. The security provided by Germany's unconditional support for Austria-Hungary was a factor in the latter's belligerent attitude in 1914. In 1882, the parallel TRIPLE ALLIANCE was formed, which brought Italy into alliance with the Dual Alliance partners.

Dual Entente *see* FRANCO-RUSSIAN ALLIANCE.

Dubček, Alexander (1921–92) Czechoslovakian politician. Born in Slovakia, Dubček grew up in the USSR. He returned to Czechoslovakia in 1938, and joined the Communist party. After fighting in the RESISTANCE during the SECOND WORLD WAR, he became a party official and returned to the USSR in the mid-1950s for further political education. He succeeded NOVOTNÝ as the party's First Secretary in 1968, and immediately introduced reforms designed to relax some of the more repressive features of communist rule, a period which became known as the PRAGUE SPRING. The reforms, coupled with his plans for an independent foreign policy, precipitated the Soviet invasion of 1968. Dubček was forced to withdraw the reforms and recant his deviation. He served as President of the Federal Assembly from 1968 to 1969, and as Ambassador to Turkey, before being expelled from the party in 1970. After the revolution of 1989 (*see* REVOLUTIONS OF 1989–91), Dubček returned to national politics as Chairman of the Czechoslovakian Parliament, a position he held until his death in 1992.

Dunkirk, treaty of (March 1947) Mutual aid treaty between France and the UK. The first European pact to be signed in the aftermath of the SECOND WORLD WAR, the treaty of Dunkirk provided for mutual military aid for fifty years in case of an attack on either country by Germany. It also provided for economic consultation between the two governments, which laid the foundations for the BRUSSELS TREATY of 1948.

Dunkirk evacuation (May–June 1940) *see* SECOND WORLD WAR.

Duppel, battle of (April 1864) *see* SCHLESWIG WAR.

E

eastern policy *see* *OSTPOLITIK*.

Ebert, Friedrich (1871–1925) German politician. Ebert joined the Social Democratic party (SPD) in 1889, and entered the Reichstag in 1912. The following year he became the party's Chairman. An anti-revolutionary, he was appointed Chancellor in November 1918 in the immediate aftermath of the collapse of the German empire. He helped to establish the WEIMAR REPUBLIC, and to quell the revolutionary situation in Germany through a pact with the army that guaranteed the latter a great deal of autonomy. The National Assembly made him provisional President of the Republic in February 1919. Despite his dislike of the harsh terms of the treaty of VERSAILLES, he accepted it, an act which ensured his vilification by many. Ebert was due to stand for election as president in 1922, but his provisional term of office was extended due to the instability of the time. He was unsuccessfully tried for treason in 1924 after allegations that he had taken part in a munitions strike during the First World War. Ebert died in office the following year.

Ebro offensive (July 1939) *see* SPANISH CIVIL WAR.

EC *see* EUROPEAN COMMUNITY.

ECSC *see* EUROPEAN COAL AND STEEL COMMUNITY.

EDC *see* EUROPEAN DEFENCE COMMUNITY.

EEC *see* EUROPEAN ECONOMIC COMMUNITY.

EFTA *see* EUROPEAN FREE TRADE ASSOCIATION.

Eichmann, Adolf (1906–62) German administrator. Eichmann worked as a salesman before joining the Austrian Nazi party in 1932 (*see* NAZISM). He moved back to Germany, and joined the Jewish department of the Nazi intelligence organisation, the SD. The head of the SD's Office for Jewish Emigration from 1935, Eichmann administered the Jewish migrations from Vienna and Prague in 1938 and 1939 respectively, and became the head of the GESTAPO's Jewish Evacuation Department in 1941. Eichmann attended the Wannsee conference of January 1942 which attempted to coordinate the FINAL SOLUTION, and was made responsible for the overall administration of the process, directing such areas as transport and gas chamber construction. He personally oversaw the deportations of Hungarian Jews in 1944. Eichmann was arrested by US troops in 1945, but he escaped and left Europe on a Vatican passport. In 1960 Israeli agents kidnapped him in Argentina and took him to Israel for trial. He was found guilty of war crimes, crimes against humanity, and crimes against the Jewish people, and executed in 1962.

emancipation of the serfs (Russia) (February 1861) Russian socio-economic reform. Serfdom had developed in many parts of Europe as a form of socio-economic management. Although practices varied between areas, it involved private, state or Church ownership of individual domestic and agricultural workers. The individual serfs had few freedoms, although owners had various obligations towards them. The practice came under attack during the FRENCH REVOLUTION, and it was abolished in many areas occupied by the French army during the FRENCH REVOLUTIONARY WARS and the NAPOLEONIC WARS. The REVOLUTIONS OF 1848 saw its abolition in the HABSBURG empire. However, it survived in Russia. After the defeat of the CRIMEAN WAR, ALEXANDER II began to address a number of long-term structural weaknesses in Russia's polity, economy and society. In 1856 he specifically addressed serfdom, and called for its reform as it was seen as economically inefficient, and as a cause for political discontent. At this stage, approximately 22,500,000 people were serfs (31 per cent of the Russian population), owned by just over 200,000 individuals, while the state owned an additional 19,000,000.

Between 1857 and 1861 the details of emancipation were developed, which fed into the emancipation edict of February 1861. The edict represented a compromise between the perceived need for reform and the vested interests of the landowners who would be losing their labour force. Individual serfs were given their freedom, and allowed to buy the land they currently worked and run it on private commercial lines. The state provided loans to help with the capital costs of purchase: while private landowners were compensated by a system of redemption payments, to be paid over forty-nine years. In practice, the costs involved meant that most of the land went into collective ownership through the *mir* system of rural communes, where conservative influences tended to retard agricultural experimentation and thus reduce productivity. The emancipation thus failed to improve the efficiency of Russian agriculture, particularly in the context of a growing population, while the income losses suffered by individual peasants created a new set of causes for social and political discontent in the countryside.

Enabling Act (March 1933) German legislation. On 5 March 1933, the Nazis (*see* NAZISM) failed to win an absolute majority in the national election which followed HITLER's appointment as Chancellor. In order to achieve full power, the Nazis introduced an enabling bill under the WEIMAR REPUBLIC's constitution, designed to give the government emergency powers without consulting the Reichstag. The bill, entitled the 'Law for removing the distress of People and Reich', was introduced to the Reichstag on 23 March. With Nazi paramilitaries in the building, only the Social Democrats voted against the bill, which was passed by 441 votes to 94. The centre and right-wing parties supported it. The act gave the government power to rule for four years without consulting the Reichstag, and the power to alter the constitution. It also undermined the role of the presidency. It thus created the legal framework for the establishment of the Nazi dictatorship. To comply with technicalities, the act was renewed in 1937, 1939 and 1943. *See also* THIRD REICH.

Engels, Friedrich (1820–95) German political theorist. Engels came from a rich cotton manufacturing family, but developed communist ideas (*see* COMMUNISM), particularly after observing industrial conditions in England, where he moved in 1842. These views were expressed and popularised in *The Condition of the Working Classes in England*, published in 1845. He met MARX in 1844, and worked with him in the radical press in Germany. He also joined the Communist League in 1847, took part in the revolution of 1848 in Baden (*see* REVOLUTIONS OF 1848), and co-wrote *The Communist Manifesto* with Marx in 1848. He moved back to England in 1849, working for his family's cotton firm until 1870. He continued to work with Marx, both by providing funds for him and by editing his writings. Engels was a founder of the SECOND INTERNATIONAL, and an adviser to the founders of the German Social Democratic party. He continued working on Marx's writings after Marx died in 1883, playing an important part in making *Capital* and other texts ready for publication.

enosis (Greek: 'union') Notion of political union between Greece and Cyprus. The concept of *enosis* emerged in both Cyprus and Greece during the nineteenth century, owing much to broader trends of nationalism and unification at a time when Cyprus became a British possession. After British control was formalised by the treaty of LAUSANNE in 1923, calls for *enosis* recommenced in various political and cultural fora. It emerged as a major political cause in the 1950s, promoted diplomatically by MAKARIOS, and through violence against the British administration by EOKA (National Organisation of Cypriot Fighters) from 1955. British interests in maintaining influence in the region led to a compromise settlement negotiated in 1959: Cyprus was made independent and allowed into the British Commonwealth. The idea of union with Greece survived this, and re-emerged in 1974 when the GREEK COLONELS organised a pro-*enosis* coup on Cyprus. However, this provoked a Turkish invasion and subsequent colonisation of northern Cyprus, which gradually led to the development of two separate states on the island, divided by a UNITED NATIONS force.

Entente Cordiale (French: 'cordial agreement') (April 1904) Agreement between France and the UK, made in April 1904. Colonial disputes between France and the UK had created tension in the 1880s and 1890s, particularly in Egypt and the Sudan (*see* IMPERIALISM). In 1899, these were diluted by talks on spheres of influence: but, in the context of apparently increasing German hostility towards both countries, the *Entente*

Cordiale was established as a more formal settlement and as a means to improve relations. Negotiated by Lord Lansdowne and DELCLASSÉ, the *Entente* formally recognised British rights in Egypt and French rights in Morocco, while also dealing with other disputed areas, such as Madagascar and Siam. The *Entente* had no military aspect, and was maintained in the early stages through increasing cultural and trade links between the two countries, and through British royal patronage. However, the MOROCCAN CRISIS of 1905 brought the partners closer together, and joint military talks began in 1906. In 1907, a colonial agreement between Russia and the UK, combined with the FRANCO-RUSSIAN ALLIANCE of 1894, effectively brought France, Russia and the UK into an alignment which became known as the TRIPLE ENTENTE. The *Entente Cordiale* influenced France's relations with the UK through the FIRST WORLD WAR and into the inter-war period and beyond. *See* treaty of DUNKIRK.

Erfurt Union Union of German states, 1850. After the failure of the FRANKFURT PARLIAMENT to produce a constitution for a unified Germany that was acceptable to Prussia, FREDERICK WILLIAM IV of Prussia established a union of German states at Erfurt in March 1850. Aiming to develop a new unified state under Prussian leadership, discussions opened in April. However, Bavaria and other influential states refused to join the union, and Austria resisted the Prussian attempt at dominance in northern Germany. Prussia was not strong enough to fight Austria over this issue, and Frederick William backed down at the Olmütz Convention of November 1850, agreeing to dissolve the Erfurt Union and restore fully the structure of the GERMAN CONFEDERATION.

Erhard, Ludwig (1897–1977) West German politician. An economist, Erhard first came to prominence as an advisor to the occupation forces on economic reconstruction in Germany after the SECOND WORLD WAR, most notably as Chairman of the Economic Executive Council of the British and American zones in 1948. He entered parliament as a Christian Democrat in 1949, and was immediately appointed Minister for Economic Affairs by ADENAUER. Helped by the general recovery in western Europe, Erhard oversaw the Federal Republic of Germany's 'economic miracle', promoting growth through policies that favoured investment, encouraged immigration, promoted non-confrontational labour relations, and provided a welfare system within a capitalist economy, a model he described as the 'social market economy'. He became Deputy Chancellor in 1957, and succeeded Adenauer as Chancellor in 1963. He was less successful in this role than he had been as a specialist, and he resigned over contested tax increases in 1966.

Ethiopian War *see* ITALO-ABYSSINIAN WAR.

EU *see* EUROPEAN UNION.

Euratom Abbreviation for the European Atomic Energy Community. Euratom was created by the treaty of ROME of March 1957 at the same time as the EUROPEAN ECONOMIC COMMUNITY (EEC), and with the same membership of Belgium, the Federal Republic of Germany (FRG), France, Italy, Luxembourg and the Netherlands. It was designed to provide integration in the important sector of atomic and nuclear energy, providing the members with the means to develop this energy source at a time of uncertainty over more traditional sources. Euratom was part of the wider structure of the early European communities, sharing the Assembly and Court of Justice with the EEC and the EUROPEAN COAL AND STEEL COMMUNITY, but, until 1967, it had its own budget, Council of Ministers and Commission, along with an advisory Scientific and Technical Committee. In 1967 Euratom was fully merged with the other communities. The membership of Euratom has been the same as that of the EEC and its successor, the EUROPEAN COMMUNITY.

European Atomic Energy Community *see* EURATOM.

European Coal and Steel Community (ECSC) European economic organisation for the coal and steel industries. The ECSC was based on the French politician Robert Schuman's plan of 1950 as a supranational body to promote and develop the key industries of coal and steel. These were seen as vital due to their significance for post-SECOND WORLD WAR reconstruction in all countries, and because supranational control of them could prevent unilateral rearmament by any members. The ECSC was established between Belgium, the Federal Republic of Germany (FRG), France, Italy, Luxembourg and the Netherlands by the treaty of Paris of April 1951, and started work in July 1952. Based in Luxembourg, and consisting of a Council of Ministers, an Assembly (using existing members of parliamentary bodies from member states), a High Authority, and a Court of Justice, the ECSC encouraged the designated industries through dropping internal tariffs, promoting a free labour market, and providing training and development schemes. In 1967 the ECSC formally merged with the other European communities, the EUROPEAN ECONOMIC COMMUNITY (EEC) and EURATOM, under the new structure of the EUROPEAN COMMUNITY. The ECSC is widely seen as a sector-based prototype for the more general EEC and later organisations.

European Community (EC) Administrative and legislative organisation for European sectoral communities. The EC was formed in 1976, based on a 1965 treaty, to provide a common administrative framework and support system for the three European communities: EURATOM, the EUROPEAN COAL AND STEEL COMMUNITY (ECSC), and the EUROPEAN ECONOMIC COMMUNITY (EEC). While each organisation maintained its own identity, the EC provided shared resources through a common European Commission, an enlarged Assembly (*see* EUROPEAN PARLIAMENT), a Council of Ministers, the ECSC's European Court of Justice, and the European Investment Bank. While working for the three communities, the EC also developed as a forum for the discussion and development of other ideas on European integration, both by sector and in general. For example, early ideas on monetary union and social conditions were discussed through EC structures; and the single market envisaged in the 1957 treaty of ROME was set up by the EC through the 1986 SINGLE EUROPEAN ACT, which also looked towards greater political integration. By the MAASTRICHT treaty of 1991, the EEC was formally renamed as the European Community, while the EUROPEAN UNION emerged as the political agency.

European Defence Community (EDC) Projected supranational military organisation. In October 1950, the French Prime Minister René Pleven proposed the formation of a joint army for the six signatories of the 1951 treaty of PARIS which had created the EUROPEAN COAL AND STEEL COMMUNITY (ECSC), Belgium, the Federal Republic of Germany (FRG), France, Italy, Luxembourg and the Netherlands. This proposal for a common army was seen largely as a way of allowing the FRG to rearm in a controlled environment. The Pleven Plan outlined a structure in which each member state would provide troops proportionate to its size, with units made up of troops from different nations. In May 1952 the six governments duly signed the European Defence Community treaty in Paris. However, despite its successful ratification in five of the countries, the plan ran into resistance in France, based predominantly on fears of German rearmament. Despite a number of attempted solutions, the National Assembly voted against the treaty in August 1954. The EDC was thus never formed. However, integrated military policy was soon encouraged by the establishment of the less controversial WESTERN EUROPEAN UNION.

European Economic Community (EEC) International economic organisation. The EEC was established by the treaty of ROME of March 1957. It was designed to provide a common trading area with no internal tariffs and freedom of movement for investment, goods and workers, which built on the sectoral integration exemplified by the EUROPEAN COAL AND STEEL COMMUNITY (ECSC). It also aimed to promote economic expansion and to enhance the living standards of populations in member states, while the political context of the post-SECOND WORLD WAR and COLD WAR period was evident in its desired aim to improve relations between member states. It originally consisted of 'the six': Belgium, the Federal Republic of Germany (FRG), France, Italy, Luxembourg and the Netherlands. The EEC began work in January 1958. In 1963 and again in 1967, UK applications to join were rejected through France's veto. In 1967 the EEC joined with the other two European communities, EURATOM and the ECSC, under the umbrella organisation of the EUROPEAN COMMUNITY (EC). After DE GAULLE's resignation from French politics in 1969, the EEC began to expand, both in size and remit: in 1973, Denmark, Ireland, Norway and the UK joined (although Norway then withdrew after a negative referendum result); in 1975 it established trading arrangements with the EUROPEAN FREE TRADE ASSOCIATION (EFTA) and with a number of African nations; and Greece joined in 1981, followed by Portugal and Spain in 1985. By the MAASTRICHT treaty of 1991, the EEC was renamed as the European Community as part of a rearrangement of the growing number of European organisations. In 1995 Austria, Finland and Sweden joined.

The EEC achieved its target of a customs union in ten years, with the system envisaged in the treaty of Rome being set up in July 1968. Agricultural products began to be subsidised in common from 1962, with a more extensive common agricultural policy in place from 1968. However, the aim of a single market was delayed, not least by the international economic crises of the 1970s; but it was finally embodied in the 1986 SINGLE EUROPEAN ACT, and introduced in 1992.

European Free Trade Association (EFTA) Intergovernmental organisation for economic cooperation, formed in Stockholm in November 1959. After the establishment of the EUROPEAN ECONOMIC COMMUNITY (EEC) in 1957, a number of the other member governments of the ORGANISATION FOR EUROPEAN ECONOMIC CO-OPERATION (OEEC) moved towards a looser structure of economic cooperation which would have trading benefits, but would not look towards political integration or supranationalism in the way that the EEC did. The result was EFTA, which began work in May 1960, consisting of Austria, Denmark, Norway, Portugal, Sweden, Switzerland (with Liechtenstein) and the UK, known collectively as 'the seven' in contrast to 'the six' members of the EEC. With Finland as an associate member from 1961, EFTA's main work was in reducing tariffs on industrial goods between the member countries. Although EFTA expanded in 1970 when Iceland joined, it quickly began to diminish in significance as its members began to move into the EEC and its successor organisations: Denmark and the UK left in 1973, followed by Portugal in 1986, although Finland gained full membership of EFTA in the same year. In 1995 Austria, Finland and Sweden all left, resulting in the dissolution of the rump of EFTA.

European Parliament Parliament of the EUROPEAN COMMUNITY (EC) and subsequently the EUROPEAN UNION (EU). In 1952 the EUROPEAN COAL AND STEEL COMMUNITY (ECSC) established an Assembly, made up of seventy-eight members from member nations' own parliaments. This expanded in 1958 after the treaties of ROME to cover EURATOM and EUROPEAN ECONOMIC COMMUNITY (EEC) affairs, taking on the name European Parliamentary Assembly, and comprising 142 members. Its functions included scrutiny of the budgets and constitutions of the communities. It expanded again in 1973, when Denmark, Ireland and the UK joined the EEC, this time to 198 seats. In 1976 the composition of the parliament was changed by the EC's Council of Ministers: from 1978, members would be directly elected by voters in member nations, rather than be nominated from existing national parliaments. The first elections under this system were held in 1979, and have been held quinquenially since then. The size of the Parliament, a title formalised by the 1986 SINGLE EUROPEAN ACT, grew with new accessions to the EC in 1981 and 1986, when Greek, Portuguese and Spanish membership took the size of the parliament up to 518 seats; while Austrian, Finnish and Swedish membership of the EU and the EC from 1995 took the total to 626. The significance of the

Parliament increased after 1986 and 1991, when the Single European Act and the MAASTRICHT treaty gave it powers of sovereignty over national parliaments in some areas.

European Union (EU) International political organisation, established in 1992. The idea of a political union had informed many of the sectoral integrations of the 1950s (*see* EURATOM, EUROPEAN COAL AND STEEL COMMUNITY (ECSC), EUROPEAN ECONOMIC COMMUNITY). This developed more fully within the EUROPEAN COMMUNITY (EC) during the 1970s and 1980s, particularly as the EUROPEAN PARLIAMENT became more significant and as the EC itself grew. In February 1992 the twelve member states of the EC – Belgium, Denmark, France, Germany, Greece, Ireland, Italy, Luxembourg, the Netherlands, Portugal, Spain and the UK – signed the MAASTRICHT treaty on European Union, which formally established the EU as an overarching body for the members' common activities. The EU maintained the EC as its economic wing (based on the 1957 EEC), while also formalising the common interests of its members in defence, security, policing and social conditions. The EU expanded further in 1995, when Austria, Finland and Sweden joined; and, in the post-COLD WAR setting, negotiations for entry with twelve other European nations, including Bulgaria, Hungary, Malta and Slovenia, began.

European Union, treaty on (1991) *see* MAASTRICHT, TREATY OF.

F

Facta, Luigi (1861–1930) Italian politician. Facta entered parliament in 1892, and held a number of ministerial posts in GIOLITTI's government, before becoming President of the Council of Ministers in February 1922. His main concern was the growing threat of MUSSOLINI's Fascists (*see* FASCISM), who took over Bologna and Milan during the summer. Facta attempted to undermine the Fascists through secret talks and by threatening forced suppression, and he requested emergency powers from VICTOR EMMANUEL III to help prevent Mussolini's threatened MARCH ON ROME. The King's refusal precipitated Mussolini's arrival in Rome and Facta's resignation in October 1922.

Falange Spanish political party. In 1933, José Antonio Primo de Rivera, Miguel PRIMO DE RIVERA's son, formed the *Falange Españole* (Spanish Phalanx) as a new movement for the radical right. Influenced by ANARCHISM and FASCISM, the Falange was opposed to republicanism, capitalism and Marxism, and promoted an Italian-influenced model of corporatism and a German-influenced model of NATIONALISM. It remained a minority grouping, consisting mainly of radical students, who were involved in street violence in Madrid and elsewhere. It became more significant after the February 1936 election, won by a POPULAR FRONT coalition, and attracted some support from Catholic and military circles. It was attacked when the SPANISH CIVIL WAR started in July 1936, with Primo de Rivera being imprisoned and subsequently executed by the government. FRANCO worked with the *Falange*, and effectively appropriated it in April 1937 in his bid to gain a political movement to focus the nationalists' war effort. He merged the *Falange* with Carlist groups (*see* CARLISM), thereby promoting a combination of traditional and modern nationalist politics: the reformed grouping was named the Traditional Spanish Phalanx (FET). The FET peaked in influence between 1939 and 1942, when, on Italian lines, its Grand Council acted as the country's legislature. During the latter stages of the SECOND WORLD WAR, the fascist aspects were diluted. It remained the only legal political party in Spain throughout Franco's dictatorship, although its actual influence was limited. The FET finally closed down in 1977, two year's after Franco's death.

fascism Political ideology. Fascism developed in Italy in the immediate aftermath of the FIRST WORLD WAR, although it drew on some older traditions in European political and cultural thought, particularly NATIONALISM and romanticism. The name came from the *Fascio di Combattimento*, a Milan-based anti-communist militia formed in 1919, who appropriated the *fasces*, a classical Roman symbol of authority. This grouping formed the basis for MUSSOLINI's political career: and it was through his dictatorship in Italy from 1922 until 1943 that fascism was first and most fully applied. It rested on a number of positive ideas: that the state was greater than any individual or agency under it, for example, and that political divisions should be suppressed in the interests of the state's strength. It also stressed militarism, nationalism and economic self-sufficiency. However, it was also strongly characterised by its oppositional and reactionary nature, as it was promoted as being against COMMUNISM, LIBERALISM, SOCIALISM and democracy. As such, it relied heavily upon propaganda, the promotion of a strong leadership, and internal terrorism against opponents and potential opponents.

Beyond Italy, fascism influenced a number of similar movements: and while its specifically national identity made the notion of international fascism contradictory, Italian values, styles and policies were imitated in a number of parties, drawing largely on youth, the middle classes and ex-servicemen. For example, fascism influenced NAZISM in Germany, the *FALANGE* in Spain, various movements in France, the IRON GUARD in Romania, and the governments of HORTHY in Hungary, PILSUDSKI in Poland, and SALAZAR in Portugal. A number of these developed ANTI-SEMITISM as a central part of their appeal, although this was not present in the original Italian model. While fascism was widely discredited by the SECOND WORLD WAR, it re-emerged on the political fringes in a number of countries from the 1970s onwards, as economic recession and colonial migration influenced some on the extreme right to adapt the inter-war ideology.

Ferry, Jules (1832–93) French politician. Ferry was a lawyer and a journalist during the SECOND EMPIRE who entered the Assembly in 1869. An opponent of the FRANCO-PRUSSIAN WAR, he was Mayor of Paris from 1870 until 1871, and subsequently one of the architects of the THIRD REPUBLIC. As Minister of Education from 1879 until 1884, Ferry led the legislative attack on sectarian education in France with a number of reforms: these included the introduction of free, compulsory, lay primary education; the establishment of girls' schools; and the closure of religious teaching orders. Ferry also served as Prime Minister from 1880 to 1881, and again from 1883 to 1885. His periods of office saw a number of general liberal reforms, such as press freedom and trade union protection, as well as colonial expansion (*see* IMPERIALISM). His policies here led to France gaining Tunisia, the French Congo, greater control of Madagascar, and Annam. He resigned in 1885 when the Chamber of Deputies refused to grant funds for war in Indo-China. He stood unsuccessfully for president in 1887. He was assassinated in 1893.

Final Solution German government's name for the attempted genocide of the European Jews, 1941–45. ANTI-SEMITISM was always central to NAZISM, and German Jews in the THIRD REICH suffered various forms of discrimination and maltreatment (*see* ANTI-SEMITISM, NUREMBERG LAWS). Moreover, HITLER spoke and wrote on a number of occasions about the prospect of massacring Jews. At the start of the SECOND WORLD WAR, Polish Jews were concentrated into ghettos and camps, while the Nazis explored forced migration and resettlement as ways of removing Jews from the territories they conquered. Mass killing as a solution developed in June 1941 as part of the German invasion of the USSR (*see* BARBAROSSA): special mobile units followed the army and carried out mass shootings of Jewish civilians along with political commissars and others. This was most probably based on a verbal order from Hitler to HIMMLER, whose Defence Unit (SS) were the primary killers. In January 1942 the killing became more clearly formalised at the Wannsee conference, under HEYDRICH's guidance, which identified approximately 11,000,000 Jews in Europe and modelled extermination as the 'final solution to the

Jewish problem'. Increasingly, specially constructed gas chambers at six camps in Poland (Auschwitz-Birkenau, Belzec, Chelmno, Lublin, Sobibor and Treblinka) were used. Through these, victims were killed more quickly than by the mass shootings and the experimental mobile gas chambers of 1941, although other methods of killing continued in various locations. The disposal of corpses was also easier in the camps than in the open shootings. From February 1942, large numbers of Jews from ghettos, concentration camps, Germany, and conquered territory were transported to these extermination camps, of which Auschwitz-Birkenau had the greatest capacity: large-scale gassings started there in June 1942. Jews in some areas fared relatively better than in others, depending on indigenous levels of anti-semitism and the form of the country's relationship with Germany: in conquered Poland, where anti-semitism had regularly been evident, some 88 per cent of the Jewish population was killed, compared to 26 per cent of Italian Jews, where more liberal traditions and the alliance with Germany afforded some protection until 1943. In the final stages of the war, the killings were stopped, and the SS attempted to destroy the evidence, although the liberation of camps by allied forces uncovered the extent of the programme. Exact figures have been impossible to establish, but the total number of casualties falls somewhere between 4,000,000 and 6,000,000. In September 1952, the Federal Republic of Germany (FRG) and Israel established the Restitution Agreement, under which the FRG's government paid 3,000,000,000 marks in compensation to be distributed amongst Israeli survivors.

In addition to the Jewish victims of the final solution, Nazi racial policy also earmarked individuals from other groups for killing on racial grounds. These included Gypsies, Slavic peoples from conquered territories (including prisoners of war), and those deemed unfit for reproduction, such as homosexuals, and the mentally and physically disabled. The concentration on the term the 'Final Solution', which related specifically to Jews, and more recently the religious term 'Holocaust', occasionally hides these other victims of Nazi racial policy.

First Coalition *see* FRENCH REVOLUTIONARY WARS.

First International (International Working Men's Association) Federation of working-class organisations, established in London in September 1864 as the International Working Men's Association (IWMA). The IWMA was established by trade unionists, liberals and socialists from various parts of Europe who recognised their growing interests in the context of nationalist risings and parliamentary reform (*see* ANARCHISM, LIBERALISM, NATIONALISM, SOCIALISM). It attracted a number of leading figures from radical politics, including MARX and ENGELS, as well as followers of MAZZINI and PROUDHON. This diversity of traditions and ideologies meant that the IWMA was always internally unstable, with socialist, liberal, anarchist and nationalist wings in perpetual struggle. In 1868–9, as it adopted a broadly socialist programme, the movement was split by differences between Marx and BAKUNIN, who favoured revolutionary tactics: these differences resulted in Bakunin's expulsion in 1872. The Association declined in influence thereafter, and broke up in 1876. It was subsequently used as a model by the SECOND INTERNATIONAL, and gained a retrospective significance as the 'First International'.

First World War (1914–18) Multinational global conflict, in which the main protagonists were the DUAL ALLIANCE partners Austria-Hungary and Germany, and the TRIPLE ENTENTE allied partners of France, Russia (until November 1917) and the UK, although many additional alliances and interventions developed around these core countries.

The conflict was rooted in long-term rivalries over IMPERIALISM, armaments, and the interests of different countries in the Balkans. With the TRIPLE ALLIANCE and the Triple Entente developing generally mutually hostile military strategies in the years before 1914, and Austro-Hungarian and Russian policies in the Balkans creating great tension (*see* BOSNIAN

CRISIS, BALKAN WARS), many commentators felt a wider conflict to be imminent. The war started over the Balkans in the summer of 1914 when the heir to the HABSBURG throne, Archduke Francis Ferdinand, was assassinated by Slav nationalists in Sarajevo. Austro-Hungarian demands to the Serbian government for action against nationalists accelerated the crisis, leading, between 28 July and 12 August, to Austria-Hungary's declaration of war on Serbia, Russia's mobilisation against Austria-Hungary, Germany's declaration of war on Russia and France, Austria-Hungary's declaration of war on Russia, and French and British declarations of war on Austria-Hungary.

The war in western Europe began with a German strategy based on the SCHLIEFFEN PLAN, aimed at the conquest of France and the Low Countries before attention shifted to the east. This started successfully, but the invasion of Belgium brought the UK into the war (*see* LONDON, TREATY OF, 1839). The advance was stopped at the MARNE in September, and Paris was never encircled. German attempts to work round the Belgian, British and French and seize key Channel ports were also stopped at Ypres and Yser in October and November. From this stage, with both sides entrenched and backed by heavy artillery, the western front became static. In the Balkans, Austria-Hungary invaded Serbia in August, but was beaten back three times before securing Belgrade in December 1914. The OTTOMAN EMPIRE joined the Dual Alliance powers in November 1914. In the east, the Austro-Hungarian invasion of Poland and the Russian invasion of Prussia and Hungary established a long front on which Russia experienced heavy defeats, as at TANNENBERG in August and the Masurian Lakes in September, before a more static line settled in December 1914.

In February 1915 the western powers attempted to open another front and release the Russian Black Sea fleet by attacking the Ottoman empire in the DARDANELLES: this costly campaign failed to open up a significant new Balkan front, although an attack on Salonika in October 1915 proved more successful. Serbia was defeated in October 1915 after Bulgaria joined Austria-Hungary and Germany. The war also extended in 1915 through Germany's use of submarine attacks on enemy merchant shipping, and through German and British use of air raids. In May 1915 Italy left the TRIPLE ALLIANCE by the treaty of LONDON of April 1915, and entered the war against Austria-Hungary (and against Germany in August 1916); while in the east, Russia lost most of Poland during the course of the year. The western front saw fresh offensives in 1916, with a German attack at VERDUN in February and a Franco-British attack on the SOMME in July, but neither campaign managed to create any significant change in the front lines, despite high casualty figures. In June 1916, the Russians staged the BRUSILOV OFFENSIVE, which failed after Germany moved troops to the eastern front. The war's only major sea battle took place between the British and Germany navies at Jutland in May, as a result of which the German fleet remained relatively inactive. Italy was beaten by the Austro-Hungarians at Asiago in June, although the allies also gained new support from Romania and Portugal, and made some advances against the Ottoman empire in Salonika and in Mesopotamia.

In April 1917 Germany's submarine attacks brought the USA into the war (extended to Austria-Hungary in December), providing the allied powers with significant new resources. The Russian Revolution of February 1917 (*see* RUSSIAN REVOLUTIONS 1917) destabilised Russia's war effort, and was encouraged by Germany, although Russia did not withdraw from the war until December, after a series of mutinies and the BOLSHEVIKS' October revolution. Further offensives on the western front, notably those in Artois and the Champagne, failed to break the German lines, although gradual expensive victories, as at Arras in May, Ypres in November, and Cambrai in November and December, set up the basis for a temporary breakthrough on Germany's front line. In the south, the Italians were beaten at CAPORETTO in November, after which Austria-Hungary temporarily ended its campaign rather than press further into Italy. The Ottoman empire continued to suffer defeats in its Asian territories through 1917. The final Russian surrender in March 1918 (*see* treaty of BREST-LITOVSK) allowed Germany to concentrate its efforts on the western front with a major offensive in April, but this was halted: and, in late September, allied attacks managed to break the main German line. In the same month, Bulgaria and the Ottoman empire surrendered, with armistices imposed in September and October respectively, while Austria-Hungary surrendered in November after being beaten by Italy at Vittoria Veneto. With mutinies in Germany's forces, and a revolution deposing WILLIAM II, Germany requested an armistice in November 1918. The settlement of the war was made in a number of treaties arising out of the PARIS PEACE CONFERENCE.

Beyond Europe, the First World War involved colonial wars in Africa, Asia and the Far East, and involved Japan as well as British colonies and dominions.

The total number of casualties caused by the war was in the region of 9,000,000, including 1,700,000 Russians, 1,700,000 million Germans, 1,300,000 French and 1,200,000 million Austro-Hungarians. The war witnessed the development of new military technologies, most notably the tank and poison gas, while the application of aerial and submarine technology to military needs extended the war to merchant and passenger shipping and to civilian and industrial settlements behind the front lines.

five year plans Series of Soviet economic plans, 1928–51, central to STALIN's policy of industrialising and modernising the USSR. After the mixed economy of Lenin's NEW ECONOMIC POLICY, Stalin moved towards a command economy in which state planning directed production and policy. Driven by a number of factors, including the country's need to catch up with the other industrial nations, and by the government's desire to crush perceived agrarian reaction, the planning process began in 1928 with the institution of the first plan. This established production targets in heavy industry, electrical power, and for the collectivisation of agriculture (which helped to pay for the high level of state investment needed for the industrial plans). The second plan, declared in 1933, continued to emphasise these sectors along with consumer goods and rearmament; while the third plan of 1938 placed a priority on defence-related industries. Planning continued after the SECOND WORLD WAR, with plans in 1946 and 1951 concentrating on reconstruction.

Broadly, the plans achieved their aims of increasing the USSR's industrial capacity and power supplies, and in exploiting mineral resources. Some of the successes included Europe's first hydroelectric dam, built on the Dneiper, as well as massive production and output increases in most of the sectors covered. Moreover, the development of new industrial areas in eastern and southern areas, such as the oil, coal and metallurgical developments in the Fergana Valley in Tashkent, and the mining and machine building plants of Kusbass, meant that much of the country's productive capacity was relatively safe from foreign aggression. In this context, the first three plans were undoubtedly significant in the USSR's victory in the Second World War. Moreover, they set the foundations for the USSR's post-war status as a major industrial nation. However, these successes were achieved at high prices. The collectivisation of agriculture led to between 10,000,000 and 14,000,000 deaths, with an additional 6–7,000,000 dying in the related Ukrainian famine of 1932–3. Labour in all affected sectors came under rigid disciplinary regimes, with excessive punishments being imposed for under-achievement, absenteeism and perceived sabotage. The long-term environmental impact was also problematic, a legacy revealed after the collapse of the USSR (*see* REVOLUTIONS OF 1989–91). Despite the mixed costs, the five year plans were adopted as a model elsewhere, including Germany in 1936 (*see* THIRD REICH), and in post-1945 Soviet-bloc countries.

Foch, Ferdinand (1851–1929) French soldier. Foch fought in the FRANCO-PRUSSIAN WAR of 1870–71, and later went on to teach and write on military strategy. He took an active role in the early stages of the FIRST WORLD WAR at the MARNE and in Flanders. After commanding the French forces at the SOMME in 1916, Foch briefly retired, but he returned in May 1917 as PÉTAIN's Chief of Staff. In 1918 he became Commander-in-Chief of the allied forces on the western front, organising the summer offensive that directly led to the German collapse and surrender. Foch was promoted to the rank of Field-Marshal in 1919. He was active at the PARIS PEACE CONFERENCE, pressing CLEMENCEAU for a harsh settlement on Germany, and helped to oversee Germany's compliance with the military clauses of the treaty of VERSAILLES.

Food and Agriculture Organisation (FAO) *see* UNITED NATIONS.

Fouché, Joseph (*c.* 1763–1820) French politician. An Oratorian, Fouché renounced the Church at the time of the FRENCH REVOLUTION of 1789. He became active in the Nantes JACOBIN club, and entered the National Convention in 1792. As a representative-on-mission during the TERROR, he was responsible for many deaths in Nantes and elsewhere, and for a fervent anti-clerical policy. His excesses here, which included the removal of crosses from churches and the posting of atheistic slogans in cemeteries, placed a rift between Fouché and ROBESPIERRE, and he was involved in the July 1794 Thermidor coup. After a period out of politics, he became Minister of Police in 1799, and served NAPOLEON in this capacity until 1810, when the Emperor removed Fouché due to his English contacts (*see* NAPOLEONIC WARS). He worked with Napoleon during the Hundred Days in 1814–15, but also helped to bring about the Bourbon restoration, and served LOUIS XVIII as Minister of Police in the summer of 1815. However, he was subsequently exiled from France as he had voted for LOUIS XVI's execution in 1793.

Fourteen Points US President Woodrow Wilson's agenda for a post-FIRST WORLD WAR peace settlement. Wilson presented the points to Congress in January 1918 as an ideal basis for peace terms in Europe, although this had not been agreed by the USA's allies, and some of the issues covered contravened existing secret treaties between the other allies, such as the treaty of LONDON of 1915. Six of the points covered general issues of principle for the future management of international relations: that there should be no more secret diplomacy; that all seas should be free; that tariffs should be removed; that all countries should disarm; that imperial powers should negotiate changes in colonial matters; and that a new international organisation should be set up to act as a forum for arbitration of disputes between countries. The remaining eight were geographically specific, although the principle of 'self-determination', to be defined in contested areas through plebiscites, underpinned many of them: in this way, the Fourteen Points recognised the decline of continental European empires, and attempted to promote the nation state as the ideal model (*see* IMPERIALISM, NATIONALISM). Under this heading, three of the points covered the Austro-Hungarian, OTTOMAN and Russian empires, all of which should give up their possessions, which would then become independent states: moreover, the point relating to the Ottoman empire recommended that the Straits be open to all shipping. Belgium, Poland and the Balkan countries were highlighted for restoration, with Poland and Serbia also gaining access to the sea (*see* POLISH CORRIDOR). Alsace and Lorraine should be returned to France (*see* FRANCO-PRUSSIAN WAR), and the areas on the Austro-Italian border should be allowed to practise self-determination before the border would be settled.

Although the Fourteen Points could never have been binding, they were taken by some politicians in the central powers as a likely basis for a relatively favourable peace: this idea was influential in the armistices of autumn 1918, and in the collapse of monarchies and institution of republics that coincided with the end of the war (*see for example* WEIMAR REPUBLIC). The points were influential at the PARIS PEACE CONFERENCE and in the resultant treaties, not least in the creation of the LEAGUE OF NATIONS, but the realities of Europe's geopolitical composition made full self-determination impossible.

Fourth Coalition *see* NAPOLEONIC WARS.

Francis Joseph (1830–1916) HABSBURG Emperor of Austria (1848–1916) and King of Hungary (1867–1916). Francis Joseph succeeded to the throne when his uncle, Emperor Ferdinand, abdicated in December 1848 (*see* REVOLUTIONS OF 1848). He strove to overturn the gains of the revolution, both by abolishing the 1849 constitution in 1851, and by taking a consistently hostile line towards the nationalities within the Habsburg empire (*see* IMPERIALISM, NATIONALISM). Preferring to rule through centralised personal channels, he also led the empire's foreign and military policy. However, failures here in the 1850s and 1860s led to a decline in Austrian influence: defeats in the FRANCO-AUSTRIAN WAR in 1859 and the AUSTRO-PRUSSIAN WAR in 1866 effectively ended Austrian power in the Italian states and the German states respectively (*see also* GERMAN UNIFICATION, ITALIAN UNIFICATION). Francis Joseph accepted the reconstruction of the Habsburg empire that followed in 1867 with the *Ausgleich*, becoming King of Hungary. His foreign policies in the 1870s were more successful, with the gaining of Bosnia-Herzegovina in 1878 (*see* BERLIN CONGRESS) and the securing of the DUAL ALLIANCE the following year. While his heir Archduke Francis Ferdinand favoured greater Slav autonomy, the Emperor remained hostile to nationalist demands, a position that hardened after the BALKAN WARS of 1912–13, and that came to a head after Francis Ferdinand's assassination in Sarajevo in June 1914. Francis Joseph's subsequent invasion of Serbia precipitated the FIRST WORLD WAR. He died in 1916, and was succeeded by his great-nephew Charles for the two remaining years of the Habsburg empire.

Franco, Francisco (1892–1975) Spanish soldier and politician. Graduating from the Infantry Academy in 1910, Franco served in the Spanish army in Morocco. Under ALFONSO XIII his career advanced, but it declined during the Second Republic after 1931. He returned to favour from 1933, particularly when he led the repression of the Asturias miners' strike in 1934. In the same year he was made Commander-in-Chief of the Spanish forces in Morocco, followed by the promotion to Chief of the General Staff in May 1935. His fortunes dipped again in early 1936 after the POPULAR FRONT's victory, and his appointment as Governor of the Canary Islands was effectively a demotion. However, Franco became involved in the coup against the government, taking a decisive role in combining Foreign Legion and native Moroccan troops and, with German help, airlifting them to the Spanish mainland to begin the SPANISH CIVIL WAR. In October 1936 the military leadership of the rebel forces declared Franco *Generalissimo* and head of state.

Combining the military with a right-wing populist movement based on the *FALANGE*, Franco led the nationalists through the war, assuming the role of dictator on the nationalist victory in 1939. Franco maintained Spanish neutrality during the SECOND WORLD WAR, although Spain did provide the AXIS powers with facilities, resources and some troops. His foreign policy after the war was anti-communist, allowing for some cooperation with the west despite his system of government having fascist trappings. Domestically, Franco, who assumed the title of *El Caudillo* (the Leader) in 1947, imposed a one-party state, run at first on corporate lines, although the economy became more liberal in the 1950s. Spain remained socially and culturally conservative, with key roles given to the Roman Catholic Church, landowners and the military. In 1969 Franco named Juan Carlos, ALFONSO XIII's grandson, as his successor, a succession that duly took place on Franco's death in 1975.

Franco-Austrian War (1859) War between France, in alliance with Piedmont-Sardinia, and the HABSBURG empire. In 1858, NAPOLEON III and CAVOUR settled the PLOMBIÈRES pact, which committed French troops to support Piedmont-Sardinia against the Habsburgs. This was turned into a more formal alliance in January 1859, after which Piedmont-Sardinia mobilised its forces. A Habsburg ultimatum insisting on demobilisation was ignored, and the empire moved against Piedmont-Sardinia in late April. The French intervention was decisive. A more efficient mobilisation than that carried out by the Habsburgs, and a larger force, led to two quick victories in Lombardy: at Magenta on 4 June and at Solferino on 20 June. These battles were very costly to both sides – at Magenta, for example, approximately 11,000 men were killed – and Napoleon III called for a peace as the Habsburg forces retreated into Venetia in July. Peace was made at the treaty of VILLAFRANCA in July. Although Cavour resigned over what he saw as a premature end to the war, the Habsburg defeats facilitated the expansion of Piedmont-Sardinia, and influenced local risings in various parts of the Italian states. *See* ITALIAN UNIFICATION.

Franco-Prussian War (1870–71) War between France and Prussia and its German allies. After the AUSTRO-PRUSSIAN WAR of 1866, tensions between France and Prussia developed, particularly over control of Alsace and Lorraine. Prussian policy under BISMARCK seemed to favour a conflict with France as a way of securing Prussian domination of central western Europe, and as a means of ensuring a unified Germany under Prussian dominance. In this context, Prussian backing for the HOHENZOLLERN Prince Leopold to become king of Spain in 1868 alienated France: and while Prussia backed down over this, the subsequent French demand that the candidature would never be raised again was managed in such a way that both governments were offended. NAPOLEON III declared war on Prussia in July 1870. The French plan for an attack on southern Germany, ideally with backing from Italy, failed to develop: and the numerically superior and well organised Prussians under MOLTKE attacked in north-west France. Despite some early successes against the Prussians, one of the French armies was defeated at Sedan in early September, at which battle Napoleon III was captured. Two days later, politicians in Paris declared the THIRD REPUBLIC, with the Prussians besieging the capital later in the month. The French were defeated in the field at Metz in late October, and Paris finally capitulated in late January 1871, ten days after Prussia and its German allies had staged the declaration of the German empire at Versailles (*see* GERMAN UNIFICATION), although the surrender was resisted by the PARIS COMMUNE, and was followed by a brief period of civil war in France. The war was settled by the treaty of Frankfurt (*see* FRANKFURT, TREATY OF) in May 1871.

Franco-Russian Alliance (1894) Military alliance between France and Russia. In the context of growing German hostility towards both France and Russia, exemplified by the creation of the TRIPLE ALLIANCE and by Germany's refusal of Russian loan requests, Russia and France began to develop links with each other. Originally financial, through French loans to Russia, these links allowed for alliance negotiations from 1891, when Germany refused to renew the REINSURANCE TREATY with Russia and when the UK seemed to be moving closer to the Triple Alliance. The secret alliance, sometimes known as the 'Dual Entente', was signed in St Petersburg in January 1894. By its terms, France and Russia agreed to assist each other in case of attack by any of the Triple Alliance powers, and agreed to mobilise if any of the Triple Alliance powers mobilised. The alliance was designed to terminate as and when the Triple Alliance ended. It formed the basis for the TRIPLE ENTENTE. The alliance ended in 1917 when the Bolsheviks renounced all of imperial Russia's treaty obligations. *See* RUSSIAN REVOLUTIONS 1917.

Frankfurt, treaty of (May 1871) Peace treaty that ended the FRANCO-PRUSSIAN WAR of 1870–71. By the treaty, the newly unified German empire (*see* GERMAN UNIFICATION) gained Alsace and Lorraine, to be administered as an imperial territory. France had to pay a 5,000,000,000 franc indemnity to Germany, and Germany established an army of occupation until the debt was repaid.

Frankfurt Parliament Representative body for the German states, 1848–49. During the REVOLUTIONS OF 1848, pressure for a unified Germany gave rise to the establishment by liberals and nationalists of a parliament for all of the German states, which would work towards creating a constitution for a new nation state to replace the GERMAN CONFEDERATION (*see* LIBERALISM, NATIONALISM). After elections in April and May 1848, the new body, composed mainly of middle-class representatives, met at Frankfurt. Under the presidency of Heinrich von Gagern, the Parliament appointed the liberal HABSBURG Archduke John as the imperial administrator. Although the Parliament attempted to establish a broadly liberal constitution, it was hampered by a number of factors, most notably its lack of revenue-raising powers, its lack of an army, disagreements between members on the borders of the projected new Germany, and the relative roles of Austria and Prussia within it. It produced a constitution in March 1849, but quickly declined when FREDERICK WILLIAM IV of Prussia refused to become emperor of the projected state. The Parliament began to fragment after this, as a number of states rejected the constitution and withdrew their members, and it was eventually forcibly dissolved in June 1849 after its radical remnant had moved to Stuttgart.

Frederick William III (1770–1840) HOHENZOLLERN King of Prussia, 1797–1840. Succeeding his father Frederick William II in 1797, Frederick William III came to the throne at a time of military crisis in Europe (*see* FRENCH REVOLUTIONARY WARS). He succeeded in keeping Prussia out of the Second Coalition against France, and, at first, out of the Third Coalition. However, the possibility of the return of Hanover to the UK in 1806 pushed him to declare war on France (*see* NAPOLEONIC WARS), which led to the disastrous defeat at the battle of Jena and the loss of a third of Prussian territory at the treaty of TILSIT in 1807. Frederick William subsequently pursued a domestic reform programme, under the guidance of HARDENBERG and STEIN, involving constitutional, religious, educational and military reconstruction, and the emancipation of the serfs. Frederick William involved Prussia against France again in 1813, with the Prussian army fighting at LEIPZIG, and Prussia joining the Fourth Coalition in 1814, and supporting the British at the battle of WATERLOO in 1815. Under Frederick William, Prussia made gains at the Congress of Vienna (*see* VIENNA, CONGRESS OF), after which the king returned to a broadly conservative policy, exemplified by his support for the CARLSBAD DECREES of 1819. He died in 1840, and was succeeded by his son FREDERICK WILLIAM IV.

Frederick William IV (1795–1861) HOHENZOLLERN King of Prussia, 1840–61. Frederick William IV succeeded his father FREDERICK WILLIAM III in 1840. He briefly favoured the idea of GERMAN UNIFICATION, and showed some sympathy to this cause during the REVOLUTIONS OF 1848, but he soon moved against it by dissolving the Prussian Assembly in December 1848. The following year he rejected the FRANKFURT PARLIAMENT's offer of a new role as emperor of a unified Germany, as it did not come from the other German states' princes. In 1850, he established the ERFURT UNION in a bid to unite Germany through royal agreement, but this collapsed due to HABSBURG opposition, and Frederick William was forced to cede Prussian leadership of Germany by the treaty of OLMÜTZ. Between 1848 and 1850, he oversaw constitutional changes, establishing the relatively liberal framework that was to last in Prussia and then in Germany until 1918, which involved male suffrage to a two-tier assembly with powers of legislation and taxation, but with a power of veto for the monarch. His policies became more inconsistent in the 1850s, as he reintroduced censorship and other reactionary measures. In 1858, Frederick William's mental illness forced him to give way to his brother William's regency. He died three years later, and was succeeded by the regent as WILLIAM I.

Free French Organisation of French military personnel, politicians and administrators working outside metropolitan France against the AXIS and VICHY powers during the SECOND WORLD WAR. In June 1940 DE GAULLE, in exile in London, began to develop the Free French Forces (FFL) as a movement which could continue to fight against Germany. It had little success at first, as it was hampered by British attacks on the French navy, and by the loyalty to Vichy expressed by most French colonial administrators. However, de Gaulle developed the movement's size and profile, particularly by working with internal RESISTANCE movements, and by organising attacks on Vichy colonial troops in 1941. In July 1942 the movement was renamed as the Fighting French Forces (FFC); and by 1943 the political and military wings were broadly recognised by the western allies as a government-in-waiting, as seen by their involvement in the CASABLANCA conference, although de Gaulle continued to be a controversial figure. The FFC were involved in the battle for France after the NORMANDY CAMPAIGN, and were the first allied troops into Paris in August 1944. Many figures involved in this movement became significant local and national politicians in France after 1945.

French Revolution (1789–99) Umbrella term for series of events in France between the late 1780s and the late 1790s. These events brought about changes in the way that France, continental Europe's most populous and culturally advanced country of the period, was governed; and they had implications and effects on the systems of government and political ideology throughout Europe and beyond.

The changes became evident in the late 1780s, when LOUIS XVI's government was facing financial crisis, as a high national debt and bad harvests had undermined the economy. In the face of resistance to new taxation and peasant risings in the countryside, Louis convened the Estates-General, a body composed of elected representatives from the three 'estates' (nobility, clergy, and the rest of the population) which had last met in 1614. Once convened at Versailles in May 1789, the Third Estate pressed for equal rights; when these were not given, it declared itself the National Constituent Assembly in June 1789, and was joined by the clergy. The government's attempts to quell this essentially middle-class revolution by force were prevented when mass risings in Paris in July 1789 led to the successful storming of the Bastille and the collapse of royal authority in the capital. This pattern was followed in many other towns and in rural areas. By early August 1789 the Assembly had secured power, and over the course of the following year introduced a number of constitutional and legal reforms, including the abolition of feudalism, the expropriation of crown and church lands, the introduction of a new paper currency, the Declaration of the Rights of Man and the Citizen, and the Civil Constitution of the Clergy of July 1790 which reorganised the Catholic Church in France. The increasing radicalism of the Assembly, particularly with this anti-clerical move, helped to polarise opinions on the Revolution, from those calling for a republic to those, including some foreign governments, wanting a full restoration. The situation was brought to a head by Louis' unsuccessful escape attempt in June 1791, and by the forced suppression of a pro-republican meeting in Paris the following month, an event that became known as the Champ de Mars massacre. A compromise was made with the declaration of a new constitution in September 1791, which Louis accepted, despite it limiting the crown's powers.

The Revolution subsequently became characterised by a more radical agenda when, in April 1792, France declared war on Austria, a declaration that helped to bring foreign enmity to the Revolution to a head, and started a series of wars that kept France at arms almost continually until 1815 (*see* FRENCH REVOLUTIONARY WARS, NAPOLEONIC WARS). Louis' opposition to the Revolution's successes made him a suspect during wartime, and he was effectively imprisoned from August 1792 as French military failures left Paris itself threatened. Fear of internal enemies at this time also contributed to the massacre of over 1,000 prisoners in Paris, including some nobles and priests, in the September massacres. Soon, however, French success at the battle of VALMY led to a period of greater confidence and radicalism, seen most clearly in the declaration of the republic and the introduction of a new REPUBLICAN CALENDAR, in late September. Louis was tried, and executed in January 1793.

The next significant period of change came when military defeats coincided with anti-conscription risings in the Vendée department, which met with brutal suppression over the following year. In this climate, the Convention handed much of its day-to-day power to smaller emergency agencies, including the Revolutionary Tribunal, the Committee of Public Safety, and the Committee of General Security. Internal political disputes were increasingly managed by this machinery of TERROR, initiated by the suppression of the GIRONDINS in June 1793, and followed by waves of judicial and extra-judicial killings of individuals and factions identified as enemies of the state and the Revolution. ROBESPIERRE emerged as the leading proponent of Terror, until he himself fell victim to the factionalism in the Thermidor coup of July 1794.

In July 1795 a new constitution established the Directory as the executive, which lasted until 1799 in a climate of domestic instability and commitment to war. The Directory used force on a number of occasions against internal dissent, including the suppression of the Vendémaire rising of October 1795, and used the army against royalists and the right in the Fructidor coup of September 1797. Two years later, leading Directors, including SIEYÈS, engineered the BRUMAIRE coup, whereby NAPOLEON was brought in as First Consul in a new executive Consulate, and the Directory was abolished.

French Revolutionary Wars Series of conflicts between France and other European states between 1792 and NAPOLEON Bonaparte's BRUMAIRE coup of 1799. Encouraged by émigrés who had left France after the revolutionary events of 1789–92 (*see* FRENCH REVOLUTION), a number of foreign governments were antagonistic towards the increasing radicalism of the French government. This was made clear by the joint HABSBURG-Prussian Declaration of Pillnitz of August 1791, requesting international consultation over LOUIS XVI's role, and suggesting armed intervention to assist the king. In December 1791 the Habsburg empire mobilised after French threats against émigré activity in Mainz and Trier; and when the empire refused to back down, France declared war in April 1792. Prussia and Piedmont joined the Habsburgs, while France also declared war on Bohemia and Hungary. In July, the Duke of Brunswick provided a focus for the anti-French war effort by declaring that the war aimed to bring about Louis' restoration. France started the war badly, with losses to the Prussians at Languy and Verdun, which exacerbated internal tensions and led to the September massacres and the commencement of the TERROR. However, the French army rallied and beat the Prussians at VALMY, a success which led to the consolidation of the Revolution through the declaration of the republic, the decision to try Louis, and, in November, the Revolutionary Manifesto which declared France's willingness to support popular revolutionary movements abroad. This period also saw French successes at Jemappes lead to the occupation of Brussels, and, in the south, the occupation of Nice and Savoy.

The war entered a new phase in the spring of 1793 when, after Louis' execution, France declared war on Great Britain, Holland and Spain. This declaration gave the nations opposed to France coherence as a coalition, subsequently styled the First Coalition. France suffered a number of significant defeats, including the battle of Neerwinden against the Habsburgs which pushed French troops out of Holland in March; the Vendean revolt against conscription which diverted resources into a civil war; and the defeat by the Spanish at Perpignan in April. France was close to collapse: but this was averted by divergent aims within the Coalition which prevented a concerted push on Paris. The French consolidated in the summer of 1793 under CARNOT through the use of conscription; and although the British navy took Toulon, France recovered enough to defeat the Habsburgs in October and to re-enter Spain and Piedmont. This laid the foundations for the major successes of the spring and summer of 1794, including the suppression of the Vendée, the removal of the Prussians and the Habsburgs from France, and the occupation of Belgium. By the treaties of BASLE of 1795, France made peace with Prussia, Holland and Spain respectively, gaining some territories and guaranteeing Prussian neutrality.

In March 1796, France concentrated on the Habsburg empire by sending two forces: a northern one under Jean Baptiste Jourdan and Jean Moreau, and one through the Italian states under Napoleon. Napoleon's small army was successful, with the Piedmontese beaten by late April, giving France access to the Alps. The Habsburgs were beaten at Lodi in May and at Lonato in August, alongside Napoleon's treaties with Naples and the Papal States. Despite some Habsburg successes against Jourdan's force, notably at Altenkirchen in September, the Italian expedition continued to go France's way, with further victories at Arcola in November and at Rivoli and Mantua in January 1797. In April, Napoleon and Archduke Charles signed an armistice at Leoben, which became formalised at the treaty of CAMPO FORMIO in October.

The war against Great Britain also developed during this period. France's ally Spain declared war on Great Britain in October 1796, and in December peace talks between France and Great Britain failed. However, the plans for an invasion of Britain failed in 1797: the Spanish fleet was defeated at Cape St Vincent in February, a small invading force which landed at Fishguard was beaten in the same month, and the Dutch fleet on its way to Ireland was beaten at Texel in October. With further successes in the Italian states and in Austria itself, the French government dropped the invasion plans in March 1798, and instead sent Napoleon to Egypt in May in order to attack British imperial holdings (*see* IMPERIALISM). After successes in Malta and, in July, at the battle of the Pyramids, Napoleon's forces were beaten by the British navy at the battle of the Nile in August. This setback encouraged other countries to re-open their wars with France: by December 1798, Great Britain, the Habsburg empire, Naples, Portugal and Russia had come together as the Second Coalition. French forces were pushed back in Switzerland, Piedmont and on the Rhine, although internal splits in the Coalition once again prevented France's defeat. In August 1799 Napoleon abandoned his army in Egypt and returned to France, where, in November, he staged his BRUMAIRE coup. The wars continued. *See* NAPOLEONIC WARS.

Friedland, battle of (June 1807) *see* NAPOLEONIC WARS.

Fundamental Laws (May 1906) *see* RUSSIAN REVOLUTION 1905.

G

Gallipoli, battle of (1915) *see* DARDANELLES CAMPAIGN; FIRST WORLD WAR.

Gambetta, Léon (1838–82) French politician. Gambetta was a lawyer who came to prominence for his attacks on the government during the last stages of the SECOND EMPIRE. Elected as a deputy in 1869, he opposed the FRANCO-PRUSSIAN WAR, and helped to establish the THIRD REPUBLIC in September 1870 on NAPOLEON III's collapse. He took the interior portfolio in the emergency Government of National Defence, and escaped from Paris during the Prussian siege in order to maintain the government, at first in Tours and then in Bordeaux. As Minister for War and effectively head of state, he raised a new army in an unsuccessful bid to retake Paris. He resigned when the remainder of the government accepted the defeat. Re-elected in 1871, Gambetta campaigned against President MACMAHON. He was made the President of the Chamber of Deputies in 1879, and formed his only government in 1881. He resigned early in 1882 due to internal factions and the lack of President Jules Grévy's support. Gambetta died later the same year.

Garibaldi, Guiseppe (1807–82) Italian nationalist and revolutionary. Garibaldi became attracted to Italian NATIONALISM in the early 1830s, and joined MAZZINI's Young Italy movement in 1834. He was involved in that year's rebellion in Genoa, for which he was sentenced to death, but he escaped to South America, where he developed his military strategy and skills.

Garibaldi returned to Italy in 1848, and took part in the risings against HABSBURG domination of the peninsula (*see* REVOLUTIONS OF 1848, ITALIAN UNIFICATION). He was involved in the unsuccessful attempt to establish a republic in Rome in 1849 and defend it against both the Habsburgs and the French, after which he left for exile in the USA with a reputation as a brave soldier and committed nationalist. In 1859 Garibaldi fought for VICTOR EMMANUEL II of Piedmont-Sardinia against the Habsburgs in Lombardy (*see* FRANCO-AUSTRIAN WAR), and then raised a republican force, known as 'the thousand', to take Sicily and Naples in 1860. He was aided in this successful campaign by local risings, and ended the movement by presenting the gains to Victor Emmanuel as part of the unified Kingdom of Italy. In 1862 he led an abortive march on Rome, during which he was captured, and in 1866 he again fought for Venetia against the Habsburgs in the AUSTRO-PRUSSIAN WAR. In 1867 he led another march on Rome, which was stopped by French intervention, finally helping to secure Rome for the Kingdom of Italy in 1870 during the FRANCO-PRUSSIAN WAR. His final military action was for the French republican army at Dijon in 1871.

Gastein, Convention of (August 1865) Agreement between the HABSBURG empire and Prussia on the future of Schleswig, Holstein and Lauenberg. After the SCHLESWIG WAR and the subsequent treaty of Vienna (*see* VIENNA, TREATY OF) of 1864, the Habsburg empire and Prussia jointly administered the disputed territories. This settlement was problematic, as it exacerbated differences between the two powers, and it almost led to war between them. In August 1865 the two sides met at Gastein to settle the problem. By the convention, Schleswig and Holstein remained technically under joint Habsburg-Prussian rule, but the administration was divided, with the Habsburgs taking Holstein and Prussia taking Schleswig. Prussia also incorporated Lauenberg. This settlement was a compromise for Prussia, particularly for BISMARCK, as it left Habsburg influence in northern Germany. This was successfully challenged in 1866. *See* AUSTRO-PRUSSIAN WAR.

German Confederation Political organisation of German states, 1815–66. The German Confederation, or *Bund*, was formed at the Congress of Vienna (*see* VIENNA, CONGRESS OF) of 1814–15 as a solution to the organisation of north central Europe after the NAPOLEONIC WARS. Based on all parties' desire for a stable and conservative region, the Confederation, which was formally established in June 1815, brought together thirty-nine of the German states as a successor to the dissolved HOLY ROMAN EMPIRE. The diverse size of the states, ranging from the large and powerful Austria to smaller states such as Anhalt and Brunswick, meant that the HABSBURG empire would always be the dominant power within the Confederation. The Confederation excluded some Germans, such as the east Prussians, and it included many non-Germans, including Czechs, Danes and Italians. The Confederation had a Diet at Frankfurt with limited powers under an Austrian presidency. Habsburg domination was exemplified by the passing of the CARLSBAD DECREES of 1819. Although the Confederation allowed the growth of some common economic links between member states, it failed to evolve into a German nation state in its own right (*see* NATIONALISM): and while the FRANKFURT PARLIAMENT gained some independence during the REVOLUTIONS OF 1848, Austrian hegemony was restored in 1850 by the Convention of OLMÜTZ. Some of the states in the Confederation backed Prussia in the SCHLESWIG WAR and AUSTRO-PRUSSIAN WAR, and the Confederation was formally dissolved in 1866 after Prussia's defeat of the Habsburg empire. It was replaced in the north of Germany by the NORTH GERMAN CONFEDERATION. *See also* GERMAN UNIFICATION.

German reunification (1990) Process by which the Federal Republic of Germany (FRG) and the German Democratic Republic (GDR) unified as a single nation state, October 1990. The FRG had never recognised the COLD WAR division of Germany: and while BRANDT's *OSTPOLITIK* and the 1972 BASIC TREATY had eased tensions over this issue, reunification remained a target for many in the west. GDR governments, and their allies in the USSR, had been hostile towards this aspiration. In the late 1980s, under the influence of *GLASNOST* and *PERESTROIKA*, changes in the GDR and eastern Europe as a whole provided a new context; while the FRG's key role in western Europe, particularly through NATO and the EUROPEAN COMMUNITY (EC), gave fresh impetus to western demands for reunification. The issue was forced by illegal migration from the GDR to the FRG, which climaxed in the autumn of 1989, and by large anti-government demonstrations in Leipzig, Berlin and elsewhere (*see* REVOLUTIONS OF 1989–91). With the New Forum acting as a focus group for opposition in the GDR, the HONECKER government was replaced by a more moderate one, which, in November 1989, introduced freedom of travel for east Germans. This helped to create an effectively unified German labour market. As checkpoints in the BERLIN WALL were opened to facilitate greater movement, groups of demonstrators breached the wall in a number of places. While the GDR's government did not necessarily intend this to lead to unification, the revolution was seized upon by Chancellor KOHL of the FRG as a propitious moment in which to promote the unification issue. This was developed in conjunction with the new GDR government, a conservative coalition, formed after the March 1990 elections. Negotiations between the two governments led to economic unification in July 1990.

The international dimension of reunification was more complicated, but this was tackled in a series of discussions in 1990. In July, Kohl and GORBACHEV negotiated the removal of WARSAW PACT forces from the GDR; while negotiations in Paris in July involving the two governments and the governments of the SECOND WORLD WAR allies France, the UK, the USA and the USSR (the 'Two plus Four' talks) established the political basis for reunification. This necessitated a guarantee on the German-Polish border, which the new Germany would accept as the existing GDR-Polish border: the FRG thus renounced its claims to east Prussia and other territories in Poland (*see also* ODER-NEISSE LINE, POLISH CORRIDOR.) This issue was settled in the Treaty on the Final Settlement with Respect to Germany in September 1990. By this, the allies also removed all their interests in Berlin. Full reunification accordingly took place on 3 October 1990, with the former GDR automatically joining NATO, the EC and other organisations. The first elections were held in December 1990.

German unification (1871) The establishment of the German empire in 1871. After the FRENCH REVOLUTIONARY WARS and the NAPOLEONIC WARS, various strands of nationalist ideology existed in the German states: but the settlement reached at the Congress of Vienna (*see* VIENNA, CONGRESS OF) in 1815 realigned the area as a federation of states of various sizes (*see* GERMAN CONFEDERATION). There was, however, some economic unification between the states, most notably the *ZOLLVEREIN* of 1832. Liberal and conservative NATIONALISM also emerged during the REVOLUTIONS OF 1848. These fed into the FRANKFURT PARLIAMENT and the ERFURT UNION, the latter confirming Prussia's potential as the most powerful of the German states as HABSBURG influence began to decline. During the 1860s tensions between the Habsburg empire and Prussia, ruled by WILLIAM I from 1861, became more pronounced. In February 1862, for example, Prussia rejected Habsburg plans for a reorganisation of the Confederation; while in the same year, the Prussian Minister President BISMARCK began to speak vociferously of Prussia's leadership of a united Germany. Although the Habsburg empire and Prussia allied in 1864 for the SCHLESWIG WAR, the two powers' approaches to the management of Schleswig and Holstein after the war brought out their differences in relation to the German states once again.

These differences developed into open conflict in 1866 (*see* AUSTRO-PRUSSIAN WAR), at the end of which Prussian dominance, at least in the north, was assured, a dominance confirmed by the creation of the NORTH GERMAN CONFEDERATION. Through these conflicts, Bismarck and

William had alienated parts of the liberal nationalist movement, most notably the Progressive party, but populist notions of a strong, unified Germany under Prussian leadership developed, and the liberals were accommodated in the Confederation's structures. Prussian success in the FRANCO-PRUSSIAN WAR of 1870–71 provided the context for the creation of this unified country: with Prussia so clearly the most powerful country in northern and western Europe, and with extensive influence in the east, a number of the princes of the southern German states accepted the Prussian and HOHENZOLLERN dominance. By royal invitation, William I took the crown of the new German empire in December 1870, with his formal proclamation as emperor coming in January 1871 at Versailles.

The Second Reich, as the German empire came to be known in a scheme which viewed the HOLY ROMAN EMPIRE as the First Reich, adopted an imperial constitution in August 1871. It established a unified state with the Prussian King serving as emperor, with reserved rights in foreign and military affairs. A federal system recognised the different states, with their representatives meeting in the Federal Council, and a popularly-elected parliament was established. The earlier models of economic union were developed in various sectors, including railways, postal services and the armed forces (*see* INDUSTRIALISATION). This system of government, with an increasing emphasis on welfare CONSERVATISM, remained in place in Germany until the end of the FIRST WORLD WAR, when the empire collapsed to be replaced by the WEIMAR REPUBLIC.

Gestapo (German abbreviation for *Geheime Staatspolizei*, Secret State Police) The political police force of the THIRD REICH. The Gestapo was developed out of a branch of the pre-Nazi Prussian police force, and quickly came to represent the Nazi government's power in everyday life through its use of arbitrary arrest, terror tactics and a culture of informing. It was run by HIMMLER from 1934, and given greater resources in 1936 when it became part of the Defence Echelon (SS). The Gestapo took on the responsibility of running concentration camps for political and, subsequently, racial prisoners, and was involved in enforcing Nazi rule in occupied countries during the SECOND WORLD WAR. The organisation was proscribed at the NUREMBERG TRIALS.

Gheorghiu-Dej, Gheorghe (Gheorghe Gheorghiu) (1901–65) Romanian politician. Gheorghiu was an electrician who became active in politics in the 1920s through trade union work. He joined the underground Communist party in 1930, and was imprisoned in 1933 for his role in a strike. He adopted the name of his prison, Dej, as a suffix during this time, during which he developed links with other activists, including CEAUÇESCU. After his release in 1944 he became General Secretary of the Communist party in 1945, along with taking the economics portfolio in the coalition government. He was active in creating the new republic in 1948, and in securing communist primacy within it. Gheorghiu-Dej strengthened his own position in the party during the early 1950s, particularly through following Stalinist-style purges, and he became First Secretary in 1955. An ally of KHRUSHCHEV, he managed to secure some relaxation of Soviet influence on Romania, both by negotiating the removal of Red Army troops in 1958, and by following a non-COMECON industrial policy. He became President in 1961, a position he held until his death in 1965. He was succeeded by Ceauçescu.

Gheorghiu, Gheorghe *see* GHEORGHIU-DEJ, GHEORGHE.

Giolitti, Giovanni (1842–1928) Italian politician. A Piedmontese civil servant, Giolitti entered parliament as a Liberal in 1882. His first office came in 1889, when he served as Treasury Minister. In 1892 he became Prime Minister, although he was forced to resign in 1893 after a banking scandal. He returned as Minister of the Interior in 1901 before forming another government from October 1903 until March 1905. He held office on two more occasions before the FIRST WORLD WAR, from May 1906 until December 1909, and from March 1911 until March 1914. These terms of office exemplified Giolitti's expertise as a coalition manager.

His administrations made a number of modernising reforms, including franchise extension, the improvement of trade union rights, and industrial regulation. He also oversaw some colonial expansion in Libya and the Dodecanese (*see* IMPERIALISM), and followed a European policy that kept Italy in the TRIPLE ALLIANCE while building relations with France. An opponent of Italian involvement in the First World War, he returned to office for the final time for a year from June 1920. This administration managed to remove D'ANNUNZIO from Fiume and solved some long-running strikes; it also made an electoral pact with MUSSOLINI that gave the Fascists parliamentary representation and provided official toleration of some fascist violence (*see* FASCISM). He lost office after the 1921 elections, but remained a deputy. He did not take part in the AVENTINE SECESSION, but grew critical of Mussolini in the last years of his life.

Girondins Political grouping of the FRENCH REVOLUTION, flourishing between 1791 and 1793. The grouping took its name from the Gironde region, where many of its members originated, although they were also known variously as Brissotins (after Jacques Brissot) and Rolandists after the most prominent office-holder, Jean-Marie Roland (Minister of the Interior in 1792 and 1793). The Girondins were first united in their calls for war (*see* FRENCH REVOLUTIONARY WARS), but soon became identified as the party of moderation – particularly in relation to the fate of LOUIS XVI – and provincial interests. They declined in influence in the spring of 1793 as France suffered military setbacks, and were expelled from the Convention in early June, an expulsion that helped to set the scene for the TERROR. The group was proscribed, and twenty-three members were executed after a trial in October 1793. After Thermidor, the Girondins were rehabilitated, and some survivors were re-admitted to the Convention.

Giscard d'Estaing, Valéry (born 1926) French politician. After military service in the SECOND WORLD WAR, Giscard d'Estaing became a civil servant, and then a Gaullist Deputy in 1956 (*see* DE GAULLE). His first major office came with his appointment as Minister of Finance in 1961, a position he held until 1966 and again from 1969 until 1974. After President POMPIDOU's death in 1974, Giscard d'Estaing beat MITTERAND in the presidential election. The early years of his office were characterised by some liberal reforms, such as the limited legalisation of abortion and the restructuring of state education, but also by an economic recession. His personal authority was weakened by factions within his government, particularly those associated with Jacques Chirac and other Gaullists. In 1978 his position was partially strengthened by the creation of the Union for French Democracy (UDF); but scandals linking him to Jean Bokassa, the controversial President of the Central African Republic, damaged his credibility. Giscard d'Estaing lost the 1981 presidential election to Mitterand. He remained the President of the UDF until 1996.

glasnost (Russian: 'openness') Soviet policy of the GORBACHEV era. In February 1986, Gorbachev formally began to promote *glasnost* as a government policy. The 'openness' he and his supporters intended was soon felt in the media, in academic research, and in the management of government business at all levels. The policy allowed the media to become far more critical than it had previously been in the Soviet period, leading to reflective and provocative coverage of such issues as the Chernobyl nuclear disaster of April 1986, and the Soviet war effort in Afghanistan. Historical research on STALIN and the abuses of his era was encouraged, with publicity being given to the evidence of the KATYN MASSACRE (to which the USSR finally admitted responsibility) and other mass killings of the period. Moreover, a number of victims of the *YEZHOVSCHINA*, including BUKHARIN, were posthumously rehabilitated. *Glasnost* was also applied to the political process, creating a growth of informed public debate on the government's activities, and to everyday bureaucratic procedures. Together with *PERESTROIKA*, *glasnost* contributed to demands for change in the USSR and eastern Europe, and played a part in bringing about the REVOLUTIONS OF 1989–91.

Goebbels, Josef (1897–1945) German politician. Rejected from military service in the FIRST WORLD WAR due to his polio-related disability, Goebbels followed a successful university career before becoming a political journalist. Increasingly attracted to NAZISM, he joined the NSDAP in 1925. Goebbels became a close colleague of HITLER. In 1926 he became the party's leader in Berlin, while maintaining his journalism. Hitler appointed him as the party's main propagandist in 1929, which allowed Goebbels to develop his skills in oratory and display. A Reichstag deputy from 1928, he became Reich Minister for Public Enlightenment and Propaganda in March 1933. Goebbels' relative intellectualism and his command of the resources of technological media, provided the Nazis with successful propaganda throughout the period of the THIRD REICH; and he was largely responsible for the construction of Hitler's popularity. Despite some decline in influence during the first years of the SECOND WORLD WAR, Goebbels returned to prominence with his calls for increased effort after STALINGRAD. He helped to manage the aftermath of the July 1944 assassination attempt on Hitler, and the following month was appointed as General Plenipotentiary for the Mobilisation of Total War. He maintained this role of controlling resources until the last days of the war. Goebbels remained with Hitler in Berlin until the latter's suicide, and, after briefly attempting to make peace with the USSR, he committed suicide.

Goering, Hermann (1893–1946) German politician. Goering served with distinction as a fighter pilot during the FIRST WORLD WAR, after which he worked as a stunt pilot. He joined the Nazi party (*see* NAZISM) in 1922, and led the Storm Division (SA) in the Beer Hall Putsch of 1923. After a period of exile, he returned to Germany and was elected to the Reichstag in 1928, becoming President of that body in 1932. He served in numerous capacities in HITLER's government, with early portfolios including air and the Prussian interior ministry. In this latter role, he was influential in developing the GESTAPO and the concentration camp system. He emerged as Supreme Commander of the Luftwaffe when it was publicly acknowledged in 1935. In 1936, Hitler appointed Goering to manage the Four Year Plan to prepare the German economy for a war footing, giving Goering a leading role in industry, agriculture and the development of synthetics. He was named as Hitler's successor in 1939, and achieved great prominence and the unique title of Reich Marshal in 1940, after the Luftwaffe's early successes in the SECOND WORLD WAR. However, the loss of the Battle of Britain in 1940 and the failure of the Luftwaffe to maintain supplies to the Eastern front (*see* BARBAROSSA) dented his prestige, while drug dependency damaged his personal efficiency. In April 1945 he left Berlin in an act that was interpreted as a plot to depose Hitler, and Hitler expelled him from all offices in his political testament. Goering surrendered himself to American forces in Austria. He was convicted of all four counts at the NUREMBERG TRIALS, and sentenced to death; but he committed suicide before his execution was due.

gold standard International banking practice. The gold standard was formally introduced in the UK in 1821 as a backing for currency, based on the assumption that a unit of currency could be exchanged for a stable unit of gold. It gradually developed as an international standard, supported by gold coins, used as a mechanism for international trade and the payment of loans and debts. By the 1890s, France, Germany and the USA were all on the gold standard: its prevalence between the industrialised nations' economies was seen as a mark of status and aspiration for industrialising nations, hence Russia's involvement in the late 1890s as a way of encouraging trade (*see* INDUSTRIALISATION). However, the stability of gold that the gold standard assumed was disrupted by the FIRST WORLD WAR; and the inflation of wartime, caused by the printing of currency beyond the value of gold reserves to help finance emergency projects, led to the gold standard's suspension. Some countries had chosen to suspend their membership of the gold standard early on in the war, as their governments had anticipated this problem. After the war, a number of countries returned to adapted versions of the gold standard: Denmark and Norway, for example, introduced gold convertibility for exports; while most other countries fixed their currencies against another gold standard country's currency. Through these forms, the gold standard was in general use again by 1928. It was increasingly unstable in this period due to deflation, and was gradually abandoned by all countries during the DEPRESSION, with Belgium, France and the Netherlands holding on until the mid-1930s. Planning for post-war economic reconstruction in 1944 at BRETTON WOODS involved an abandonment of the gold standard.

Gomulka, Wladyslaw (1905–82) Polish politician. Gomulka joined the Communist party in 1918, and became a member of its Central Committee in 1931. He was twice imprisoned for his communist activism in the 1930s. During the SECOND WORLD WAR he worked for the Polish RESISTANCE, becoming Secretary General of the Polish Workers' Party in 1943. He served in the post-war Government of National Unity as minister in charge of the former German territories, but was dismissed in 1948 for allegedly promoting Polish NATIONALISM. He was imprisoned for this non-Stalinist line from 1952 until 1955, but returned to favour and prominence after KHRUSHCHEV's denunciation of STALIN in 1956. Gomulka became the party's First Secretary in 1956. His period of office was initially characterised by social and economic reforms, including the maintenance of private land ownership, relative religious freedom, and the promotion of individual rights, but this liberalism was stifled from the early 1960s. In 1970 Gomulka resigned after price rises led to riots in a number of cities.

Gorbachev, Mikhail (born 1931) Soviet politician. Gorbachev joined the Communist party in 1952, and worked for it while practising as a lawyer and agricultural planner. He joined the Central Committee in 1971, and was rapidly promoted as an agricultural expert under the patronage of ANDROPOV. Gorbachev developed a broadly reformist power base during CHERNENKO's brief term of office, and became General Secretary after Chernenko's death in 1985. In 1986 he promoted the twin ideas of *GLASNOST* and *PERESTROIKA* for economic and administrative improvements, and followed a broadly conciliatory line in foreign affairs, enabling the USSR to reduce its defence expenditure (*see* COLD WAR). Gorbachev improved his position by removing a number of older members of the government, including GROMYKO, in 1988, and he assumed the presidency in the same year. His term of office was characterised by many reforms, notably the growth of individual freedoms, the release of political prisoners and the abolition of the party's protected role, and he oversaw the inauguration of a new Congress of People's Deputies, which elected Gorbachev president in 1989. In the bulk of the REVOLUTIONS OF 1989–91, Gorbachev rejected intervention, thus facilitating the collapse of the Soviet bloc. In 1990 he was awarded the Nobel Peace Prize. However, the pressures for decentralisation within the USSR, particularly that from Russia, led to a Communist coup against Gorbachev in August 1991: and while it failed, it weakened his position. In December 1991, with the framework for the post-Soviet Commonwealth of Independent States in place, Gorbachev resigned. His attempt to return to Russian politics in 1996, when he ran for president, ended in defeat.

Gottwald, Klement (1896–1953) Czechoslovakian politician. After serving in the Austro-Hungarian army during the FIRST WORLD WAR, Gottwald joined the Communist party in 1921. He became a member of its Central Committee in 1925, and its General Secretary in 1927. During the 1930s he worked for the THIRD INTERNATIONAL in Czechoslovakia. He moved to Moscow after the MUNICH AGREEMENT of 1938, remaining there until 1945. He then returned to Prague as a member of the provisional government, and formed a coalition, with BENEŠ as President, after elections in 1946. Gottwald organised a communist coup in February 1948, assuming the presidency himself (*see* COLD

WAR). His period in office was characterised by Stalinist political structures and state terrorism, and by a close economic relationship with the USSR. Gottwald died in office in 1953.

Grammos, Mount, battle of (August 1949) *see* GREEK CIVIL WAR.

Great Depression *see* DEPRESSION, GREAT.

Great Purge *see* *YEZHOVSHCHINA*.

Greek Civil War War between communist and monarchist factions in Greece, with external involvement, 1944–45, 1946–49. During the Second World War, Greek RESISTANCE to the AXIS invasion had been provided mainly by the communist National People's Army of Liberation (ELAS), the military wing of the National Liberation Front (EAM), who planned for a communist republic after the war (*see* COMMUNISM). However, resistance also came from royalist groups dedicated to the restoration of George II. The splits between these groups became evident as soon as the occupation ended, and in October 1944 British troops were sent to Athens to help the restoration, and to support the interim monarchist government. They were involved in fighting the following month, which broke out over attempts to purge the army of communists. A compromise truce in February 1945 was based on the promise of reforms, a plebiscite on the monarchy and the dissolution of ELAS. Little action followed: and when the plebiscite supported a restoration in October 1946, some communists recommenced their attack on the government forces under the banner of the Democratic Army of Greece. The Civil War then took on major international significance as a key flashpoint in the COLD WAR: the UK withdrew its military commitment, due to costs; the USA provided economic and military aid to the government (*see* MARSHALL PLAN); while communist governments in Albania, Bulgaria and Yugoslavia supported the rebels. The communists gradually lost, as they failed to gain enough peasant support, and their supplies were restricted after Yugoslavia's break from the USSR in 1948. The government forces finally won the war in the battle of Mount Grammos in August 1949. Approximately 25,000 people were killed in the war.

Greek colonels Label used to describe the military dictatorship of Greece, 1967–74. In April 1967 a group of high-ranking Greek army officers, led by Georgios Papadopoulos and Stylianos Pattakos, staged a coup in order to prevent PAPANDREOU from forming a liberal government. Presenting it as a necessary precaution to prevent COMMUNISM spreading in Greece, the coup was welcomed by CONSTANTINE II, who worked with the colonels in their imposition of martial law. However, in December 1967 Constantine staged his own abortive coup against the colonels. The seven-year period of military rule was characterised by censorship, suppression of political debate and opposition, and human rights abuses. In March 1972 Papadopoulos made himself Regent, but then declared Greece a republic with himself as President in 1973. He was replaced by General Phaidon Gizikis in November 1973. In July 1974 the government sponsored a military coup against MAKARIOS in Cyprus in an attempt to achieve *ENOSIS*: but the failure of this, and the subsequent Turkish invasion of Cyprus, undermined the ruling group's authority and credibility. In late July, the government resigned, and Greece returned to constitutional rule. A referendum in late 1974 confirmed its status as a republic. In August 1975 leading members of the military dictatorship were tried for the abuses that took place during their period in office, with Papadopoulos and others being given life imprisonment.

Greek-Turkish War (1921–22) War between Greece and Turkish nationalists, 1921–22. At the end of the FIRST WORLD WAR, the treaty of SÈVRES was rejected by Turkish nationalists, who, under the leadership of Kemal (*see* ATATÜRK), committed themselves to resisting the imposition of the treaty's territorial clauses in Asia Minor. In March 1921 Greece sent an armed force to Smyrna to regain the territory. After some early successes against Turkish guerrilla attacks, they began their advance on the nationalists' capital of Ankara in June 1921. In August, however, the over-stretched

Greeks were beaten by Kemal's forces at Sakhgaria River and forced into retreat. An attempt at arbitration by the British and French governments was unsuccessful, as the Turks would not accept an armistice without the total withdrawal of Greek forces: and in September 1922 the Turks entered Smyrna. The Greeks were pushed out, while Greek civilians were massacred and large sections of the town destroyed. The Turkish threat to advance into the European territories given to Greece at Sèvres led to a major confrontation with the UK: the British government strengthened its garrison at Chanak in order to hinder Kemal's access to the Straits. However, the potential conflict was prevented by an Anglo-Turkish meeting at Mudiana, at which the British agreed to renegotiate the 1920 settlement in return for a cessation of Turkish hostilities. This led to the treaty of LAUSANNE in July 1923. As well as contributing to a territorial realignment, the war led to the collapse of the Greek government and CONSTANTINE I's abdication, while the nationalist movement in Turkey used its victory as the base for the overthrow of the OTTOMAN Sultan and the establishment of a new republic in October 1923.

Greek War of Independence (1821–29) War between Greeks and OTTOMAN forces, with interventions from France, Russia and the UK, that led to the establishment of Greece as an independent state. After the FRENCH REVOLUTION, liberal and nationalist ideologies were assimilated by some Greek elites in the Ottoman empire (*see* LIBERALISM, NATIONALISM). In 1814, Greek merchants and administrators formed the secret Friendly Society in Odessa to develop the idea of Greek independence. In March 1821, General Alexandros Ypsilantis led a small liberal nationalist army into Moldavia and Wallachia, while popular rebellions also broke out in southern Greece. Ypsilantis' army was beaten by Sultan Mahmud II's forces at the battle of Dragashan in June 1821, but the southern revolts led to further fighting. By late 1821 the Greek rebels were dominant, and in January 1822 they declared independence and published a liberal constitution. Although the QUADRUPLE ALLIANCE powers were at first opposed to the rebellion, various strategic interests elicited different responses: for example, Russia saw the revolt as an opportunity to gain influence in the Balkans (*see* PANSLAVISM), while the UK saw intervention as a way to check Russian advances. The Greek cause attracted much liberal sympathy throughout Europe, particularly after the campaign of the Sultan's ally Ibrahim Pasha began in July 1822. The civilian and religious massacres involved in this war forced the powers to act. In April 1826 Russia and the UK signed the St Petersburg Protocol, committing them to mediate and promote Greek autonomy; and in July 1827 France, Russia and the UK signed the treaty of London which formalised the protocol (and also dented the HOLY ALLIANCE by dividing Russia from its partners). When the Sultan refused to allow mediation, a combined allied fleet blockaded southern Greece and defeated the Turkish fleet at the battle of NAVARINO. In January 1828 Ioannis Kapodistrias assumed the presidency of Greece. Turkish resistance to independence was finally overcome by a Russian invasion, with the Turkish withdrawal starting in August 1828. With allied backing for an independent Greece confirmed in November 1828, the new state was formally created by the treaty of ADRIANOPLE of September 1829 between Russia and the Ottoman empire. The territorial and political settlements were made at an allied conference in London in 1832. The frontiers were set, excluding Crete and Thessalonika, and a hereditary monarchy was established, with Prince Otto of Bavaria becoming the first king in 1833. The settlement did not prevent the continuation of factional conflict, and it left many territorial issues unresolved.

Gromyko, Andrei (1909–89) Soviet politician. A professional economist, Gromyko joined the Communist party in 1931. He moved into the diplomatic service, becoming Ambassador to the USA in 1943. Present at the TEHRAN CONFERENCE, the YALTA CONFERENCE and the POTSDAM CONFERENCE of the SECOND WORLD WAR, Gromyko stayed in Washington until

1946, thereafter representing the USSR on the UNITED NATIONS Security Council until 1949. He was recalled to Moscow to become deputy Foreign Minister to MOLOTOV, a post he held until 1957, excepting a brief spell as Ambassador to London. He then succeeded Molotov as Foreign Minister, staying in office until 1985. GORBACHEV removed him from this post, making him instead President of the Supreme Soviet and thus head of state. He retired in 1988, and died the following year.

Guadalajara, battle of (March 1937) *see* SPANISH CIVIL WAR.

Guernica, bombing of (March 1937) *see* SPANISH CIVIL WAR.

Guizot, François (1787–1874) French politician. A history professor, Guizot served LOUIS XVIII's government in various capacities from the restoration of 1814 until 1820, but then fell from favour due to his LIBERALISM. He returned to prominence in 1830 as a supporter of LOUIS-PHILIPPE, whom he served as Minister of the Interior and, from 1832 until 1837, as Minister of Public Instruction. In this office he helped to reform state education. In 1840 he served as Ambassador to London, before being made Foreign Minister, and then Prime Minister in 1847. However, his repressive measures against the press, and his resistance to political reform, directly fed the reform movement that underpinned the French revolution of 1848 (*see* REVOLUTIONS OF 1848). Louis-Philippe dismissed Guizot in February 1848. After an unsuccessful coup attempt in 1851, Guizot retired from public life.

H

Habsburg dynasty Central European royal family. The Habsburg family dominated central Europe for much of the medieval and early modern periods, ruling Austrian territory from the thirteenth century, Bohemia and Hungary from the sixteenth century, and holding the crown of the HOLY ROMAN EMPIRE from the mid-fifteenth century. They also had extensive Iberian interests. In the eighteenth and nineteenth centuries, they also added Italian interests, notably control of Tuscany from 1737 and Modena from 1803. Habsburg power in the Italian states was ended in 1860 (*see* ITALIAN UNIFICATION), while their role in Hungary was diminished by the *AUSGLEICH* of 1867. The dynasty lost its last crown in 1918 when Emperor Charles abdicated at the end of the FIRST WORLD WAR.

Hammarskjøld, Dag (1905–61) Swedish diplomat. An economics professor and banker, Hammarskjøld worked as an advisor to the Swedish Foreign Ministry before joining the Ministry as an under-secretary and then, from 1951, a minister. Alongside this work for the government, he also worked for the UNITED NATIONS (UN) from 1947. In 1953 he became the second Secretary-General of the UN, succeeding LIE. In his first term of office, he led the UN's response to the Suez crisis of 1956, and he was re-elected for a second term in 1957. He promoted peace initiatives in the Middle East, and he ensured that the UN had a role in managing European decolonisation from Africa (*see* IMPERIALISM). He was killed in an aeroplane crash in Africa in 1961, and was awarded the Nobel Peace Prize posthumously the same year.

Hardenberg, Karl, Prince von (1750–1822) Prussian politician. A regional administrator, Hardenberg came to prominence in 1806 when he advised FREDERICK WILLIAM III to continue the war against France (*see* FRENCH REVOLUTIONARY WARS). He left office in 1807, but emerged again in 1810 as State Chancellor. In the context of Prussia's defeat by the French and subsequent territorial losses at the treaty of TILSIT, Hardenberg and STEIN advised Frederick William on a course of reforms to modernise and reconstruct Prussia. These included various economic reforms, and improvements in the state's administrative forms. Hardenberg claimed that such moves could pre-empt revolution on the French model. He was also involved with foreign affairs, representing Prussia at the Congress of Vienna (*see*

VIENNA, CONGRESS OF). He stayed in office until his death in 1822, even after the King moved away from this liberal phase.

Havel, Václav (born 1936) Czechoslovakian and Czech activist and politician. A playwright and theatre worker, Havel came to prominence in 1977 as a signatory and leading spokesman for Charter 77, an intellectual petition against human rights abuses and the lack of intellectual freedom in Czechoslovakia (*see* COLD WAR). He was imprisoned a number of times for his activities between 1977 and 1989. In 1989 he was a founder member of Civil Forum, an organisation that argued publicly against the Communist government, and he played a role in the 'velvet revolution' that forced the resignation of President Gustav Husák in December 1989 (*see* REVOLUTIONS OF 1989–91). Despite his original reluctance to take a leading political role, Havel was elected President of Czechoslovakia by the National Assembly after Husák's fall, securing the position with a popular mandate in the following year's election. He resigned in 1992 over the imminent separation of Czechoslovakia into two republics, but returned as the President of the Czech Republic in the 1993 election.

Helsinki conference (1973–75) *see* CONFERENCE ON SECURITY AND COOPERATION IN EUROPE.

Herzl, Theodor (1860–1904) Hungarian zionist activist (*see* ZIONISM). A successful writer and journalist in Vienna, Herzl became convinced of the need for a separate Jewish homeland during the rise of ANTI-SEMITISM in Austria and France in the 1890s, particularly that centred around the DREYFUS AFFAIR, on which he reported for a Vienna newspaper. Herzl developed his ideas in his 1896 publication *The Jewish State*, and convened existing zionist groups as the World Zionist Congress in Basel in 1897. He became the first President of the World Zionist Organisation, campaigning until his death in 1904 for Israel to be established as a nation state.

Hess, Rudolf (1894–1987) German politician. After serving in the FIRST WORLD WAR, Hess became attracted to NAZISM in Munich. He joined the Nazi party in 1920, and participated in the Beer Hall Putsch of 1923. He was imprisoned with HITLER for this. The two men became close in prison, with Hess acting as Hitler's secretary, a role he maintained after their release. He entered the Reichstag in 1932, the same year in which he was made the party's deputy leader. Hitler appointed Hess as Minister without Portfolio in June 1933, and as Deputy *Führer* in 1934. Hess was involved in party appointments, and helped to promote Hitler's personality cult at rallies. In 1939 he was named as second in line after GOERING to succeed Hitler. His influence waned during the early years of the SECOND WORLD WAR, and in May 1941 he flew alone on an abortive peace mission to the UK which has yet to be satisfactorily explained. He was immediately disowned by Hitler for this move. After an internment in the UK, he was convicted of conspiracy and crimes against peace at the NUREMBERG TRIALS, and sentenced to life imprisonment. He served this term at Spandau prison in West Berlin, where he died in 1987.

Heydrich, Reinhard (1904–42) German security officer. After his dishonourable discharge from the German Navy in 1931, Heydrich joined the Nazi party and the Defence Unit (SS) (*see* NAZISM). His rapid promotion came after he was noticed by HIMMLER. In 1933 he headed the security services in Bavaria, and he took a leading role in the NIGHT OF THE LONG KNIVES in 1934. In the same year he was promoted to run the GESTAPO, from which he developed a remit for Jewish affairs and internal security. He helped to organise the *Kristallnacht* attacks on Jewish properties in 1938. He organised the commandos responsible for killing Jews, Poles and political commissars during BARBAROSSA, and was subsequently involved in writing the paper on the 'FINAL SOLUTION to the Jewish problem' that formed the basis of the Wannsee conference of January 1942, which he chaired. He also organised camps and transportations. In September 1941 he was appointed Protector of Bohemia and Moravia. He died in June 1942 as a result of wounds received the previous month in an assassination attempt by Czechoslovakian RESISTANCE fighters backed by the British government. The German authorities carried out severe reprisals for his death, including the destruction of the villages of Lezaky and Lidice and their populations.

Himmler, Heinrich (1900–45) German politician. After brief military service in the FIRST WORLD WAR, Himmler joined the Nazi party (*see* NAZISM) in 1921, and played an active role in the Beer Hall Putsch. He joined the Defence Unit (SS) in 1925, becoming its leader in 1929. From here, he developed this bodyguard into a powerful elite force. Himmler supervised the NIGHT OF THE LONG KNIVES in June 1934, after which the SS gained its independence from the Storm Division (SA). He was given command of the GESTAPO in 1934, and in 1936 he brought together all internal security and police forces under his command. This role extended into occupied territories during the SECOND WORLD WAR, with Himmler's extensive use of state terrorism and its threat making him one of the most powerful Nazis. As head of the SS, he had the main overall responsibility for the FINAL SOLUTION. His position was consolidated after the July 1944 assassination attempt on Hitler, and he was made Commander-in-Chief of the home forces. After brief spells commanding forces on both the western and eastern fronts in late 1944 and early 1945, Himmler began informal peace talks with BERNADOTTE in April 1945. Hitler expelled him from the party, and Himmler fled from Berlin. He was arrested by British troops in May 1945, but committed suicide in captivity before interrogation.

Hindenburg, Paul von (1847–1934) German soldier and politician. Hindenburg fought in the AUSTRO-PRUSSIAN WAR of 1866 and the FRANCO-PRUSSIAN WAR of 1870–71. He remained in the army until his retirement in 1911 at the rank of general, but rejoined in 1914 at the outbreak of the FIRST WORLD WAR. After the battle of TANNENBERG in 1914 he was promoted to Field-Marshal with command of the Eastern Front. As Chief of the General Staff from 1916, Hindenburg, with his colleague LUDENDORFF, had extensive political and economic powers. After negotiating the Treaty of BREST-LITOVSK with Russia, he co-led the March 1918 western offensive. By the autumn, with the allies gaining ground in the west and Germany's eastern allies collapsing, he successfully advised WILLIAM II to abdicate, after which Hindenburg sued for peace. He retired for a second time in 1919, but re-entered public life in 1925 as a conservative presidential candidate after EBERT's death (*see* WEIMAR REPUBLIC). He won the election, and served his seven-year term. From 1930 he worked with BRÜNING, frequently using presidential decrees to bypass the Reichstag. He stood again in 1932 as the only person likely to beat the Nazis' presidential candidate, HITLER. He did so, winning the election on the second ballot, but was increasingly ineffective due to his age and health. After working with conservative chancellors PAPEN and Kurt von Schleicher, he appointed Hitler in January 1933 on Papen's advice. Sympathetic to some aspects of NAZISM, he remained in office until his death in August 1934, although he played very little part in the running of the government. He was buried at Tannenberg.

Hitler, Adolf (1889–1945) German politician. Born in Austria, Hitler lived in Linz and Vienna until 1913, before moving to Germany. He joined the Bavarian army in 1914, serving throughout the FIRST WORLD WAR. Disillusioned by the German surrender, Hitler moved towards extremism, and in 1919 he joined the German Workers party. He became the party's leader in 1921, and was influential in its renaming as the National Socialist German Workers party (NSDAP) (*see* NAZISM) and in focusing its interests in NATIONALISM, anti-COMMUNISM and ANTI-SEMITISM. Hitler led the Nazis' unsuccessful coup, the Beer Hall Putsch of 1923, becoming convinced of the need for legal access to power during his subsequent prison sentence. His main writings, the two volumes of *Mein Kampf*, were produced during this period. Along with colleagues such as HESS and GOEBBELS, Hitler rebuilt the party from 1925, developing his oratorical skills alongside increasingly professional propaganda and paramilitary activities. After a good showing against HINDENBURG in the 1932 presidential election, Hitler was recognised as a major player in German politics; and in January 1933 Hindenburg appointed him as Chancellor of a coalition government. Hitler's position was strengthened after the Reichstag fire of February 1933 and the ENABLING ACT gave the government emergency powers, leading to the replacement of the coalition with a predominantly Nazi administration. The party itself was purged of Hitler's opponents and potential opponents in the NIGHT OF THE LONG KNIVES of June 1934. In August 1934, on Hindenburg's death, Hitler combined the posts of Chancellor and President under the title *Führer* (leader), and replaced the WEIMAR REPUBLIC with the THIRD REICH.

As the head of an administratively complex and illogically structured government, Hitler was involved in most areas of domestic, economic, foreign and military affairs, playing roles in the development of expansionist foreign and military policies that worked against the VERSAILLES settlement (*see* APPEASEMENT, AXIS, MUNICH AGREEMENT, RHINELAND, REMILITARISATION). After securing the pragmatic NAZI-SOVIET PACT in 1939, Hitler ordered the invasion of Poland that precipitated the SECOND WORLD WAR. From this point on, his main interests were military and strategic, although he was clearly involved with the authorisation of the FINAL SOLUTION, if not its actual execution. After early successes in western Europe, Hitler authorised the shift to the east in Operation BARBAROSSA of 1941, taking personal command of the war against the USSR in December 1941. Hitler's own position, propaganda and reputation kept him immune from blame for some of Germany's military reverses thereafter, although the reverses of 1944 caused some of his opponents in the military to attempt to assassinate him. He survived this, but committed suicide in Berlin in April 1945 as the Red Army approached.

Hohenlinden, battle of (December 1800) *see* NAPOLEONIC WARS.

Hohenzollern dynasty Prussian and German royal family. The family provided monarchs of Prussia from 1701, through which it became the most powerful royal family in the German states. On GERMAN UNIFICATION, the Prussian monarchs became monarchs of Germany, with the Hohenzollern dynasty thus ruling the new German empire until its dissolution at the end of the FIRST WORLD WAR. The last Hohenzollern monarch, WILLIAM II, abdicated in 1918.

Holocaust *see* FINAL SOLUTION.

Holy Alliance (September 1815) Christian-based personal alliance system between European rulers in the post-NAPOLEONIC WARS period. In May 1815, during the Congress of Vienna (*see* VIENNA, CONGRESS OF), ALEXANDER I of Russia wrote a pact for all Christian rulers to sign. It was duly signed as the Holy Alliance in late September 1815 by the HABSBURG, Prussian and Russian rulers, with most other European rulers joining subsequently: only the Pope, the British Prince Regent and the Ottoman Sultan stayed out. The terms of this loose alliance were vague and mystical, but were broadly based on all rulers practising Christian principles in their mutual dealings and in their domestic government. The Alliance was not taken seriously by many of its signatories, and had very little political or diplomatic relevance: this was provided by the QUADRUPLE ALLIANCE of November 1815. However, it increasingly came to embody the reactionary and anti-revolutionary interests of the three main monarchs.

Holy Roman Empire Political organisation of the HABSBURG and German states, originating in the ninth century and ending in 1806. The Holy Roman Empire survived the medieval period, but declined in influence throughout the early modern period. Dominated by the Habsburg dynasty, it was, by the middle of the seventeenth century, a loose federation of over three hundred states, many of which developed strong political, economic and religious links beyond the territory of the Empire itself. Its fabric was threatened by the growing strength of Hanover and Prussia. It was eventually destroyed in the aftermath of the FRENCH REVOLUTION. France gained territory from the Empire during the FRENCH REVOLUTIONARY WARS and the NAPOLEONIC WARS, and Napoleon's institution of the CONFEDERATION OF THE RHINE in 1806 formally ended the Empire's existence. Its last Emperor, the Habsburg Francis II, who had reigned since 1792, revoked this title.

Honecker, Erich (1912–94) German and East German politician. Honecker joined the German Communist party in 1929, and worked for its youth wing. Remaining in Germany after HITLER's accession to power, he was arrested in 1935, and spent the remainder of the THIRD REICH in custody. At the end of the SECOND WORLD WAR, he remained in what became the German Democratic Republic (GDR), and returned to an active role in communist politics. After running the GDR's national youth movement from 1949 until 1958, Honecker joined the Politburo, and soon emerged as ULBRICHT's deputy. He succeeded Ulbricht as the party's First Secretary in 1971, and became head of state in 1976. His domestic policies were focused on improving the GDR's industrial output. Despite making some western connections, Honecker remained close to the USSR internationally (*see* COLD WAR), although he failed to embrace GORBACHEV's reforms after 1985. He resigned in October 1989 in the face of mass demonstrations (*see* GERMAN REUNIFICATION, REVOLUTIONS OF 1989–91), and moved to the USSR. He subsequently returned to Germany for trial on corruption and human rights charges, but he was released in 1993 for health reasons.

Horthy, Miklós (1868–1957) Hungarian admiral and politician. After serving as FRANCIS JOSEPH's aide-de-camp before the FIRST WORLD WAR, Horthy served in the Austro-Hungarian navy, achieving the post of Commander-in-Chief in 1917. He moved into party politics after the war, serving briefly as Minister for War, and then leading a nationalist revolt (with Romanian support) against KUN's communist government in 1919. Horthy became head of state in post-HABSBURG Hungary in January 1920, officially accepting the role as a regency for the exiled King Charles: but he resisted Charles' attempts at forcing a restoration in 1921, and assumed increasingly dictatorial power. His policies and style were influenced by FASCISM and later NAZISM. Having agreed the terms of the treaty of TRIANON in June 1920, Horthy attempted to restore Hungary's lost territories: his main successes, with German assistance, came in 1938 and 1940 with the regaining of parts of southern Slovakia. In 1941 Horthy allied Hungary with Germany, and provided troops for the war in Yugoslavia and the USSR (*see* BARBAROSSA). However, in 1944 he attempted to negotiate a separate peace for Hungary, an act which precipitated a German invasion of Hungary and Horthy's imprisonment. He fell into American hands at the end of the war, and was released in 1946, despite Yugoslavian pressure for his trial. He spent the rest of his life in exile, dying in Portugal in 1957.

Hoxha, Enver (1908–85) Albanian politician. Hoxha became active in communist politics during his studies in France in the 1930s. He returned to Albania in 1936, and was a founder member and First Secretary of the Communist party in November 1941, during the Italian occupation of Albania (*see* SECOND WORLD WAR). He led the RESISTANCE movement, a position which set the basis of his leadership of the post-war provisional government. Hoxha quickly shaped this government into a communist dictatorship, closely modelled on STALIN's rule. He purged the party of TITO's sympathisers in 1948, and remained faithful to Stalinism even after KHRUSHCHEV's denunciation of Stalin in 1956. Under Hoxha, Albania followed a strictly isolationist foreign policy, with few links developed to either east or west; while domestically it remained an economically poor country, with a strict system which suppressed religion and individual liberties. Hoxha died in office in April 1985.

Hundred Days *see* NAPOLEON BONAPARTE; NAPOLEONIC WARS.

Hungarian rising (October–November 1956) Unsuccessful anti-Soviet revolution in Hungary. In the context of KHRUSHCHEV's movement away from Stalin's policies and legacy, liberal and democratic ideas began to circulate in many parts of eastern Europe under Soviet domination (*see* COLD WAR, IMPERIALISM). In Hungary these became clearly expressed within the ruling Communist party, and Khrushchev responded by effectively dismissing RÁKOSI in July 1956. Pressure for less cosmetic reforms grew, particularly in the early autumn after bad harvests, and student and worker demonstrations in Budapest and elsewhere provided a focus for change. In late October, violent clashes grew out of these demonstrations, with both the Hungarian police and the Red Army involved, before a cease-fire was brokered under which the Red Army withdrew. This was followed by the creation of a new government under NAGY as Prime Minister, who quickly introduced various liberal reforms. However, his call for Hungarian neutrality on Austrian lines (*see* AUSTRIAN STATE TREATY), and for Hungary to withdraw from the WARSAW PACT, resulted in a Soviet clampdown: aided by the party's First Secretary, KÁDÁR, Warsaw Pact forces re-entered Budapest in early November and put down the rising by force. Resistance continued, in the form of fighting, strikes and non-violent demonstrations, but Kádár was successfully established as the head of a new communist government. At least 3,000 Hungarians were killed in the fighting and in subsequent executions, and over 200,000 people left Hungary. Nagy himself was arrested and later executed. The UNITED NATIONS debated the issue, but had no real opportunity to intervene. The incident demonstrated that the tensions of the Cold War had outlived Stalin, and that the creation of the Warsaw Pact in 1955 had been intended in part to allow the USSR to maintain its domination of eastern Europe through troop placements.

I

imperialism The domination of one geopolitical area by a stronger one. Although the word 'imperialism' was not applied to this process until the late nineteenth century, the political and economic relations involved in imperialism have been evident throughout the post-1789 period. However, it is important to stress that the motivations behind imperialism have varied greatly between different imperial powers and over time, and that, certainly before the 1870s, imperial development by any one power tended to be pragmatic rather than driven by any clear or unified policy. Over the period from 1789 to 1999, it is possible to see two distinct forms of imperialism undertaken by European powers: inter-European, or continental; and extra-European, or overseas.

INTER-EUROPEAN IMPERIALISM

Throughout the period, parts of continental Europe itself have been subject to imperial control and contestation. French expansion during the FRENCH REVOLUTIONARY WARS and NAPOLEONIC WARS created an empire for France that stretched, by 1812, from the Danish border in the north into parts of Spain and the Italian states in the south, with the Illyrian provinces giving France a presence in the Balkans. While these acquisitions were new, they put France on a footing with three other major European empires: the HABSBURG empire, the OTTOMAN EMPIRE and the Russian empire. These four had in common their economic and strategic interest in maintaining control over smaller national populations. This form of inter-European imperialism altered dramatically over the course of the nineteenth century, both through military activity – for example, the French empire was dismantled by the peacemaking of 1814 and 1815, while the 1878 BERLIN CONGRESS that followed the RUSSO-TURKISH WAR confirmed the independence of Montenegro, Romania and Serbia from the Ottoman empire – and by the growth of NATIONALISM as a political and economic force. ITALIAN UNIFICATION, for example, reduced the Habsburg empire, as did GERMAN UNIFICATION, which in itself created a new German empire. However, despite nationalism as an anti-imperial force, a number of nations with traditions or notions of independence remained under imperial control, such as Poland (split between the German, Habsburg and Russian empires), and Finland under Russian control.

This form of continental imperialism was a significant factor in the origins of the FIRST WORLD WAR, as Austro-Hungarian and Russian rivalries in the Balkans led to conflict. As a result of this, it was deliberately diluted in the peace settlement, with the idea of self-determination (*see* FOURTEEN POINTS, PARIS PEACE CONFERENCE) being applied in a number of areas to promote nationalism rather than imperialism. The reconstruction or creation of, for example, Czechoslovakia, Hungary, Poland, and the Kingdom of the Serbs, Croats and Slovenes (subsequently Yugoslavia) were evidence of this. The imperial aspects of the RUSSIAN CIVIL WAR can also be seen in this context, with Estonia, Finland, Latvia and Lithuania all emerging from the old Russian empire. Moreover, the First World War can be seen to have effectively destroyed the Austro-Hungarian, German, Ottoman and Russian empires. However, continental imperialism re-emerged very quickly: it was evident in the USSR's consolidation as, effectively, a new Russian empire, as in the Ukraine and Belarus; and it was evident in Germany's expansion during the THIRD REICH, which went beyond the basic idea in NAZISM of unifying all Germans by spreading into Czechoslovakia, Poland and the USSR. After the SECOND WORLD WAR, the main aspect of this form of imperialism was the USSR's effective control of large parts of eastern Europe: and while this did not take the form of direct conquest and rule from the centre, the use of communist parties and Russocentric economic and military ties made it a form of indirect imperialism (*see* COMECON, COMINFORM, WARSAW PACT). The collapse of communist and Soviet domination of this area during the REVOLUTIONS OF 1989–91, and the collapse of the USSR itself, brought this system to an end, and saw a number of new nation states emerge, such as Belarus, Moldova and Ukraine.

EXTRA-EUROPEAN IMPERIALISM

The acquisition of overseas territories for a combination of political, strategic and economic purposes was carried out by a number of European states before 1789. While Great Britain was a leading power here, France at various times had interests in Africa, India, North America, the Caribbean and the East Indies, for example, while Spain and Portugal both had southern American interests. Overseas possessions were contested during the FRENCH REVOLUTIONARY WARS and the NAPOLEONIC WARS, during which time a number of territories changed hands, with Denmark, France, the Netherlands and Sweden all losing out to the UK. During the wars, and throughout the subsequent decades, many parts of the Portuguese and Spanish empires declared themselves independent (for example, Uruguay from Spain in 1814, and Brazil from Portugal in 1822), although Africa, Asia and the Pacific soon replaced the Americas as areas for more extensive European imperialism. Again, while the UK was the leading power here, by the end of the 1850s France had extended its power in north and west Africa and the Pacific, Portugal had gained Macao, Portugal and the Netherlands had consolidated their control of parts of the East Indies, and Russia had moved into central Asia.

Overseas imperialism developed greatly from the 1880s, characterised at this time by rivalries between different European powers, and influenced by the growth of INDUSTRIALISATION which created new economic opportunities and constraints. In this period, Belgium, France, Germany and Italy all became involved, with the UK, in the 'scramble for Africa', a phase which left virtually the whole of Africa in some form of imperial relationship by 1914. France also continued to develop its Asian interests in Indo-China, as did the Netherlands in the East Indies and Germany in the Pacific. As with continental imperialism, overseas imperialism was a factor in causing the FIRST WORLD WAR; and the peace settlement involved colonies and possessions being taken from the defeated nations and run, under LEAGUE OF NATIONS auspices, as MANDATES. While imperial factors remained influential before and during the SECOND WORLD WAR, with some fresh imperialism in Africa (*see* ITALO-ABYSSINIAN WAR) the post-1945 period was largely characterised by decolonisation, as the costs of imperialism outstripped its benefits, and as nationalist movements in a number of colonised areas became more influential. Decolonisation was violent on occasions, as in the French withdrawal from Indo-China from 1946 to 1954 and Algeria from 1954 until 1962, and the Dutch withdrawal from Indonesia between 1947 and 1949. At other times it was more peaceful. By the late 1990s the vast majority of European overseas possessions had become independent or taken by larger local powers. A number of colonial territories survived as such, with France, for example, controlling Martinique and French Guiana, and Portugal controlling Macao until the end of 1999. Many of the former imperial powers have maintained strong links with their former colonies, helped by linguistic, religious and cultural ties; while processes of inward migration from former colonies to former imperial powers has had a significant impact upon European demography.

industrialisation Label applied to the shift in an area's predominant form of economic activity from agricultural to industrial. While the phrase 'industrial revolution' has become largely superseded in analyses of the British experience between the 1780s and the 1840s, as it disguises the continuities that existed and exaggerates the speed with which changes took place, it is clear that by the 1850s the UK's economy had many industrial characteristics, including a significant manufacturing sector reliant on steam rather than water for power, a national transport network, and exploitable supplies of investment capital, labour and raw materials. In continental Europe, such changes were slower to emerge; but from the 1860s, changes were discernible in a number of countries. For example, railway building programmes in France under NAPOLEON III and the German states facilitated the greater movement of goods, while customs unions, such as the pre-existing *ZOLLVEREIN*, helped the movement of capital and products. While the British experience had been unplanned, a number of continental governments deliberately pursued industrialisation in the 1860s and 1870s, seeing it as the basis for economic strength and imperial development (*see* IMPERIALISM), while the development of the nation state (*see* GERMAN UNIFICATION, ITALIAN UNIFICATION, NATIONALISM) aided production, transport, investment and retailing. By the 1890s parts of Austria-Hungary, France, Germany, Italy and Russia has sophisticated industrial economies, outstripping British performances in a number of areas (notably in steel production, electrical engineering, chemicals and pharmaceuticals). While industrialisation remained a significant feature of most countries' economies in the first half of the twentieth century, it was aggressively promoted in the USSR under STALIN (*see* FIVE YEAR PLANS), and in the eastern European countries under Soviet influence after the SECOND WORLD WAR. Here, it was linked not just to economic and military needs, but also to the notion of modernisation. In the latter part of the twentieth century, industry remained as a significant part of the European economy, with many areas devoted to industrial manufacture. However, it must be seen here as one part of the continent's economy, alongside the survival of agriculture, and the development of post-industrial sectors, such as leisure, tourism, services and finance.

Inkerman, battle of (November 1854) *see* CRIMEAN WAR.

Inönü, Ismet (Mustafa Ismet) (1884–1973) Turkish soldier and politician. An officer in the OTTOMAN army, Ismet was involved in the YOUNG TURKS movement of 1908. He served in the FIRST WORLD WAR, after which he joined Kemal's (*see* ATATÜRK) national resistance movement. He acted as Chief of the General Staff and commander of the army during the GREEK-TURKISH WAR. He then served as Kemal's Foreign Minister, leading the Turkish delegation that negotiated the treaty of LAUSANNE in 1923, before becoming Prime Minister of the new republic in the same year. He assisted Kemal's westernisation programme, and took the name Inönü in 1935 in commemoration of two battles at Inönü from the Greek-Turkish War. He became President after Atatürk's death in 1938, ruling with dictatorial powers until after the SECOND WORLD WAR, which he managed to keep Turkey out of until March 1945. Inönü then oversaw some limited political reforms, including the creation of a party system. He lost the 1950 election, and led the Republican People's party in opposition until 1961, when he took office as Prime Minister again a year after a military coup had overthrown MENDERES' government. He left office in 1965 after another election defeat, and remained leader of the opposition until another coup in 1971 suspended party political activity.

International, First *see* FIRST INTERNATIONAL.

International, Second *see* SECOND INTERNATIONAL.

International, Third *see* THIRD INTERNATIONAL.

International Bank for Reconstruction and Development *see* BRETTON WOODS CONFERENCE; UNITED NATIONS.

International Labour Organisation (ILO) *see* LEAGUE OF NATIONS; UNITED NATIONS.

International Monetary Fund *see* BRETTON WOODS CONFERENCE.

International Working Men's Association *see* FIRST INTERNATIONAL.

Iron Curtain *see* COLD WAR.

Italian campaign (July 1943–May 1945) Allied campaign of the SECOND WORLD WAR against the AXIS. After allied successes in North Africa, Italy was targeted for invasion as a way of attacking the Axis from the south. Allied planners hoped that this would not only destroy the Italian war effort, but would also divert German resources away from the eastern front and from north-west Europe. In July 1943 allied successes in Sicily forced the Fascist Grand Council to depose MUSSOLINI, and the new Italian government under BADOGLIO made peace with the allies in September as they began to land on the mainland at Reggio and Salerno. The peace terms forced Italy to declare war on Germany, a move which the Germans countered by disarming Italian troops and effectively occupying Italy. The allied advance, involving American, British, Polish and other troops, slowed down in December 1943 as the Germans consolidated their front line and offered strong resistance, particularly at Cassino. In January 1944 the allies landed 500,000 troops at Anzio, behind the German lines, which diverted German resources from other parts of Europe. Cassino was taken in May 1944, an allied victory that led fairly quickly to the fall of Rome in June – the day after the NORMANDY CAMPAIGN had opened the western European front – and Florence in August: but once again, the German winter line in the Apennines stalled the allies. In April 1945, however, the allies broke through, taking Milan. The Germans surrendered on 1 May. Throughout the campaign, the allies were assisted by Italian partisan groups using guerrilla tactics against the Germans. *See* RESISTANCE.

Italian unification Establishment of the kingdom of Italy as a nation state. The diverse movement for unification of the Italian states grew out of the settlement of the Congress of Vienna (*see* VIENNA, CONGRESS OF), which left HABSBURG influence in the northern states and in the duchies of Tuscany, Modena and Parma. Various strands of nationalist and liberal ideology (*see* LIBERALISM, NATIONALISM) developed from this time on through different groups, with some abortive risings, such as that in Piedmont in 1820. In 1847 CAVOUR named his nationalist journal *Il Risorgimento* ('resurrection' or 'resurgence', a name which became symbolic of the movement towards unification) and there were nationalist strands visible in the various unsuccessful Italian revolutions of 1848 (*see* REVOLUTIONS OF 1848), notably in the Piedmontese attacks on Austrian troops, and Charles Albert of Piedmont-Sardinia's declaration of support for the anti-Habsburg revolts in Lombardy and Venetia (*see* AUSTRO-PIEDMONTESE WAR). In the 1850s Piedmont-Sardinia – under Cavour's premiership – became the leading state in the movement towards Italian nationhood, with his cultivation of support from many of the smaller Italian states and the military backing of France through the Pact of PLOMBIÈRES (1858). Through military action against Austria (*see* FRANCO-

AUSTRIAN WAR) and the southern expeditions of GARIBALDI, the kingdom of Italy was declared in March 1861. Over the next decade, the areas that had remained outside the new kingdom were incorporated: Venetia in October 1866, after the decline of Austrian power; and the Papal States in October 1870 after the withdrawal of French support.

The general identification of Italian unification with the notion of *risorgimento* disguises the contested nature of the final settlement, not least the power of the northern industrial Piedmont over southern agricultural areas, or the dependence on external factors such as French assistance and Habsburg decline. The linguistic situation was a famous example of this: in 1870, only approximately 2.5 per cent of the population of Italy could speak Italian. However, seen alongside GERMAN UNIFICATION, the Italian experience was evidence of a growing belief in the idea of the nation state as a desirable political structure.

Italo-Abyssinian War (1935–36) Colonial war between Italy and Abyssinia (*see* IMPERIALISM). MUSSOLINI's Fascist government in Italy expressed its desire for an enlarged African empire at a number of points from the mid-1920s. Abyssinia was seen as a target, as its conquest would add to the Italian possessions of Eritrea and Italian Somaliland to provide a significant east African block. Abyssinia was also attractive for historical reasons, as an Italian invasion in 1896 had been beaten. In 1934 Mussolini aggravated relations with Abyssinia by authorising border incursions: and when one of these, at Walwal, led to casualties in December 1934, the pressure for intervention hastened. Despite the LEAGUE OF NATIONS' arbitration offers, Italy invaded Abyssinia in October 1935. The League condemned the attack as an act of aggression against another member state, and established a scheme of sanctions against Italy: the majority of members agreed not to provide Italy with arms, rubber or loans. The scheme was flawed by its exclusion of petroleum products, iron and coal, and was further weakened when some member states, including Germany and the USSR, ignored it. The brutality of the invasion shocked many in Europe, particularly due to the obvious imbalance of the two sides' weaponry: Italy used tanks, aircraft and gas against the poorly equipped Abyssinian army, which had to rely on guerrilla tactics. In December 1935 the British Foreign Secretary Samuel Hoare and the French Prime Minister LAVAL planned a partition of Abyssinia, although this was rejected by their governments. In April 1936 the Italians under BADOGLIO won the decisive battle at Marchew, with Addis Ababa being occupied in May. The Abyssinian Emperor Haile Selassie moved into exile in the UK; and the Italians quickly established a colonial infrastructure. Italy subsequently left the League. The war also helped to destroy the STRESA FRONT, and gave some momentum to APPEASEMENT. Abyssinia itself remained under Italian rule until 1941, when the Italians were defeated by the British: Selassie was subsequently restored.

Italo-Turkish War (1911–12) War between Italy and the OTTOMAN EMPIRE. Italy declared war on the Ottoman empire in September 1911 in a bid to gain colonial territories in North Africa, specifically Tripoli, and in the Aegean Sea (*see* IMPERIALISM). The war was rooted in the Italian government's perceived need to develop as a colonial power, and the timing was linked to the general growth of European interest in north Africa (*see* MOROCCAN CRISES), although the Italian Prime Minister GIOLITTI was ambivalent about the war. In November 1911 Italian forces occupied Tripoli. In May 1912 the Italians also occupied the Dodecanese islands. The war was settled in Italy's favour in October 1912, by which time the Ottoman government was under pressure from the Balkan League of Bulgaria, Greece, Montenegro and Serbia (*see* BALKAN WARS). The treaty of Ouchy recognised Italy's gains. Although relatively limited, the war gave Italy a colonial role, albeit a minor one, and also extended Italian influence deep into the Balkans, creating a possible source of friction between Italy and its TRIPLE ALLIANCE partners, Austria-Hungary and Germany. The war further weakened the Ottoman empire, presenting the Balkan League governments with their opportunity to fight against Turkish influence in their region. It also created a strain on Italian resources, particularly in garrisoning Tripoli.

J

Jacobins Radical political grouping of the FRENCH REVOLUTION, flourishing between 1789 and 1794, which took its name from the former Paris monastery of the Jacobins in which it met. The Paris grouping was part of a national network of sympathetic clubs and corresponding societies. Many key politicians from the Constitutional Assembly and its successor bodies were Jacobins, including DANTON, MARAT and ROBESPIERRE. It became the most influential grouping in France during 1793, with policies associated with the TERROR largely emanating from Jacobins' discussions and implemented by leading Jacobins in the Convention and on the key committees. After the coup of Thermidor, the Paris club declined in influence, and was closed down in November 1794. Provincial Jacobin clubs were closed down in 1795.

Jaruzelski, Wojciech (born 1923) Polish soldier and politician. Having been deported to the USSR as a child, Jaruzelski fought for the Red Army's Polish division during the SECOND WORLD WAR. He stayed in the Polish army, rising to the rank of general by 1956. Entering parliament in 1961, he served as Chief of the General Staff from 1965 until 1968, and then became Minister of Defence, a post he held until 1983. Prime Minister and First Secretary of the party from 1981, he led the government during Poland's economic and political crises that were centred around SOLIDARITY. He responded to the crisis, and to the threat of a Soviet invasion, by leading a military coup and ruling Poland through martial law until 1983. In 1985 Jaruzelski became Chairman of the Council of State, gradually becoming more liberal and helping the negotiations that re-established Solidarity (*see* REVOLUTIONS OF 1989–91). He retired in 1990. In 1996 the Polish government decided to drop charges against him for his declaration of martial law.

Jaurès, Jean (1859–1914) French politician. A philosopher, historian and journalist, Jaurès entered the Chamber of Deputies in 1885 as a republican. He shifted to the left, particularly in the context of labour disputes in the early 1890s, and became a leading socialist orator and spokesman in his second and third terms as a deputy from 1893 to 1898 and 1902 to his death in 1914. A supporter of Alfred Dreyfus (*see* DREYFUS AFFAIR), he founded the socialist daily *L'Humanité* in 1904, and helped to form a united Socialist party out of the various left-wing groups in 1905. Following the SECOND INTERNATIONAL's line, he refused to participate in coalitions, and so never held office. In his later years, he opposed French colonial expansion (*see* IMPERIALISM) and military build-up, and attempted to promote peaceful cooperation between French and German workers. He was assassinated by a nationalist in July 1914.

Jemappes, battle of (November 1792) *see* FRENCH REVOLUTIONARY WARS.

Jena, battle of (October 1806) *see* NAPOLEONIC WARS.

Joachim I Napoleon *see* MURAT, JOACHIM.

Joffre, Joseph (1852–1931) French soldier. Joffre joined the army in 1870, and immediately served in the defence of Paris during the FRANCO-PRUSSIAN WAR. He later served in colonial campaigns in Asia and Africa (*see* IMPERIALISM), before leading military engineering projects from 1904 to 1906, and working as a tactical planner from 1911. He commanded the French army at the start of the FIRST WORLD WAR, beginning with ill-fated attacks in Lorraine and the Ardennes before regaining the initiative by stopping the German advances at the MARNE in September 1914 and at Ypres the following month. After unsuccessful attacks in 1915, Joffre became further discredited due to the costly battles of VERDUN and the SOMME, and in 1916 BRIAND promoted him to Marshal of France, a position which took him out of the military leadership. He served the Ministry of War in a number of posts from 1918 until his full retirement in 1930.

John Paul II (Karol Wojtyla) (born 1920) Pope from 1978. After studying theology illegally in Cracow during the German occupation in the SECOND WORLD WAR, and providing forced labour for the Germans, Wojtyla was ordained in 1946. He rose to the positions of bishop in 1958, archbishop in 1964 and cardinal in 1967. He was elected to the papacy in 1978 after John Paul I's brief tenure. He quickly established the practice of travelling to visit Catholic communities throughout the world, particularly in Africa, Asia, Latin America and eastern Europe. He followed conservative lines on Catholic doctrine, especially relating to contraception and homosexuality, and made a number of conservative appointments within the Church's hierarchy which also served to centralise Catholic practice. However, he also promoted the Church's social responsibility, and attempted to promote peace and dialogue in politically sensitive situations, including the Falklands War of 1982, Poland throughout the 1980s, Ireland, and the Gulf War of 1990. He survived an assassination attempt in 1981.

July Monarchy *see* LOUIS-PHILIPPE; REVOLUTIONS OF 1830.

July Plot (1944) *see* HITLER; RESISTANCE.

Jutland, battle of (May 1916) *see* FIRST WORLD WAR.

K

Kádár, János (1912–89) Hungarian politician. Kádár joined the illegal Communist party in 1932, remaining active throughout the 1930s and the SECOND WORLD WAR, during which he fought in the RESISTANCE. He served as Minister of the Interior in RÁKOSI's government from 1948 until 1950, but fell from grace himself in 1951, and was imprisoned until 1954. He re-emerged after Rákosi's fall, becoming First Secretary of the party in October 1956. Kádár supported NAGY and the HUNGARIAN RISING of 1956 to begin with, but soon moved to an anti-reformist stance. He left Budapest, and signed the invitation to the Soviet government to return WARSAW PACT troops to the capital. He then served as Prime Minister until 1958, a period in which he led the suppression of those involved in the rising. He was Prime Minister again from 1961 until 1965, during which time he promoted a more liberal agenda. As First Secretary, he helped to introduce a new economic policy in 1968, a line which attracted some western investment and approval. He retained this post until 1988, when, in a worsening economic climate, he moved to the nominal post of party president. He died in July 1989.

Kalisch, treaty of (February 1813) *see* NAPOLEONIC WARS.

Kamenev, Lev (Lev Rosenfeld) (1883–1936) Soviet politician. A law student involved in left-wing politics, Kamenev left Moscow for Paris in 1902, where he met LENIN and TROTSKY. He spent the rest of the pre-FIRST WORLD WAR period in Russia and Switzerland. In Russia in 1914 he entered the Duma, but was exiled for his opposition to the war. Kamenev returned to Petrograd after the February revolution of 1917 (*see* RUSSIAN REVOLUTIONS 1917), and took a leading role in the Congress of Soviets, from which position he opposed the BOLSHEVIKS' take-over after the October revolution. In 1918 he became Chairman of the Moscow Soviet, joining the POLITBURO the following year. After Lenin's death, he worked with STALIN and ZINOVIEV against Trotsky, but soon shifted to an anti-Stalin position with Trotsky. For this, he lost his Moscow post in 1926 and his place on the Politburo in 1927. Kamenev was arrested in 1935, and started a five-year prison sentence before being charged with KIROV's murder at the first major show trial in 1936 (*see* *YEZHOVSHCHINA*). He was executed the same year. In 1988, under the influence of *GLASNOST*, the Soviet courts rehabilitated him.

Karamanlis, Constantine (1907–98) Greek politician. After practising law, Karamanlis entered parliament in 1935. He took on various ministerial posts in the aftermath of the SECOND WORLD WAR, a period in which he developed good links with the USA through his management of MARSHALL PLAN funds. He was appointed Prime Minister by King Paul in 1955, developing the new National Radical Union as a conservative party. He helped to improve Greece's relations with the EUROPEAN ECONOMIC COMMUNITY (EEC). He resigned in 1963, and refused to work with the GREEK COLONELS after the coup of 1967, preferring instead to leave Greece for Paris. Karamanlis returned to Greece in 1974, and, as Prime Minister again until 1980, played a leading role in overseeing the country's transition towards a republic. He also helped to secure accession to the EEC in 1979. He served as President from 1980 until 1985, and again from 1990 until his resignation in 1995.

Károlyi, Mihály (1875–1955) Hungarian politician. Count Károlyi, from a leading landed family, entered parliament as a liberal in 1905. He argued for greater autonomy for Hungary and other parts of the HABSBURG empire, and for a less pro-German foreign policy. During the FIRST WORLD WAR, he led the Independence party, a position which led to his appointment as Prime Minister in October 1918 as a pro-allied figure. In November 1918 he became provisional President of the new republic, introducing social and economic reforms. Károlyi was overthrown by KUN's communist coup in March 1919, and lived in exile until 1946. He then returned to Hungary briefly, serving as a diplomat until 1949, when he left again for a voluntary exile.

Katyn massacre Name given to the killing of over 15,000 Polish prisoners-of-war by Soviet forces in 1940. In 1939, when the USSR invaded eastern Poland (*see* NAZI-SOVIET PACT, SECOND WORLD WAR), thousands of Polish army officers were interned. In 1943, when the German army reached the Katyn forest near Smolensk, they discovered the mass grave of over 4,000 of the officers, all of whom had been shot. The German and the Soviet governments accused each other of the killings, but a Red Cross investigation suggested that they had been carried out by the Soviets, presumably to destroy the basis for an independent political leadership in Poland. STALIN's denial of responsibility caused a break in relations between the USSR and the Polish government-in-exile, led by SIKORSKI, and influenced Polish-Soviet relations after the SECOND WORLD WAR. In April 1990, under the influence of *GLASNOST*, the Soviet government admitted that Stalin had authorised the killings.

Kautsky, Karl (1854–1938) Czech-born politician and theorist. Kautsky was born in Prague, moving to Austria and joining the Social Democratic party in 1875. He founded and edited the socialist newspaper *Die Neue Zeit* from 1883, and worked as ENGELS' secretary in London from 1885 until 1890. Kautsky played a leading role, with BERNSTEIN, in the reformulation of the party's programme in 1891, and remained active both in that party and in the SECOND INTERNATIONAL. He opposed the FIRST WORLD WAR, and condemned the development of Marxism-Leninism during the Russian Revolution (*see* RUSSIAN REVOLUTIONS 1917). After the war he moved to Vienna, where he remained until the *ANSCHLUSS* in 1938, when he settled in Amsterdam. He died the same year.

Kellogg-Briand Pact International agreement of August 1928, also known as the Pact of Paris. In 1927, in the context of an apparent improvement in international relations after the LOCARNO treaties and Germany's admission to the LEAGUE OF NATIONS, the French Foreign Minister BRIAND suggested to the USA's Secretary of State, Frank Kellogg, that their two countries should make a pact against war. Kellogg expanded the idea to include other countries. In August 1928, representatives of a number of nations, including Belgium, France, Germany, Italy, the UK and the USA, met in Paris to sign the Pact, which was subsequently adopted by over sixty governments. The Pact renounced certain types of war and established an arbitration process in case of disputes: and while it mirrored some of the League's responsibilities, it included the USSR and the USA, neither of which were members of the League. The pact was largely cosmetic, as it allowed for wars of self-defence, including imperial defence, and no system of punishment or enforcement was created.

Kerensky, Alexander (1881–1970) Russian politician. After a training in law, Kerensky entered the Duma in 1912 as a moderate socialist, serving at the same time as the Deputy Chairman of the Petrograd soviet. He supported the Russian Revolution of February 1917 (*see* RUSSIAN REVOLUTIONS 1917), and took office in Prince Lvov's provisional government: first as Minister of Justice in March 1917, then as Minister of War in May. Kerensky became Prime Minister in July 1917, and took command of the armed forces in August. Despite pressure from various quarters for Russia to withdraw from the FIRST WORLD WAR, Kerensky decided to pursue the fight, and committed troops and resources to unsuccessful new offensives. He also failed to deal with the confused state of agrarian land ownership, which lost him further support, as did his involvement with KORNILOV before the latter's coup attempt in August 1917. By the time the BOLSHEVIKS staged their coup in October 1917, Kerensky had little support. He left Russia in 1918, and spent the rest of his life in exile.

KGB (Russian: *Komitet Gosudarstvennoi Bezopasnosti*, Committee for State Security) USSR's intelligence and secret police service, 1954–91. The KGB was established in 1954 as part of the reorganisation of Soviet state agencies after STALIN's and BERIA's deaths. The KGB incorporated the old NKVD, and was given a greater remit in internal and external espionage, including a special role in the communist countries of eastern Europe (*see* IMPERIALISM, WARSAW PACT). As such, it played a key role in suppressing political discontent and debates. Under GORBACHEV's policies of *GLASNOST* and *PERESTROIKA*, and the culture of criticism and liberalisation that they informed, the KGB's role diminished. It was formally abolished in 1991 after leading officers had been involved in the coup attempt against Gorbachev.

Khrushchev, Nikita (1894–1971) Soviet politician. Khrushchev joined the Communist party in 1918, and fought in the Red Army during the RUSSIAN CIVIL WAR, before moving into mining management. In the early 1930s he began to ascend the party's hierarchy, with appointments on the Central Committee in 1934 and in the Moscow party structure in 1935 securing him recognition. In 1938 he became the leading figure in Ukrainian politics. He joined the POLITBURO in 1939, and fought during the SECOND WORLD WAR, seeing action at STALINGRAD and in the Ukraine. In 1949 he became secretary of the party's Central Committee, and an agricultural advisor to STALIN. After Stalin's death in 1953, Khrushchev emerged from the power struggle with MALENKOV, MOLOTOV and Lazar Kaganovich, as First Secretary in October 1953. He secured his position, and global recognition, when he publicly denounced Stalin in 1956, and became Prime Minister after BULGANIN in 1958. Internationally, Khrushchev's record was inconsistent, with some liberal and progressive steps, such as dialogue with the USA and the establishment of the 1963 Nuclear Test Ban Treaty, countered by suppression of the HUNGARIAN RISING in 1956, the stationing of nuclear missiles in Cuba in 1962, and other crises in the COLD WAR. Domestically, he introduced some partially successful economic reforms within the context of a planned economy, including grain expansion and the development of a consumer goods industry; while the terror of Stalin's period was diluted, and anti-clericalism and ANTI-SEMITISM were promoted. In October 1964, with worsening relations with China and a poor economic climate, Khrushchev was deposed.

Kirov, Sergei (1886–1934) Soviet politician. A BOLSHEVIK activist in the 1905 and 1917 Russian Revolutions (*see* RUSSIAN REVOLUTION 1905, RUSSIAN REVOLUTIONS 1917), Kirov went on to organise the Red Army's victory in the Caucasus in the RUSSIAN CIVIL WAR. As the head of the Communist party in Azerbaijan, he helped to organise the establishment of the Transcaucasian Soviet Republic in 1922. He then moved to Leningrad as party leader, working closely with STALIN until 1934, when he spoke against some of Stalin's policies at the party congress. He was murdered in December 1934, probably on Stalin's orders. KAMENEV and ZINOVIEV confessed to Kirov's murder in the first of the show trials which began the *YEZHOVSHCHINA*.

Kohl, Helmut (born 1930) West German and German politician. Kohl joined the Christian Democratic Union (CDU) in 1947, and was active in its youth wing. After gaining a PhD and working in industry, he entered the Rhineland parliament, rising to the post of Minister-President of the Rhineland Palatinate in 1969. He became the CDU's leader in 1973, taking the office of Chancellor in 1982 at the head of a coalition government. His position was confirmed in elections in 1983 and 1987. Kohl pursued pro-French, pro-American and pro-European policies, while also maintaining *OSTPOLITIK*. This combination, and his negotiating skills, allowed Kohl to develop the opportunities that arose from the German Democratic Republic's (GDR) revolution of 1989 (*see* REVOLUTIONS OF 1989–91) into GERMAN REUNIFICATION within NATO and the EUROPEAN UNION in 1990. Kohl's government won the first elections in the reunified Germany, held in 1990, and retained power in the 1994 elections. In 1998 the CDU lost the election, and Kohl resigned his state and party posts. After his resignation, evidence emerged of his involvement in financial irregularities while in office.

Kolchak, Alexander (1874–1920) Russian admiral and politician. A career sailor, Kolchak fought in the Russo-Japanese War of 1904–5, and the FIRST WORLD WAR, during which he took command of the Black Sea fleet with the rank of Vice-Admiral. An opponent of the Russian Revolutions of 1917 (*see* RUSSIAN REVOLUTIONS 1917), Kolchak acted as one of the leaders of the disparate White Russian forces that gathered in Siberia in 1918. He served as Minister of War in the Whites' All Russian Government, and achieved some initial military successes in the RUSSIAN CIVIL WAR. In November 1918 became Supreme Ruler, resigning the leadership in December 1919. Early in 1920 he was captured by the BOLSHEVIKS and executed.

Kornilov, Lavrenti (1870–1918) Russian soldier. Kornilov fought in the Russo-Japanese War of 1904–5, and served as a commander in the FIRST WORLD WAR. He worked with KERENSKY's Provisional Government after the Russian Revolution of February 1917 (*see* RUSSIAN REVOLUTIONS 1917), and was promoted to the post of Commander-in-Chief in July 1917. After apparently ambiguous discussions with Kerensky in August 1917, Kornilov attempted to organise a military coup in Petrograd in order to suppress the extreme left as Russia's war effort worsened. The coup was halted by a railway strike, and Kornilov was arrested. The coup attempt helped to undermine Kerensky and to strengthen the Bolsheviks. Kornilov escaped to join the White forces in the RUSSIAN CIVIL WAR. He was killed in battle in 1918.

Kosovo War (1999) Conflict between NATO and Yugoslavia. In March 1999, NATO began a series of air strikes against Serbian military and civil targets in an attempt to force MILOSEVIC's government to end its campaign against ethnic Albanians in Kosovo. While the campaign, Operation Allied Force, was led by the USA and the UK, European member states Belgium, Denmark, France, Germany, Italy, the Netherlands, Norway, Portugal and Spain also contributed aircraft. Initially, the attacks influenced the Serbian forces to accelerate their campaign against the Kosovo Albanians, causing a major refugee crisis in neighbouring countries. In May, the UNITED NATIONS' International Criminal Tribunal for the former Yugoslavia (*see* YUGOSLAVIA, DISSOLUTION) indicted Milosovic for the campaign against the Albanians. The Serbians backed down in June, after losing Russian sympathy, and after the United Nations established an acceptable model for peacekeeping.

Kossuth, Lajos (1802–94) Hungarian politician. A liberal nationalist, Kossuth sat in the Hungarian Diet from 1825 until

1827, and again from 1832 until 1836, while also working as a journalist. He was imprisoned twice in the late 1830s, but rejoined the Diet in 1847. Kossuth helped to focus nationalist feeling against HABSBURG domination in March 1848, and was one of the architects of the March Laws which limited Hungary's links with Austria and introduced liberal economic reforms (*see* REVOLUTIONS OF 1848). He served as Minister of Finance in the Hungarian government, and from April 1849, as Governor of Hungary. Despite his declaration of Hungary's independence, his marginalisation of non-Magyar nationalities and ethnic groups lost him much internal support, and his government fell in August 1849 under pressure from Austrian and Russian intervention. Kossuth left Hungary, and spent the next eighteen years attempting to promote the Hungarian nationalist cause, through international campaigning work and through attempted revolutions planned from Italy in 1859, 1861 and 1866. He opposed the *AUSGLEICH* of 1867, and retired from politics after it had been passed. He remained in exile, dying in Turin in 1894, although he was quickly embraced as a nationalist icon in death.

Kosygin, Alexei (1904–80) Soviet politician. From a background in the textile industry, Kosygin came to prominence in the Communist party in the late 1930s, particularly through his role as Mayor of his native St Petersburg from 1938 to 1939. He joined the party's Central Committee in 1939 with an industrial portfolio, and was involved in the eastward transfer of industrial plant and infrastructure during the SECOND WORLD WAR (*see also* FIVE YEAR PLANS). He took on various ministerial posts after the War, including the portfolios for finance in 1948, for light industry from 1949 until 1953, and for economic planning in 1956. Deputy Prime Minister from 1960, he succeeded KHRUSHCHEV as Chairman of the Council of Ministers in 1964, maintaining this prime ministerial role alongside BREZHNEV as First Secretary. His attempts to develop the Soviet economy through decentralisation of industry and the promotion of consumer goods were not successful in the short term, although they set a precedent for later developments. He also achieved some diplomatic successes in Asia and over arms control. Kosygin's influence declined in the last years of his tenure of office. He retired in 1980.

Kristallnacht (German: 'crystal night') German pogrom of 9–10 November 1938. Following the assassination of Ernst vom Rath, an official at Germany's Paris Embassy, by a German Jewish refugee, the Nazi government organised a night of action against Jews throughout Germany and Austria. Initiated by Goebbels, coordinated by HEYDRICH and executed by security forces and party activists, the attacks targeted individuals, homes, business premises, schools and synagogues, with damage on properties ranging from broken windows – hence the name attached to the events – to arson. Around seventy individuals were killed, and between 20,000 and 30,000 arrested and sent to concentration camps. In the aftermath, the Jewish community was charged 1,000,000,000 marks compensation for Rath's killing, and insurance payouts for the damage were taken by the government. The pogrom was not popularly supported, and drew condemnation from many foreign governments. It is generally seen as a defining moment in the escalation of Nazi ANTI-SEMITISM. *See also* FINAL SOLUTION.

Kronstadt, mutiny (October 1905) *see* RUSSIAN REVOLUTION 1905.

Kulturkampf (German: 'struggle of cultures') Period of tension between the Roman Catholic Church in Germany and the German and Prussian governments, 1871–87. With long-term roots stretching back to the Reformation, tensions between Catholics and Protestants in the German states became more pronounced in the 1860s in response to POPE PIUS IX's anti-liberal stance. After GERMAN UNIFICATION in 1871, BISMARCK exacerbated these tensions by initiating a series of anti-Catholic laws. They were motivated by a combination of factors, most significantly his need to gain liberal support in parliament, and the potential threat that Catholics were perceived to pose to the nation state due to their loyalties to the supranational church and the sympathies they might have with Catholics in Austria-Hungary, France and Poland. Anti-Catholic laws started in 1871, gaining a higher profile in 1872 when the Jesuit order was banned from Germany, and in the laws of May 1873 introduced by Falk which restricted the Church's freedom to appoint and educate clergy in Prussia. In 1874, civil marriages and the civil registration of births, deaths and marriages were introduced, and in 1875 most Catholic orders were dissolved, and grants to parishes were withheld unless the clergy complied with all of the new laws.

With Pius IX condemning these acts, and the vast majority of the clergy resisting them and facing prison or exile, the *Kulturkampf* failed in its aims, and Catholic solidarity developed in such a way that the Centre party hugely increased its electoral support. In 1878 Bismarck began to scale down the anti-clericalism, helped both by the election of Pope Leo XIII, and by the realisation that continued persecution could create permanent splits in the new empire; although the introduction of ANTI-SOCIALIST LAWS from 1878 suggests that the government's desire to persecute minority groups in order to secure itself had not diminished. By the end of 1887, when Germany re-established formal links with the Vatican, all of the anti-Catholic laws had been repealed.

Kun, Béla (1886–*c.* 1939) Hungarian politician. A lawyer and journalist, Kun was taken as a prisoner of war by the Russian army in 1916. He became a communist during his imprisonment, and when he returned to Hungary in 1918 he founded the country's first Communist party. In March 1919 he helped to bring about the downfall of KÁROLYI's government; and, with backing from the Social Democrats, he established a government. This government pushed through many radical laws, including the nationalisation of land and industry and anti-clerical legislation, but it failed to win popular support, and relied heavily on internal terror. Kun also committed troops and resources to the battle against Romanian and Czechoslovakian occupation of disputed territories. These pressures, combined with those from HORTHY's nationalist movement, led Kun's government to collapse in August 1919, as Romanian troops entered Budapest. Kun moved to the USSR, working for a while as the head of the THIRD INTERNATIONAL. He disappeared during Stalin's purges (*see* *YEZHOVSHCHINA*), although his exact fate is uncertain. He was rehabilitated in 1958.

Kursk, battle of (July 1943) SECOND WORLD WAR battle between Germany and the USSR. The strategic railway town of Kursk, taken by Germany in November 1941 (*see* BARBAROSSA), was retaken by the Red Army in February 1943, after the victory at STALINGRAD. Kursk then became the centre of a large salient the Red Army made into Germany's eastern front line. In the spring of 1943, HITLER and his military aides developed a plan to attack this salient in a pincer movement which would regain Kursk and cut off the Soviet front line. Delays in the plan gave the Red Army time to construct defences along the front, and to move tanks, anti-tank guns, missile launchers and approximately 1,300,000 troops into the salient. The attack began on 5 July, with northern and southern pincer movements backed up by aerial bombardment. The northern attack was repulsed by superior Soviet defences after only ten miles. The southern attack reached Prokorova, approximately twenty-five miles into Soviet-held territory, where the largest tank battle in history then took place on 12 July: with around 900 tanks on each side, this engagement involved close range fighting with great destruction. On 15 July, five days after the allied landings in Sicily (*see* ITALIAN CAMPAIGN), Hitler abandoned Kursk in order to concentrate on southern Europe: and while the fighting continued until 23 July, the Germans lacked any new supplies. The defeat left the Germans behind their starting lines and severely depleted of men and material; while Soviet tanks and aircraft production, and greater manpower reserves, left the initiative with the Red Army. From July 1943 onwards, the Germans were on the defensive in the east.

L

Laibach, Congress of (January–May 1821) Continuation of the Congress of TROPPAU of 1820. After agreeing in principle at Troppau to armed intervention against revolutions, the HABSBURG empire, Prussia and Russia concerned themselves at Laibach with the revolutions in the Italian states (*see* NEAPOLITAN RISING, PIEDMONTESE RISING). After hearing from King Ferdinand of Naples, the powers approved Habsburg military intervention to help crush the revolution. This intervention was ineffectually resisted by the UK's observer at Laibach. The Congress's authorisation of armed intervention in another state demonstrated that the original terms of the QUADRUPLE ALLIANCE had been left behind, and that the Habsburg empire, Prussia and Russia were acting more generally as an anti-revolutionary block. *See also* CONGRESS SYSTEM.

Languy, battle of (August 1792) *see* FRENCH REVOLUTIONARY WARS.

Lateran Accords (February 1929) Bilateral agreements between the Italian government and the Roman Catholic Church. Relations between Church and state had been poor since ITALIAN UNIFICATION, with the issue of political power aggravated by the state requisitioning papal land holdings. The church refused to recognise the kingdom of Italy. Under MUSSOLINI, the Fascist government began to build some links with the papacy, the latter seeing the Fascists as a valuable anti-communist organisation. By 1929 both sides were able to take this cooperation further, leading to the signing of the Lateran Accords by Mussolini and Pope Pius XI. The government gave the Church a compensation payment for the lost territories and their earning potential since 1860, and recognised Roman Catholicism as the only religion in Italy. It gave the papacy some temporal sovereignty by establishing the Vatican City as an independent state, allowed Catholic teaching in state schools, and outlawed divorce. In return, the Church recognised the kingdom of Italy, and barred clergymen from joining political parties. The Accords brought political credit to the government in general and to Mussolini in particular, as they apparently reconciled Catholics to the state. The Accords were confirmed in 1946 when the new republic was established in Italy, and were amended in 1984.

Lausanne, treaty of (July 1923) Peace treaty between the allied powers and Turkey, which superseded the treaty of SÈVRES of 1920. After the OTTOMAN Sultan Mohammad VI accepted the treaty of Sèvres when the British occupied Constantinople, a republican nationalist movement based in Ankara and associated with Kemal (*see* ATATÜRK) continued to stress rejection of the treaty. This movement subsequently beat back the Greek invasion of Asia Minor in 1922 (*see* GREEK-TURKISH WAR): and, after precipitating a confrontation with the British at Chanak, the nationalists managed to secure the promise of renegotiation of the 1920 settlement. This took place at Lausanne in July 1923. The major change from Sèvres was the restoration of Eastern Thrace and the part of Anatolia that Sèvres had given to Greece, while the treaty also recognised Turkish control of Armenia. The reparations demanded at Sèvres were dropped. Beyond that, most of the clauses of Sèvres were confirmed, including the loss of Palestine and Syria as MANDATES, the loss of Cyprus to the UK and the Dodecanese islands to Italy, and the demilitarisation of the Dardanelles.

Laval, Pierre (1883–1945) French politician. After practising as a lawyer, Laval entered the Chamber of Deputies as a socialist in 1914. He lost his seat in 1919, but returned as an independent in 1924, before entering the Senate in 1927. He held various ministerial posts in the 1920s, including the public works, justice, and labour portfolios, before becoming Prime Minister in 1931 for a year. He served as Prime Minister and Foreign Minister from 1934 until 1936, during which time he showed his shift to the right through his pro-Italian stance over the ITALO-ABYSSINIAN WAR, which forced him to resign. He re-emerged in 1940 as a supporter of the VICHY government, helping to secure the suspension of the THIRD REPUBLIC. He served as PÉTAIN's deputy until December 1940, when he was dismissed, but was reinstated in 1942 with German backing, which set him up as effective dictator of Vichy. During this time, he attempted to limit the extent of German control over France by complying with some German policies, such as deporting French Jews and sending forced labour east. Laval attempted to re-establish a national assembly in the summer of 1944, but he was arrested by the German authorities. After an escape and a period in exile, he returned to France in 1945, where he was tried for treason and executed.

League of Nations International organisation, 1920–46. The idea for an international arbitrational organisation developed during the FIRST WORLD WAR, and was given a high priority by its inclusion in US President Woodrow Wilson's FOURTEEN POINTS. The idea was accepted by the PARIS PEACE CONFERENCE in April 1919, and the covenant of the League of Nations was included in the resultant peace treaties. It came into being in 1920, although, despite Wilson's role, the USA did not join. Based in Geneva, the League comprised of an Assembly, a Secretariat and a Council, which included four permanent members: the British empire, France, Italy and Japan. It also built up a range of specialist and technical committees and bodies, such as the International Court of Justice, the International Labour Organisation, the Mandates Commission (*see* MANDATES), and committees working on refugees, drugs, slavery and other international issues. As well as these specialised branches, the League was dedicated to promoting peace through collective security, working on the principle that member states would use the League for arbitration rather than settle differences by war. It also pressed for openness in all bilateral and multilateral diplomacy, and for disarmament. The League did not have its own armed force: it favoured economic sanctions. The constitutional demand for unanimity on major issues also hampered its effectiveness.

With fifty-three members by 1923, the League enjoyed some early successes in arbitrating contested issues between some member states, including Finland and Sweden in 1920, and Bulgaria and Greece in 1925, although it was less successful in dealing with the CORFU INCIDENT in 1923. Germany joined in 1926 after the treaty of LOCARNO, gaining a permanent seat on the Council. The League's influence as an arbitrational body declined in the early 1930s: it was unable to promote peace between China and Japan in 1933, while Germany and Japan both left in the same year. While the USSR's membership from 1934 added a major power, the 1935 ITALO-ABYSSINIAN WAR further damaged the League's credibility: Italy refused to arbitrate; the sanctions package imposed on Italy was ineffective; and the bilateral secret diplomacy of Hoare and LAVAL undermined the League's call for open diplomacy. Italy left in 1937. The League was similarly largely ineffective over the SPANISH CIVIL WAR, and failed to prevent Germany's invasion of Czechoslovakia in 1939, or the USSR's invasion of Finland in the same year (*see* SECOND WORLD WAR). Although the specialist committees continued to work, the Assembly stopped meeting in 1939, and the League was formally wound up in 1946: the UNITED NATIONS took over its remaining specialist responsibilities, and replaced it as an international body.

Lebensraum (German: 'living space') Concept in German nationalist politics. The notion of *Lebensraum* developed in the late nineteenth century, during Germany's period of colonialism (*see* IMPERIALISM), as a theoretical explanation of Germany's quest for colonies: based on the assumption that Germany was running out of space, and that as industrialisation had led to over-population in relation to resources, new areas were sought for exploitation. After the FIRST WORLD WAR, the concept became more focused on eastern Europe, particularly the territories lost by Germany and Austria at the treaties of VERSAILLES and ST GERMAIN: these, it was argued, could be annexed by Germany to provide greater agricultural resources. The concept became strongly associated with NAZISM and HITLER's ideas, in which they were clearly underpinned by economic theories of self-sufficiency, and by racial assumptions: Germans, in this view, had greater rights to the space and resources than Jews, Poles or Slavs. Military policy in the east from 1938 provided the opportunity for the German government to develop *Lebensraum* into policy. The invasion of western Poland in 1939 was followed by a 'Germanisation' programme in which natives were forcibly migrated eastwards and into ghettos and camps (*see* FINAL SOLUTION), while ethnic Germans living in these areas, and Germans from the Reich itself and from other areas, were settled in the conquered areas: for example, some 200,000 Germans were resettled in Poland between 1939 and 1941.

Leipzig, battle of (16–19 October 1813) Battle of the NAPOLEONIC WARS between France and its allies on one side, and the HABSBURG empire, Prussia, Russia and Sweden on the other, sometimes known as the Battle of the Nations. After retreating from Russia in 1812, NAPOLEON continued to engage with Russia and Prussia in eastern Europe. However, the alliance systems of the treaties of Kalisch and Teplitz created a powerful and large allied force, which Napoleon faced at Leipzig on 16 October 1813. The first day of fighting was indecisive, despite the allies' numerical superiority of approximately 220,000 against Napoleon's force of 185,000 French and German soldiers. However, the arrival of the Swedish force of 150,000 on the second day turned the tide, leading to the desertion of many of the Germans from Napoleon's side, and by the fourth day Napoleon was forced to retreat rather than be fully surrounded. The French suffered approximately 38,000 casualties and lost 30,000 men as prisoners, while the allied losses were in the region of 50,000. Napoleon also lost over 300 cannon and much of his logistical support. The battle led to the allies gaining control of the German states, and to Napoleon's hasty retreat back to France in November. Coming with the British successes in the Peninsular War, which led to their invasion of southern France in October, Leipzig was the decisive battle that signalled Napoleon's first fall.

Lenin, Vladimir (Vladimir Ilyich Ulyanov) (1870–1924) Russian and Soviet politician. Ulyanov became active in revolutionary politics in the late 1880s. He was arrested in 1895 and exiled to Siberia in 1897, before leaving Russia for western Europe in 1900. He developed his political theories in debates, books, pamphlets and journalism. By 1903, by which time he had adopted the pseudonym 'Lenin', his key idea that an elite party should spearhead a revolution in order to bring about socialism led to a split in the Russian Social Democrat party in exile, with Lenin emerging as leader of the BOLSHEVIK faction. He returned to Russia during the Revolution of 1905 (*see* RUSSIAN REVOLUTION 1905), but soon left again for Switzerland, where he continued to write and provide leadership for the Bolsheviks. After the February 1917 revolution (*see* RUSSIAN REVOLUTIONS 1917) the German army allowed him through Germany to Russia, as they felt that he might help to undermine the Russian war effort. In Petrograd, he published his *April Theses*, calling for an overthrow of the provisional government and the seizure of power by the Bolsheviks, as opposed to the more traditional Marxist model of waiting for the democratic bourgeois stage to collapse. This intervention changed the shape of the revolutionary events in Russia. He left Russia for Finland briefly after the failed rising of July 1917, but returned in October and co-organised the revolution against KERENSKY's government. After the success of this rising, Lenin quickly consolidated his position as Chairman of the Council of People's Commissars, from which he used increasingly dictatorial powers to establish a centralised state under Bolshevik rule. He authorised the closure of the Constituent Assembly in January 1918, withdrew Russia from the FIRST WORLD WAR (*see* treaty of BREST-LITOVSK), provided leadership during the RUSSIAN CIVIL WAR, authorised terror against opponents and suspected opponents, and promoted the economic experiment of WAR COMMUNISM, involving forced nationalisation and confiscation of assets. He changed the party's name to the Communist party, and in 1919 he established the THIRD INTERNATIONAL to promote COMMUNISM abroad. In 1921 he replaced war communism with the NEW ECONOMIC POLICY.

Lenin's health deteriorated from the early 1920s, and he began to suffer strokes in 1922. However, he remained the leader of the party and the country until his death in 1924. He achieved a posthumous personality cult, evident in the changing of Petrograd's name to Leningrad, and the public display of his embalmed corpse in Moscow's Red Square, a display which survived the REVOLUTIONS OF 1989–91.

Leningrad, siege of (1941–44) *see* BARBAROSSA; SECOND WORLD WAR.

liberalism Political and economic ideology. Liberalism emerged by name in the early nineteenth century, when it was adopted by Spanish political reformers, although it was rooted in British political discourse of the seventeenth century, and in some aspects of the American Revolution and FRENCH REVOLUTION of the late eighteenth century. Key features of liberalism as it developed, essentially as a reformist and oppositional ideology, included an emphasis on individuals' rights and liberties and an antipathy to state interference, along with a belief in the value of constitutions to regulate the relationship between government and people. It also had an economic aspect, particularly in British models, based on freedom of trade. Liberalism was espoused by radicals and revolutionaries in a number of continental struggles in the first half of the nineteenth century, including the SPANISH RISINGS of 1820–23, and the REVOLUTIONS OF 1848 in Belgium, France and elsewhere: here, liberalism and NATIONALISM came close together. As a partisan ideology, liberalism subsequently declined in influence in continental Europe, particularly as most European governments accommodated some form of constitutionalism by the end of the nineteenth century. It also lost ground to SOCIALISM as a more radical reformist ideology. However, a number of its premises as they have related to the rights of the individual, the role of the state and the nature of sovereignty, have become basic assumptions in democratic systems throughout the continent. The REVOLUTIONS OF 1989–91 against communist governments throughout eastern Europe, many of which had liberal and constitutional agendas, stressed liberalism's broad acceptance as an underlying feature of democracy.

Lie, Trygve (1896–1968) Norwegian politician. After working as a lawyer, Lie entered the Norwegian parliament in 1935. He served as Justice Minister from 1935 until 1939, then briefly as Minister of Supplies before the German invasion of Norway (*see* SECOND WORLD WAR). Lie joined the Norwegian government-in-exile in London, serving as Foreign Minister from 1941 until 1946. He emerged as a leading figure in the UNITED NATIONS (UN) at its first assembly in 1946, and was elected as the organisation's first Secretary-General. Re-elected in 1950, he organised the UN's military intervention in the Korean War of 1951–53, which lost him the USSR's support. He retired from the UN in 1953, and returned to Norwegian politics, holding portfolios for industry and commerce in the 1960s.

Ligny, battle of (June 1815) *see* NAPOLEONIC WARS.

Little Entente Eastern European alliance system, 1920–39. The Little Entente emerged out of three bilateral treaties signed in the aftermath of the FIRST WORLD WAR: the Czechoslovakia-Kingdom of the Serbs, Croats and Slovenes treaty of 1920, and the Czechoslovakia-Romania and Romania-Kingdom of the Serbs, Croats and Slovenes treaties of 1921. The alliances were designed to check any attempt from Austria or Hungary to revoke the treaties of ST GERMAIN and TRIANON of 1920. The three treaties were brought together by a tripartite treaty signed in Belgrade in 1929, leading to such formal structures as military talks, internal economic cooperation and a permanent council, established in 1933. However, the Little Entente was constrained by its concentration on the perceived Austrian and Hungarian threats, while the German threat to the 1920 settlement was underplayed. Yugoslavia's cooperation with Germany from 1935 undermined the Little Entente, and it formally ended in February 1939 after its failure to offer any resistance to the German annexation of the Sudeten area of Czechoslovakia in 1938. *See* MUNICH AGREEMENT.

Litvinov, Maxim (Meier Wallakh) (1876–1951) Soviet politician and diplomat. Litvinov joined the Social Democratic party in 1898, and left Russia in 1902 after a period of imprisonment. He was active in revolutionary politics in exile in France and the UK, and was appointed as the diplomatic representative to London after the November Revolution (*see* RUSSIAN REVOLUTIONS 1917). He returned to Russia in September 1918 when the British government deported him. Litvinov served as Deputy Foreign Commissar from 1921 until 1930, and as Foreign Commissar until May 1939. He pursued a policy in favour of collective security against the threat of FASCISM, and helped to improve the USSR's diplomatic credibility by establishing relations with the USA in 1933, by taking the USSR into the LEAGUE OF NATIONS in 1934, and by negotiating the Franco-Soviet mutual aid agreement of 1935. In May 1939 STALIN replaced Litvinov with MOLOTOV. Litvinov subsequently served as the USSR's Ambassador to Washington from 1941 until 1943. He retired in 1946.

living space *see LEBENSRAUM.*

Locarno, treaties of (December 1925) Series of multilateral treaties on European frontiers and security, negotiated from October 1925. After the tension of the RUHR occupation, France and Germany began to work for a greater cooperation. In this context, STRESEMANN initiated discussions which led to the Locarno treaties. The main treaty recognised Germany's borders with Belgium and France as established by the treaty of VERSAILLES, with Italy and the UK acting as guarantors of this settlement. By this, Germany effectively dropped its claims to Alsace and Lorraine and other disputed territories. For its eastern borders, Germany signed treaties with Czechoslovakia and Poland guaranteeing that any future territorial claims would be settled by negotiation, not violence. To provide some security to these eastern countries, France duly signed mutual guarantee treaties with them to guard against any German denunciation of this promise. Germany also signed treaties on future arbitration with Belgium and France.

The Locarno treaties were widely welcomed as evidence of Germany's rehabilitation after the FIRST WORLD WAR, and helped Germany to gain admission to the LEAGUE OF NATIONS in 1926. Stresemann and the chief French negotiator, BRIAND, jointly won the Nobel Peace Prize for the treaties. In 1936, Germany's reoccupation of the Rhineland broke the western treaty, while moves against Czechoslovakia and Poland in 1938 and 1939 broke its eastern commitments. *See* APPEASEMENT, MUNICH AGREEMENT, SECOND WORLD WAR.

Lodi, battle of (May 1796) *see* FRENCH REVOLUTIONARY WARS.

Lonato, battle of (August 1796) *see* FRENCH REVOLUTIONARY WARS.

London, treaty of (July 1827) *see* GREEK WAR OF INDEPENDENCE.

London, treaty of (May 1839) Multilateral treaty on Belgium. During the Belgian Revolution of 1830 (*see* REVOLUTIONS OF 1830) and the subsequent war between Belgium and Holland, ambassadorial representatives of France, the HABSBURG empire, Prussia, Russia and the UK met in London on a number of occasions to attempt to settle the crisis. Their suggestions were rejected by the Dutch. However, after Holland's withdrawal from Belgium in 1832, and their subsequent recognition of Belgian independence from the United Kingdom of the Netherlands, the powers worked on a final territorial settlement. This was signed at London in May 1839. By the treaty, Belgium was formally established as an independent and neutral state, and its independence was guaranteed by the powers. The treaty also established Luxembourg – which Belgium claimed – as a duchy.

London, treaty of (May 1852) Multilateral treaty on the future of Denmark. After the revolution against Danish rule in Holstein (*see* REVOLUTIONS OF 1848), and the subsequent Prussian intervention that led to war with Denmark until 1850, an international conference on Denmark's borders and status was held in London. In May 1852, France, the HABSBURG empire, Prussia, Russia, Sweden and the UK signed the protocol whereby Denmark was left intact, with an agreed succession, while Schleswig and Holstein were left with limited autonomy in union with Denmark. This agreement was ended in 1864. *See* SCHLESWIG WAR.

London, treaty of (May 1913) Peace treaty that settled the first BALKAN WAR. Drawn up by representatives of the powers who feared that the Balkan War might expand, the treaty was a speedy response to the Balkan League's victory over the OTTOMAN EMPIRE. The Turkish losses were confirmed, and divided between the League partners. Bulgaria gained much of Thrace and access to the Aegean, and part of eastern Macedonia; Greece gained southern Macedonia and the port of Salonica; Montenegro gained parts of the Sanjak of Novibazar; while Serbia gained Kosovo, part of Macedonia, and the north eastern section of the Sanjak of Novibazar. The treaty also created Albania as an independent state. This settlement failed to calm the region: in June 1913, Bulgaria, dissatisfied with its treatment under the treaty, attacked its former allies, thus starting the second Balkan War.

London, treaty of (April 1915) Secret FIRST WORLD WAR treaty between the TRIPLE ENTENTE and Italy. The treaty promised Italy territorial gains if it entered the war against Austria-Hungary. The gains included long-disputed territory on the Italo-HABSBURG borders known to the Italians as *Italia Irredenta*, including Trentino, South Tirol and Trieste, as well as parts of the Dalmatian coast. Italy was also promised areas from the OTTOMAN EMPIRE, including parts of Albania and the Dodecanese islands, as well as African colonies. Italy duly entered the war in May 1915, although this failed to dent the central powers' war effort significantly. The terms of the treaty were revealed in 1918 by the BOLSHEVIKS as part of their repudiation of their inherited military obligations. It was widely condemned for its secrecy and its lack of regard for self-determination (*see* FOURTEEN POINTS). The PARIS PEACE CONFERENCE awarded Italy only some of the territories covered by the treaty. The broken promise of London fed into post-war Italian dissatisfaction, and was influential on both D'ANNUNZIO and MUSSOLINI.

Louis XVI (1754–93) Bourbon King of France, 1774–92. Louis XVI succeeded his grandfather Louis XV in 1774, and enjoyed some popularity in the first part of his reign, particularly through his backing of the Americans in their war of independence. However, his government's financial problems were significant, and by the late 1780s his inability to deal with these decisively led directly to the meeting of the Estates-General in 1789, and to that body's declaration of a National Assembly (*see* FRENCH REVOLUTION). In the context of popular riots, and his own return to Paris from Versailles in October 1789, Louis accepted the National Assembly and worked with it as a constitutional monarch. However, his anti-revolutionary sympathies were made evident in June 1791, when he attempted to escape from France. He was captured at Varennes, returned to Paris, and suspended until he accepted the new constitution, which he did in September. He subsequently failed to follow the constitution, exemplified by his dismissal of his ministers in June 1792, after which his position became even more tenuous. In late June 1792, his quarters in the Tuileries Palace were stormed; and in August 1792, when a similar rising occurred, the Assembly suspended the monarchy. As the course of the FRENCH REVOLUTIONARY WARS turned against France, pressure for more decisive action against internal opponents grew, culminating in the abolition of the monarchy and the declaration of the republic in September 1792. In December Louis was tried by the Convention for crimes against the revolution. Found guilty unanimously, he was sentenced to death: and despite some discussion of a reprieve and of holding a popular referendum on his sentence, he was executed in January 1793.

Louis XVIII (1755–1824) King of France, 1814–24. The brother of LOUIS XVI, Louis left France in 1791 (*see* FRENCH REVOLUTION), and assumed the title of regent on his brother's execution in 1793, and the title of king on the death of Louis XVI's son Prince Louis (who, had he reigned, would have been Louis XVII) in 1795. He was involved in émigré politics as the pretender to the throne during the revolutionary and Napoleonic periods. In 1814 he renounced some of his earlier objections to the changes brought about by the revolution and NAPOLEON, and negotiated a restoration with TALLEYRAND, which involved the king accepting the constitutional charter. Louis duly took the throne in 1814, but left France on Napoleon's escape from Elba, returning only after the battle of WATERLOO the following year. At first his reign was broadly in line with the constitutional assumptions, and many of the recent changes were maintained. However, he did introduce some reactionary changes, including the re-establishment of Roman Catholicism as the state religion. In 1820, the assassination of Charles, Duke of Berry, created a focus for repression of republicanism and the curtailment of press freedoms, which served to undermine Louis XVIII's commitment to constitutional monarchy. He died in 1824, and was succeeded by his younger brother, CHARLES X.

Louis Napoleon *see* NAPOLEON III.

Louis-Philippe (1773–1850) King of the French, 1830–48. The son of the Duke of Orleans, Louis-Philippe originally supported the FRENCH REVOLUTION of 1789, and fought in the FRENCH REVOLUTIONARY WARS against the HABSBURG empire. In 1793 he was implicated in a plan to establish a constitutional monarchy, and he left France. He returned after NAPOLEON's fall, keeping a low political profile until the French Revolution of 1830 (*see* REVOLUTIONS OF 1830) when he emerged as a potential replacement for CHARLES X, acceptable to both monarchists and liberals. Parliament duly appointed him as king in July 1830 when Charles abdicated. Louis-Philippe, whose reign became known as the July Monarchy, followed generally cautious policies, and oversaw some liberal reforms of the reactionary policies introduced by his two predecessors LOUIS XVIII and Charles X, including the disestablishment of Catholicism. Louis-Philippe lost popularity after 1840, particularly through his links with the anti-reformist politician GUIZOT, and abdicated in February 1848 in response to riots in Paris (*see* REVOLUTIONS OF 1848). He moved to England, and lived there in exile until his death in 1850.

Ludendorff, Erich von (1865–1937) German soldier and politician. Ludendorff joined the army in 1882. When the FIRST WORLD WAR began, Ludendorff led the capture of Liège, before being transferred to the eastern front where, with HINDENBURG, he led the defeat of the Russian army at TANNENBERG. From 1916 he worked with Hindenburg as effective military dictator of Germany, helping to organise a total war effort. He planned the spring offensives of 1918 that carry his name, but when these failed, he began to argue for an armistice and the creation of a republic in order to gain favourable peace terms. He left Germany for Sweden when the war ended, but returned in 1919, when he became active in right-wing politics in the WEIMAR REPUBLIC. A Nazi member of the Reichstag from 1924 to 1928, he helped to reconstruct the party after its proscription. He also stood as the Nazis' candidate in the 1925 presidential election against Hindenburg. His final years in public life were characterised by an increasingly eccentric nationalist agenda against supposed Jewish and masonic plots.

Lunéville, treaty of (February 1801) Treaty between France and the HABSBURG empire during the NAPOLEONIC WARS. After losing the battles of Marengo and Hohenlinden to France in 1800, the Habsburg empire faced its peacemaking with France in a far weaker position than it had held at the treaty of CAMPO FORMIO in 1797. As a result, Lunéville confirmed the French gains of Campo Formio, including control of Belgium, Luxembourg and areas of northern Italy. However, the Habsburgs had to concede the gains of Campo Formio, and also had to recognise the independence of France's dependent republics: the Batavian, Cisalpine, Ligurian and Helvetic. Habsburg influence in the Italian states was further limited by the cession of Tuscany to Parma as the Kingdom of Etruria. The treaty thus consolidated France's European empire from the former Netherlands in the north to the Cisalpine border with the Papal States in the south. *See* IMPERIALISM.

Luxemburg, Rosa (1871–1919) Polish-born German revolutionary politician. Luxemburg gained German citizenship in 1898 through marriage. Having been involved in radical politics in Poland, she joined the German Social Democratic party in 1898, and emerged as a leading proponent of its revolutionary wing against the revisionist ideas of BERNSTEIN. In 1905 she formed a syndicalist wing of the party with Karl Liebknecht (*see* SYNDICALISM), and became a high-profile activist. Luxemburg and Liebknecht publicly opposed the FIRST WORLD WAR, and formed the Spartakists in 1915 as an anti-war wing of the party. She was imprisoned for her anti-war stance from 1915 until 1918, spending her time in prison writing on political issues. Released in November 1918, she recommenced her active role in the Spartakists. Favouring a national rising against the new WEIMAR REPUBLIC, she was involved in the local rising in Berlin in January 1919. Along with Liebknecht, she was captured by right-wing paramilitaries and murdered.

Lutzen, battle of (May 1813) *see* NAPOLEONIC WARS.

M

Maastricht, treaty of (February 1992) Treaty on European Union, signed by all member states of the EUROPEAN COMMUNITY (EC) in February 1992. After the successful passing of the SINGLE EUROPEAN ACT in 1986, and the subsequent movement towards a single market, the EC developed a new treaty to hasten both monetary union and political cooperation between member states. The treaty was produced at Maastricht in December 1991, and signed in February 1992. It formally established the EUROPEAN UNION (EU) as political body, and committed the EU to further development of common policies for all members in such areas as social conditions, justice, security and foreign policy, although it also stressed that the national identity of member states should be maintained. The treaty also set up bodies to organise and implement monetary union and a single currency, and enhanced the powers of both the Council of Ministers and the EUROPEAN PARLIAMENT. Compromise over specific issues was allowed through the use of opt-out clauses, which, for example, Denmark and the UK took on the single currency. The wide-ranging issues involved in the treaty caused debates in many member countries when the treaty had to be ratified. It was rejected by referendum in Denmark, although accepted on a second ballot, and accepted only narrowly in a referendum in France. The treaty represented a major revision of the original treaty of ROME of 1957 and the 1986 SINGLE EUROPEAN ACT.

MacMahon, Patrice (1808–93) French soldier and politician. MacMahon came to prominence in the CRIMEAN WAR in 1854. In 1859 he led the French army against HABSBURG forces at Magenta and Solferino (*see* FRANCO-AUSTRIAN WAR), after which he was created Marshal of France and Duke of Magenta. He also served the SECOND EMPIRE as a colonial administrator, as Governor-General of Algeria from 1864 until 1870. He returned to fight in the FRANCO-PRUSSIAN WAR, and was captured, along with NAPOLEON III, at Sedan. He was released, and led the French army in its repression of the PARIS COMMUNE in 1871. In 1873, the royalist MacMahon was elected President of the THIRD REPUBLIC, and he worked for a restoration, focused around the Duc de Broglie. In May 1877 he dismissed the republican Prime Minister Jules Simon, and replaced him with Albert de Broglie: the unpopularity of this act was shown by the republican gains at the subsequent election, which set the tone for two years of struggle between royalists and republicans. MacMahon resisted the option of staging a coup, and resigned in January 1879.

Madrid, siege of (1936–39) *see* SPANISH CIVIL WAR.

Magenta, battle of (June 1859) *see* FRANCO-AUSTRIAN WAR.

Maginot Line French fortifications. The line was built along the Franco-German border between 1929 and 1934, and named after the Minister of Defence, André Maginot. It consisted of a series of heavily defended artillery placements fronted by anti-tank defences, and stretched from the Franco-Belgian border to the Franco-Swiss border. The Belgian government refused to extend it along the Belgian-German border, which allowed the Maginot Line to be outflanked when Germany attacked its western neighbours through the Ardennes in 1940. *See* SECOND WORLD WAR.

Makarios III, Archbishop (Mihail Khristodolou Mouskos) (1913–77) Cypriot cleric and politician. Mouskos was ordained in 1946 after studying in Athens, and became Bishop of Kitium in 1948. Two years later he was made Archbishop of Cyprus, and assumed the title of Makarios III, along with the political role that went with the archbishopric. At first he favoured union with Greece (*ENOSIS*), and he was exiled by the British for his links with the *enosis* movement. Makarios then helped to negotiate the establishment of an independent Cyprus as a republic within the British Commonwealth, and became its first President in 1960. He remained unpopular with the pro-*enosis* movement, surviving a number of assassination attempts and, in 1974, a military coup backed by the military government in Athens (*see* GREEK COLONELS) which removed him from office for five months. The coup precipitated the Turkish invasion of Cyprus: and on his return Makarios was unable to reunite the island. He remained President of Greek Cyprus until his death in 1977.

Malenkov, Georgi (1902–88) Soviet politician. After serving in the Red Army during the RUSSIAN CIVIL WAR, Malenkov joined the Communist party in 1920. He became a close ally of STALIN, working with him on the forced collectivisation of agriculture and in running the purges of the 1930s (*see YEZHOVSHCHINA*). During the SECOND WORLD WAR Malenkov served on the State Defence Committee. He joined the POLITBURO and became Deputy Prime Minister in 1946, and was widely seen as Stalin's successor. When Stalin died in 1953, Malenkov became Prime Minister and First Secretary, but quickly lost the party post to KHRUSHCHEV. After some attempts to promote economic diversification, he was attacked by Khrushchev as a revisionist, and he resigned in 1955. He served as Minister for Electrical Energy until 1957, when he became a target during the destalinisation process. He was expelled from the party, and sent to manage a hydroelectric plant in Kazakhstan. He moved back to Moscow in retirement, and died in 1988.

mandates LEAGUE OF NATIONS trusteeships of defeated powers' extra-European colonies after the FIRST WORLD WAR. The mandate system was developed at the PARIS PEACE CONFERENCE as a way of managing the colonial possessions of the German and OTTOMAN empires. The territories were awarded to various victorious countries under League of Nations trusteeship, with a Permanent Mandates Commission to oversee their management. Middle Eastern mandates were designated to be prepared for self-government, including Transjordan, Iraq and Palestine (under the UK) and Syria and Lebanon (under France), while African and Pacific mandates were scheduled either as permanent or as integral parts of the country taking up the mandate. In Africa, Germany's possessions were awarded to Belgium, France, South Africa and the UK, while Pacific possessions were awarded to Australia, Japan and New Zealand. In 1946 the UNITED NATIONS Trusteeship Council inherited the League's work in this area. *See also* IMPERIALISM.

Mannerheim, Carl (1867–1951) Finnish soldier and politician. Mannerheim served in the Russian army from 1889 until 1917, fighting in both the Russo-Japanese War of 1904–5 and the FIRST WORLD WAR. After the Russian Revolution (*see* RUSSIAN REVOLUTIONS 1917) he returned to Finland to lead a nationalist campaign against Russian domination of Finland. With German assistance, Mannerheim led the recapture of Helsinki from communists. Finland declared its independence in December 1917, and Mannerheim, as acting head of state from 1919, led the Finns against the Red Army in the RUSSIAN CIVIL WAR. In 1921 Mannerheim retired from military service. He returned to prominence in 1931 as the President of the Defence Council, where he helped to reorganise the Finnish army and designed the Mannerheim Line of defences on the Finnish-Soviet border. When the USSR attacked Finland in 1939, Mannerheim resumed command of the army, and led a four-month resistance before Finland was defeated (*see* SECOND WORLD WAR). In June 1941 Mannerheim allied Finland with Germany, and allowed the German army to use Finnish territory as a base for its attacks on the USSR. President from 1944, Mannerheim signed an armistice with the USSR in September and joined the war against Germany in March 1945. He retired in 1946.

Mantua, battle of (January 1797) *see* FRENCH REVOLUTIONARY WARS.

Marat, Jean-Paul (1743–93) French politician and journalist. A physician and writer on medical matters, Marat was one of the most consistently radical figures of the FRENCH REVOLUTION, both through his journalism, and through his actions on the Paris Commune and the Convention from 1792. He helped to organise the September massacres of 1792, and was a strong supporter of the death penalty for LOUIS XVI. He was tried for an anti-GIRONDINS pamphlet in 1792, but was acquitted. He was subsequently instrumental in organising the mass risings that led to the expulsion of the Girondins from the Convention and their subsequent suppression. In July 1793 he was assassinated by Charlotte Corday for his role in suppressing the Girondins. Radical revolutionaries adopted him as a martyr.

March on Rome (October 1922) Incident in Italian political history. In late October 1922, MUSSOLINI's Fascists (*see* FASCISM) occupied buildings in northern Italian cities, in a prelude to a projected 'march on Rome' to take the capital. The Prime Minister, FACTA, asked VICTOR EMMANUEL III to declare martial law to prevent the coup, but the King, influenced by other politicians, preferred to accommodate Mussolini rather than risk a civil war. He invited Mussolini to form a government. Mussolini's train journey to Rome from Milan was followed by a purely ceremonial march in Rome by thousands of blackshirts, most of whom had also travelled by train. The 'march' quickly entered fascist mythology as an armed seizure of power.

Marengo, battle of (June 1800) *see* NAPOLEONIC WARS.

Marne, first battle of (September 1914) Battle of the FIRST WORLD WAR along the river Marne. The German strategic aim of defeating France quickly (based on the SCHLIEFFEN PLAN) depended upon the encirclement of Paris. In early September, the first and second German armies were within thirty miles of Paris on a line along the Marne. The French, under JOFFRE, attacked the flank of the first army as it headed south, which helped to create a major break in the German line between the first and second armies. With British support, the French then turned on the second army. The two German armies retreated, leaving Paris untouched. The battle, which cost over 500,000 lives, thus helped to stop the German advance; it also helped to establish the entrenched positions which each side took on the western front, and the static, attritional nature of the next three years of war. German vulnerability here was linked to Russia's quick mobilisation, not foreseen by Schlieffen, which diverted resources to the east (*see* TANNENBERG). In July and August 1918, the Marne was also the scene of the final German offensive of the war, the successful counter to which began the German retreat and ultimate surrender.

Marshall Plan American economic assistance programme for European countries. The Marshall Plan was announced in

June 1947 by George Marshall, the US Secretary of State. Formally named the European Recovery Program, the plan offered economic assistance ('Marshall Aid') to European countries which provided their own recovery programme. The plan was welcomed by the authorities in France, Germany, Italy, the UK and other countries in western and southern Europe, who formed the ORGANISATION FOR EUROPEAN ECONOMIC COOPERATION (OEEC) in April 1948 to administer the aid. The plan was rejected by the Soviet government as evidence of the USA's agenda for the economic and political domination of Europe. This had the effect of keeping eastern European countries out of the programme, and of further consolidating early COLD WAR divisions. Between 1948 and 1952, $17,000,000,000 of aid was provided for industrial, agricultural and trade recovery. The programme was successful in stimulating the recipients' economies. In 1953 Marshall was awarded the Nobel Peace Prize for the scheme.

Marx, Karl (1818–83) German philosopher and political theorist. Educated in history, philosophy and law in Berlin, Marx became involved in radical politics and worked in Germany as a radical journalist and editor. He moved to Paris in 1843, where he met ENGELS, and then to Brussels until 1848. During this period he became involved in the League of the Communists, and co-wrote *The Communist Manifesto* with Engels in 1848 (*see* COMMUNISM). He returned to Cologne briefly during the REVOLUTIONS OF 1848, but left for London when his newspaper was closed down. He remained in London for the rest of his life, spending his time researching and writing, and living on journalism fees and Engels' support. He developed his theories on capitalism, class struggle, materialism and history during this time: and while he produced no single text outlining his philosophy, he wrote widely on these issues. In 1867 the first volume of *Capital* was published, which helped to spread his influence in the growing socialist and communist movement of the period (*see* SOCIALISM). He remained politically active, particularly through the FIRST INTERNATIONAL from 1864 until 1876. Much of his work, including the last two volumes of *Capital*, was published after his death, with Engels' assistance, and his reputation as the foremost scientific theorist of capitalism and the inevitability of communism was established as his ideas were taken up by radicals throughout Europe. Marxism, as his theories became known, was established as the founding philosophy of Soviet communism, and hence became a key ideology of twentieth-century Europe.

Masaryk, Jan (1886–1948) Czechoslovak diplomat and politician. The son of Tómas MASARYK, Masaryk served in the Austro-Hungarian army during the FIRST WORLD WAR. He moved into diplomacy immediately after the war, serving as an assistant to BENEŠ at the PARIS PEACE CONFERENCE. From 1925 until 1938 he was Czechoslovakia's Minister in London, resigning over the MUNICH AGREEMENT. He remained in London during the SECOND WORLD WAR, joining the Czechoslovakian government-in-exile in 1940, and holding the posts of Foreign Minister and Deputy Prime Minister. He returned to Prague in 1945, and kept the foreign affairs portfolio in GOTTWALD's government: but he increasingly found himself at odds with the USSR's growing influence on Czechoslovakia (*see* COLD WAR), seen most clearly in his opposition to the Soviet veto on Czechoslovakia applying for aid under the MARSHALL PLAN. He remained in office after the Communist coup of February 1948, but died the following month in a fall from a window.

Masaryk, Tómas (1850–1937) Czech and Czechoslovakian academic and politician. An academic at the Czech University in Prague from 1882, this intellectual political activist worked consistently for greater Czechoslovakian autonomy. He represented the Young Czech party in the Vienna parliament from 1891 until 1983, returning in 1907 as a founder of the Czech Realist party, which favoured a reorganisation of the HABSBURG empire along federal lines with increased cooperation between ethnic groups (*see* IMPERIALISM). After the FIRST WORLD WAR started, Masaryk moved to London, where he led the Czech National Council and publicised his cause through teaching, writing and negotiations with politicians. In 1917 he went to Russia to form a Czech Legion of prisoners of war to fight for the Russians, before moving on to the USA to continue his campaign, which by now envisaged full independence for a unified Czech and Slovak state. He won the support of President Woodrow Wilson, and of émigré communities in the USA, and was accepted as president-elect of the new state, which was formally created through the PARIS PEACE CONFERENCE. Masaryk returned to Prague in December 1918, and was elected President. He helped to promote stability and democracy in the new state. Masaryk was re-elected twice before retiring in 1935.

Masurian Lakes, battle of (September 1914) *see* FIRST WORLD WAR.

Matteotti affair Italian political scandal. In June 1924 the General Secretary of the Italian Socialist Unity party, Giacomo Matteotti, disappeared. He had been an opponent of the Fascist government (*see* FASCISM), writing and speaking against their abuses and methods, and fascist implication in his disappearance was suspected. His body was then found buried outside Rome: he had been stabbed to death. The murder sparked widespread opposition to the government, and non-Fascist deputies attempted to get King VICTOR EMMANUEL III to dismiss MUSSOLINI. When he failed to respond, many deputies left parliament in the AVENTINE SECESSION. Mussolini used the crisis as a context for increasing the government's power through stricter censorship and steps against opposition parties. Although Mussolini denied having ordered the killing, he accepted some responsibility. Matteotti became seen as a martyr, both within and outside Italy.

Matteotti, Giacomo *see* MATTEOTTI AFFAIR.

Mazzini, Giuseppe (1805–72) Italian revolutionary. An early member of the secret nationalist society the Carbonari, Mazzini was exiled from Piedmont in 1831 (*see* NATIONALISM). In exile in France, he founded Young Italy as a nationalist organisation, and developed his ideas on the need for Italy to be unified as a republic, with revolutionary activity and education necessary to remove foreign and royal control from the peninsula. He organised an abortive rising in Piedmont in 1832, and was sentenced to death in absentia. In 1837 he moved to London, returning to the Italian peninsula occasionally. Mazzini was involved in the REVOLUTIONS OF 1848 in Milan and Rome, and briefly held office as one of the triumvirate in the republican government of Rome from late 1848 until PIUS IX was restored the following summer with French assistance. Mazzini's influence began to decline after the failures of 1849, as the *Risorgimento* began to emerge as the model for unification, involving royal support. He attempted to organise a number of risings in the 1850s, but they all failed. However, his influence on later notions of Italy as a united nation was significant. *See also* ITALIAN UNIFICATION

Mediterranean agreements (March and December 1887) Series of agreements involving Austria-Hungary, Italy, Spain and the UK on the Mediterranean area, including North Africa, the Balkans, the Adriatic Sea and the Aegean Sea (*see also* IMPERIALISM). In the mid-1880s the Mediterranean and the Balkans again became the focus of international tension. Russian interest in Bulgaria was renewed after conflicts in the region (notably between Serbia and Bulgaria in 1885 over Bulgaria's annexation of Eastern Roumelia), while imperial rights in northern Africa led to a worsening of relations between France and both Italy and the UK. In this context, BISMARCK encouraged the interested parties to offer mutual support, which led in February 1887 to the signing in London of the first Mediterranean Agreement between Italy and the UK (with Austria-Hungary and Spain joining subsequently). By this, each partner agreed mutually to work for stability in the Mediterranean, with the offer of aid in case of aggression against the status quo. This was clearly aimed at French ambitions in North Africa. In December 1887 a second agreement was made between Austria-Hungary, Italy and the UK, this time over Bulgaria and the

OTTOMAN EMPIRE. The signatories stated their support of the Ottoman empire, and offered aid in maintaining the status quo in Bulgaria and the Straits. This agreement was countered by the REINSURANCE TREATY of 1887, which gave German backing to Russia's Balkan aspirations. Taken together, the agreements illustrated Germany's aim to keep France and Russia away from any alliance with the UK by exacerbating their differences. The apparent British support for the TRIPLE ALLIANCE that the Mediterranean agreements implied helped to bring France and Russia closer together (*see* FRANCO-RUSSIAN ALLIANCE). The agreements were not renewed in the 1890s.

Menderes, Adnan (1899–1961) Turkish politician. After training as a lawyer, Menderes entered Turkish politics in 1932 as a representative of the Republican People's party. In December 1945 he founded the Democratic party, and led it to its election victory of 1950. As Prime Minister, Menderes followed a reformist economic and administrative policy, which helped to alienate some conservative sections of Turkish society. He also attempted to develop Turkey's western links, most notably by leading the country into NATO in 1952, and negotiating with the UK for Cyprus' independence in 1959 (*see ENOSIS*). In 1960 Menderes assumed dictatorial powers in the face of an economic crisis, which brought opposition against him to a head. He was deposed by a military coup in May 1960, and subsequently tried for treason for his extra-constitutional powers. He was executed in 1961. In 1990 Menderes was rehabilitated.

Mendès-France, Pierre (1907–82) French politician. Mendès-France was elected to the Chamber of Deputies as a socialist representative in 1932. After a brief spell as Under-Secretary at the Treasury in 1938, he served in the air force from 1939 until 1943, joining Charles DE GAULLE in London in 1941. He held the economics portfolio in the French government-in-exile, and went on to represent France at the BRETTON WOODS conference in 1944. After the SECOND WORLD WAR, Mendès-France stayed out of government, and became a significant critic of right-wing trends and of French colonial policy (*see* IMPERIALISM). He served as Governor of the International Monetary Fund from 1947 until 1958. In June 1954 Mendès-France became Prime Minister of a coalition government, and quickly negotiated the French withdrawal from Indochina. He also initiated some withdrawal from Tunisia, but alienated his socialist coalition colleagues by increasing French military involvement in Algeria. Domestically, his brief government attempted some financial reforms. His government collapsed in February 1955 when the left withdrew. Mendès-France held office as a minister of state in 1956, but remained out of office as a critic of the government throughout the Fifth Republic. He retired in 1973.

Mensheviks Russian political party. The Mensheviks, a name taken from the Russian term for 'minority', emerged as a faction of the Russian Social Democratic Workers' party at the 1903 Congress in London when they lost a vote over the control of *Iskra*, the party's paper, to the BOLSHEVIKS (although the Mensheviks won votes on other matters). The Mensheviks retained close links to orthodox Marxism, particularly in their emphasis on the inevitable evolution of a socialist state after a liberal revolution, and also differed from the more radical Bolsheviks by attempting to build up a mass party. After some experience of working with soviets in the 1905 Revolution (*see* RUSSIAN REVOLUTION 1905), the Mensheviks became an independent party in 1912. Despite some early involvement with the 1917 Revolution (*see* RUSSIAN REVOLUTIONS 1917), particularly in the Petrograd soviet, the Mensheviks subsequently joined the provisional government and backed many of KERENSKY's policies, acts which alienated them further from the Bolsheviks. The Mensheviks declined sharply in influence after the Bolshevik coup of November 1917, and the party was formally closed down in 1921.

Metaxas, Ioannis (1871–1941) Greek soldier and politician. After military training in Germany, Metaxas served in the BALKAN WARS of 1912–13, by the end of which he was Chief of General Staff. He went into self-imposed exile due to his opposition to Greek involvement in the FIRST WORLD WAR, but subsequently returned and entered national politics as a leading member of the pro-restoration Monarchist party. After gaining ministerial experience in various posts from 1928, Metaxas helped to secure the restoration in 1935, which was followed by his own rise to political dominance. In 1936 he became Minister of War and Prime Minister, before establishing (with royal support) a dictatorship that summer through the adjournment of parliament and the granting of emergency powers. His dictatorship was characterised by some fascist-style aspects (*see* FASCISM), including his use of the title *Archigos* (leader), and in 1938 he took the position of head of government for life. Domestically, Metaxas initiated reforms in a number of areas, including education, administration and the military. He managed to secure Greek neutrality when the SECOND WORLD WAR began, then led the successful defence of Greece against the Italian invasion of October 1940. He died before the German invasion.

Metternich, Clemens (1773–1859) German-born Austrian diplomat and politician. Metternich followed his father into the HABSBURG diplomatic service, serving at Dresden, Berlin and Paris, before being appointed Foreign Minister in 1809, a post he held until 1848. In this role, Metternich promoted links with France after the Habsburg defeat at the battle of Wagram, but switched to an alliance with Russia in 1813 to check NAPOLEON's power. Metternich, Chancellor from 1812 and created a prince in 1813, was one of the architects of the Congress of Vienna (*see* VIENNA, CONGRESS OF) of 1814–15, and helped to influence the post-Napoleonic settlement of a balance of power backed up by the CONGRESS SYSTEM. Domestically and internationally, he favoured an anti-liberal policy which restricted opportunities for the discussion of reform and NATIONALISM, and which used force against perceived threats to order (*see also* LIBERALISM). This was exemplified by his introduction of the CARLSBAD DECREES of September 1819 against revolutionary activities, by his development of a strong internal security system in the Habsburg empire, by his work at the Congress of TROPPAU in 1820, and by the use of Habsburg troops in various risings in the Italian states in the 1820s. Metternich's international influence declined relatively in the 1830s, as the Habsburg empire began to lose ground in the German states to Prussia. He was forced to resign when he became a focus of the discontent that developed into the REVOLUTIONS OF 1848 throughout the Habsburg empire. He moved to England briefly, before retiring to the Rhineland.

Metz, battle of (October 1870) *see* FRANCO-PRUSSIAN WAR.

Milosevic, Slobodan (born 1941) Serbian and Yugoslav politician. Milosevic worked in business alongside his advancement in the Belgrade Communist party in the 1970s and 1980s. In 1987 he became General Secretary of the Serbian Communist party, and in 1989 President of Serbia. In this role he incorporated Kosovo into Serbia in 1989, and attempted to maintain the federal structure of Yugoslavia in the face of growing national and ethnic diversification in the late 1980s and early 1990s (*see* YUGOSLAVIA, DISSOLUTION). Despite using the Yugoslav army against both Slovenia and Croatia in 1991 and 1992, he was instrumental in restructuring the federation after their withdrawals, and that of Macedonia. In 1992 he became the first President of the new federation. Milosevic gave his government's support to the Serb rebels in Bosnia-Herzegovina when that republic declared independence in 1992, providing logistical and financial support. In 1994 he ended his support in the face of NATO air strikes and the UNITED NATIONS-backed economic sanctions against Serbia, and cooperated with the Dayton peace agreement that ended the war in Bosnia. Increasingly nationalistic and anti-democratic, Milosevic led the campaign against Kosovo Albanians that led, in March 1999, to renewed NATO intervention (*see* KOSOVO WAR). In May 1999 the International Criminal Tribunal for the former Yugoslavia indicted him for his anti-Albanian policies, although he survived in office despite this charge and the NATO bombing.

Mitterand, François (1916–96) French politician. After a distinguished record in the SECOND WORLD WAR, which included an escape from German captivity and RESISTANCE work in France, Mitterand entered politics in 1946 as a Socialist deputy. He gained ministerial experience in eleven of the Fourth Republic's governments, but opposed the creation of the Fifth Republic in 1958 due to its right-wing and centralising tendencies. Mitterand helped to develop a left-wing block, and emerged as its main spokesman, running unsuccessfully for president against DE GAULLE in 1965. In 1971 he became Secretary of the Socialist party, and ran unsuccessfully for president again in 1974. He finally won the presidency in 1981, defeating the incumbent GISCARD D'ESTAING, and was backed by a left-wing majority in the National Assembly to carry out a reformist programme. However, the subsequent recession damaged the left's standing, and after 1986 Mitterand had to dilute his programme and work with the right-wing Prime Minister, Jacques Chirac. Mitterand's foreign policy promoted European integration, and he worked closely with the West German Chancellor KOHL. In 1988 Mitterand defeated Chirac to regain the presidency for a second term, which lasted until 1995. The last years of his tenure, during which he was suffering from cancer, were dogged by a number of political scandals.

Mollet, Guy (1905–75) French politician. Mollet joined the socialists in 1923, and worked as a teacher before the SECOND WORLD WAR. During the war, he fought with the RESISTANCE, and, in 1944, was appointed as the government's representative in the liberated Pas-de-Calais. He became a Deputy in 1945, and party leader in 1946. Mollet served in a number of the coalition governments of the Fourth Republic, and was Prime Minister of the longest-lasting of these, from January 1956 until May 1957. In this role he attempted unsuccessfully to solve the Algerian crisis, and was also involved in planning the Anglo-French intervention in the Suez Canal zone (*see* IMPERIALISM). Mollet opposed the early Fifth Republic, and attempted to unify anti-Gaullist parties against it. He retired in 1971.

Molotov, Vyacheslav (Vyacheslav Skriabin) (1890–1986) Soviet politician. Skriabin joined the BOLSHEVIKS in 1905, and was exiled for his activities a number of times. In 1912 he assumed the name Molotov. He was one of the leading Bolsheviks in Petrograd in 1917, and as a member of the Military Committee he helped plan the October coup (*see* RUSSIAN REVOLUTIONS 1917). He worked closely with both LENIN and STALIN. In 1928 he helped to run the first of the FIVE YEAR PLANS, and he was appointed Prime Minister in 1930, a position he maintained throughout the period of *YEZHOVSHCHINA*. In 1939 Molotov took on the USSR's foreign policy brief, and quickly negotiated the NAZI-SOVIET PACT in August 1939. In 1942 he negotiated the Anglo-Soviet Pact, and he was an influential figure at the YALTA CONFERENCE and POTSDAM conferences in 1945. In the early years of the COLD WAR, Molotov oversaw the consolidation of Soviet influence in eastern Europe (*see* IMPERIALISM), the rejection of the MARSHALL PLAN, and the BERLIN BLOCKADE. He lost his foreign affairs post in 1949, but re-emerged in 1953 as one of the triumvirate which succeeded Stalin. His influence declined as KHRUSHCHEV rose to prominence, although he briefly held office as Minister of State Control from 1956 until 1957. However, Khrushchev expelled him from the party in 1957 after Molotov was implicated in a coup attempt. He served as the USSR's Ambassador to Mongolia until 1960, and then as a representative on the International Atomic Energy Agency until he retired in 1962. Molotov was readmitted to the party shortly before his death.

Moltke, Helmuth von (senior) (1800–91) Prussian and German soldier. Moltke joined the Prussian army in 1822, and the General Staff in 1832. His gradual advancement led to his appointment as Chief of the General Staff in 1857. Applying theories and practices from various military settings, and blending them with the technological and military logistics of his period, Moltke reorganised the Prussian army and its methods. This included the development of a strong, elitist General Staff; the use of heavy artillery; and the use of railways for quick troop movements. These strategies were influential in Prussia's military campaigns, most notably against Denmark (*see* SCHLESWIG WAR), Austria (*see* AUSTRO-PRUSSIAN WAR), and France (*see* FRANCO-PRUSSIAN WAR). On GERMAN UNIFICATION, Moltke was made a Field-Marshal, a Count, and the Chief of the Imperial General Staff. He retired in 1888.

Monnet, Jean (1888–1979) French economist, politician and administrator. A civil servant, Monnet worked on the Inter-Allied Maritime Commission from 1915, and then served as an economics advisor at the PARIS PEACE CONFERENCE and as Deputy General Secretary of the LEAGUE OF NATIONS from 1919 until 1923. He returned to international and collaborative work in the SECOND WORLD WAR in various capacities, including chairing the Franco-British Economic Cooperation Committee in 1939, and working for the British Supply Council in Washington until 1943. Monnet then joined DE GAULLE's government-in-waiting, and served as Minister of Commerce from 1944. In 1946 de Gaulle appointed him to design and implement a plan for France's economic recovery: the Monnet Plan, which ran from 1947 until 1952, helped France to regain its pre-war wealth through a mixed economy programme. Monnet then became most prominent through his work with Robert Schuman for European integration. He presided over the EUROPEAN COAL AND STEEL COMMUNITY (ECSC) from 1952 until 1955, and then founded and chaired the Action Committee for the United States of Europe until his retirement in 1975.

Montreaux Convention (July 1936) Multilateral agreement on the Straits. In late 1935, the Turkish government began to fear that Italy might develop imperial interests in Asia Minor beyond its possession of the Dodecanese Islands (*see* IMPERIALISM, treaty of LAUSANNE). This came in the light of the ITALO-ABYSSINIAN WAR. The states bordering the Black Sea, along with France, Greece, the UK and Yugoslavia, duly met at Montreaux to discuss the possibilities. The resulting convention aimed to deter Italian aggression in the region, and to provide Turkey with greater defences, by allowing Turkey to remilitarise the Straits: this aspect of the convention was thus a revision of the treaty of Lausanne. The convention also established greater restrictions on military ships' access to the Straits.

Moroccan crises (1905–06, 1911) Two international crises centred on imperial interests in Morocco (*see* IMPERIALISM). In 1904 France and Spain developed plans for protectorates in Morocco. By not involving Germany in the discussion of these plans, the two imperial powers contravened the 1880 treaty of Madrid on Morocco's management. The German government took this opportunity to make a stand against France, aiming also to weaken the *ENTENTE CORDIALE*. The German chancellor, BÜLOW, advised WILLIAM II to visit Morocco: while he was there, William spoke in favour of Moroccan independence, which the German government followed up by calling for an international conference on the issue under the 1880 agreement. The French Foreign Secretary DELCLASSÉ resigned over the issue in June 1905, but the French case was revived at the conference itself, held at Algerçiras in Spain from January to April 1906. Here, Italy, Russia, Spain, the UK and the USA backed France, leaving Germany defeated. The conference agreed that France and Spain should work with the Sultan of Morocco, but gave both powers roles in Morocco's police force and banking structures. The conference also led to increased military cooperation between France and the UK.

The second crisis developed in 1911, by which time the increased links between France, Russia and the UK (*see* TRIPLE ENTENTE) had convinced some in the German government that Germany was being encircled, which created a context for further agitation. In May 1911 French troops intervened in a revolt in Fez, the capital of Morocco. Germany claimed that this contravened Algerçiras, and made demands for financial and territorial compensation to cover Germany's losses which would accrue if France took Morocco over. In July the German gunboat *Panther* visited Agadir. This act brought hostility from the UK, and led to Franco-German discussions between July and November. The result was that Germany recognised France's right to establish a protectorate (which it did in 1912), while Germany received financial compensation and part of the French Congo. Although this crisis did not lead directly to war, it did increase tensions between Germany and the Triple Entente powers, and contributed to an increase in shipbuilding. *See also* FIRST WORLD WAR.

Moscow, retreat from (October 1812) *see* NAPOLEONIC WARS.

Munich agreement 1938 multilateral agreement on German territorial demands on Czechoslovakia. In 1938 the German government and the ethnic German Nazi movement within the Sudeten area of Czechoslovakia stepped up their campaign for the inclusion of the area in Germany. The British Prime Minister, Neville Chamberlain, met HITLER twice to work out a compromise. In late September MUSSOLINI brokered a final meeting between himself, Chamberlain, Hitler and the French Prime Minister DALADIER at Munich. The agreement reached at this conference allowed for Germany to gain the Sudeten area, while all four powers guaranteed the rest of Czechoslovakia against aggression. The meeting also resulted in a bilateral statement between Hitler and Chamberlain on the need for Germany and the UK to avoid war in future. Czechoslovakia was excluded from the conference, as was the USSR, one of Czechoslovakia's allies.

The Munich agreement was generally welcomed at the time in the western countries as it averted war. The agreement directly influenced the NAZI-SOVIET PACT of August 1939, as it suggested to the USSR that France and the UK were not prepared to fight over eastern Europe. The agreement was destroyed in March 1939 when Germany invaded the rest of Czechoslovakia, and the other three guarantors did not act in the country's defence. It has been defended as a useful time-buying exercise, but has also come to be seen as an emotive symbol of APPEASEMENT, as it allowed Germany significant territorial advantages without the use of force. *See also* SECOND WORLD WAR.

Murat, Joachim (1767–1815) French soldier, and King of Naples (1808–15). A cavalry volunteer in 1787, Murat came to prominence through his work with NAPOLEON in suppressing the Vendémiaire coup of 1795 (*see* FRENCH REVOLUTION). He also provided military backing for Napoleon's BRUMAIRE coup of 1799, and secured his position by marrying Caroline, Napoleon's sister, in 1800. Murat led the French cavalry in all of Napoleon's campaigns from 1800 until 1807. In 1808 he suppressed the rising in Madrid. He then succeeded Joseph Bonaparte as King of Naples, taking the title Joachim I Napoleon. In 1812 Murat returned to active service in Napoleon's Russian campaign, commanding the cavalry and subsequently the whole army. He returned to Naples after this failure, and negotiated with the allies over his throne as Napoleon abdicated. During the Hundred Days, Murat attempted to lead an Italian rising behind Napoleon, but this was suppressed by HABSBURG troops. Murat escaped to France, but Napoleon did not use him at Waterloo. In 1815 Murat returned to Calabria in an attempt to reclaim his throne from the restored King Ferdinand, but was caught and executed.

Mussolini, Benito (1883–1945) Italian politician. A socialist before the FIRST WORLD WAR, Mussolini shifted to the right in the context of Italian dissatisfaction over the peace settlement (*see* PARIS PEACE CONFERENCE). Mussolini organised *Fascio di Combattimento*, paramilitary groups involved in fighting communists and trade unionists, which he formed into the National Fascist party (PNF) (*see* FASCISM). After some gains in the 1921 election, Mussolini exploited the unstable situation by engineering his way into the premiership through the MARCH ON ROME in 1922. Over the next four years he gained dictatorial powers, so that by 1926, as *Duce* (leader), he was responsible only to the monarch. This success was gained through electoral manipulation, state terrorism (*see* MATTEOTTI AFFAIR), and through the failure of other parties to withstand fascism (*see* AVENTINE SECESSION). Mussolini also consolidated his position in 1929 through the LATERAN ACCORDS, and through reducing the franchise.

Mussolini's policies gained some economic successes for Italy, particularly through public works schemes, but other schemes, notably the 'battles' for various sectors of the economy, were less successful. Diplomatically, Mussolini also gained some successes, especially through the LOCARNO treaties of 1925 and through preventing the prospective *ANSCHLUSS* in 1934, but other aspects were adventurous and expansionist, and earned him international condemnation: these included the ITALO-ABYSSINIAN WAR, the backing of the rebels in the SPANISH CIVIL WAR, and the invasion of Albania in 1939. From 1936, Mussolini increased his links with Nazi Germany, as exemplified in the AXIS, although Italy did not enter the SECOND WORLD WAR until 1940, in part because the country was not prepared for the struggle, having become exhausted from costly interventions elsewhere. When Italy did join, Mussolini's campaigns in Africa and the Balkans required German support, and were thus costly to the Axis. In July 1943, Victor Emmanuel and leading members of the Fascist Grand Council deposed Mussolini before the allies' ITALIAN CAMPAIGN. He was rescued by a German military operation, and installed as a German puppet dictator of the Salò Republic. In April 1945 he was captured by Italian partisans (*see* RESISTANCE) during an escape attempt, and executed after a summary trial.

Mustafa Ismet *see* INÖNÜ, ISMET.

Mustafa Kemal *see* ATATÜRK, KEMAL.

N

Nagy, Imre (1896–1958) Hungarian politician. Nagy served in the HABSBURG army in the FIRST WORLD WAR, and was captured by the Russians in 1916. He became a communist in Russia, and was active in the RUSSIAN CIVIL WAR. He returned to Hungary in 1921, but moved back to the USSR in 1930 to study agriculture. In 1944, he returned to Hungary, and became Minister of Agriculture, overseeing significant land reforms. He served briefly as Minister of the Interior, but then left politics during the RÁKOSI period to teach economics. In 1953, with backing from MALENKOV, Nagy became Prime Minister, and introduced some social, political and economic reforms. He fell from grace in 1955, and was expelled from the party. However, when the HUNGARIAN RISING began in October 1956, he returned to office, and led the government's liberal reform programme and its attempt at independence from the WARSAW PACT. When the rising was crushed by the USSR's intervention, Nagy surrendered to the Soviets, but was returned to the Hungarian authorities and executed in 1958. He was rehabilitated in 1990.

Napoleon Bonaparte (1769–1821) French soldier and politician. Born in Corsica, Napoleon joined the French army in 1785 as an artillery officer. He came to prominence during the FRENCH REVOLUTIONARY WARS when he led the lifting of the British siege of Toulon. His JACOBIN links worked against him briefly, but his suppression of the Vendémiaire revolt of October 1795 earned him greater recognition from the government (*see* FRENCH REVOLUTION), and he was rewarded with the command of the French army in the Italian states. Here, he led the army to significant victories, and set the peace terms of the treaty of CAMPO FORMIO in 1797. Napoleon's leadership of the French campaign in Egypt in 1798 was less successful. The following year he became a leading political figure when SIEYÈS chose him to lead the BRUMAIRE coup of November 1799, which replaced the 1795 constitution. Napoleon's role as a popular military figure had influenced Sieyès, but Napoleon quickly established himself as the effective dictator of France, making himself First Consul in 1800 and then consul for life in 1802. During this period Napoleon instituted a number of administrative reforms, most notably in the reconstruction of France's local government system (*see CODE NAPOLEON*). He also reached an agreement with the Roman Catholic Church in 1801, which helped to legitimise his rule. In 1804 Napoleon consolidated his rule by declaring himself Emperor.

The rest of his reign was characterised by further military commitments (*see* NAPOLEONIC WARS) as he established a French empire in Europe (*see* IMPERIALISM). By 1807, with the treaty of TILSIT, this covered large parts of south-west and northern Europe, with other territories in the Italian states and the Adriatic, and dependencies in the CONFEDERATION OF THE RHINE, the Grand Duchy of Warsaw, and the Italian states. Napoleon's influence began to decline from 1808, when, in an attempt to starve the UK through the CONTINENTAL SYSTEM, he invaded Spain and Portugal. This overcommitment was exacerbated by his invasion of Russia in 1812, which, after an initial victory at Borodino, failed, and Napoleon was forced to retreat. In 1813 he was beaten at the battle of LEIPZIG, and was given very little chance of recovery when the HABSBURG empire, Prussia, Russia and the UK allied against France in March 1814. The following month Napoleon abdicated on the advice of NEY, fearing that the army would no longer serve him. By the treaty of Fontainebleu of 1814, Napoleon renounced his claim to the throne, but was allowed to keep the imperial title for life. He was exiled to Elba with a pension. However, he escaped in February 1815 in an attempt to regain the French empire, and, for his 'Hundred Days', he resumed command of the army and restarted his military campaigns. He was defeated at the battle of WATERLOO in June 1815, and was exiled to St Helena, where he died in 1821.

Napoleon III (Charles Louis Napoleon Bonaparte) (1808–73) French politician. NAPOLEON's nephew, Louis Napoleon was exiled from France in 1815, and took on the role of Bonapartist pretender in 1832. He staged two unsuccessful attempts at military risings against LOUIS-PHILIPPE, in 1836 and 1840, for the latter of which he was imprisoned. He escaped to England, returning to France after the 1848 February revolution (*see* REVOLUTIONS OF 1848), and winning a seat in the National Assembly. Backed by monarchists, and with huge popular support, he won the presidential election of December 1848. In 1851 he staged a coup which suspended the SECOND REPUBLIC's constitution, and claimed the role of president for ten years. The following year, in line with his longer-term aims as pretender, he established the SECOND EMPIRE, and created himself hereditary emperor, taking the title Napoleon III. This move was supported in a plebiscite. Domestically, Napoleon III's reign saw INDUSTRIALISATION and commercial expansion, public works schemes, and the legalisation of trade unions. However, his foreign policies were less successful. He involved France in the CRIMEAN WAR, and, through the Pact of PLOMBIÈRES of 1858, committed himself to support Italian independence, which led to the FRANCO-AUSTRIAN WAR in 1859. Napoleon III's interests in IMPERIALISM led to the disastrous establishment of an empire in Mexico in 1863. He was also unable to cope with Prussia's emergence during the 1860s, and led France into the FRANCO-PRUSSIAN WAR in 1870. The Prussians captured him after the battle of Sedan in September 1871: two days later the empire was overthrown by republicans and the THIRD REPUBLIC declared. Napoleon III moved to England, where he died in 1873.

Napoleonic Wars (1799–1815) Series of conflicts between France and other nations during the period of NAPOLEON's domination of French politics, from the BRUMAIRE coup of 1799 until his final defeat in 1815. They were, in effect, continuations of the FRENCH REVOLUTIONARY WARS which had been in progress since 1792. The label is an umbrella term for a number of regionalised and international conflicts.

In 1799, with France being beaten in Egypt, Great Britain brought together the HABSBURG empire, Naples, Portugal and Russia as the Second Coalition. This force won some victories, notably the Habsburgs in the German states and the Russians in the Italian states, but after BRUMAIRE Napoleon was able to halt these hostile advances. In 1800 the French beat the Habsburgs at Marengo and Hohenlinden, leading to the treaty of LUNÉVILLE the following year. Russia, with objectives at variance with those of both Great Britain and the Habsburg empire, also left the Coalition in 1800. The UK made peace with France at the treaty of AMIENS in 1802, bringing an end to this phase of the wars by which post-revolutionary France had consolidated its position as a major power and built up territorial gains on its western border, in the Italian states, and in the German states (*see* IMPERIALISM). However, the peace did not last for long: in May 1803 the UK re-declared war on France, to be joined in 1804 by the Habsburg empire, Russia and Sweden as the Third Coalition. The French developed plans for the invasion of the UK, but these were destroyed after the battle of Trafalgar of October 1805, in which the French and Spanish fleets were beaten by the Royal Navy. This defeat confirmed Napoleon's continental ambitions, evident from his crossing the Rhine in September 1805. With Prussia on the verge of joining the Coalition, Napoleon effectively destroyed the grouping by beating the Habsburgs and Russia at AUSTERLITZ in December. The Habsburgs subsequently made peace at PRESSBURG. In 1806 Prussia re-entered the fighting, only to be beaten by France at Jena and Auerstadt in October, and the Coalition finally collapsed in 1807 after Napoleon's victory over Russia at Friedland in June led to the treaty of TILSIT, which also dealt with Prussia. By this time Napoleon had established the CONFEDERATION OF THE RHINE as an alliance system of medium-sized German states.

In November 1806 Napoleon revised the French war effort against the UK by declaring the economic blockade of the CONTINENTAL SYSTEM. In an attempt to enforce this in the north Atlantic, France invaded Portugal (with Spanish complicity) in November 1807. This war spread to Spain in the summer of 1808, when a number of popular risings against the French were exacerbated by Napoleon's attempt to establish his brother Joseph as king. With British support, the Peninsular War thus developed as a major southern commitment for France which was to last until 1814. The French were pushed out of Portugal in late 1808. In 1809 Napoleon had to divide his attentions between Spain and the Habsburg empire, after the latter took the opportunity of the southern diversion to attack Bavaria and the Grand Duchy of Warsaw. Napoleon was successful in this campaign, defeating the Habsburgs at Wagram in July 1809 and gaining further Italian and Balkan territories in the subsequent treaty of Vienna, but the French continued to lose ground to the British armies, notably at Salamanca in July 1812, and to the Spanish guerrillas.

In December 1810 Russia recommenced trade with the UK, a step which led Napoleon to prepare for a new war in the east. After securing Prussian support in February 1812, Napoleon led an invading army into Russia in June. After some early victories, which led to the capture of Smolensk in August, the French fought the Russians at Borodino (with some 28,000 French and 15,000 Russian casualties) in September: and while neither side won, the battle left the Russians unable to defend Moscow, which Napoleon entered in mid-September. However, ALEXANDER I's government refused to negotiate with the French, leaving the invasion unsuccessful and the French army severely overstretched. In October, Napoleon accordingly began the retreat from Moscow, a two-month process in which the army had to cope with further fighting, winter conditions and disease. This retreat was disastrous for the French, who lost approximately 600,000 men through illness, combat and desertion out of an original force of 700,000.

In February 1813 Prussia and Russia signed the treaty of Kalisch, which formed the basis of the Fourth Coalition when the Habsburg empire, Sweden and the UK subsequently joined. Napoleon fought a number of battles in eastern and central Europe after leaving Russia, which included some victories, as at Lutzen and Bautzen against the Russians and the Prussians in May 1813. However, the French were defeated at Vittoria in Spain in June, and the British army crossed the Franco-Spanish border in October. Meanwhile, the Habsburgs, Prussia and Russia had united their efforts through the treaty of Teplitz in September, by which each state agreed to provide at least 60,000 troops, and agreed not to make separate peace with France. This alliance formed the basis for the decisive battle of LEIPZIG in mid-October, which pushed Napoleon back towards France. He recrossed the Rhine in early November. The Coalition powers continued to press in on France, their efforts confirmed by the treaty of CHAUMONT in March 1814 which committed them to fight until France was reduced to its 1791 borders. After a number of battles, Paris was taken in late March. Napoleon abdicated, and the French monarchy was restored under LOUIS XVIII. Peace was made by the treaty of PARIS of May 1814. In November the powers assembled at the Congress of Vienna (*see* VIENNA, CONGRESS OF) to begin to resolve the territorial and political legacy of twenty-two years of conflict.

The final phase of the Napoleonic Wars began in March 1815, when Napoleon escaped from his exile on Elba and returned to France. Louis XVIII fled, and Napoleon reclaimed power and rebuilt his army. His 'Hundred Days' were dominated by his attempt to split the British, Dutch and Prussian forces that had assembled in Belgium. After beating the Prussians at Ligny on 16 June, he was halted by the British, Dutch and Prussians at the battle of WATERLOO on 18 June. Napoleon abdicated again, this time to be exiled to St Helena, and the treaty of PARIS of November 1815 settled the conflict.

National Socialism *see* NAZISM.

nationalism Political ideology. Nationalism, as it emerged out of the FRENCH REVOLUTION at the end of the eighteenth century, was based on the assumption that the 'nation' was the primary determinant in any group of people's identity, and that the nation as a unit should be promoted and protected. While this was effectively ignored for conquered areas during the FRENCH REVOLUTIONARY WARS and the NAPOLEONIC WARS, its influence began to grow during this period of major conflict. Although it did not influence the peacemaking process at the Congress of Vienna (*see* VIENNA, CONGRESS OF) in 1814 and 1815, where inter-European IMPERIALISM was re-established, movements dedicated to gaining some form of national identity gained some successes shortly thereafter, as in the GREEK WAR OF INDEPENDENCE of 1821–29, and the Belgian revolution a year later (*see* REVOLUTIONS OF 1830). However, most nationalist movements were minority affairs, based predominantly amongst liberal, middle-class, urban elites, and the various nationalist strands in the other revolutions of 1830 and the REVOLUTIONS OF 1848 were generally unsuccessful. However, these revolutions did establish major challenges to the European empires, challenges that were informed both by LIBERALISM and by nationalism, and by the middle of the century some of the key ideas of nationalism were spreading. While nationalist groups in different areas varied in their exact understanding of what constituted the nation, with language, culture, history, traditions and religion, for example, variously taken as significant, there was some common ground in their opposition to imperialism and external control.

Another form of nationalism that emerged in the third quarter of the century was based on powerful states enlarging themselves in the name of a nation; and it was this form, influenced by CONSERVATISM, that was most influential in achieving the tangible results of nation creation, particularly by Piedmont-Sardinia (*see* ITALIAN UNIFICATION) and Prussia (*see* GERMAN UNIFICATION). In the new Italy and the new Germany, the nation was actively promoted as a common cause for all members of the population: and while this caused conflicts with the supranational Roman Catholic Church (*see* *KULTURKAMPF*), it helped to create strong states. From this time, the creation of smaller nations was also seen as a potentially useful diplomatic tool, exemplified by the 1878 changes in the Balkans against the OTTOMAN EMPIRE. *See* BERLIN CONGRESS.

After the FIRST WORLD WAR, some of these nineteenth-century concepts of nationalism, combined with the pragmatic need to weaken the defeated powers, informed the peacemaking (*see* FOURTEEN POINTS, PARIS PEACE CONFERENCE). The new or re-created states, such as Czechoslovakia, Hungary, Poland, and the Kingdom of the Croats, Serbs, and Slovenes (subsequently Yugoslavia), apparently consolidated the idea that the nation state was the most desirable and efficient form of geopolitical organisation. Despite subsequent wars and further continental imperialism, particularly that practised by Germany from 1939 to 1942 (*see* SECOND WORLD WAR) and the USSR during the COLD WAR, this assumption remained influential throughout the twentieth century. It could be seen, for example, in the REVOLUTIONS OF 1989–91, in the emergence of many former Soviet republics as nations in their own right (such as Belarus, Estonia and Ukraine), and in the fragmentation of Yugoslavia from 1992 (*see* YUGOSLAVIA, DISSOLUTION). Moreover, it remained a significant political cause for some marginal nationalities pressing for separatism, such as the Basques in Spain. This, combined with the challenges created by decolonisation and related migration, and by European integration, has maintained nationalism as a contested issue.

Nations, battle of the *see* LEIPZIG, BATTLE OF.

NATO (North Atlantic Treaty Organisation) Military alliance. After the alliance systems of the treaty of DUNKIRK and BRUSSELS TREATY in 1947 and 1948, and in the context of growing COLD WAR tensions, the USA and a number of European nations formed NATO as a western defence alliance against the USSR. It was established by the North Atlantic Treaty, signed in Washington in April 1949 by representatives of Belgium, Canada, Denmark, France, Iceland, Luxembourg, the Netherlands, Portugal, the UK and the USA. By this, each member agreed to provide support to any other member that was attacked in an area defined as the signatories' territories and island possessions north of the Tropic of Cancer. NATO was based in France, and run by a Military Committee (made up of officers from member nations) and the North Atlantic Council (made up of appropriate ministers).

Although it was not drawn into any conflicts until 1994, the existence of NATO meant that US-backed forces were based permanently throughout western Europe under a single, integrated military command: from 1955, they were faced by the Soviet-dominated equivalent, the WARSAW PACT. NATO expanded in the 1950s, with Greece and Turkey joining in 1952, and the Federal Republic of Germany (FRG) in 1955, although it was weakened in the 1960s, first by Greece's withdrawal in 1964, and then by France's withdrawal from the command structure in 1966. Greece rejoined in 1979, while Spain joined in 1982. At the end of the Cold War, NATO reduced some of its forces and redeveloped its functions along peace-keeping and humanitarian lines, while extending its influence through contacts with nations from the disintegrating Warsaw Pact, along with Sweden and Finland. This was seen clearly in the London declaration of 1990, which set an agenda for greater cooperation with the Warsaw Pact. It was in this period that NATO forces were first used in conflict: first in the Bosnian Civil War (*see* YUGOSLAVIA, DISSOLUTION) in 1994 as part of the UNITED NATIONS force; and as an alliance against Serbia for the KOSOVO WAR of 1999. In the same year, the Czech Republic, Hungary and Poland became the first of the former Warsaw Pact members to join NATO.

Navarino, battle of (October 1827) Naval battle of the GREEK WAR OF INDEPENDENCE. After the 1827 treaty of London, by which France, Russia and the UK agreed to mediate between the Greek rebels and the OTTOMAN government, the allies developed a joint naval force to blockade Turkish-controlled ports and encourage the Turks to negotiate. The Turks responded by developing a joint force with their Egyptian allies. On 20 October 1827, the allied fleet sailed to the Turkish supply base at Navarino to attempt mediation. When the Turks fired on a British ship, a full-scale battle developed. Within hours the Turks lost sixty ships and approximately 8,000 men. This defeat severely weakened the Turkish war effort, which was finished off in 1828 by the Russian invasion. Navarino was the last major sea battle fought under sail.

Nazi-Soviet Pact (August 1939) Bilateral non-aggression treaty between Germany and the USSR, signed in Moscow in August 1939. In the context of the German invasion of Czechoslovakia in March 1939, and of the USSR's war with Japan from May 1939, STALIN attempted to improve relations with France and the UK in a strategic revival of the TRIPLE ENTENTE. However, mutual suspicion between politicians in all three countries, and some of the USSR's terms, made such a settlement difficult to establish. HITLER, meanwhile, appreciated that a pact with the USSR would provide some security for an attack on Poland. Accordingly, and against the tone of each government's ideology and propaganda, the foreign ministers RIBBENTROP and MOLOTOV agreed a treaty in August 1939. The published aspects of the treaty committed the two countries to mutual non-aggression, and each government to neutrality if the other became involved in a war with a third party. Both governments also agreed not to join any other alliance against the other party. The secret clauses of the treaty provided mutual recognition for each government's territorial ambitions in eastern Europe and the Baltic. Germany recognised the USSR's interests in eastern Poland, Estonia, Finland and Latvia; while the USSR recognised Germany's interests in western Poland and Lithuania. In the first half of September, Germany and the USSR invaded Poland from east and west, dividing the country close to the CURZON LINE. The USSR also invaded the Baltic republics, with Germany relinquishing Lithuania in return for more of Poland. The Pact was destroyed in June 1941, when Germany invaded the USSR (*see* BARBAROSSA). For both governments, the Pact, which shocked many in western Europe, allowed for wars of conquest in the area between Germany and the USSR, apparently without an immediate threat of escalation. *See also* SECOND WORLD WAR.

nazism Political ideology associated with the National Socialist German Workers party (NSDAP), named from the German abbreviation of 'National Socialist'. The ideology developed in the early 1920s out of the debates and discourse within the party, and became strongly associated with HITLER, the party's leader from 1921. In the early stages, as expressed in the party's programme of February 1920, the ideology combined aspects from a number of different strands. It incorporated some long-term nationalist (*see* NATIONALISM) and militaristic strands from the nineteenth century, but restated them in the context of Germany's defeat in the FIRST WORLD WAR and subsequent losses through the treaty of VERSAILLES: for example, it stressed the need to unite all ethnic Germans in a 'Greater Germany', with the restoration of lost territory and the right to unite with Austria (*see ANSCHLUSS*). The programme also contained strong statements on race and nationality, with an explicit ANTI-SEMITISM and statements on citizenship and immigration. There were also some socialist aspects (*see* SOCIALISM), with plans for state welfarism and the nationalisation of major businesses. These features of the early ideology, which shared some ground with FASCISM, were adapted over time: in particular, some of the socialist elements were diluted. Hitler's *Mein Kampf*, published in two volumes in 1925 and 1928, came to be seen as a fuller statement of nazism: and after Hitler's consolidation as leader, the ideology became virtually indistinguishable from his own views and their dissemination through various media. However, it remained reactionary (against, for example, Versailles, COMMUNISM, and some features of modernism), racist, militaristic and nationalistic, with a major emphasis on the role of the leader and on the natural superiority of the 'pure' 'Aryan race'. Nazism became the orthodox ideology of Germany during the THIRD REICH, but was proscribed, along with the party, at the end of the SECOND WORLD WAR. Neo-nazism, drawing heavily both on the ideology and aesthetics of the NSDAP, emerged in many parts of Europe and elsewhere in the economic crises of the late 1970s, and has continued to influence a number of small political groups.

Neapolitan rising (1820–21) Rebellion in Naples. In July 1820 a group of military officers who had backed MURAT's abortive rising in 1815 staged a rebellion against the recently restored king, Ferdinand. They were influenced by NATIONALISM and LIBERALISM, and by the SPANISH REVOLUTION of January 1820. Like the military leaders in Spain, the rebels demanded a liberal constitution for the Kingdom of the Two Sicilies. With risings also taking place on Sicily, Ferdinand agreed to the rebels' demands, although the rebellion soon attracted a popular following which created pressure for more radical reforms. The issues were discussed by the Quintuple Alliance powers (*see* QUADRUPLE ALLIANCE) at the Congress of TROPPAU, where the HABSBURG empire, Prussia, and Russia agreed to the principle of intervention in other countries' affairs. The Congress of LAIBACH formalised this by allowing METTERNICH to send Habsburg troops into Naples in February 1821. The rebels were quickly defeated, and Ferdinand was able to abandon the promised constitution.

Neerwinden, battle of (March 1793) *see* FRENCH REVOLUTIONARY WARS.

Neuilly, treaty of (November 1919) Peace treaty between the allied powers and Bulgaria at the end of the FIRST WORLD WAR, one of the treaties written during the PARIS PEACE CONFERENCE. Territorially, Bulgaria ceded to Greece the remnant of western Thrace that it had retained by the treaty of LONDON of 1913, thus losing direct access to the Aegean sea; while Romania was given southern Dobrudja, and the new Kingdom of the Serbs, Croats and Slovenes gained some small parts of borderland. Bulgaria was set reparations payments, both in cash and in kind. The Bulgarian army was reduced to a maximum size of 20,000 volunteers. The relatively generous terms of this treaty were linked to the victorious allies' desire to minimise potential territorial disputes in the Balkans.

New Economic Policy Soviet economic strategy, introduced in 1921. As the BOLSHEVIKS' authority was weakened by food shortages, riots and mutinies during the RUSSIAN CIVIL WAR, LENIN introduced the New Economic Policy (NEP) in March 1921 as a temporary measure to restore some stability to the country's economy in place of WAR COMMUNISM. NEP introduced a mixed economy by returning some small firms to the private sector, allowing private enterprise in food and other goods, and, from 1924, it involved a currency reform. The policy proved popular with the agricultural sector, as it allowed farmers to sell their surplus products privately. Although the state kept control of heavy industry, wholesale, and international trade, NEP was seen to work, as it quelled some of the dissent of the war communism period. However, it also led to unemployment, and was disliked by many communists as a betrayal of ideology (*see* COMMUNISM): the appearance of the bourgeois 'nepmen' and rich peasants was particularly offensive here. Although Lenin had viewed NEP as a necessary concession, it was gradually diluted under STALIN, and was formally abandoned in 1929 with the introduction of planning and collectivisation. *See* FIVE YEAR PLANS.

Ney, Michel (1769–1815) French soldier. After joining the French army in 1787, Ney gained advancement during the FRENCH REVOLUTIONARY WARS, and was promoted to the rank of general. A close ally of NAPOLEON, he helped to mastermind France's campaigns in the German states from 1799, and was made Marshal of France in 1804. He continued to fight in France's major campaigns in the NAPOLEONIC WARS, and was widely acclaimed for his decisive role at the battle of Friedland in 1807. The following year Napoleon created him Duc d'Elchingen. In the Russian campaign, Ney commanded the rearguard action as the French army retreated from Moscow in 1812. After fighting on into 1814, Ney's advice to Napoleon on the decline in the army's support was influential in the Emperor's decision to abdicate. Ney duly backed the restored LOUIS XVIII, and led the party sent to arrest Napoleon at the start of the 'Hundred Days'. However, he changed sides once again, and joined Napoleon in the Belgian campaign, fighting at the battle of WATERLOO. He was subsequently court-martialled after Napoleon's defeat, and executed in Paris in 1815.

Nicholas I (1796–1855) ROMANOV Tsar of Russia, 1825–55. Nicholas I succeeded his brother ALEXANDER I in 1825, and quickly crushed the DECEMBRIST CONSPIRACY that had staged its revolt in the aftermath of Alexander's death. This repressive approach came to characterise much of his reign, seen most obviously in his increase of censorship, his retardation of education, and his creation of a secret police force within an enlarged central bureaucracy. Nicholas was unsympathetic to the nationality issue within the Russian empire (*see* IMPERIALISM), using force against the revolution in Poland (*see* REVOLUTIONS OF 1830). He also backed the HABSBURG government's repression of the revolution in Hungary (*see* REVOLUTIONS OF 1848). Nicholas I also oversaw the introduction of some limited reforms, including the codification of Russia's laws from 1833, and a limited emancipation of the serfs on state land from 1838, but he was unprepared to pursue such policies. His foreign policies brought Russia some territorial and strategic gains, most notably through the treaty of ADRIANOPLE that ended the RUSSO-TURKISH WAR in 1829, but his Balkan policies led to clashes with France and the UK which, in 1854, precipitated the CRIMEAN WAR. Russia's defeat here, which Nicholas I did not live to see, demonstrated the country's relative military and industrial backwardness. He was succeeded by his son, ALEXANDER II.

Nicholas II (1868–1918) ROMANOV Tsar of Russia, 1894–1917. Nicholas succeeded his father ALEXANDER III in 1894. He characterised his reign by an emphasis on the autocratic and divine role of the Tsar, which exacerbated tensions in Russian politics. In the first eleven years of his reign he made few concessions to calls for reform, concentrating instead on promoting the historical significance of the Romanov dynasty, and attempting to recreate early Russian forms in cultural life. Nicholas' foreign policy was marked by a shift towards France in Europe, and eastern expansion into Korea and Manchuria, which led to war with Japan in 1904. It was in the context of this war that discontent over food supplies and prices precipitated revolutionary activity in a number of centres (*see* RUSSIAN REVOLUTION 1905). Nicholas responded to the demands for concessions by establishing a *duma* (parliament) and making some constitutional concessions, but these were limited by the 'Fundamental Laws'. Between 1905 and the outbreak of the FIRST WORLD WAR in 1914, Nicholas showed preferences for reactionary and conservative ministers, although some important land reforms were introduced by STOLYPIN. He also became increasingly influenced in all his decisions by his wife Alexandra, and her controversial adviser RASPUTIN. In 1914 Nicholas led Russia into war against Austria-Hungary and Germany over the Balkan crisis, taking personal command of the army in 1915. This removed him from the intrigues of St Petersburg, and placed him in a position of responsibility for all military failures. His reputation suffered further through allegations of his pro-German sympathies. Nicholas abdicated in March 1917 after the February revolution (*see* RUSSIAN REVOLUTIONS 1917). He was killed, along with all of his family, by BOLSHEVIKS in July 1918. In July 1998 his rediscovered remains were ceremonially buried in St Petersburg.

Night of the Long Knives (1934) Nazi purge of party and external opponents, 29 June–2 July 1934. As HITLER attempted to consolidate his power in Germany, particularly through his planned merger of the offices of chancellor and president on HINDENBURG's imminent death, the leadership of the Storm Division (SA), particularly Röhm, began to call for radical reforms in land, industry and the armed forces. This faction, which included approximately 4,000,000 SA members, was thus proving a liability to Hitler, particularly in his relations with the army. During June 1934, Hitler and other leading Nazis, including Goering and Himmler, developed plans for a purge of the party, to rid it of the SA and other internal opponents. On the night of 29 June arrests and shootings began, which lasted until 2 July. The killings were carried out by members of the GESTAPO and the Guard Unit (SS), with logistical support from the army. As well as the SA figures, the victims included political opponents such as Gregor Strasser and Kurt von Schleicher. On 13 July, Hitler announced the killings in the Reichstag, claiming that they had been carried out to prevent a coup. He gave the action its name, the 'Night of the Long Knives', and acknowledged seventy-seven deaths, although the real number is unknown: some estimates place it as high as 1,000. The purge diminished the SA, strengthened the SS, and helped to consolidate Hitler's own position.

NKVD (Russian: *Norodny Komitet Vnutrennykh Del*, People's Commissariat for Internal Affairs) The USSR's secret police and internal security agency, 1934–46. The NKVD was formed in 1934 as an umbrella organisation for all aspects of the USSR's internal security, including the observation of all political debates, the interrogation and trial of those arrested for political crimes, and the management of punishments for those found guilty, including executions and the running of prisons and labour camps. The NKVD's powers peaked during *YEZHOVSCHINA* in the 1930s, and under BERIA during the SECOND WORLD WAR. In 1946 it was reorganised, and from 1954 its duties were merged with those of the KGB.

Normandy campaign (June–August 1944) First stage of Allied invasion of north-west Europe in the SECOND WORLD WAR. After aerial bombardment of German positions and infrastructure, and false intelligence to promote the idea that the invasion was planned further north in the Calais region, the allies launched an invasion of Normandy from southern England on 6 June 1944 (D-Day). Landing on five beaches along a thirty-mile front, American, British, Canadian and other allied troops, supported by air and sea attacks, established beach-heads before moving on to take key targets in Normandy, including Cherbourg and Caen. With supplies coming through artificial harbours and a submarine oil pipeline, the allied armies pushed out of Normandy in late July, heavily defeating a brief German counter-attack at Avranches in early August. The success of this campaign opened the western allies' way to Paris, which the Germans surrendered in late August, and formed the foundation of the subsequent NORTH-WEST EUROPE CAMPAIGN. By September 1944 the allies had lost approximately 225,000 troops in the campaign, the Germans 500,000.

North Atlantic Treaty Organisation *see* NATO.

North German Confederation Political organisation of northern German states, 1867–71. The North German Confederation was established by the treaty of PRAGUE of August 1866 which ended the AUSTRO-PRUSSIAN WAR. It involved federal unification of all of the German states north of the river Main, with the newly enlarged Prussia as the dominant state. The Confederation stretched from the Belgian border in the west to the Russian border east of Königsberg, and from Schleswig in the north to the Main in the south. The individual states were allowed to maintain some independence: for example, no monarchs were deposed, and administrative, constitutional and judicial matters were largely left intact. A Federal Council and Assembly were set up, and a number of social and economic reforms were introduced. However, Prussia's dominance was ensured in a number of ways. The Prussian king automatically held the presidency of the Confederation, with powers in foreign and military policy; Prussia had the largest number of votes in the Council; and the Prussian king had the power to veto all laws passed by the Assembly. It was dissolved in 1871 on the declaration of GERMAN UNIFICATION.

North-west Europe campaign (September 1944–May 1945) Western allies' military campaign against Germany in the SECOND WORLD WAR. After the success of the NORMANDY CAMPAIGN, allied forces advanced into north-west Europe on a wide front from the Channel coast to the Franco-Swiss border, aiming to push the Germans out of Belgium, France, Luxembourg and the Netherlands, which would then allow for a western invasion of Germany. In early September, Brussels and Antwerp were both taken, laying the foundation for the conquest of the rest of Belgium and the Netherlands: while Belgium and the southern Netherlands were taken, the attempt to push into the north across the lower reaches of the Rhine initially failed at Arnhem in September. While the Americans, Canadians and French had pushed the Germans out of most of France by this time, Hitler ordered a counter-attack through the Ardennes in northern Luxembourg and eastern Belgium in December. This, the last German offensive on the western front, was aimed at retaking Belgium and dividing the allies. However, after some initial successes, the offensive was weakened by a lack of supplies, while allied resistance managed to absorb the attack. The last Germans were pushed back out of the Ardennes in mid-January 1945, the German army having suffered approximately 100,000 losses (dead, injured, and taken prisoner). Having entered Germany in October, American forces crossed the Rhine at Remagen in March, with the British also crossing further north. From there, the different armies continued to concentrate on separate parts of Germany: the British moving towards the Baltic through Hamburg and the Americans aiming for Dresden, paralleling the Soviet attack from the east. In April, American and Soviet forces linked at Torgau on the Elbe. On 4 May, following HITLER's suicide, the German armies in north-west Europe surrendered at Lüneberg.

Novara, battle of (May 1821) *see* PIEDMONTESE RISING.

Novara, battle of (March 1849) *see* AUSTRO-PIEDMONTESE WAR.

Novotný, Antonin (1904–75) Czechoslovakian politician. Novotný joined the Communist party in 1921 while working in munitions. He was imprisoned by the Germans from 1941 until 1945. He subsequently became a leading politician in Czechoslovakia after the SECOND WORLD WAR. He was involved in the Communist coup of 1948, and became the party's First Secretary in 1953 after GOTTWALD's death. He also served as President from 1957. He was relatively isolated within eastern Europe during the KHRUSHCHEV period in the USSR, as he remained a Stalinist, committed to heavy industry. These policies led to a recession in the early 1960s, accompanied by student-led unrest, after which Novotný began to liberalise, but these reforms came too late. Throughout the mid-1960s, disquiet with Novotný mounted, culminating in the PRAGUE SPRING of 1968. Novotný resigned from his party and state posts in March when the army refused to occupy Prague.

Nuremberg laws German legislation of 1935. At the 1935 Nazi party (*see* NAZISM) rally in Nuremberg, the government announced two major pieces of legislation which were designed to limit German Jews' political and personal freedoms. The Reich Law on Citizenship removed Jews' German nationality by limiting that status to people of 'Aryan' blood. The Law for the Protection of German Blood and Honour barred marriages and non-marital sexual relations between Jews and non-Jews. Both laws, which were enforced from September 1935, were designed to marginalise Jews, and helped to make concrete Nazi propaganda and ideology on race and ethnicity. The laws were followed by supplementary decrees on various issues which further limited Jews' rights and opportunities. *See also* ANTI-SEMITISM.

Nuremberg trials Judicial trial of German and Austrian Nazis (*see* NAZISM), 1945–47. The principle that the leading Nazis should be tried for their actions was accepted by the Allied governments during the SECOND WORLD WAR, and in May 1945 the model to be used was agreed. This involved France, the UK, the USA and the USSR each supplying two judges and a team of prosecutors. The accused were to be tried with any of four charges: crimes against peace; war crimes; crimes against humanity; and conspiracy. The trials were held at Nuremberg for propaganda reasons, as the city had been the site of the Nazi party's rallies. In all, 177 individuals and a number of organisations, including the GESTAPO and the Guard Unit (SS), were tried. The main trial, featuring twenty-one of the leading Nazis such as GOERING, HESS, RIBBENTROP and SPEER, lasted from November 1945 until September 1946, and resulted in eleven death sentences.

The exact legality of the trials has continued to raise questions on a number of grounds. For example, the Allied powers provided all the judges; some of the charges were poorly defined and lacked precedents in international law; and the defence that individuals were acting under order was not accepted. Moreover, the absence of such key figures as the late GOEBBELS, HEYDRICH, HIMMLER and HITLER, and the absence of EICHMANN, meant that much information remained undisclosed. However, despite these issues, the trials widely publicised and recorded the abuses of the THIRD REICH, including some of the details of BARBAROSSA and the FINAL SOLUTION.

O

October Manifesto (October 1905) *see* NICHOLAS II; RUSSIAN REVOLUTION 1905.

Oder-Neisse Line German-Polish border from 1945. The line, following the rivers Oder and Neisse, was accepted as a temporary border between Germany and Poland by the allies in the planning for post-war Europe at the YALTA CONFERENCE and POTSDAM CONFERENCE of the SECOND WORLD WAR. It came into force in May 1945, having the effect of shifting Poland westwards at Germany's expense to compensate for the establishment of the new Polish-Soviet border approximately on the CURZON LINE. Although this was seen as temporary by the allies, the Polish government quickly moved to make the territorial settlement permanent by forcing over 6,000,000 Germans out of the re-acquired areas (and East Prussia), and replacing them with Poles, and by promoting the Polish language and culture. The German Democratic Republic (GDR) recognised the border in 1949, but the Federal Republic of Germany (FRG) did not accept the settlement until 1970 when BRANDT's policy of eastern reconciliation (*see OSTPOLITIK*) formed the context for the treaty of Warsaw, which confirmed the two countries' mutual acceptance of the 1945 border. The border was not affected by GERMAN REUNIFICATION in 1990. *See also* POLISH CORRIDOR.

Organisation for Security and Cooperation in Europe *see* CONFERENCE ON SECURITY AND COOPERATION IN EUROPE.

Organisation for European Economic Cooperation (OEEC) Intergovernmental body for post-SECOND WORLD WAR economic recovery and development. When the US government announced the MARSHALL PLAN in June 1947, the governments of the European nations which would receive the aid were obliged to establish a body which would coordinate and channel the assistance. This was established in April 1948 as the OEEC, consisting originally of Austria, Belgium, Denmark, France, Greece, Iceland, Ireland, Italy, Luxembourg, the Netherlands, Norway, Portugal, Sweden, Turkey, the UK, and the western zones of Germany. The OEEC's decisions were made by Council, on which each member government had equal voting rights. It began work on reorganising trade agreements (influenced here by the smaller BENELUX UNION model), on promoting the recovery of production, and on distributing Marshall Aid. In 1949 the Federal Republic of Germany (FRG) formally joined, as did Spain in 1959; while north American interests in the OEEC's work were represented by Canada and the USA's associate member status from 1950. The OEEC provided a forum for the discussion of future models of continent-wide economic collaboration, which led to the formation of both the EUROPEAN ECONOMIC COMMUNITY (EEC) and the EUROPEAN FREE TRADE ASSOCIATION (EFTA). In 1960 the OEEC restructured itself in the light of the emergence of the EEC and EFTA, becoming the Organisation for Economic Cooperation and Development (OECD): with Canadian, US and, from 1964, Japanese membership, the new body took on a global remit.

Organisation for Security and Cooperation in Europe *see* CONFERENCE ON SECURITY AND COOPERATION IN EUROPE.

Orlando, Vittorio (1860–1952) Italian politician. A law professor, Orlando entered the Italian parliament in 1897. He gained ministerial experience in a number of posts, including education (1903–5), justice (1907–9 and 1915–16), and the interior (1916–17). Orlando formed a government in 1917 after the Italian defeat at CAPORETTO, and he remained Prime Minister until 1919. As President of the Chamber of Deputies, Orlando represented Italy at the PARIS PEACE CONFERENCE, but was unable to secure the territories covered by the 1915 treaty of LONDON, and resigned. In the early 1920s Orlando supported MUSSOLINI, but he resigned in 1925 in protest over the Fascists' tactics (*see* FASCISM). In 1931 he also resigned his chair at the University of Rome rather than swear an oath to Mussolini. Orlando returned to positions of influence towards the end of the SECOND WORLD WAR, when he became President of the Chamber of Deputies in 1944 after Mussolini's fall from power. He served as President of the Constituent Assembly from 1946 until 1947, and was made a life senator the following year.

Ostpolitik (German: 'eastern policy') Federal Republic of Germany's (FRG) policy towards the German Democratic Republic (GDR) in the late 1960s and early 1970s. Associated predominantly with BRANDT, *Ostpolitik* represented a shift in the FRG's attitudes towards the GDR. Whereas previous policy had been based on non-recognition of the COLD WAR division of Germany, including a non-acceptance of the Polish-German border (*see* ODER-NEISSE LINE), and a lack of diplomatic relations with the GDR and any country that recognised it (except the USSR), Brandt attempted to promote a more pragmatic line. This was designed to ease relations, both inter-German and international. The concrete results of *Ostpolitik* included non-aggression treaties with Poland and the USSR in 1970, which also signalled the FRG's acceptance of territorial changes in those countries' favour at the end of the SECOND WORLD WAR, and the BASIC TREATY of mutual recognition between the FRG and the GDR in December 1972.

Ottoman empire African, Asian and European empire ruled by Sultans based in Istanbul (Constantinople) from the mid-fifteenth century. The empire peaked in size and influence during the sixteenth century, but declined throughout the eighteenth, nineteenth and early twentieth centuries, losing much of its European territory (*see* GREEK WAR OF INDEPENDENCE, STRAITS CONVENTION, RUSSO-TURKISH WAR, BERLIN CONGRESS, BALKAN REBELLIONS, ITALO-TURKISH WAR, BALKAN WARS, FIRST WORLD WAR). Alth-ough the empire survived the First World War, it was overthrown in 1923 by Kemal's (*see* ATATÜRK) republican movement. The new republic of Turkey became its successor state.

Ouchy, treaty of (October 1912) *see* ITALO-TURKISH WAR.

P

Pact of Steel *see* AXIS.

panslavism Ideology promoting common interests of all Slavic peoples in Europe, which emerged in the mid-nineteenth century. In the context of growing NATIONALISM, a number of Slav intellectuals began, from the 1820s, to promote the idea of some form of union between Slavs, with language and heritage seen as unifying features. This had anti-imperial implications, as Slavs were spread over the HABSBURG, OTTOMAN and Russian empires: these were clearly expressed in the first Slav congress, held in Prague in 1848 (*see also* IMPERIALISM). However, the position of Russia, as a Slav empire, limited the viability of this movement: while most non-Russian Slavs looked to Russia for leadership in achieving union, successive Russian governments were more cautious. Moreover, the religious differences between Catholicism and Orthodoxy complicated the supposed interests that panslavs believed all Slavs to have in common. The differences between Russian and panslav agendas were underlined in Russia's suppression of the POLISH REVOLUTION (1863–64): and while Russia promoted an apparently panslavist line in foreign policy on occasions, exemplified in its backing of the Balkan nationalities against the Ottoman empire during the BALKAN REBELLIONS and RUSSO-TURKISH WAR in the late 1870s, the ideology was more justification than motivation. Panslavism survived in various forms into the twentieth century, as seen in the BALKAN WARS of 1912–13, although it was diluted by the creation of new Slav nations after the FIRST WORLD WAR. *See* PARIS PEACE CONFERENCE.

Papadopoulos, George *see* GREEK COLONELS.

Papandreou, George (1888–1968) Greek politician. A lawyer and moderate socialist, Papandreou held various posts in the Greek government between 1922 and 1935, before his opposition in the Social Democratic party during METAXAS' dictatorship. He was active in the RESISTANCE in the early stages of the SECOND WORLD WAR, before leaving Greece in 1942. In 1944 Papandreou returned to Greece as the Prime Minister of a coalition government, but military objections prevented this from lasting. He remained active in opposition, and in 1961 founded the popular Centre Union party. He was Prime Minister briefly in 1963, and for a further seventeen months after an election victory in February 1964. However, his inability to solve the *ENOSIS* crisis, and his unpopularity with CONSTANTINE II and the military over his reformist plans, constrained his administration, and he resigned in July 1965. In 1967 the GREEK COLONELS' coup was largely aimed at Papandreou's imminent election victory. The colonels held Papandreou under house arrest until his death in 1968.

Papen, Franz von (1879–1969) German politician. Papen served as a diplomat and an officer before the FIRST WORLD WAR. During the war he served as a military attaché in Mexico and Washington, before returning to Germany. He entered politics in 1921 as leader of the Centre party, and sat as a representative in the Prussian legislature until 1932. In June 1932, he was HINDENBURG's choice as Chancellor, a position he held without a parliamentary majority. During this time he helped to undermine the labour movement, opposition parties, and democracy, particularly through his establishment of emergency rule in Prussia. From July 1932 he worked with HITLER in an attempt to dilute the Nazi leader's radicalism, and used some of his industrial contacts to provide the Nazi party with funds (*see* NAZISM). Papen was replaced as chancellor in September 1932 when Hindenburg rejected his calls for martial law, but returned as Vice-Chancellor to Hitler in January 1933 after helping to persuade Hindenburg to accept Hitler. He survived the NIGHT OF THE LONG KNIVES, but lost his post in 1934, and thereafter served the THIRD REICH as a diplomat: in Austria from 1934 until 1938, where he helped to coordinate the *ANSCHLUSS*; and then in Turkey until 1944. Acquitted at the NUREMBERG TRIALS, he served two years' imprisonment from 1947 after his denazification trial.

Paris Commune (1871) Radical municipal administration of Paris at the end of the FRANCO-PRUSSIAN WAR. In March 1871, German troops entered Paris as part of the preliminary peace settlement that had ended the war. The new French head of state, THIERS, ordered the disarmament of the National Guard in Paris: but this, combined with Parisians' economic hardships, sparked a rising against both the German occupation and the French government. On 18 March, a group of radical politicians and National Guard occupied the *Hôtel de Ville*, and quickly organised elections for a Paris Commune. The Commune was proclaimed on 28 March as the city's governing body, with a membership made up of working- and middle-class representatives from a variety of political groupings: radicals, revolutionaries, socialists, anarchists and conservatives were all evident (*see* ANARCHISM, CONSERVATISM, SOCIALISM). The Commune organised workshops and cooperatives and established a minimum wage, while also organising a military campaign against the government forces based at Versailles: the Germans withdrew to leave the matter to Thiers' government. French troops led by MACMAHON bombarded Paris, and entered it on 21 May, leading to a week of street fighting in which up to 25,000 communards were killed, both in battle and summarily as prisoners. This localised civil war also involved the killing of hostages by the communards, most notably the bishop of Paris. The Commune was suppressed on 28 May, with the loss of approximately 1,000 government troops. 40,000 communards were arrested in the aftermath.

Paris Peace Conference (January–May 1919) International conference at the end of the FIRST WORLD WAR. Opening in Paris in January 1919, the conference was called to draw up the specific peace terms relating to Austria, Bulgaria, Germany, Hungary and Turkey, and to establish some more general structures and principles in international relations for the post-war period. It was attended by delegates from thirty-two different states and a number of governments-in-waiting from new states, but was dominated by the leaders of the four main victorious powers: CLEMENCEAU of France, David Lloyd George of the UK, Woodrow Wilson of the USA, and to a lesser extent ORLANDO of Italy. Wilson was seen as a key figure, particularly as his FOURTEEN POINTS had been publicised before the Conference as a basis for the wider settlement. These countries' governments had diverse agendas at Paris, linked to their levels of involvement in the war and their interests in the geopolitics of the peace settlement. The governments of the defeated countries were not invited to send delegates. The conference met a number of times in full session, with smaller groups working out specific details. The individual peace treaties were signed at NEUILLY, ST GERMAIN, SÈVRES, TRIANON and VERSAILLES. As well as producing these treaties, the Conference set up the LEAGUE OF NATIONS as an agency of international arbitration, and established the principle that the defeated countries' colonies should be taken over by the League and by individual countries as MANDATES.

Paris, Pact of (1928) *see* KELLOGG-BRIAND PACT.

Paris, treaties of (February 1947) Series of peace treaties that ended the SECOND WORLD WAR between twenty-one allied nations and Germany's allies. The peace conference began work in July 1946 on settlements with Bulgaria, Finland, Hungary, Italy and Romania. The treaties were signed in the following February. Bulgaria's 1939 border with Yugoslavia was confirmed, as was its possession of south Dobrudja. Finland ceded Petsamo to the USSR, and was limited to its 1940 borders; while Hungary lost Transylvania to Romania, and was restricted to its borders as set by the treaty of TRIANON of 1920. Italy suffered the greatest losses of the five. Trieste was made a free city, while the Istrian peninsula and the town of Zadar went to Yugoslavia, and the Dodecanese islands went to Greece, while Italy had to give up all claims to African colonies (*see* IMPERIALISM). Romania, despite gaining Transylvania, lost Bessarabia and northern Bukovina to the USSR. The limited territorial settlements reflected both the realities of the Red Army's presence in eastern Europe in the early COLD WAR period, and the fact that the five countries had all fought against Germany in the closing stages of the war.

Paris, treaty of (May 1814) Peace treaty between France and the allies of the Fourth Coalition that ended the NAPOLEONIC WARS. With NAPOLEON in exile after the treaty of Fontainebleau, and the monarchy restored, the treaty of Paris was a relatively lenient settlement designed to promote stability in France. France was reduced to its 1792 frontiers rather than the 1791 model of the treaty of Chaumont, which left Avignon, Savoy and parts of Flanders in France, but meant the loss of all annexed territories in the Italian states, the German states, the Netherlands and Switzerland. France kept some of the colonies gained during the FRENCH REVOLUTIONARY WARS and the Napoleonic Wars (*see* IMPERIALISM), and was allowed to keep the proceeds of Napoleon's looting. The leniency was also evident in the fact that it excluded indemnity, occupation and disarmament clauses. The treaty deferred a final settlement of the legacy of the wars to a congress to be held in Vienna (*see* VIENNA, CONGRESS OF). The settlement was revised by the treaty of PARIS of 1815 after the battle of WATERLOO.

Paris, treaty of (November 1815) Peace treaty between France and the coalition powers of the HABSBURG empire, Prussia, Russia and the UK which settled the 'Hundred Days' phase of the NAPOLEONIC WARS. Due to the ease with which NAPOLEON had regained power, this treaty was designed to be more punitive than its predecessors, the treaty of PARIS of May 1814, and the resolutions of the Congress of Vienna (*see* VIENNA, CONGRESS OF) of June 1815. However, it was still relatively lenient due to the victorious powers' desire for the apparently fragile restoration of LOUIS XVIII to take root. France was reduced to its 1789 borders, thus wiping out virtually all of the territorial gains of the FRENCH REVOLUTIONARY WARS and the Napoleonic Wars, although internal annexations, such as Venaissin and Montbéliard, were left intact (*see* IMPERIALISM). The treaty also imposed an indemnity of 700,000,000 francs and an allied army of occupation until the debt was paid in full, which France achieved in 1818.

Paris, treaty of (March 1856) Peace treaty between France, the HABSBURG empire, Piedmont-Sardinia, Turkey and the UK on one side, and Russia on the other, which ended the CRIMEAN WAR of 1853–56. The Black Sea was demilitarised, and the STRAITS CONVENTION of 1841 restored through the closure of the Straits to warships. Russia suffered territorial losses, with Moldavia and Wallachia returning to the OTTOMAN EMPIRE, and southern Bessarabia to Turkey, while Russia also lost its rights over Orthodox Christians in the Ottoman empire. The Danube was placed under international control with freedom of navigation. As well as these specific clauses, the treaty's significance lay in its underlining of Russia's relative weakness by the middle of the nineteenth century compared to its post-NAPOLEONIC WARS position. The London agreement of 1871 subsequently ended the neutralisation of the Black Sea after a period of relative stability in the region.

Pašić, Nikola (1845–1926) Serbian politician. After entering Serbia's legislature in 1878, Pašić founded the Radical party in 1881, and was exiled for six years from 1883 due to his opposition to the monarchy. He became Prime Minister in 1891 for a year, then served as Ambassador to Russia from 1893 until 1894. Exiled again in 1899, Pašić returned in 1903 and helped to organise the restoration of the monarchy. He served as Prime Minister again from 1904 until 1908, and from 1910 to 1918. During this latter period he helped to secure territorial expansion for Serbia through the BALKAN WARS, but also fell foul of Austria-Hungary, and Francis Ferdinand's assassination in 1914 by Serbs led to the Austro-Hungarian declaration of war. Pašić led a government-in-exile in Corfu, and managed in 1917 to secure an agreement with Slovene and Croat representatives that, after the war, the three nations would unite as the Kingdom of Serbs, Croats and Slovenes under the Serb monarchy. On this basis, Pašić led the unified delegation to the PARIS PEACE CONFERENCE in 1919. He became Prime Minister of the new kingdom in 1921, a position he held (with one small interruption) until 1926, when he resigned over ethnic tensions related to his pro-Serb policies. He died later the same year.

Pattakos, Stylianos *see* GREEK COLONELS.

Peninsular War *see* NAPOLEONIC WARS.

People's Will *see* POPULISM.

perestroika (Russian: 'restructuring') Soviet policy of the GORBACHEV era. In February 1986, Gorbachev began formally to promote *perestroika* alongside *GLASNOST* as a necessary measure to improve the economic and political performance of the USSR. *Perestroika*, as Gorbachev outlined it – most fully in his 1987 book of that same title – recognised that the Soviet economy (and the economies of the USSR's eastern European allies in COMECON) was underperfoming, that there were too many inefficiencies in the country's economic and political systems, and that too many resources were being devoted to a COLD WAR nuclear arms race with the USA. Under the umbrella term of *perestroika*, Gorbachev and his supporters attempted to reform these problems. Although central planning remained integral, a mixed economy was encouraged, along with a greater delegation of responsibility away from the centre in industry, agriculture and party affairs, and the greater use of a meritocratic and democratic system within the Communist party. Alongside *glasnost*, *perestroika* contributed to a climate of change in the USSR and eastern Europe. Its impact upon party systems directly precipitated the unsuccessful coup against Gorbachev of August 1991; and the debates it engendered contributed to the REVOLUTIONS OF 1989–91 and the dissolution of the USSR.

Perpignan, battle of (April 1793) *see* FRENCH REVOLUTIONARY WARS.

Pétain, Philippe (1856–1951) French soldier and politician. During the FIRST WORLD WAR, General Pétain became a national hero for his leadership of the French forces at VERDUN in 1916. The following year he was made Commander-in-Chief of the French forces on the western front. Promoted to Marshal of France in 1918, Pétain remained involved in military affairs after the war, while also developing his interests in right-wing politics. He served on the Higher War Council from 1920 until 1930, saw further action in Morocco in 1925, and served as Minister of War in 1934. In March 1939 Pétain returned from retirement to serve as Ambassador to Spain. He was recalled to Paris in May 1940 and appointed Deputy Prime Minister to REYNAUD, before succeeding to the premiership in June with the aim of negotiating peace with Germany. He then helped to establish the VICHY government in unoccupied France, and served as its head of state from 1940, with virtually dictatorial powers. After Germany occupied Vichy France in 1942, Pétain remained as a puppet figure, and he left France with the German army in 1944. In 1945 he gave himself up to the French authorities and was convicted of treason. DE GAULLE intervened to have his death sentence commuted to a life sentence. He died in 1951.

Piedmontese rising Nationalist and constitutionalist rebellion, 1821. In March 1821 a group of military officers, influenced by the SPANISH RISINGS of 1820–23, staged a rising in Piedmont, with the aims of gaining a constitution and of removing Austrian influence from northern Italy (*see* IMPERIALISM, LIBERALISM, NATIONALISM). In this, the Piedmontese rising can be seen to have had an Italian nationalist agenda as well as a local constitutionalist one. The King of Piedmont-Sardinia, Victor Emmanuel I, abdicated immediately, and his regent, his son Charles Felix, declared his support for the liberal Spanish constitution of 1812. The rising was discussed by the Quintuple Alliance powers at the Congress of LAIBACH; and, in the context of the NEAPOLITAN RISING of 1820, the alliance members authorised HABSBURG intervention against the rebels. In May 1821, Habsburg troops beat the rebel army at Novara, and entered Turin. The constitution was abandoned, and the secret societies which had provided fora for the discussion of liberal and nationalist ideas were suppressed.

Pillnitz, Declaration of (August 1791) *see* FRENCH REVOLUTIONARY WARS.

Pilsudski, Józef (1867–1935) Polish soldier and politician. Born in Russian Poland, Pilsudski was exiled to Siberia for his Polish nationalist activism in 1887 (*see* NATIONALISM). From 1892 he became involved in socialist politics and journalism. He consistently exploited Russian problems in the hope of gaining ground for Polish independence, notably in his attacks on Russian institutions in Poland during the RUSSIAN REVOLUTION 1905. During the FIRST WORLD WAR he raised a Polish legion to fight against the Russians. However, he was interned by the German government in 1917 when it became clear that his main interest after the Russian Revolution of 1917 (*see* RUSSIAN REVOLUTIONS 1917) was Polish growth and independence. On his release he became head of state of the newly independent Poland, a position he held until a constitution was established in 1922. He continued with his military role, leading the Polish forces in the RUSSIAN CIVIL WAR of 1919–20. Pilsudski retired in 1923, but led a military coup in 1926 in protest over the country's democratic failings and political corruption. He established a limited dictatorship, holding the offices of Prime Minister from 1926 until 1928 and again in 1930, and that of Minister for War until his death in 1935.

Pius IX (Giovanni Mastai-Ferretti) (1792–1878) Pope, 1846–78. Elected in 1846, Pius IX began his pontificate with an attitude that suggested sympathies towards LIBERALISM and NATIONALISM in the Italian states, most notably by giving amnesties to political prisoners in 1846, and by introducing a constitution in response to the REVOLUTIONS OF 1848. However, he was forced to flee Rome in 1848 when he refused to declare war on the HABSBURG empire, and he stayed in Naples during the brief existence of the Roman Republic. In 1850 Pius IX was restored with French military assistance, and soon implemented a number of reactionary policies, and introduced a number of conservative doctrines. In 1854, for example, he promulgated the doctrine of the Virgin Mary's Immaculate Conception, while in 1860 Catholics were barred from collaborating with the new Italian government in the former Papal States. Pius IX's reactionary stance was furthered by his *Syllabus Errorum* of 1864, which condemned liberal and progressive political ideologies, and by the acts of the Vatican Council of 1869–70, most obviously its declaration of papal infallibility, which strained relations between Church and state in a number of countries (*see KULTURKAMPF*). In 1870, Rome was occupied by Italian troops and made the capital of Italy when the French garrison left (*see* ITALIAN UNIFICATION), and Pius IX saw out the rest of his papacy without leaving the Vatican.

Pius XII (Eugenio Pacelli) (1876–1958) Pope, 1939–58. Pacelli worked for the Vatican's diplomatic service until his election to the papacy in March 1939. During this time he developed a special interest in Vatican-German relations, serving as nuncio to Bavaria in 1917, then to Germany from 1920 until 1930, when he was made a cardinal and Secretary of State. He negotiated the Church's concordat with the Nazi government in 1933 on behalf of Pius XI. As Pope from March 1939, Pius XII attempted to promote a neutral line during the SECOND WORLD WAR, and was involved in relief projects for prisoners of war: but his failure to condemn the FINAL SOLUTION, added to his pre-war compromises with the Nazis, earned him a great deal of criticism. He failed even to respond to some calls to excommunicate Catholics taking part in the genocide. After the SECOND WORLD WAR, he spoke out against the growth of communism in eastern Europe, and in 1949 excommunicated Catholics who were members of the Communist party. Because of these political issues, Pius XII's papacy has been one of the most controversial of the modern period.

Plekhanov, Georgi (1856–1918) Russian politician and theorist. In the 1870s, Plekhanov was active in the populist (*see* POPULISM) movement in Russia, both in Land and Freedom and, from 1879, in Black Redistribution. He was exiled in 1880, remaining in Geneva until 1917. There, he became attracted to MARX's views on a revolution led by the industrial workforce, and through his writings and his leadership of Liberation of Labour (the first Russian Marxist grouping, founded in 1883), he advocated and modelled a democratic revolution to be followed by a socialist one (*see* COMMUNISM, SOCIALISM). In 1898 he became involved with the Social Democrats, joining the MENSHEVIKS after the 1903 split. Despite the influence of his writings, he remained isolated from LENIN, particularly when the latter advocated a socialist revolution involving workers and peasantry rather than waiting for the democratic stage to have established itself. Plekhanov returned to Russia after the February 1917 Revolution (*see* RUSSIAN REVOLUTIONS 1917), but did not hold enough influence to prevent the BOLSHEVIK revolution in October. He moved to Finland, where he died the following year.

Pleven Plan *see* EUROPEAN DEFENCE COMMUNITY.

Plevna, battle of (July–December 1877) *see* RUSSO-TURKISH WAR.

Plombières, Pact of (July 1858) A secret agreement between France and Piedmont-Sardinia, negotiated by CAVOUR and NAPOLEON III. The Pact committed France, in the event of HABSBURG aggression, to sending 200,000 troops to help Piedmont-Sardinia push Habsburg forces out of Lombardy and Venetia: in return, France would gain Savoy and Nice. Cavour's subsequent mobilisation of the Piedmontese army in March 1859 precipitated an Austrian ultimatum, which set up the opportunity for French intervention (*see also* FRANCO-AUSTRIAN WAR). For France, the Pact provided an opportunity to gain disputed territories and to ensure a say in the future development of a united Italy: in particular, it allowed Napoleon III to show his solidarity with the Papal States. For Piedmont, the Pact brought in the external strength needed to overturn Habsburg interests in the Italian states. *See also* ITALIAN UNIFICATION.

Poincaré, Raymond (1860–1934) French politician. After practising as a lawyer, Poincaré was elected as a deputy in 1887. He held two ministerial posts, that of education from 1893 to 1894, and finance from 1894 until 1895. In 1903 he was elected to the Senate, and after briefly holding the finance portfolio in 1906, he became Prime Minister in 1912, and then President in 1913. His main interests at this time were diplomatic and military, and he worked to strengthen the DUAL ALLIANCE and the *ENTENTE CORDIALE* in case of a war with Germany (*see* TRIPLE ENTENTE). He retained the presidency until 1920, promoting coalition governments during the FIRST WORLD WAR and a hard line on Germany at the PARIS PEACE CONFERENCE. In 1920 he returned to the Senate, and became Prime Minister again in 1922 (while also Foreign Minister), causing economic and diplomatic problems by authorising the occupation of the RUHR in 1923. He resigned in 1924, but returned for his final spell of office as the head of a coalition government in 1926, which achieved some economic and currency stability through emergency measures. He retired in 1929.

Polish Corridor Territory awarded to Poland by the treaty of VERSAILLES, 1919. Before the PARIS PEACE CONFERENCE, the re-creation of an independent Poland with access to the Baltic was part of President Woodrow Wilson's agenda (*see* FOURTEEN POINTS). The treaty of Versailles subsequently awarded a parcel of land, which became known as the Polish Corridor, to Poland. The corridor ran north through Posen and part of western Prussia, with the key German port of Danzig at its end, although the city itself was placed under the control of the LEAGUE OF NATIONS. While this settlement helped to strengthen the revived Poland's status and economy, it was contested in Germany, as it deprived Germany of Danzig, split eastern Prussia from the rest of Germany, and left many ethnic Germans in Polish territory. As such, demands for its restitution became central to nationalist politics in inter-war Germany: it was, for example, specifically targeted by the Nazis as an aspect of the Versailles settlement that should be revised (*see* NAZISM). In September 1939 Germany invaded the corridor as part of its attack on Poland (*see* SECOND WORLD WAR). The area was returned to Poland after the Second World War. *See* ODER-NEISSE LINE.

Polish partitions (1772, 1793, 1795) Divisions of the Commonwealth of Poland-Lithuania by the HABSBURG empire, Prussia and Russia. In 1772, these three used the opportunity created by internal strife in Poland to divide parts of the country between them. The Habsburgs took southern Galicia, Prussia took West Prussia, while Russia took Poland's southeastern region around Witebsk. Russian influence throughout Poland grew at this time. Further territorial acquisitions, which were justified historically by the governments of the respective powers, were made in 1793 after Poland had briefly attempted to assert its independence and introduced a new constitution. This second partition left Russia with gains in Belarus and Ukraine, and Prussia with southern Prussia and the port of Gdansk. A rebellion against this loss was staged in 1794, but its suppression led to the division of the rest of Poland between the three powers. By the third partition of 1795, West Galicia went to the Habsburgs, Prussia took New East Prussia (including Warsaw), and Russia gained Lithuania and Volhynia. This redrawing of the map destroyed Poland, and significantly enlarged the territories of the Habsburg empire, Prussia and Russia. This settlement was partially reversed in 1807, when NAPOLEON created the Grand Duchy of Warsaw, but Poland was repartitioned in 1815 at the Congress of Vienna (*see* VIENNA, CONGRESS OF). *See also* IMPERIALISM.

Polish Revolution (1863–64) Rising against Russian rule in the Kingdom of Poland. Under the rule of ALEXANDER II, some concessions to Polish NATIONALISM were made. In this context, nationalists made further demands through demonstrations that became increasingly confrontational from 1861, and through religious and agricultural fora. In April 1861 over 100 Poles were killed in agricultural demonstrations, and a state of emergency was established in October 1861. Although the Russians made some concessions in 1862, the crisis was precipitated in January 1863 by the introduction of conscription of Poles for the Russian army. The organised rebels, with provisional government structures and strongholds in rural areas, staged a series of attacks on Russian garrisons and columns using guerrilla tactics. Prussia stated its support of Russia in the crisis, and provided some troops to help put down the rising; but while other powers condemned Russian policy, they did not provide practical aid to the rebels. Although the rising spread into parts of the Ukraine and Lithuania, it was eventually defeated in April 1864, with the main leaders executed in August. It was followed by a renewed Russification policy in Poland, which included the abolition of the Polish throne, a policy which showed the fundamental weaknesses of PANSLAVISM as long as Russia was an imperial power. This anti-nationalist policy was mirrored in Prussian Poland. *See* IMPERIALISM, NATIONALISM.

Politburo Abbreviated title of the Political Bureau of the Communist Party, the most senior decision making agency in Russia and the USSR from 1917 until 1952. The Politburo was established by the BOLSHEVIKS during the 1917 Revolutions (*see* RUSSIAN REVOLUTIONS 1917) as a small, powerful body that could make and enforce decisions quickly. Its status was enhanced in 1919, when LENIN established it as a body of five men working above the Communist party's central committee. Under STALIN's leadership its role was reduced, and it was abolished in 1952. Subsequent models of decision making, however, closely reflected the old Politburo model, and the name remained in common usage in the USSR and other communist countries until the REVOLUTIONS OF 1989–91. *See also* COMMUNISM.

Pompidou, Georges (1911–74) French politician. A teacher before the SECOND WORLD WAR, Pompidou served in the French RESISTANCE, and from 1944 worked with DE GAULLE as an economics and education advisor. A member of the Council of State from 1946 until 1954, he briefly left politics to work in banking, but remained close to de Gaulle, and returned as an advisor in 1958. He helped to draft the Fifth Republic's constitution in 1958, and negotiated the end of the Algerian War in 1961. In 1962, de Gaulle appointed Pompidou as Prime Minister. de Gaulle dismissed him in July 1968 after the violent demonstrations of that spring. In 1969, after de Gaulle's retirement, Pompidou was elected to the presidency. His five years in office were characterised by a continuity of Gaullist domestic policies, and by the promotion of economic stability. However, he shifted from his predecessor's stance on the enlargement of the EUROPEAN ECONOMIC COMMUNITY (EEC), and ended the veto on the UK's membership. Pompidou died in office in 1974.

Popular Front Label applied to anti-fascist coalition governments of the 1930s. In

1936, the THIRD INTERNATIONAL promoted the model of 'popular front' as a form of government in which communists could work with socialists, radicals and liberals against FASCISM. This line was seen as a realistic way of limiting fascism and promoting leftist issues. Only two European countries actually established such coalitions: France in 1936, under BLUM, which linked socialists, liberals, and radicals with some communist support; and Spain after the February 1936 election under AZAÑA. In both countries, the governments introduced social and economic reforms, and attempted to limit the activities of *Action Française* and *Falange* respectively. The French experiment was weakened in 1937 when the communists withdrew their backing in protest over Blum's non-interventionist line towards the SPANISH CIVIL WAR: it totally collapsed in the wake of the 1938 MUNICH AGREEMENT and the 1939 NAZI-SOVIET PACT. The radicalism of the Spanish popular front precipitated the military coup that started the Spanish Civil War, and the splits within the government became apparent during the war itself.

populism Russian political movement of the late nineteenth century. Populism emerged as a radical intellectual response to Russia's problems in the aftermath of the CRIMEAN WAR. With a need for significant change evident, most obviously exemplified by the government's EMANCIPATION OF THE SERFS in 1861, populists argued that Russia needed to move towards SOCIALISM, but that, contrary to MARX's model, it could avoid a capitalist phase if the peasants could be mobilised. In order to achieve this, and working under the influence of BAKUNIN and Alexander Herzen, approximately 3,000 young intellectuals moved to rural areas in the early 1870s to live as peasants and offer propaganda, education and guidance. The unsympathetic reaction from the peasantry and the authorities caused the movement to fail. In 1876, leading populists regrouped under the more organised structure of Land and Freedom, which, in 1879, split further into moderate and radical wings, known as Black Redistribution and People's Will respectively. The latter used terrorist tactics to publicise their cause, including, in 1881, the assassination of ALEXANDER II. Although the movement failed, some of its survivors formed the Social Revolutionary party in 1902; while the revolutionary tactics of the People's Will influenced the BOLSHEVIKS.

Potsdam Conference (July–August 1945) Inter-allied planning conference after the SECOND WORLD WAR in Europe. Following the unconditional surrender of Germany in May, the Potsdam Conference was staged to allow the three main victorious allies to discuss post-war developments and future strategies. STALIN and President Harry Truman represented the USSR and the USA respectively, while the UK was represented by Winston Churchill, Prime Minister until late July, thence by his successor, Clement Attlee. On Germany, the Conference agreed to establish a joint Allied Control Commission of American, British, French and Soviet representatives, which would manage Germany in the transition from war to peace, while new democratic structures were developed: these would include revived political parties, the outlawing of NAZISM and FASCISM, legislative and educational reconstruction, and the restoration of local government. Alongside this, Germany was to be demilitarised, and plans were made for leading politicians, soldiers and planners to be tried by a joint military tribunal (*see* NUREMBERG TRIALS). Reparations were to be taken in kind by each of the four allies from its own zone of occupation; and Berlin would be divided into four allied sectors. Beyond the interim management of Germany, the leaders at Potsdam confirmed the western movement of Poland agreed in principle at the YALTA CONFERENCE, thus confirming German territorial losses in the east (*see* ODER-NEISSE LINE). In an effort to avoid the tensions caused by nationalities after the FIRST WORLD WAR, the leaders agreed to arrange and implement the forced migration of ethnic Germans from Czechoslovakia, Hungary and Poland. In relation to the continuing war in the Far East, the Potsdam Declaration was issued to warn Japan to surrender immediately or face major destruction.

Prague, treaty of (August 1866) Peace treaty that ended the AUSTRO-PRUSSIAN WAR of 1866. After the battle of SADOWA, a provisional peace treaty signed at Nikolsburg outlined the main clauses of the peace. This was confirmed at Prague in August. Prussia annexed Schleswig and Holstein, which the HABSBURG empire had gained from Denmark in 1865 after the SCHLESWIG WAR, along with the kingdom of Hanover, the electorate of Hesse-Cassel, the duchy of Nassau, and Frankfurt. The GERMAN CONFEDERATION was dismantled, and replaced north of the river Main by the NORTH GERMAN CONFEDERATION. These changes in the German states greatly enhanced Prussia's strength and territory, and firmly established it over Austria as the dominant German state. *See* GERMAN UNIFICATION.

Prague Spring (1968) Name popularly applied to the reformist policies of DUBČEK's government in Czechoslovakia, January–August 1968. After a period of growing criticism of the USSR's domination of Czechoslovakia, the Communist government began to embrace limited reforms in January 1968 when Dubček became First Secretary. He promoted the discussion of such issues as economic decentralisation, increased political and individual freedoms, and a free media, which were clarified in the party's Action Programme of April 1968. While stressing that the Communist party would still have the leading role, this manifesto called for party and state reforms, decentralisation in industry and agriculture, a federal realignment to improve Slovakia's status, and increased rights of association, speech and travel. This programme proved to be attractive domestically, where it facilitated a growth of political debate, and to some other eastern European governments – notably those of CEAUÇESCU in Romania and TITO in Yugoslavia – as a model for minor reform.

However, it proved to be unacceptable to the USSR. After failing to convince Dubček's government to retrench, BREZHNEV initiated a WARSAW PACT invasion of Czechoslovakia in August. The huge force, composed of units from Bulgaria, the German Democratic Republic (GDR), Hungary, Poland and the USSR, was not opposed, although many Czechoslovakians used forms of passive resistance and obstruction to register their opposition. Up to 200 people were killed. The invasion was justified by the 'Brezhnev doctrine', which asserted the Pact's right to use force to save COMMUNISM in individual countries. Dubček was eased out to be replaced in April 1969 by the more orthodox Gustav Husák. Internationally, the incident increased COLD WAR tensions: the reforms had been welcomed in the west as evidence of communism's decline, and the Soviet intervention was widely seen as an unjustifiable act of aggression. As with the intervention in the HUNGARIAN RISING of 1956, the incident illustrated that one of the Warsaw Pact's key roles was essentially imperial. *See* IMPERIALISM.

Pressburg, treaty of (December 1805) Treaty between France and the HABSBURG empire during the NAPOLEONIC WARS. After losing the battle of AUSTERLITZ, the Habsburgs had to cede ground to France in the subsequent treaty. Due to the scale of France's victory, the treaty went further than the previous treaties between the two countries, CAMPO FORMIO of 1797 and LUNÉVILLE of 1801. The Habsburg empire lost territory, including Venetia, to NAPOLEON's Kingdom of Italy, and the Tyrol to Bavaria, and lost influence in the German states by having to recognise the independence of Württemberg, Bavaria and Baden. The treaty thus consolidated the growing French empire, further undermined Austria's role, and effectively ended the HOLY ROMAN EMPIRE. *See also* IMPERIALISM.

Primo de Rivera, Miguel (1870–1930) Spanish soldier and politician. Primo de Rivera fought in Morocco, Cuba and the Philippines. From 1915, he served as military governor in three important centres: Cadiz until 1919, Valencia until 1922, and finally Barcelona. From here, he launched a successful coup in September 1923 with the support of ALFONSO XIII, and established a temporary military directory in an attempt to stabilise Spain and move it towards FASCISM. This involved the dissolution of parliament, censorship of the press, suppression of the opposition, and the imposition of central control on administrative matters. He was backed by the Catholic Church and the army as well as the monarchy. In December 1925 the military stage was replaced by the civilian directory, with Primo de Rivera retaining personal control through the premiership. His government introduced various public works and welfare schemes, which managed to command some cross-party support and working-class backing, but it gradually alienated the military and the middle classes: and, by the end of the 1920s, the expense of such an interventionist programme undermined Primo de Rivera's rule further. After three unsuccessful coup attempts, he resigned in January 1930 and moved to Paris, where he died three months later. His son Antonio remained active in Spanish politics as a founder of the *FALANGE*.

Proudhon, Pierre Joseph (1809–65) French political theorist and activist. Proudhon worked as a printer before moving into journalism and writing on political theory. He won some fame for his 1840 critique *What is Property?*, and had some brief contacts with MARX. Proudhon played an active role in the French revolution of 1848 (*see* REVOLUTIONS OF 1848). He wrote extensively for a number of newspapers, and won a seat in the Constituent Assembly, but his ideology prevented him from becoming an effective parliamentarian. In 1849 he established the unsuccessful People's Bank as an experiment in free credit and non-exploitative investment. The same year he was sentenced to three years in prison for his press attacks on President Louis Napoleon (*see* NAPOLEON III). He returned to writing and journalism on his release. In 1858 he left France for Belgium to escape another prison sentence, returning in 1862, three years before his death. Proudhon's writings provided the most developed case for ANARCHISM to that date, advocating small-scale communities based on cooperation, the end of money, and the destruction of all forms of authority, to be achieved through agreement rather than revolution. Although his views were rejected by Marx, they remained influential in French socialist, trade union and anarchist groups, and were significant in the PARIS COMMUNE of 1871. His writings also influenced left-wing groups in other European countries, including Spain and Russia.

Q

Quadruple Alliance (November 1815) Cooperation treaty between the HABSBURG empire, Prussia, Russia and the UK, signed at the end of the NAPOLEONIC WARS. Established on the same day as the treaty of PARIS of 1815, the Quadruple Alliance was the continuation into peacetime of the main alliance that had beaten France. The Alliance had two main aims: first, to uphold the treaty of Paris for twenty years, by force if necessary, including the exclusion of the Bonaparte family from the French throne; and second, to provide a forum for the discussion of international issues which were of concern to all members (*see* CONGRESS SYSTEM). The different approaches of the individual powers were obvious from the start, in particular in the UK's resistance to the idea of the alliance powers intervening in any other country, a factor which limited the Congress System's value. The Alliance was renewed, with French inclusion, as the Quintuple Alliance at the Congress of AIX-LA-CHAPPELLE in 1818, and was effectively dissolved after the Congress of VERONA in 1822.

Quintuple Alliance *see* QUADRUPLE ALLIANCE.

Quisling, Vidkun (1887–1945) Norwegian soldier and politician. Quisling entered politics in 1931 after his retirement from the army. He held the defence portfolio from 1931 until 1933, but his dislike of democratic structures, his fear of COMMUNISM, and his admiration for NAZISM led him to establish the electorally insignificant National Unity party in 1933. In

December 1939 Quisling visited HITLER to encourage a German invasion of Norway, and maintained contact with German intelligence up to the invasion in April 1940 (*see* SECOND WORLD WAR). The Germans set Quisling up as their puppet governor in Norway, with the official post of Prime Minister from 1942. Although he had little real influence, he collaborated in all areas, including the deportation of Norwegian Jews (*see* FINAL SOLUTION). Quisling was tried for treason after Norway's liberation, and was executed in October 1945.

R

Radetzky, Josef (1766–1858) Austrian soldier. Radetzky joined the HABSBURG army in 1784, and saw active service in the Balkans in 1788, before serving throughout the FRENCH REVOLUTIONARY WARS and the NAPOLEONIC WARS, fighting at Marengo, Wagram, LEIPZIG and other battles. In 1809 he became Chief of the General Staff, a position he kept until 1829. In 1831 he was made Commander-in-Chief of the Habsburg forces in Lombardy. In this role he was heavily involved in the Austrian suppression of the REVOLUTIONS OF 1848 in the northern Italian states. In the AUSTRO-PIEDMONTESE WAR, having lost Milan after five days of fighting, Radetzky consolidated his troops and moved on to beat the Piedmontese at the battle of Custozza. In 1849 he also led the recapture of Venice, thus reconfirming Habsburg hegemony in the region. He served as the Habsburg empire's Governor-General of Lombardy-Venetia until his retirement in 1857.

Rákosi, Mátyás (1892–1971) Hungarian politician. Rákosi held minor office in KUN's government after the FIRST WORLD WAR, but left Hungary shortly before HORTHY took power, and stayed in the USSR until the mid-1920s. He then returned to Hungary, with Soviet backing, to reconstruct the communist movement, but was subsequently imprisoned. In 1940 he was traded with the USSR for some historically significant flags, and he emerged as the leader-in-waiting of the Hungarian communist movement during the SECOND WORLD WAR. In 1944 Rákosi returned to Hungary, serving as Deputy Prime Minister and as General Secretary of the Communist party. In this role he helped to set up a Stalinist government in Hungary. His influence declined after STALIN's death in 1953, and he was removed from office in favour of NAGY. Rákosi was returned to power briefly in 1955, but his unpopularity was a liability, and he was once again recalled to the USSR in the face of growing dissent that became the HUNGARIAN RISING of 1956. Rákosi remained out of office thereafter.

Rapallo, treaty of (April 1922) Bilateral treaty between Germany and the USSR. During a European conference on economics at Genoa, the Soviet and German representatives met at Rapallo. Building on secret military agreements between the two countries, whereby Germany was re-developing its military infrastructure in the USSR in contravention of the treaty of VERSAILLES, the treaty established full diplomatic relations between the two countries. Germany thereby became the first country formally to recognise the Soviet government. The two governments agreed to abandon all claims for territory and economic losses that were still left over from the FIRST WORLD WAR, and agreed to cooperate with each other in economic matters. The treaty was received with surprise by other European governments.

Rasputin, Grigori (*c.* 1869–1916) Russian mystic. A peasant holy man, Rasputin became an influential figure at the ROMANOV court from 1907. His main appeal to NICHOLAS II and Tsarina Alexandra lay in his apparent ability to stop their son Alexei's haemophiliac bleeding. His influence extended to political and religious appointments, with the Tsarina in particular unable to accept any criticism of his decisions. In 1915, when Nicholas II left St Petersburg to command the army at the front in the FIRST WORLD WAR, Rasputin and Alexandra effectively ruled Russia, making a number of disastrous political appointments and dismissals. Their decisions hindered Russia's war effort, and caused widespread disillusionment with the monarchy and the Church. Rasputin's dissolute lifestyle was widely publicised, and press reports claimed variously that he was Alexandra's lover, and that he was being funded by Germany. In December 1916 Rasputin was murdered by a group of aristocrats.

Rathenau, Walther (1867–1922) German industrialist and politician. After coming to prominence as an industrialist through his family electrical firm, AEG, which he chaired from 1915, Rathenau was appointed to plan Germany's war economy in 1916. He helped to manage labour and the supply of raw materials for the rest of the FIRST WORLD WAR. In 1918 he entered party politics as a founder of the Democratic party, and he became a financial advisor to the new German government. Rathenau served as Minister of Reconstruction from 1921 and as Foreign Minister in 1922. In this post he achieved a number of successes, including the treaty of RAPALLO with Soviet Russia. He was assassinated in June 1922 by a nationalist paramilitary group.

Reinsurance Treaty (June 1887) Bilateral treaty between Germany and Russia. In 1887, relations within the Three Emperor's Alliance (*see DREIKAISERBUND*) deteriorated, particularly between Austria-Hungary and Russia over the two empires' Balkan interests. In this context, BISMARCK established the Reinsurance Treaty with Russia as a way of signalling continued German support and friendship, and as a way of keeping Russia and France apart. The treaty confirmed neutrality between the two powers, with the exceptions that Germany would not remain neutral if Russia attacked Austria-Hungary, and Russia would not remain neutral if Germany attacked France. Germany also committed itself to support Russia's interests in Bulgaria. The treaty apparently conflicted with the MEDITERRANEAN AGREEMENTS of 1887, and it was allowed to end in 1890 when CAPRIVI replaced Bismarck.

Reparations, German (1919–32) Compensation payments established as part of the post-FIRST WORLD WAR settlement. The treaties arising out of the PARIS PEACE CONFERENCE included reparations clauses for the defeated nations. Those affecting Germany, outlined in the treaty of VERSAILLES, were the most problematic. The treaty did not set a figure, but established a Reparations Commission to establish the details. The Commission agreed to charge Germany only for war damage rather than for the whole cost of the war. In April 1921 the Commission established the figure of £6,600,000,000, to be paid in cash and goods over thirty-seven years. Despite the payments aggravating the political tensions of the WEIMAR REPUBLIC, Germany began to pay, but the size of the task created problems: and, as early as January 1922, Germany gained a moratorium on payments. In January 1923, a slippage in coal repayments led to the RUHR OCCUPATION, a crisis which caused the Commission to reconsider reparations. In August 1924, the Dawes Plan restructured the payments: this was based on a five-year period of low repayments, designed to allow investment in Germany, along with a £40,000,000 loan, and a reorganisation of the banking system. This provided some stability, but had to be revised again in 1929 when the higher rates returned. The Young Plan reduced the reparations bill to only 25 per cent of its original total, and spread the payments to 1988. However, the DEPRESSION limited Germany's capacity to pay, and the whole system was scrapped in 1932. In all, Germany paid approximately 12 per cent of the 1921 sum.

Republican calendar (France, 1793–1806) Calendar introduced during the FRENCH REVOLUTION. As part of the establishment of the republic after the fall of LOUIS XVI, the Convention introduced a new calendar in place of the predominant western Julian system. It was designed to reinforce the changes brought about in France since 1789, and to enhance the shift away from religious and monarchist cultural symbols. The Christian numbering system of years was replaced with a new republican one, with the first year of the republic labelled as Year 1. The months were restructured and renamed after features of the climate, while ten-day weeks were introduced to marginalise Sundays. The system was never fully accepted in France. NAPOLEON returned France to the Julian calendar. A number of major events during the revolutionary period, including the Thermidor and BRUMAIRE coups that respectively ended ROBESPIERRE's rule and started Napoleon's government, took their names from the republican calendar.

resistance Umbrella term for opposition within AXIS and occupied countries during the SECOND WORLD WAR. The apparent simplicity of the term 'resistance' disguises the great political differences that existed both among and between different groups, differences that became apparent in the latter stages of the war. However, opposition to German and Italian domination provided sufficient unity in most cases for the duration of the war: clearly, the brutality of the occupations inspired levels of commitment not seen in the FIRST WORLD WAR. Groups developed varying degrees of contact with external allies, most notably the UK, the USSR and governments-in-exile; and different groups were involved in different types of resistance, including guerrilla warfare, acts of terrorism against Nazi officials, sabotage, espionage for external allies, and providing hiding places for escaped prisoners of war and persecuted individuals.

Resistance within Germany and Italy took various forms; and the wartime experiences should not be taken out of the longer-term context of peacetime opposition within these countries, where partisan and democratic expression of political views that differed from NAZISM in Germany and FASCISM in Italy were proscribed. However, forms of resistance specific to the war effort developed during the course of the war, particularly in Germany, ranging from the distribution of anti-war propaganda to the more dramatic attempts to assassinate HITLER. The July 1944 attempt, carried out by plotters within the military, was timed to coincide with a coup and a request for an armistice: but Hitler survived, and the plotters were suppressed. In Italy, resistance to the German presence developed after the fall of MUSSOLINI in 1943, and partisans, particularly in the north, used guerrilla tactics against both German troops and Italian fascists who fought with them: as well as helping to drive the Germans out of Milan and Turin, communist partisans caught and killed Mussolini in April 1945.

In other parts of Europe, resistance developed in various forms, particularly after June 1941, when Operation BARBAROSSA broke the NAZI-SOVIET PACT which had prevented communists from resisting. In France, this was fairly slow to emerge, particularly as the VICHY state provided a semblance of autonomy: but with the growth of DE GAULLE'S FREE FRENCH movement, and the German occupation of Vichy France in 1942, resistance grew. In early 1943, de Gaulle's National Resistance Council provided some coordination. French resistance organisations were used by the western allies during the NORMANDY CAMPAIGN and the NORTH-WEST EUROPE CAMPAIGN. In the USSR, resistance groups emerged in the wake of Barbarossa, using guerrilla tactics to disrupt the German invasion similar to those used by the Polish home army that developed in 1939. In Greece, communist guerrillas fought against occupying troops from 1941 until 1944; while in Yugoslavia, communist partisans under TITO and royalist CHETNIKS under Draza Mihailovic both caused major problems for the occupation.

The actions of these groups were carried out despite the heavy penalties imposed upon individuals involved, and their families and neighbours: in particular, German reprisals for single acts of terrorism or sabotage frequently involved massacres. Also, the viability of individual groups depended to a great extent on external aid, particularly logistical: the British backing of Tito over Mihailovic, and the USSR's abandonment of the Polish home army in 1944, are examples of this. Finally, it must be stressed that differences which were sometimes disguised by the need to concentrate on a single enemy quickly emerged when that enemy was defeated: the GREEK CIVIL WAR of 1944, the suppression of the Chetniks in Yugoslavia, and the struggles between communist and non-communist organisations in France and Italy, exemplify this trend.

Restitution Agreement (1952) *see* FINAL SOLUTION.

Revolutions of 1830 Series of revolutions in various parts of continental Europe, with some common ground in LIBERALISM, NATIONALISM, and anti-IMPERIALISM. The main centres were France, Belgium, Poland, and some of the Italian states. Although circumstances and conditions differed between the separate movements, they did share some common features: in particular, they were broadly middle-class and liberal in origin, and were predominantly concerned with modernising the legacy of the 1815 settlement (*see* VIENNA, CONGRESS OF) in such areas as electoral reform, constitutionalism, economic liberalism and nationalism. While events in different countries can be dealt with separately, it is important to remember that they were mutually influential, and that the imperial powers working against the revolutions, such as the HABSBURG empire, saw parallels between events in different parts of the continent. *See* IMPERIALISM.

FRANCE

The 1830 revolution in France began after the July elections had produced a strongly liberal Chamber of Deputies. CHARLES X and his leading minister, Polignac, rejected the results, and issued the reactionary St Cloud Ordinances on 22 July, which restricted the franchise, overturned the election result, and increased state control of the press. These were greeted with riots in Paris from 27 July, which, by the end of the month, had put the capital in the hands of the revolutionaries. Charles abdicated in favour of his grandson, the Duke of Bordeaux; but the leading politicians of the revolution, including THIERS, TALLEYRAND and Lafayette, worked to bring in the Duke of Orleans as King LOUIS-PHILIPPE. The new king accepted the constitutional nature of the revolution. In mid-August, a new constitution was published, which enlarged the electorate, increased press freedoms, limited the church's political role, and abolished hereditary peerages. This constitutional monarchy, often known as the July Monarchy, lasted until 1848. *See* REVOLUTIONS OF 1848.

BELGIUM

Influenced by the events in Paris, in August 1830 leading Belgian politicians staged a rebellion against Dutch domination of the United Kingdom of the Netherlands, established in 1815. Risings against the Dutch took place in Brussels and elsewhere. The Dutch responded with an attempt at royal mediation without the excessive use of force, although King William did seek military support from abroad during his negotiations. In late September, the States General accepted a separation of Belgium from the Netherlands, and a provisional government in Brussels organised elections to a new congress. In November the congress duly declared Belgian independence, and voted for a constitutional monarchy. Foreign intervention was limited by the London Conference of December 1830, which accepted independence: but the Dutch did not accept this settlement. In February 1831, Leopold of Saxe-Coburg accepted the Belgian throne, and the congress introduced a new liberal constitution. Holland invaded Belgium in August 1831, but was forced back by an Anglo-French intervention: and, in December 1832, Holland finally accepted Belgian independence after the French took Antwerp. The issue was finally settled by the treaty of LONDON of 1839.

GERMAN STATES

In September 1830, influenced by the developments in France and Belgium, nationalist and liberal risings in various states, notably Brunswick, Hanover, Hesse-Cassel and Saxony, led to a series of liberal constitutions. The most radical change came in Brunswick, where the new constitution granted in 1832 addressed many of the abuses of the post-1815 settlement. There was no significant revolutionary activity in the two main German states, Austria and Prussia, both of which promoted something of a reaction in 1832 by legislating against press freedoms in the Frankfurt parliament. A brief rising in Frankfurt itself fed into the formation of a new nationalist group, Young Germany.

POLAND

The Polish revolution was less successful than those of France and Belgium. It began in November 1830 when a group of military officers in Warsaw, backed by students and secret societies, rebelled against Russian domination and established a provisional government which, in January 1831, declared Polish independence. Russia responded with military force the following month: and without intervention from any other powers, and with little popular support within Poland, the rebels were quickly beaten. The Russians retook Warsaw in September 1831, and established a severe anti-nationalist regime.

ITALIAN STATES

In February 1831, under the influence of the French Revolution of 1830 and drawing on older traditions of liberalism and constitutionalism, risings began in the Duchy of Modena, against Pope Gregory XVI in the Papal States, and against Baron Wenklein in Parma. They were led by military officers and other middle-class individuals. The following month, the Habsburgs provided troops to help crush the risings at the request of Gregory XVI. The revolutionary administrations that emerged in many of the cities and towns were unable to cooperate fully with each other, despite a provisional federation as the United Provinces of Central Italy in February 1831, and the risings were easily put down. The longest-lived, that in Romagna, was finally suppressed by the Habsburgs in January 1832. Although these risings failed, they did give rise to a new wave of Italian liberalism and nationalism, most obviously seen in the formation of Young Italy by MAZZINI in January 1832.

In addition to these events, there were also rebellions and risings in parts of Russia, the OTTOMAN EMPIRE and Switzerland, while Portugal and Spain both experienced the start of civil wars in this period (*see* CARLISM). Overall, the varying successes of these revolutions – ranging from constitutionally and internationally guaranteed independence for Belgium to a worsening of imperial repression in Poland – can be explained in part by the attitudes taken to them by other countries. The Belgians needed French and British help, while Habsburg and Russian resistance to developments in the Italian states and Poland respectively limited those revolutions. The events of these years directly influenced later revolutions, most obviously in 1848, and fed into the growing concept of nationalism as embraced by some in the Italian states (*see* ITALIAN UNIFICATION), the German states (*see* GERMAN UNIFICATION) and the Russian empire.

Revolutions of 1848 Series of revolutions in various parts of continental Europe. With a common context in poor economic conditions linked to harvest failures of 1845 and 1846, and in the growth of LIBERALISM and NATIONALISM amongst the middle classes, the main centres of revolution were France, the Italian states, Austria, Hungary and the German states, with smaller risings also taking place in Belgium, the Netherlands, Prague and elsewhere. Although the revolutions were not organisationally linked, events in one country tended to influence events in others: and, as in the REVOLUTIONS OF 1830, the French experience provided something of a model.

FRANCE

In January 1848 the government banned one of a series of banquets organised by reformists in Paris for late February. On the day of the cancelled event, large crowds assembled and erected barricades. After some violent clashes with the army, LOUIS-PHILIPPE abdicated and a provisional government was formed, which duly declared the Second Republic on 24 February. This government introduced manhood suffrage and instituted public works and relief schemes in an attempt to solve the country's unemployment problems. In May a moderate republican government was formed after elections: but when a rising in Paris attempted to push the government into a more radical approach, the government responded by closing political clubs and removing radicals from positions of influence in the police force and National Guard. When, in late June, the national workshops which had been set up in February were dissolved, to be replaced by conscription, widespread rioting took place in Paris. It took four days for the government to restore order in clashes that left approximately 1,500 dead. Despite the institution of the new constitution in November, the revolutionary mood seemed to have passed by December when Louis Napoleon (*see* NAPOLEON III) won the presidential election. Over the next two years he oversaw a number of counter-revolutionary acts, including the suppression of republican clubs, the crushing of riots in Paris and Lyon, and, in May 1850, the restriction of the franchise to about two thirds of its 1848 total. In December 1851 Louis Napoleon staged his coup which ended the Second Republic.

ITALIAN STATES

The anti-imperial, nationalist and liberal movements that had grown since the Napoleonic period in many parts of the Italian states gave rise to a series of revolutions in 1848. They began in January, with anti-HABSBURG riots in Milan and pro-independence risings in Sicily, the latter forcing Ferdinand II to grant a constitution, which he then also applied to Naples. Very quickly, rulers in many other states granted constitutions in response to liberal agitation, including Charles Albert of Piedmont-Sardinia, the Grand Duke of Tuscany, and Pope PIUS IX. In March a revolt in Venice led to its establishment as a republic, while a new anti-Habsburg rising in Milan forced the Habsburg army under RADETZKY to withdraw from Lombardy. The Lombard rebels were then backed by Piedmont-Sardinia (*see* AUSTRO-PIEDMONTESE WAR). These risings inspired some discussion of a unified Italy (*see* ITALIAN UNIFICATION), but differences between politicians in the different states were not resolved at this time. In April, Sicilian rebels declared the island's independence. The counter-revolution began to gain an upper hand in the summer, when the Piedmontese were beaten at Custozza; but in November a rising in the Papal States forced Pius to leave Rome, where MAZZINI declared a republic in February 1849. However, further Habsburg victories in March 1849, followed by French military intervention in the Papal States and the Neapolitan recapture of Sicily in April and May respectively, represented the end of the major risings. The Venetian republic collapsed in August 1849.

AUSTRIA

While Habsburg rule was the target of some of the Italian risings, there were also revolutions in Austria itself. On 12 March 1848, influenced by events in Paris, riots in Vienna led to METTERNICH's resignation. In late April, Ferdinand I granted a moderate constitution: but further rioting in Vienna in May led to the institution of a more far-reaching constitution (which included adult male suffrage) and Ferdinand's departure from the capital. A new Constituent Assembly was formed, which implemented the constitution. In July, Ferdinand returned to Vienna, where renewed riots in August were suppressed. Another wave of discontent surfaced in October in the context of rising prices and internal disputes in the Assembly: and the city was held by radicals for three weeks before the revolution was suppressed with the loss of over 2,000 lives. Prince Felix Schwarzenberg formed a new administration: but while the Habsburgs had survived, Ferdinand abdicated in favour of his nephew FRANCIS JOSEPH in December. He introduced a new moderate constitution in March 1849, but this was dropped in December 1851.

HUNGARY

The Habsburg monarchy was also the target of a liberal-nationalist revolution in Hungary. In March 1848 the Hungarian Diet accepted the demands from KOSSUTH and others for constitutional reform, which led to the liberal April Laws and the establishment of a National Assembly. This body became more anti-Habsburg during the summer, notably by refusing to send troops for the Habsburg army, but it also began to develop its own empire through the annexation and attempted Magyarisation of Croatia and parts of Romania. This provided Vienna with an opportunity to attack the Hungarian revolution, with Austria backing Croatia to invade Hungary in September, and declaring war itself the following month. With Kossuth acting in a presidential role, Hungary enjoyed some successes, and in April 1849 the Assembly declared Hungarian independence. This brief success came to an end in August, when Austria, with the threat of Russian aid, beat Hungarian troops at Vilagos, which led to Kossuth's exile and the collapse of Hungarian independence.

GERMAN STATES

Local and regional revolutions took place in Bavaria and Saxony early in 1848, and in March the rulers of many of the smaller states granted constitutions in the face of reformists' demands and popular risings. Some of the worst violence took place in Berlin, where 250 were killed in mid-March, forcing FREDERICK WILLIAM IV to grant a constitution and allow a constituent assembly. In late March, reformist politicians from a number of states coordinated their efforts and established a National Assembly at Frankfurt (*see* FRANKFURT PARLIAMENT), which met in May and made some attempts to define and establish a unified Germany. In October 1848, Frederick William moved against the radical Assembly, which was closed in December, although he then granted a moderate constitution for Prussia in the following April. The Frankfurt Parliament collapsed in June 1849.

The revolutions of 1848 were highly significant, even though they were relatively unsuccessful in the short-term. By 1851 most of the pre-1848 rulers, or successor members of their families, were back in power: only the French monarchy was never restored. The independence movements in Hungary, Prague, Sicily and Venice all failed; while the liberal constitutions of 1848 were largely replaced by far more restrictive constitutions. The events fed into new forms of CONSERVATISM, which was concerned after its apparent triumphs less with counter-revolution and more with constructing strong economies in individual countries. However, the longer-term impact can be seen in the continued growth of liberalism throughout the rest of the century, in the rapid development of nationalism that led to GERMAN UNIFICATION and ITALIAN UNIFICATION by the early 1870s, and in the rise of SOCIALISM and COMMUNISM which built upon the popular elements of the revolutions in France and elsewhere. *See also* IMPERIALISM.

Revolutions of 1989–91 Series of revolutions in eastern European countries. Circumstances and contexts varied, along with the levels of violence, from country to country: for example, the variations between the 'bloodless' revolution in the German Democratic Republic (GDR) which facilitated GERMAN REUNIFICATION in under a year, the violent conflict in Romania that formed the backdrop for what was essentially an internal coup, and the disintegration of Yugoslavia (*see* YUGOSLAVIA, DISSOLUTION) can be hidden by the liberal usage of the concept of revolutions against COMMUNISM and Soviet IMPERIALISM. However, the shared timing, the changes caused to communist political culture by GORBACHEV's promotion of *GLASNOST* and *PERESTROIKA* from 1985, the presence of common factors, and the dominant themes of anti-communism, anti-Soviet imperialism, LIBERALISM and NATIONALISM, gave the events across Europe a degree of unity. Taken together with the more general disintegration of the USSR and its main imperial agencies, the WARSAW PACT and COMECON, the revolutions were broadly seen to be factors in the end of the COLD WAR.

USSR

Evidence of major changes to the USSR's system became apparent soon after Gorbachev's accession in 1985. Through *glasnost* and *perestroika*, and through developing relations with the USA, his administration embraced reform and revision. This became particularly evident in 1988, when the constitution was reformed to allow for greater democratic involvement, and was accelerated by the growth and effectiveness of independence movements in some of the republics, notably Azerbaijan, Estonia, Latvia and Lithuania. In early spring 1990, after Gorbachev had declared the COLD WAR over, the government abolished the Communist party's leading role. The Union continued to fragment under nationalist pressure in Lithuania, which declared its independence in March 1990, Russia (under YELTSIN's leadership) and the Ukraine. Although the Soviet government used force against Latvian and Lithuanian national movements in January 1991, the republics continued to press for a break-up of the Union, while anti-government demonstrations in Moscow, and Georgia's declaration of independence, also signalled the spread of the revolutionary mood. Although Gorbachev survived a communist coup in August, he became increasingly reliant on the support and sympathy of Yeltsin; and, under mounting pressure from independence movements, and from reformists in government, the Commonwealth of Independent States was established in December 1991 as a successor federation to the USSR. Through this, the bulk of the republics consolidated their independence.

POLAND

The gradual easing of martial law under JARUZELSKI that had been introduced in December 1981 (*see* SOLIDARITY), and the increasing toleration of the Catholic Church (*see* JOHN PAUL II) and Solidarity, created an increasingly reformist environment in Polish politics by the late 1980s. Solidarity became more amenable to the idea of working with the government from 1986, and began negotiations with them in December 1988 after a series of strikes had shown the growth of discontent in Poland. The government legalised Solidarity in March 1989, in time for limited elections in June, in which Solidarity won a significant parliamentary presence. Despite internal splits, this created a base for the premiership of Tadeusz Mazoviecki in July 1989, and the presidency on WALESA from December 1990. In this period, political parties proliferated, causing a degree of electoral confusion by the end of 1991.

CZECHOSLOVAKIA

The revolution in Czechoslovakia was among the least violent. Not only did the country have relatively recent democratic traditions, but the PRAGUE SPRING of 1968 stood as an example of recent liberal and anti-Soviet activism, and informed an increasingly large dissident underground movement. The country's 'velvet revolution' occurred after anti-government demonstrations in Prague and other cities in 1989, which found focus in the oppositional Civic Forum movement. These demonstrations forced the communist government to resign in November 1989. A provisional government composed of communists and Civic Forum members established itself in December, under HAVEL's presidency, which became the basis for a reformist coalition election victory in June 1990. Nationalist and ethnic issues were addressed very quickly, with Czechoslovakia splitting into two nations (the Czech Republic and Slovakia) in January 1993.

ROMANIA

The most violent of the revolutions took place in Romania. Anti-government demonstrations in Timisoara in December 1989 were met by force from the government, with over seventy demonstrators killed. Demonstrations in other cities, and an increasingly radical movement in Timisoara, brought the tensions to a head: and while CEAUÇESCU promised reforms, he was quickly abandoned by his government and by the army, who began to side with the demonstrators. Ceauçescu was subsequently arrested and executed after a televised show trial by reformists within the government working under the title of the National Salvation Front. This formed the basis for a new government, which won elections in May 1990, although the continuity of personnel and approach from the old government suggested that the revolution had been a speedy, pragmatic palace coup rather than evidence of a genuine change of direction. This was illustrated in June 1990, when the government used miners as a paramilitary force against demonstrators in Bucharest.

In addition to these events, major changes took place in Hungary, where the new constitution of March 1989 removed the Communist party's leading role and where an election in March

1990 established a democratic coalition government; in Bulgaria, where constitutional changes created a new electoral system in early 1990, through which the communists, re-formed as socialists, returned to power in June 1990; and in Albania, where constitutional reforms were introduced in January 1990 in response to demonstrations and liberal pressure, and where the new Democratic party won the first major elections, in March 1992. The events in Albania and Yugoslavia (*see* YUGOSLAVIA, DISSOLUTION) demonstrate that the events of 1989–91 were not just anti-Soviet in motivation.

For events in the GDR, *see* GERMAN REUNIFICATION.

Reynaud, Paul (1878–1966) French politician. After serving in the FIRST WORLD WAR, Reynaud was elected as a Deputy in 1919. During the 1930s he held a number of ministerial posts, most notably the finance portfolio from 1938 until 1940, during which time he promoted some economic stability in France. An opponent of APPEASEMENT, he succeeded DALADIER as Prime Minister in March 1940, but resigned three months later when his deputy, PÉTAIN, urged an armistice with Germany. Reynaud was imprisoned by the VICHY government and, from 1943 until the end of the SECOND WORLD WAR, was interned in Austria. He re-entered politics in 1946 in the National Assembly, and served as Finance Minister in 1948 and as Deputy Prime Minister from 1953 until 1954. In 1958 Reynaud chaired the committee which produced the Fifth Republic's constitution. He retired in 1962.

Rhineland, remilitarisation Act of treaty revision by the German government, March 1936. By the treaty of VERSAILLES, the strategic and important industrial area of the Rhineland had been demilitarised: Germany was barred from having any military fortifications, infrastructure or troops in the area, from Germany's western borders with Belgium, France, Luxembourg and the Netherlands on the west of the Rhine, to a line drawn from north to south approximately thirty miles east of the Rhine. The area was also to be occupied by allied troops for fifteen years. This settlement was never satisfactory to Germany: not only did it form a block on internal defence options, but it also left key industrial areas around Essen, Cologne and Koblenz unprotected in any future war. The demilitarisation was confirmed by Germany in the LOCARNO treaties of 1925, although STRESEMANN managed to negotiate an early end to the allied occupation: the last troops left in 1930, five years ahead of the Versailles schedule. In March 1936 the Nazi government took the bold step of remilitarising the area by sending in some 22,000 troops. The act was defended by HITLER as being a necessary defence against perceived Franco-Soviet aggression. Despite the fact that the act broke both Versailles and Locarno, and threatened the founding assumptions of the STRESA FRONT, the remilitarisation brought no resistance from other countries. France was unable to respond without support, the UK did not favour military action, and the Stresa Front and Locarno guarantors were divided at the time over the ITALO-ABYSSINIAN WAR. Fears that armed intervention would have led to a major war thus prevented French resistance. The remilitarisation of the Rhineland was the Nazi government's first territorial revision of Versailles; and French and British failure to react has been seen as a key act in the policy of APPEASEMENT.

Ribbentrop, Joachim von (1893–1946) German politician and diplomat. Ribbentrop joined the Nazi party (*see* NAZISM) in 1932, and was thus viewed as a latecomer by many of his colleagues, but he became very close to HITLER, and helped to manage the negotiations between Hitler and PAPEN that led to Hitler's appointment as Chancellor in 1933. From 1933 he ran the Ribbentrop Bureau as a Nazi foreign affairs unit which worked independently of the foreign ministry, through which he negotiated the 1935 ANGLO-GERMAN NAVAL AGREEMENT. As Ambassador to the UK from 1936, he attempted to persuade the British government of the two countries' common interests. Hitler recalled him in 1938 and appointed him as Foreign Minister, a position he held until the collapse of the THIRD REICH in 1945. His notable successes in this role were the NAZI-SOVIET

PACT of August 1939, and Germany's 1940 pact with Italy and Japan. Later in the SECOND WORLD WAR, Ribbentrop was involved in negotiating the deportation of Jews from Germany's allies (*see* FINAL SOLUTION). He was arrested by British troops in June 1945, and charged on all four counts at the NUREMBERG TRIALS. Found guilty of all charges, he was executed in October 1946.

Riga, treaty of (March 1921) Peace treaty between Poland and Russia. Poland had invaded the Ukraine in April 1920 in an attempt to regain historically disputed territories to the east of the CURZON LINE, hoping that the wider RUSSIAN CIVIL WAR would facilitate a victory. However, the Red Army countered, and regained ground quickly, entering Poland itself and pressing towards Warsaw in August. A provisional treaty was signed in October 1920. The final settlement was made at Riga in March 1921. By the treaty, Russia lost part of its Ukrainian and Belorussian territory as Poland moved its eastern frontier beyond the Curzon line. The settlement was reversed by the USSR's invasion of Poland after the NAZI-SOVIET PACT of 1939.

Risorgimento *see* ITALIAN UNIFICATION.

Rivoli, battle of (January 1797) *see* FRENCH REVOLUTIONARY WARS.

Robespierre, Maximilien de (1758–94) French politician. Robespierre was a lawyer from Arras who entered national politics in 1789 when he was elected to the Third Estate of the Estates-General (*see* FRENCH REVOLUTION). A JACOBIN, he soon emerged as a radical member of the National Assembly and it successors, the Constituent Assembly and the Convention. He was also active on the Paris Commune and as a journalist. He called for LOUIS XVI to be tried after his attempted escape from France, and supported the abolition of the monarchy and, subsequently, Louis' execution. He was also influential in the suppression of the GIRONDINS in June 1793, and became effective dictator of France during the TERROR through his work on the Committee of Public Safety and the Revolutionary Tribunal. Late in 1793, he promoted the Cult of the Supreme Being. His collapse came in July 1794 in the Thermidor coup, when a number of his opponents united, with some popular backing, to denounce his methods in the Convention and order his arrest. He was executed the following day.

Romanov dynasty Russian royal family. The Romanovs emerged as the most powerful royal family in Russia in 1613, and provided all of the subsequent monarchs. The dynasty lost power in March 1917 when NICHOLAS II abdicated during the RUSSIAN REVOLUTIONS 1917.

Rome, treaties of (March 1957) Two treaties establishing European organisations: the EUROPEAN ECONOMIC COMMUNITY (EEC) and EURATOM. The treaties were drafted, with a great deal of influence from SPAAK, following the Messina conference of 1955 on closer cooperation between the six members of the EUROPEAN COAL AND STEEL COMMUNITY (ECSC), Belgium, France, the Federal Republic of Germany (FRG), Italy, Luxembourg and the Netherlands. The first treaty established the EEC as a common trading area for the six signatories and any future members; the second established Euratom as a forum for the common development of atomic energy. The treaties also established the European Commission to administer the organisations, and a European Court to enforce the organisations' laws. The treaties also gave each member country the power of veto over new applicants, and expanded the ECSC's Assembly. *See* EUROPEAN PARLIAMENT.

Rommel, Erwin (1891–1944) German soldier. Rommel served in the German army in the FIRST WORLD WAR. He stayed in the army after the war, and came to HITLER's attention after 1933. In 1940, Rommel successfully commanded a tank division in the invasion of France (*see* SECOND WORLD WAR), after which he was given the command, as a general, of the Afrika Korps, in Hitler's attempt to support the Italian campaign in North Africa. After some successes, he was forced to lead the German retreat from Africa after the battle of El Alamein and the American Torch landings. Rommel served in Italy in 1943 before being appointed, in January 1944, to inspect and strengthen the defences on the French coast in case of an allied invasion. He was a commander in the subsequent German defence against the NORMANDY CAMPAIGN in June 1944, after which he attempted to persuade Hitler to sue for peace. In July 1944 he was wounded in an air attack. In October 1944 he was advised by the GESTAPO that his name had been linked with the assassination attempt against Hitler. He died soon afterwards, probably by committing suicide when faced with the alternative of being convicted of treason. He was given a military funeral, the official line being that he had died of his wounds.

Ruhr, occupation of (1923–25) Incident in Franco-Belgian-German relations. Since the late nineteenth century, the Ruhr had been central to Germany's industrial economy: it was the country's leading coalfield, and housed much of its iron and steel production (*see* INDUSTRIALISATION). In January 1923, after Germany missed some of its REPARATIONS payments to Belgium and France, those countries, under POINCARÉ's leadership, despatched technicians into the Ruhr to seize goods, with troops to protect them. This occupation was condemned by the LEAGUE OF NATIONS, and by the governments of the USA and the UK. The German government responded by ordering the region's workforce to resist passively through strikes and non-cooperation, and withheld further reparations payments. This response aggravated the situation: in the Ruhr itself, the occupying forces punished activists and imported their own labour, thus worsening relations with the local population; while the loss of the Ruhr's resources, particularly its coal, damaged the German economy. This contributed directly to the hyperinflation and high unemployment of 1923. In September 1923 the new German Chancellor, STRESEMANN, restarted reparations payments and ended his predecessor's policy of passive resistance, and managed to broker a conference on reparations as a whole, which led to the Dawes plan. Despite the acceptability of this new reparations scheme, the occupation forces remained in the Ruhr until mid-1925, when an improvement in Franco-Belgian-German relations led to their removal. *See* LOCARNO treaties.

Russian Civil War (1917–22) Umbrella term for series of conflicts throughout many parts of the Russian empire, 1917–22. Immediately after the BOLSHEVIKS gained power in November 1917 (*see* RUSSIAN REVOLUTIONS 1917), some anti-Bolshevik agencies and individuals began to organise armed resistance and plan counter-revolutionary attacks. Labelled as 'White' Russians, these groups drew heavily from aristocrats and imperial military officers. Meanwhile, a number of nationalist and ethnic separatist groups used the opportunity of the revolutionary situation to press their claims for independence; while Russia's deserted allies from the FIRST WORLD WAR, France, Japan, the UK and the USA, also intervened in various attempts to overthrow the Bolsheviks and to reopen the eastern front. Moreover, Germany remained involved in some of the fighting in 1918, particularly in the Ukraine and the Baltic. The single label of 'civil war' thus underplays the diversity of the conflicts involved.

Anti-Bolsheviks began to organise their forces soon after the revolution, establishing strongholds such as those in the Caucasus under KORNILOV and DENIKEN from early 1918, and in western Siberia under KOLCHAK. The Bolshevik government responded by giving TROTSKY the defence portfolio, and allowing him significant resources to fight against the counter-revolutionaries, such as a conscription scheme into the new Red Army in May 1918. In the spring and summer of 1918, France and the UK intervened with warships and supplies through Murmansk and Archangel, while German support for nationalist movements in Finland and the Ukraine aggravated the imperial problems inherited by the Bolsheviks, a situation made worse in May 1918 when Armenia, Azerbaijan and Georgia all declared their independence from Russia. In May the Czech Legion of former prisoners of war also entered the conflict by attacking the Bolsheviks in Siberia and taking control of the Trans-Siberian railway. These rapid but essentially uncoordinated developments gave the Bolsheviks enemies on many fronts, but left them in control of Russia's major cities, its industrial area, and its largest population concentrations. In the summer of 1918 the various White forces gained some ground, and established provisional governments in Archangel and at Omsk, although the latter was suppressed in November. The Red Army then enjoyed successes in the Baltic and the Ukraine, taking Kiev in February 1919, before having to face a new White offensive in the east under Kolchak in March. Soon after this, however, allied support for the Whites began to decline, as France and the UK began to withdraw their forces and supply lines. The Red Army beat Kolchak's offensive in June, but Denikin continued to control parts of the south, gaining Odessa and Kiev in late August 1919 before being pushed back in the autumn. The Red Army also had to defend Petrograd in late September from a Finnish-backed attack.

From here, the Red Army's superiority and the fragmentation of the Whites marked a steady decline of the anti-Bolshevik forces: Omsk fell in November, Kiev in December, Archangel in February 1920, the same month in which Kolchak was executed by the Bolsheviks. The Bolsheviks faced two new challenges in April: a Polish invasion of the Ukraine, which led to the loss of Kiev in May; and a new White offensive, under Piotr Wrangel, in the south. The Poles were pushed back in June and July, with the Red Army almost reaching Warsaw in August before a cease-fire (*see* treaty of RIGA); while Wrangel was beaten in November, with many of the Whites leaving Russia through the Crimea. Fighting continued in the far east into 1921, while the Red Army's invasion of Georgia in February 1921 marked the Bolsheviks' concern with maintaining parts of the Russian empire. The brutal suppression of the Kronstadt mutiny in March 1921 was another Bolshevik victory in their war against the opposition that had developed to their rule.

The Bolshevik victory in the war consolidated their rule, and set the pattern for an enlarged federal republic under Russian hegemony. The new government also managed to regain some of the territory lost at BREST-LITOVSK in 1918, in Belarus and the Ukraine. They managed to achieve it through centralised planning, and through the extensive use of terrorist tactics on the populations of the areas in which they were fighting. The economic policies of WAR COMMUNISM also helped. The anti-Bolshevik forces suffered from divergent interests, aims and ideologies, seen most clearly in the clash between the monarchist and imperial tendencies of such leaders as Denikin and the nationalist agendas of some of the forces which fought for them. In this situation, alliances were extremely fluid and unpredictable. In all, the fighting and related diseases killed some 800,000 people, while the deaths caused by war-related famines, epidemics and terrorist tactics by all sides totalled as many as 10,000,000. *See also* IMPERIALISM.

Russian Revolution 1905 A series of related risings, strikes and revolts that effected some political change in the tsarist system. The internal instability of the Russian empire became apparent in the early twentieth century, influenced by agrarian stagnation, high taxes, poor living and working conditions in industrial cities, and a lack of political reform that could have gone with the growth of an urban society. Rural riots and industrial strikes from 1902 demonstrated the growth of discontent. These problems were exacerbated from February 1904 when the Russo-Japanese war began, as military defeats, conscription and the over-commitment of resources created new strains. From late 1904, pressure for liberal and constitutional political reform was growing in many sectors. The tense situation was aggravated in January 1905 when troops fired on a peaceful demonstration in St Petersburg, killing approximately 1,000 civilians: this 'Bloody Sunday' massacre pushed many discontents into more radical action, as it illustrated a growing gulf between Tsar and people, as well as the government's willingness to use force. A series of strikes and peasant revolts began throughout the country, while nationalist groups in parts of the empire, such as Poles and Finns, also staged risings (*see* IMPERIALISM). The agitation increased through the spring and summer, with many pressure groups forming, such as workers' soviets (councils) in many cities and towns, and the All-Russian Peasant Union. A naval mutiny on the *Potemkin* at Odessa in June suggested that the military might not be reliable. In August, NICHOLAS II confirmed his commitment to reform, but little was done. The pace was forced by a new series of strikes in October, notably a general strike which immobilised the army. Nicholas responded with his October manifesto, promising an elected parliament (*Duma*), as well as general liberal reforms in the areas of religion and the press. The manifesto satisfied some groups, but strikes and demonstrations continued, as did mutinies (as at Kronstadt in October): and in December the Moscow soviet staged a major uprising, which was suppressed in January 1906 with some 1,000 casualties.

Partial solutions to the causes of the revolution came in 1906 and 1907. The *Duma* was constituted, for example, and the Prime Minister STOLYPIN introduced agrarian reforms that brought some change in the rural economy. However, the effectiveness of the Duma was limited by Nicholas' declaration of the 'fundamental laws' in May 1906, which left strong executive power in the hands of the tsar: and new electoral laws of June 1907 limited the electorate. The government also introduced new provincial courts to suppress the risings, which sentenced hundreds of individuals involved in them to death. The short-term gains of the 1905 revolution were thus largely negated by 1907. However, the predominantly disorganised events of 1905–6 did provide experience and models of administration to the soviets, and provided examples of military, rural, ethnic and industrial discontent that were not fully answered or destroyed. While the Social Democrats failed fully to get involved in 1905, despite some agitation and propaganda by LENIN and TROTSKY, the events showed up some of the fault lines in Russia that were relevant in the Revolutions of 1917. *See* RUSSIAN REVOLUTIONS 1917.

Russian Revolutions 1917 Series of events that involved the removal of the Tsarist government and its replacement with a BOLSHEVIK-led Soviet republic. Long-term weaknesses in Russian polity, society and economy had not been solved by the revolution of 1905 (*see* RUSSIAN REVOLUTION 1905), and the subsequent restatement of Tsarist authority had shown that constitutional reform was unlikely. Between then and 1917, conditions worsened for the majority of Russians: urban living and working conditions continued to be poor; and while STOLYPIN's agricultural reforms brought some improvements in the rural areas, landownership was still problematic. These long-term issues were exacerbated by Russia's involvement in the FIRST WORLD WAR, which made massive demands on the population through conscription and high casualty figures: the Russian war dead by early 1917 stood at approximately 1,600,000. The loss of working men through this conflict further dislocated local and national economies, a situation aggravated by inflation. NICHOLAS II's decision to act as Commander-in-Chief in 1915 removed him from Petrograd, leaving Tsarina Alexandra and her advisor RASPUTIN with unaccountable power over ministerial appointments: the instability and discontinuity that these actions caused in government impacted upon the war effort.

This fraught situation, aggravated by food shortages, demonstrations and strikes in Petrograd in early March 1917 brought a variety of tensions more fully into public view: involving workers striking over pay and conditions, women complaining about prices, and, crucially, soldiers and sailors, these popular disturbances elicited a violent response from the government. Taken together, they showed that the Russian economy, as well as its polity, was failing to cope with the impact of the war. However, the suppression failed to deter demonstrators, who continued to take to the streets. In this climate, a committee of the *Duma* established itself as a provisional government between 12 and 14 March. Calling for Nicholas's abdication, this body attempted to use constitutional reform to establish order; while the simultaneous re-emergence of soviets in Petrograd and elsewhere formed a focus for popular revolution. On 15 March, Nicholas abdicated: and when his brother Grand Duke Michael refused the crown, the provisional government under Prince Lvov assumed power. This phase of the revolutionary activities, labelled the 'February revolution' after its timing in the Julian calendar, can broadly be seen as a liberal and constitutional phase. It led to a period of reform, including the abolition of the death penalty, the calling of elections for a constituent assembly, and the freedom of religion. However, the provisional government did not introduce land reform, and committed itself to the war effort, thus leaving two significant causes of discontent in place.

Revolutionary activity continued after the apparent success of the February revolution. The Bolsheviks began to play a significant role, particularly after LENIN's return to Russia from exile in April: his subsequent calls for land reform, an end to the war, and for power to be taken by soviets offered an alternative to the liberal reforms of the provisional government. The growing relationship between the soviets, the Bolsheviks and sections of the armed forces added weight to this alternative. In the countryside, local peasant groups were taking direct action despite the lack of land reforms, with violent disorders and seizures of private land: this process was fed by a wave of desertions from the army as new offensives were organised, which the provisional government attempted to stop by reintroducing the death penalty. In mid-July the Bolsheviks attempted to force the situation by organising demonstrations of soldiers and sailors in Petrograd: these were suppressed with force. The provisional government, under KERENSKY from late July, was weakened by its unclear involvement with KORNILOV's coup attempt in September, and by worsening military conditions.

In late October the Bolsheviks began formal planning for a coup, establishing a Military Revolutionary Committee under TROTSKY. After Kerensky failed to move against the Bolsheviks, they took control of strategic locations in Petrograd on 7 November, and arrested the bulk of the provisional government's ministers. On 8 November this coup was announced to the All-Russian Congress of Soviets, which had assembled in Petrograd and which had a Bolshevik majority. The Bolsheviks, under Lenin's leadership, took effective control, and gained some support with immediate decrees on land reform and peace. By mid-November, after an abortive counter-coup by Kerensky, the Bolsheviks also controlled Moscow and other cities, with further areas coming under their control in December and January 1918. In December, Lenin rejected the model of a coalition government, and quickly established a Bolshevik power base, consolidated by the formation of a new secret police force in December, the Cheka, and by the establishment of the Red Army in January 1918. The Bolsheviks also secured a cease-fire with Germany in late December, although the peace talks proved to be problematic (*see* treaty of BREST-LITOVSK). Bolshevik power was further strengthened in January 1918 when the new Constituent Assembly, which had been established by the provisional government, first met: lacking a Bolshevik majority, it was closed down after one day. Another key change came in March 1918, when the new government moved to Moscow; while the execution of Nicholas and his family in July took the revolution further.

Bolshevik power was far from secure in 1918. The new government faced continued military conflict with Germany, military resistance from disaffected Russians backed by Russia's deserted allies, enormous ethnic and nationalist discontent throughout the disintegrating Russian empire (*see* RUSSIAN CIVIL WAR), internal political factionalism, and economic problems (*see* WAR COMMUNISM). However, the main acts of the revolution were over by then, and the basic structure of the Soviet state was in place.

Russo-Turkish War (1806–12) War between Russia and the OTTOMAN EMPIRE.

Wars between the two empires in the late eighteenth century (1768–74 and 1787–92) had maintained mutual tensions over territories, and had led to some territorial realignments, with Russia gaining the Crimea, and, by 1792, establishing the Russo-Ottoman border at the Dneister and giving Russia navigation rights in the Straits. Russian interest in the Ottoman empire remained, driven by territorial ambitions in Bessarabia, Moldavia and Wallachia, and by ethno-religious links with the Christians in the Ottoman empire. In 1806, Turkey declared war on Russia over the territorial issue. Russia invaded through Moldavia, and gained ground both on the Black Sea coast and far into Wallachia and Bulgaria, capturing Bucharest in 1811. Peace was made at the treaty of Bucharest in May 1812, at a time when Russia needed to concentrate its military resources on NAPOLEON's invasion (*see* NAPOLEONIC WARS). By the treaty, Russia gained Bessarabia, thus extending its Black Sea coastline. Conflict between the two empires was revived during the GREEK WAR OF INDEPENDENCE.

Russo-Turkish War (1877–78) War between Russia, supported by Romania, Serbia and some nationalist groups in the Balkans, and the OTTOMAN EMPIRE. After the Ottoman empire's continued prosecution of its war against Serbia and Montenegro, and its suppression of the BALKAN REBELLIONS, Russia declared war in April 1877. Having assured Austro-Hungarian neutrality by the treaty of Budapest, which promised the HABSBURG empire Bosnia and Herzogovina if Russia won the war, Russia attacked the Ottomans in the Balkans and the Caucasus. The main conflict took place around Plevna, which the Russians and their Romanian allies besieged from July until December 1877 with the loss of approximately 26,000 men. In the Caucasus, the Russians conquered Kars in November 1877. With the Russians advancing on the Ottoman empire's eastern border, and further defeats in early 1878 at Sofia and Plovdiv, the Ottomans sued for peace in March 1878. Peace was made at SAN STEFANO in March 1878, although the unacceptability of this treaty's terms to other European countries led to a renegotiation of the peace through the BERLIN CONGRESS of July 1878.

S

Sadowa, battle of (July 1866) Battle in the AUSTRO-PRUSSIAN WAR of 1866. Although Austria had started the war well by defeating Italy at the battles of Custozza and Lissa, they had not come to a main encounter with the Prussian army. This came on 3 July, when the Austrian army under Ludwig von Benedek was attacked at Sadowa (Könnigratz) on the plain of Bohemia by MOLTKE's Prussian army. Moltke attacked from the north and the north-east, and quickly broke up the Prussian force by attacking its flanks. The battle demonstrated the superiority of some of Prussia's military initiatives, notably the use of railways and the deployment of breech-loading rifles. The battle effectively ended the war, with peace signed at the treaty of PRAGUE in August 1866.

St Cloud Ordinances (July 1830) *see* CHARLES X; REVOLUTIONS OF 1830.

St Germain, treaty of (September 1919) Peace treaty between the allied powers and Austria at the end of the FIRST WORLD WAR, one of the treaties written during the PARIS PEACE CONFERENCE. The collapse of the Austro-Hungarian empire and the HABSBURG monarchy at the end of the war left Austria as an independent republic for the peace terms. Territorially, the treaty confirmed many of the changes that had taken place in the aftermath of the war, but also added some new changes. Austria lost Trentino and South Tyrol to Italy; Bohemia and Moravia to the new state of Czechoslovakia; Galicia to the revived Poland; Bukovina to Romania; and Dalmatia, Slovenia, Bosnia and Herzegovina to the new Kingdom of the Serbs, Croats and Slovenes. Hungarian independence was also confirmed; while Carinthia was subject to a plebiscite, in which it gained a pro-Austrian majority in 1920. Austria was thus greatly reduced territorially, demographically, and industrially. The treaty barred *ANSCHLUSS* with Germany (a proscription which was mirrored in the treaty of VERSAILLES), reduced the Austrian army to a maximum of 30,000, and imposed reparations payments. As with the treaty of Versailles, the treaty of St Germain exacerbated many territorial issues in the region, not least the ceding of territory to Czechoslovakia that became the focus for German agitation. *See* MUNICH AGREEMENT.

St Petersburg Protocol (April 1826) *see* GREEK WAR OF INDEPENDENCE.

St Vincent, Cape, battle of (February 1797) *see* FRENCH REVOLUTIONARY WARS.

Sakhgaria River, battle of (August 1921) *see* GREEK-TURKISH WAR.

Salamanca, battle of (July 1812) *see* NAPOLEONIC WARS.

Salazar, Antonio (1889–1970) Portuguese politician. After lecturing in economics, Salazar was appointed Finance Minister in Antonio Carmona's military government in 1926. He resigned when his requests for special powers were rejected, but resumed office in 1928 with a freer hand. Through this post he imposed some stability on the Portuguese economy, for which he achieved popularity (*see also* DEPRESSION, GREAT). In 1932 Carmona made him Prime Minister, and the following year Salazar, with military and Church backing, introduced a new fascist-style constitution, declaring the 'New State' (*Estada Novo*) (*see* FASCISM). Salazar combined the premiership with other posts, including defence from 1936 until 1944, and foreign affairs from 1936 until 1947. He provided some assistance to the nationalist rebels in the SPANISH CIVIL WAR, but ensured Portuguese neutrality during the SECOND WORLD WAR. Salazar was convinced of Portugal's need for an empire, and committed troops to the defence of Angola and Mozambique in colonial wars that outlived him (*see* IMPERIALISM). He suffered a stroke in 1968, and died in office in 1970.

San Stefano, treaty of (March 1878) Peace treaty between Russia and the OTTOMAN EMPIRE that ended the RUSSO-TURKISH WAR of 1877–78. Russia used the opportunity provided by the peace treaty to attempt to reshape the Balkans in Russian interests. Russia gained a larger Black Sea coastline through territorial gains in the Caucasus and in Bessarabia. Austria-Hungary was offered protection rights over Bosnia and Herzegovina, which had been agreed secretly before the war started. But Russia broke with its pre-war promises by restructuring Bulgaria into a large state: stretching from the Black Sea into Macedonia, and as far south as the Aegean coastline, and designated to be occupied by Russia for two years, this was clearly an attempt to circumvent the problematic Straits (*see* STRAITS CONVENTION). The treaty also gave most of Dobrudja to Romania, and enlarged independent Serbia and Montenegro. As well as causing some concern in the Balkans, the treaty was unacceptable to Austria-Hungary and the UK, and Russia was forced to renegotiate the area at the BERLIN CONGRESS in July. The Berlin settlement superseded San Stefano.

Schacht, Hjalmar (1877–1970) German politician and banker. Schacht entered politics in 1919 as a co-founder of the Democratic party. In 1923 STRESEMANN appointed him to solve the inflation crisis (*see* REPARATIONS, WEIMAR REPUBLIC), which he did through the introduction of the *Rentenmark*. This success earned him the presidency of the Reichsbank, from where he negotiated the Dawes plan. He resigned in 1929. Schacht moved to the right politically in the later 1920s, and joined the Nazi party in 1930. In 1933 Hitler reappointed him to the Reichsbank, and in 1934 made him Minister of Economics, giving him an involvement in managing the rearmament programme, public works schemes and bilateral trade links. In 1937 Schacht resigned his ministerial post, although he retained his Reichsbank position until 1939. During the SECOND WORLD WAR Schacht gradually moved away from Hitler, and he was imprisoned in 1944. Schacht was acquitted at the NUREMBERG TRIALS, but served a two-year prison sentence imposed by a denazification court. After his release he returned to banking.

Schleswig War (1864) War between the HABSBURG empire and Prussia against Denmark over the disputed territories of Schleswig and Holstein. After the Vienna settlement of 1815 (*see* VIENNA, CONGRESS OF), Schleswig (with a mainly Danish population) and Holstein (predominantly German) had remained under Danish rule, although Holstein was incorporated in the GERMAN CONFEDERATION. Anti-Danish risings in the provinces during the REVOLUTIONS OF 1848 precipitated Prussian intervention: and the subsequent 1852 treaty of LONDON, which left both duchies with some autonomy in union with Denmark, failed to provide a permanent solution to the dispute. In 1864 King Christian IX of Denmark, whose succession had been disputed by Germans, authorised the annexation of Schleswig, which contravened the 1852 settlement. In February the Habsburg empire and Prussia jointly declared war on Denmark, and invaded. The Danish army was beaten at Duppel in April, and defeated in July. In June, a conference in London had proposed various models for the future administration of the territories, which fed into the treaty of Vienna (*see* VIENNA, TREATY OF) in October 1864, and the convention of Gastein (*see* GASTEIN, CONVENTION OF) in August 1865.

Schlieffen, Alfred von *see* SCHLIEFFEN PLAN.

Schlieffen Plan German army's strategic plan, developed and revised between 1895 and 1905 by the Chief of General Staff, Alfred von Schlieffen. After the FRANCO-RUSSIAN ALLIANCE of 1894, Schlieffen began to develop a plan to allow Germany to fight on two fronts. Assuming that any continental war with contemporary weaponry would be over very quickly, Schlieffen advocated a reversal of orthodox thinking which prioritised Russia, by calling for a quick offensive war against France. This would be carried out by major attacks through Belgium, Luxembourg and the Netherlands, which would bypass the Franco-German border defences, while a minor attack was staged through Alsace to draw the main French resistance. The northernmost army would then pass to the west of Paris before turning east and north again to meet with the other armies, thus cutting the capital off. With France defeated in six weeks before Russia would have fully mobilised, Germany would then be able to concentrate on the east. The plan influenced German defence policies from the late 1890s. Its disregard for the neutrality of Belgium, Luxembourg and the Netherlands was not seen to be problematic for the military. When the FIRST WORLD WAR started in August 1914, Germany's unsuccessful western offensive incorporated some key elements of the Schlieffen Plan.

Schumann Plan *see* EUROPEAN COAL AND STEEL COMMUNITY.

Second Coalition *see* NAPOLEONIC WARS.

Second Empire (France) System of government in France, 1852–70. Following his coup of December 1851 and the subsequent plebiscite which confirmed him as president for ten years, Louis Napoleon (*see* NAPOLEON III) developed a new constitution, which was published in January 1852. This set up the framework of an authoritarian state, with a senate, councils of states, and an elected but relatively powerless legislative body, under a powerful presidency. In February 1852, Louis Napoleon re-introduced press censorship and removed the Orleanist family from France; and in November he oversaw the introduction of an empire, with himself as Emperor, for which he assumed the title Napoleon III. The first eight years of the Second Empire were characterised by this conservative and reactionary start to the period, with the army and the Catholic Church promoted, and political opponents subject to punishment without trial. Napoleon III also pursued an adventurous foreign policy throughout the period, as exemplified by the CRIMEAN WAR, French involvement in ITALIAN UNIFICATION, and an unsuccessful and embarrassing imperial war in Mexico. From 1859 France became markedly more liberal, in response to the growth of opposition (particularly after the 1863 elections) and developments in the economic sphere (*see* INDUSTRIALISATION). In this period the government oversaw the development of commerce, banking, industry, agriculture and the railways, while education was also improved. The political system gradually became more representative and inclusive, with the publication of debates from 1860, ministers being open to question from 1867, the ending of press censorship in 1868, the introduction of a parliamentary system in 1869, and the publication of a more liberal constitution in 1870. The Empire was overturned as a result of France's defeat in the FRANCO-PRUSSIAN WAR of 1870–71: when Napoleon III was captured at Sedan in September 1870, politicians in Paris abandoned the imperial constitution and declared a new republic. *See* THIRD REPUBLIC.

Second International International federation of socialist and labour organisations (*see* SOCIALISM). It was formed in Paris in 1889 as forum for groups in different countries to discuss ideologies and strategies. It gained a genuinely international membership, with parties from Africa and Australasia joining alongside European organisations. From 1900, when the International Socialist Bureau was formed, it had an administrative section. As with the International Working Men's Association (*see* FIRST INTERNATIONAL), the diversity of the Second International's composition meant that it had little internal stability, and some significant splits emerged, such as those between anarchists (*see* ANARCHISM) and socialists, between parties from imperial countries and those from colonies, and between internationalists and nationalists. The International advocated the boycotting by socialists of coalition governments formed by non-socialist parties, although some members saw such cooperation to be a useful step in gaining power and experience. In 1904 there were splits evident over BERNSTEIN's model of gradualism; and from 1907, over the position that socialists should take in time of war. The International effectively dissolved in July 1914, but was reformed in 1923 and again in 1951 as a forum for parties and organisations throughout the world, although the Soviet-run THIRD INTERNATIONAL took on some of its functions.

Second World War (1939–45) Multinational global conflict, in which the main protagonists were the AXIS partners Germany, Italy, Japan and their allies (including, effectively, the USSR until 1941) against the allied powers of France, the UK and its empire, the USA (from 1941), and their allies, particularly the USSR from 1941. In addition, a number of other alliances and interventions developed around these core combatants.

The conflict was rooted in a number of areas. Traditional quests for increased power in Europe and beyond were exacerbated by the settlement that had ended the FIRST WORLD WAR. The territorial aspects of the various peace treaties of 1918–20, including VERSAILLES, ST GERMAIN and BREST-LITOVSK, left strained international relations over territories throughout Europe. The need to revise the treaties that had affected Germany and the Germans was a major cause for the Nazis (*see* NAZISM), and HITLER consistently called for their revision so that Germany could rearm and regain lost territories and acquire *LEBENSRAUM*. This tense situation was exacerbated by a number of factors, including the failure of the LEAGUE OF NATIONS to prevent aggression, the rise of COMMUNISM and FASCISM as apparently oppositional ideologies, and the long-term failure of APPEASEMENT to prevent war rather than simply defer it.

Conventionally, the war is seen to have started in September 1939, with the German invasion of Poland and the subsequent declarations of war on Germany by France and the UK under the terms of their March 1939 guarantee to Poland. However, this date overlooks the conflict between Japan and China, which began in full in 1937, and, within Europe, the German invasion of the bulk of Czechoslovakia in March 1939 (*see* MUNICH AGREEMENT), and the Italian invasion of Albania in April. However, the Polish invasion, secured for Germany by the NAZI-SOVIET PACT, made the war continental in scope. Using *BLITZKRIEG* techniques, Germany conquered western Poland by the end of September; while the Soviet invasion of eastern Poland in mid-September led to the country's partition roughly along the CURZON LINE at the end of the month. This division was followed by oppressive military rule in both parts of the country. In November the war spread to the Baltic states with the USSR's successful invasion of Finland: Estonia, Latvia and Lithuania were subsequently invaded in June 1940. In April 1940, Germany turned its attention to the west by invading Denmark and Norway, followed by Belgium and the Netherlands in May. The former campaign was designed to secure the North Sea and to guarantee iron ore supplies; the latter to gain access to the English Channel and to set up an invasion of France which outflanked the MAGINOT LINE. After British and other allied troops escaped to the UK from Dunkirk in late May and early June, the German campaign against France led to the collapse of the THIRD REPUBLIC and France's surrender in late June. The country was divided between an occupied zone and the German-backed French government based at VICHY. With Italy declaring war on France and the UK in June, this stage of the war in western Europe ended with the UK isolated, albeit with imperial resources to call on. However, German plans for an invasion of the UK failed when the aerial campaigns of the battle of Britain between June and September 1940 failed to give Germany the necessary superiority. The planned invasion, Operation Sealion, was called off in October: although naval and submarine activity in the Atlantic from 1940 was designed to disrupt the UK's supply routes from the USA. Moreover, the aerial bombing of cities and towns throughout the UK maintained German pressure.

In eastern Europe and the Balkans, further developments in 1940 included the division of Romania between the USSR and Germany between June and October, and the Italian invasion of Greece in October: Italy also extended its African commitments at this stage, although defeats here in December 1940 and January 1941 led to German assistance under ROMMEL. German interests in the Balkans in support of its partner also led to its invasion of Greece and Yugoslavia in April; while British interests led to their supply of men and resources to Greece, and a British build-up of troops in north Africa.

The next decisive stage of the war began in June 1941 when Germany invaded the USSR in Operation BARBAROSSA. While the breaking of the 1939 pact was not a surprise, the timing of the attack was: and, with support from Finland, Hungary and Romania, Germany's invasion of Belorussia, Lithuania and the Ukraine led to early successes which helped to provide further economic gains for Germany. The USSR immediately allied with the UK, providing a source of supplies. Along with the German conquest of Poland, Barbarossa was heavily influenced by Nazi racial policy as well as by more traditional assumptions on territorial gains, and the first mass killings of Jews and other civilians took place under the umbrella of this campaign. *See* FINAL SOLUTION.

The war became global in December 1941 when Japan attacked both the US naval base at Pearl Harbor in Hawaii, and British holdings in Malaya. The UK and the USA immediately declared war on Japan, which was followed by Japan's partners Germany and Italy declaring war on the USA. The implication of these developments for the European conflict was that, as in 1917, the USA became directly involved in the continental war, leading to its supply of troops, resources and equipment which were influential in subsequent campaigns in north Africa, Italy and western Europe. The USA also provided supplies for the USSR, an arrangement formalised in May 1942.

Axis dominance began to slip in 1942, influenced by allied bombing raids on German towns and cities, the defeat of Axis forces in north Africa in November, and the start of the successful Soviet counter-attack at STALINGRAD in the same month. German withdrawals from Soviet territory began, a defeat hastened by Soviet success at KURSK. In July 1943 allied landings in Sicily (*see* CASABLANCA) marked the start of the ITALIAN CAMPAIGN, which forced MUSSOLINI's deposition in July and, after landings on the mainland in September, the defeat of Italy, which resulted in Italy joining the allies against Germany. This second continental front was, however, slowed down by the German defensive campaign throughout the peninsula. With the Red Army gaining ground throughout conquered Soviet territory into 1944, and the long-running siege of Leningrad ending in January 1944, Germany was under increasing pressure. This was exacerbated by defeats on various fronts in 1944: in Italy, where Rome fell to the allies in June; in the east, with the Soviet invasion of Romania in April and Yugoslavia in October and British successes in Greece; and in the west, where the NORMANDY CAMPAIGN of June 1944 established a bridgehead for the invasion of France, the Low Countries and Germany itself (*see* NORTH-WEST EUROPE CAMPAIGN). Despite the German counter-attack in the Ardennes from December 1944, a German defeat was imminent: the advance of well supplied forces from all sides, the loss of resources, and the loss of allies (such as Hungary in February 1945) left Germany with few opportunities. Moreover, Nazi rhetoric in favour of a fight to the end, and allied policy from Casablanca in 1943 of fighting on until Germany surrendered unconditionally, ensured that the conflict continued into the streets of Berlin itself. Hitler's suicide on 30 April 1945 heralded the end, with his successor DÖNITZ formally authorising the surrender on 7 May. In the Far East, the war continued until the Japanese surrender in mid-August 1945, hastened by the USA's use of two atomic bombs. Peace was settled between the allies and Germany's European allies in the 1947 treaties of PARIS, between the western allies and Germany in 1951, between the USSR and Germany in 1955, and with Austria in 1955 (*see* AUSTRIAN STATE TREATY). Final outstanding issues that were complicated by Germany's post-war division into two states were settled after GERMAN REUNIFICATION in 1990.

The Second World War was the most expensive and the most bloody in history. Apart from the massive costs borne by all combatant nations, the human costs were unprecedented. Statistics of the casualty rates vary between different sources, but approximate figures of 50,000,000 people killed in the war, or died as a result of injuries, are broadly used. In Europe the casualty rates for a number of nations demonstrate the war's impact: the USSR, for example, lost somewhere between 7,000,000 and 13,000,000 military personnel, and up to 8,000,000 civilians; over 2,000,000 Polish civilians were killed; while German military losses were over 3,000,000. The extensive use of aerial bombardment of civilian areas, as well as mass killings linked to Nazi racial policy, allowed for these figures. Moreover, the movements of refugees and prisoners, and the territorial settlements which arose out of the war, caused extensive demographic dislocation, such as the 6,000,000 Germans who moved from Poland to Germany (*see* ODER-NEISSE LINE), the 500,000 Ukrainians leaving Poland for the Ukraine by 1947, and the million or so 'displaced persons' who left Germany for Israel, the UK, France and the Americas after the war. Moreover, despite the allies' common cause against Germany, their different views on the peacetime settlement for Europe helped to create fault lines in the alliance (*see* TEHRAN CONFERENCE, YALTA CONFERENCE, POTSDAM CONFERENCE): these became more pronounced once occupation troops were located in the various countries re-taken from Germany. *See* COLD WAR.

secret police *see* GESTAPO; KGB; NKVD.

Sedan, battle of (September 1870) *see* FRANCO-PRUSSIAN WAR.

Sevastopol, siege of (September 1854–September 1855) *see* CRIMEAN WAR.

Sèvres, treaty of (August 1920) Peace treaty between the allied powers and Turkey at the end of the FIRST WORLD WAR, one of the treaties written during the PARIS PEACE CONFERENCE. Territorially, Greece gained parts of Anatolia and Eastern Thrace, while many middle eastern areas, including Iraq, Palestine and Lebanon, were made MANDATES through the LEAGUE OF NATIONS. The treaty also limited Turkey's military capability by demilitarising the Dardanelles and the Bosphorous and placing them under international control, and by reducing the size of Turkey's armed forces. The treaty was rejected by many in Turkey, including the parliament, and directly led to Kemal's (*see* ATATÜRK) armed struggle against the territorial losses (*see* GREEK-TURKISH WAR). After the nationalists' successes, the Chanak crisis, and the establishment of the new Turkish republic, the settlement was renegotiated and replaced by the treaty of LAUSANNE in 1923.

Sieyès, Emmanuel (1748–1836) French priest and politician. Sieyès helped to focus the political and constitutional debates that surrounded LOUIS XVI's summoning of the Estates-General for 1789 with two pamphlets, notably *What is the Third Estate?*. He was elected as a member of the Third Estate for the 1789 meeting of the Estates-General, and helped to shift that meeting's attention away from the royal agenda by calling for the estates to meet together or not at all, and in drafting the Tennis Court Oath (*see* FRENCH REVOLUTION). During the constitutional monarchy he played a leading role in administrative matters in the Constitutional Assembly, and helped to draft the Declaration of the Rights of Man and the Citizen. He was a member of the Convention, and, after Thermidor, of the Committee of Public Safety. Under the Directory, he was a member of the Council of 500, and, after a spell as France's Ambassador to Berlin, was elected to the position of Director in 1799. It was from this position that he helped to engineer NAPOLEON's successful coup of BRUMAIRE (November 1799) and to establish the Consulate. Under the Empire he was created a Count, and served on the Senate. He was exiled in 1814, but returned to France in 1830 under LOUIS-PHILIPPE.

Sikorski, Wladyslaw (1881–1943) Polish soldier and politician. After studying engineering, Sikorski fought against Russia with PILSUDSKI in the FIRST WORLD WAR, but was interned by the Germans for his Polish nationalist agenda. He fought in the defence of Warsaw during the RUSSIAN CIVIL WAR, and was made Chief of the General Staff in 1921. He was briefly Prime Minister from December 1922 until May 1923, but his influence declined under PILSUDSKI's government as he was seen as too liberal. In 1939 he returned to the premiership briefly after the German invasion (*see* SECOND WORLD WAR), but then left Poland for France and the UK, taking an army and a government-in-exile with him. He worked well with the British authorities, and also made some links with the USSR, including an agreement in July 1941, but these relations were destroyed by the revelation of the KATYN MASSACRE. Sikorski was killed in an air crash in Gibraltar in 1943.

Single European Act (December 1986) Legislation adopted by all member nations of the EUROPEAN COMMUNITY (EC). As the EC grew in size through new accessions in 1973, 1981 and 1985, and extended its remit and responsibilities through the work of the EUROPEAN PARLIAMENT, the Council of Ministers and other agencies, pressure grew within the EC for some form of standardising legislation that would bind all member states to common aims. Moreover, a common law was seen as a way of focusing the development of a single market, one of the key aims of the 1957 treaty of ROME which established the EUROPEAN ECONOMIC COMMUNITY (EEC), but which had not been introduced. The Single European Act, signed by all member states in December 1986, attempted to address these issues. Under the act, 1992 was set as the target for the introduction of the single market, with all internal tariffs and obstacles to the flow of capital, labour and investment to be removed by then. The act also changed the voting procedures of the Council of Ministers and the European Parliament, and committed members to work towards closer political union. *See* EUROPEAN UNION.

Six Weeks War *see* AUSTRO-PRUSSIAN WAR.

socialism Political and economic ideology. With precedents from at least the seventeenth century, socialism emerged in the later stages of the FRENCH REVOLUTION, and, more formally, in the first decades of the nineteenth century. It was an ideology very closely related to the changing economic context of INDUSTRIALISATION, and while it developed into a number of strands, they all had common ground in the context of urban working-class culture and its economic corollaries. As such, it was underpinned by ideas of community and cooperation, and by the assumption that humans could live harmoniously together if societies recognised differences in need and abilities, and organised themselves on collective lines so that all members could have basic equalities. One of the earliest strands to emerge was utopian, advocated by Charles Fourier, Robert Owen and PROUDHON (and thus related to ANARCHISM); while, particularly in the 1840s, a more practical and radical strand emerged, advocating revolutions in order to achieve socialism, a tradition identified with MARX and ENGELS. This was supplemented in the later nineteenth century by a parliamentary and evolutionary approach to socialism, associated with BERNSTEIN, which reflected the growth of socialist parties throughout Europe, and recognised the pragmatic value of their gaining power through cooperation with existing structures. The different approaches to socialism were evident in the debates of the SECOND INTERNATIONAL, formed in 1889. During and immediately after the FIRST WORLD WAR, socialism became essentially a moderate left-wing ideology: not only were many of its basic assumptions being appropriated by liberals and even conservatives in many countries, but the BOLSHEVIKS' successes (*see* RUSSIAN REVOLUTIONS 1917) had shown COMMUNISM as a more radical ideology. Socialism thus gained parliamentary and governmental respectability in most European countries throughout the twentieth century, although it suffered a decline in the 1980s and 1990s, both through the emergence of a new CONSERVATISM, and through the collapse of communism in the REVOLUTIONS OF 1989–91.

Solferino, battle of (June 1859) *see* FRANCO-AUSTRIAN WAR.

Solidarity (*Solidarnosc*) Polish trade union and political movement. Solidarity was formed in the Gdansk dockyards in late 1980 as a focus for free trade unionism and political protests that had developed throughout Poland that year over food prices and other political and economic issues. Its leader, the Gdansk electrician WALESA, became a national figure, and helped to negotiate a number of political, economic and religious reforms with the Polish government. In December 1981, however, when faced with a potential BREZHNEV doctrine-inspired invasion of Poland, President JARUZELSKI's declaration of martial law included the proscription of Solidarity and the imprisonment of its leadership. Solidarity remained active as an underground organisation during the last years of communist rule in Poland, and began to re-emerge during the late 1980s. The government dropped the ban on Solidarity in 1989 (*see* REVOLUTIONS OF 1989–91) and its candidates were successful in the elections of that June. Solidarity declined in influence after the fall of communism, although Walesa went on to become President.

Somme, battle of (July–November 1916) FIRST WORLD WAR battle on the river Somme. Planned as a Franco-British offensive by generals Haig and JOFFRE, the attack on the German trenches along the Somme was designed to dilute the German campaign at VERDUN. It began with a week-long artillery bombardment on the German lines, followed by infantry attacks. However, the German machine-gun positions were left largely intact, and approximately 19,000 allied troops were killed on the first day of fighting. With tanks introduced in September, along with new infantry attacks, the allies managed to gain approximately ten miles of territory by November before the battle ended. However, this involved no significant strategic gains. The allies suffered approximately 615,000 casualties, the Germans 500,000. The Somme was also the scene of a German offensive in March 1918.

Spaak, Paul-Henri (1899–1972) Belgian politician. A lawyer, Spaak entered Belgian politics in 1932 as a socialist deputy. He served as Prime Minister from 1938 until 1939, and moved to London as Foreign Minister for the Belgian government-in-exile during the SECOND WORLD WAR. In this post he helped to establish the BENELUX UNION. Spaak served as President of the UNITED NATIONS' first general assembly in 1946 before returning to Belgian politics as Prime Minister again from 1947 until 1949. He continued to combine his national and international roles, presiding over the Assembly of the COUNCIL

OF EUROPE from 1949 until 1951, before taking Belgium's foreign affairs portfolio again from 1954 until 1957. A leading advocate of European economic integration, Spaak chaired the Spaak Committee set up in 1955 to explore ways in which sectoral integration could be widened after the initial successes of the EUROPEAN COAL AND STEEL COMMUNITY (ECSC). Its report in 1956 helped to establish models used in the framing of the 1957 treaties of ROME. After a four-year spell as Secretary-General of NATO from 1957, Spaak served as Belgian Foreign Minister again from 1961 until his retirement in 1966.

Spanish Civil War (1936–39) Civil war between the government and nationalist rebels in Spain. Between 1931 and 1936, various long-term tensions in Spanish politics and social and economic affairs came to a head. The fall of PRIMO DE RIVERA's dictatorship and the subsequent fall of the monarchy (*see* ALFONSO XII) led to a period of republican government, in which politics became increasingly polarised between left and right, and in which popular disturbances, such as those in Barcelona in January 1933, and in the Asturias and Catalonia in October 1934, kept regional, class and economic differences in focus. In February 1936, a POPULAR FRONT government was formed, whose radical agenda on such issues as land and the role of the Church further alienated the right. In July 1936 a number of generals staged a coup against the government, led by FRANCO in the Balearics and Morocco, and by Emilio Mola in Spain itself. The coup failed, as the government responded with force, and as popular defence groups in Catalonia, the Basque region and elsewhere opposed the rebellion. Moreover, while some sections of the military backed the coup, the bulk of the navy and the air force remained loyal to the government. The failed coup thus quickly developed into a major civil war, in which the republicans initially held the advantage in much of the south as well as Catalonia, Aragon and Asturia, while the nationalist rebels secured Morocco, Galicia, Castile and Navarre, as well as some strategic cities in the south, such as Cadiz and Seville.

The civil war quickly assumed an international dimension. The French and British governments officially worked towards establishing a non-intervention agreement in August 1936, by which twenty-seven countries pledged to leave the war to Spain. However, this agreement had little real impact, and three signatories became heavily involved: Germany and Italy, whose backing for the nationalists included supplies, aerial support and troops; and the USSR, which provided some support for the republicans, with the THIRD INTERNATIONAL developing international brigades for foreign volunteers. Portugal also provided facilities and supply lines for the nationalists. External interests, although fluctuating, were crucial to the subsequent course of the war.

In late 1936 the nationalists extended their control of Castile by taking Toledo and attacking Madrid, but the republicans' defence of the capital was successful. With Franco declared 'head of state' by the rebels in October 1936, the nationalists had a relatively unified identity: this was enhanced in April 1937, when all parties were merged under the auspices of the *FALANGE*. The republicans, however, were divided along political lines between communists, socialists, liberals and anarchists (*see* ANARCHISM, COMMUNISM, LIBERALISM, SOCIALISM). They also suffered regional problems, particularly over Catalonia, where fighting between separatist militias and government troops took place in the spring of 1937.

By March 1937, the nationalists controlled the whole of western Spain, as well as Andalusia, Old Castile and Navarre, although their advance on Madrid was repelled at Guadalajara. However, the strength of the nationalists and their backers was demonstrated in March 1937, when the key town of Guernica was destroyed in a German aerial bombardment. The republicans were also weakened in this period by the Soviet-backed suppression of anarchists, and by the loss of Bilbao and Santander, which cut into their previous stronghold in Asturias. A republican offensive at Tereul in December 1937 was unsuccessful, and was followed in early 1938 by a nationalist attack through Aragon, which isolated Catalonia by April 1938. In May 1938 the government attempted to open negotiations with Franco, but these failed, as did their offensive on the Ebro which aimed to reclaim Aragon. In January 1939 the nationalists finally conquered Barcelona, and the republicans' peace terms were rejected. Madrid fell in late March, after an anti-communist rebellion by the National Defence Council forced another internal split on the government's side. The war ended in April 1939, with Franco assuming office as head of state. His dictatorship lasted until his death in 1975.

Approximately 500,000 people died as a result of the Spanish Civil War (although some estimates place the figure closer to 1,000,000). Many of these casualties were civilian and religious victims of political suppression carried out by both sides, such as the 6,800 Catholic priests executed by republicans, and the thousands of workers and unionists executed by nationalists.

Spanish Revolution (1868–74) Period of political instability in Spain, from the deposition of Queen Isabella II in 1868 to the restoration of her son, Alfonso XII, in 1874. Relations between crown and state remained problematic in Spain after the Carlist War of 1833–40 (*see* CARLISM) and the REVOLUTIONS OF 1848. In the 1850s, a fresh outbreak of partisan strife became focused on the largely middle-class progressive and liberal parties who were pressing for liberal reforms; while opposition to the monarchy also emerged in some sections of the army, whence General Juan Prim organised an unsuccessful coup in 1866. In September 1868 Prim staged another coup, this one successful, which forced Isabella to leave Spain. The provisional republican government of liberals and progressives attempted to control some of the extremes that emerged in this revolution centred on the democrats, for example by introducing universal suffrage, freedom of the press, and freedom of religion: but the military demands of a colonial war in Cuba, and the increasingly revolutionary tactics of the republicans in local and regional federalist committees, led the government to use force and distance itself from the democrats.

In 1869 the provisional government introduced a new constitution, which contained a number of liberal strands from 1812 (*see* LIBERALISM, SPANISH RISINGS) but also maintained the monarchy. The succession was problematic, with other European countries taking an active interest (*see* FRANCO-PRUSSIAN WAR), but in 1870 the throne was accepted by Amadeo of Savoy. There followed three years of unstable constitutional monarchy and political violence. In August 1872, the radical government exacerbated the weaknesses of the 1870 settlement through anti-clerical measures and by attempting to limit the army's political power. In this climate, Amadeo abdicated in February 1873. A republic was declared in April 1873. This experiment was, however, weakened by federalist republican risings in Andalusia, Catalonia and elsewhere, which damaged national unity and tested army loyalty, and by the re-emergence of the Carlists, who effectively set up a rival state in northern Spain and engaged the army in a number of battles in 1873 and 1874. In this context, a group of politicians and soldiers managed to organise the restoration of the monarchy in 1874 by bringing Isabella's son Alfonso to the throne as Alfonso XII. The republic was replaced with a partially constitutional monarchy, a system which managed temporarily to defuse the various revolutionary and reactionary strands in Spanish politics.

Spanish risings (1820–23) Liberal and constitutional revolution against King Ferdinand VII. In 1812, during Spain's war of independence against France (*see* NAPOLEONIC WARS), the *Cortes* had created a constitution heavily influenced by LIBERALISM, with clauses on land reform, administrative control and popular sovereignty. Ferdinand VII abolished this constitution on his restoration in 1814. Over the next six years liberal and radical movements developed, particularly in the military and through masonic lodges, and there were a number of small-scale rebellions. In January 1820 the situation came to a head: the government's bankruptcy, and its insistence on continuing with colonial wars in South America (*see* IMPERIALISM), alienated a number of individuals and agencies. In Cadiz, a declaration in favour of the 1812 constitution by officers waiting to go to South America led to a military rebellion, which was paralleled in a number of provincial centres. With the rest of the army refusing to stop the rebellions, Ferdinand was forced to step down and reintroduce the constitution. In March 1821 his dismissal of a liberal ministry led to popular revolts in Cadiz, Corunna and elsewhere. Ferdinand attempted to stage a military coup in July 1822, but this failed when the troops in Madrid attacked the plotters, and Ferdinand became effectively a prisoner of the government. He was deposed in February 1823 after further popular riots; but by this time the Congress of VERONA had authorised French military intervention. This began in April 1823, and was met with little resistance. Ferdinand was restored, and the constitution of 1812 abandoned once again.

Although it ultimately failed, and despite the many splits that existed within the revolutionary movement in Spain, these risings were significant as the first major radical challenge to the post-1815 settlement of Europe. They proved influential on a number of other liberal revolutions of the period, including those in Piedmont, the Two Sicilies and Russia (*see* PIEDMONTESE RISING, NEAPOLITAN RISING, DECEMBRIST CONSPIRACY). They also continued to influence the development of liberal politics in Spain throughout the rest of the nineteenth century. *See* SPANISH REVOLUTION .

Speer, Albert (1905–81) German politician. Speer joined the Nazi party in 1931 while working as an architect (*see* NAZISM). He became a friend of HITLER, and helped design a number of party rallies from 1933 onwards, the success of which led Hitler to commission him to redesign Berlin and other cities. In 1942 Speer moved into the more immediately influential role of Minister for Armaments and War Production. By establishing a centralised coordination process over previously confused structures, he managed to increase production and maintain food supplies until early 1945, despite the impact of allied bombing (*see* SECOND WORLD WAR). This was achieved in part through the use of forced labour and a plunder economy. Speer pleaded guilty at the NUREMBERG TRIALS, although he claimed that as an economist and technician he was removed from political processes; he was convicted for war crimes and crimes against humanity. He served his twenty-year sentence in Spandau prison from 1946. He spent his later years writing on the Nazi period.

Stalin, Josef (Josef Djugashvili) (1879–1953) Soviet politician. Born in Georgia, Djugashvili was expelled from a seminary in 1899 due to his political views. He became an active revolutionary soon after this, joining the BOLSHEVIKS in 1903. His activities included terrorist attacks and bank robberies. He was exiled to Siberia twice, escaping both times, and travelled in Europe during his absences from Russia. In 1912 he adopted the name 'Stalin'. Imprisoned from 1913 until 1916, he returned to Petrograd after the February Revolution of 1917 (*see* RUSSIAN REVOLUTIONS 1917) and edited the Bolsheviks' newspaper *Pravda*. He was active in the October Revolution, and, as a close ally of LENIN, was a founder member of the POLITBURO in 1919, a member of the Revolutionary Military Council from 1920, and Commissar for Nationalities until 1923. During the RUSSIAN CIVIL WAR he helped to organise the defence of Petrograd, and was also involved in the battle for Tsaritsyn, which was later renamed Stalingrad. During the later stages of the war, Stalin began to consolidate his own position in the Communist party, by developing his post of General Secretary of the Central Committee.

After Lenin's death in 1924, and despite Lenin's warnings, Stalin emerged as the leading figure in the party and the government, successfully beating TROTSKY in the leadership struggle. From here, Stalin developed the idea of 'socialism in one country', aiming to develop the USSR's economic and military strength, and to consolidate the party's role. These themes were enacted through FIVE YEAR PLANS for heavy industrial production from 1928, through the forced collectivisation of agriculture, and through the extensive and arbitrary purging of opposition in political, military, social and economic life (*see* YEZHOVSHCHINA). These policies entailed millions of casualties. In 1939, Stalin helped to settle the NAZI-SOVIET PACT with Germany, which allowed the USSR time to rearm and provided it with territorial gains in eastern Europe. When Germany attacked the USSR in Operation BARBAROSSA in 1941, Stalin promoted himself as the country's saviour. Taking the roles of Prime Minister, Commissar of Defence, and Marshal of the USSR, he developed a strong leadership style and played a leading role at the key conferences of TEHRAN, YALTA and POTSDAM. After the SECOND WORLD WAR Stalin committed the USSR to an imperial role in eastern Europe through economic, political and military links which helped the COLD WAR to escalate (*see* IMPERIALISM). Domestically, this period saw the further establishment of his hero status and the re-emergence of his repressive tactics towards opponents, real or suspected. He died in office in 1953. In 1956, his successor KHRUSHCHEV denounced Stalin's rule, an act that began a vigorous 'destalinisation' process which was designed to marginalise his memory and significance. The critical questions about Stalin raised at this time, and furthered in the 1980s by *GLASNOST*, eventually showed that his government was responsible for the deaths of over 40,000,000 people.

Stalingrad, battle of (September 1942–February 1943) SECOND WORLD WAR battle between the USSR and Germany (with Romanian support). Stalingrad (Tsaritsyn until 1928, Volgograd from 1961) was a strategic target for the Germans in their 1942 campaign which built on the successes of the southern attack of Operation BARBAROSSA. Stalingrad's munitions and vehicle industries, developed as part of the FIVE YEAR PLANS, and its role as a centre for river and railway transport, meant that its capture would bring military and economic advantages. The town was attacked in September 1942 as part of the German advance into the Caucasus. By October the Germans had secured the bulk of Stalingrad, but had failed to cross the Volga. This left the Soviet artillery positions on the river's east bank intact. In November, the Soviets under ZHUKOV launched a counter-attack by building up artillery and troops around Stalingrad, surrounding the Germans and subjecting them to heavy artillery bombardments. Meanwhile, fighting inside Stalingrad itself continued, with the Germans facing heavy resistance on a house-by-house basis. In January 1943 the Soviet attack intensified, and the German line was pushed back close in to Stalingrad itself by the end of the month. Despite evacuating some troops through an airlift, and despite Hitler's order that the Germans should fight to the death, General Friedrich von Paulus surrendered on 2 February. The German and Romanian casualties numbered approximately 146,000, while 90,000 were taken as prisoners (including the bulk of the surviving officers). Germany also lost significant amounts of material. The defeat not only stopped the German penetration of Soviet territory: it also marked the start of their retreat from the south-east, which was hastened after their unsuccessful offensive at KURSK in July 1943.

Stambolisky, Alexander (1879–1923) Bulgarian politician. From a rich farming background, Stambolisky studied agriculture in Germany before returning to Bulgaria. He was involved in peasant politics from the late 1890s, and in 1908 entered parliament as a leading member of the Agrarian National Union. In 1915 he was imprisoned for his opposition to Bulgarian involvement in the FIRST WORLD WAR, but he was released towards the end of the war and immediately became a focus for reform. He helped to persuade King Ferdinand to abdicate, and declared a provisional republic with himself as President in 1918. Stambolisky represented Bulgaria at the signing of the treaty of NEUILLY in 1919. He also became Prime Minister in that year. He ran the country as a pro-agrarian dictatorship, with land and tax reforms designed mainly to assist the farming sector. In June 1923 he was deposed in a right-wing coup, precipitated by the army's decline in influence and Stambolisky's attempts to improve relations with the Kingdom of the Serbs, Croats and Slovenes. Stambolisky was murdered five days after the coup.

Stein, Heinrich von (1757–1831) Prussian politician and administrator. A civil servant from a wealthy background, Stein was appointed as Chief Minister of Prussia by FREDERICK WILLIAM III in October 1807, after the Prussian military collapse in the NAPOLEONIC WARS had shown up problems in the country's structures. Stein approached his post with a reformist agenda, introducing a period that became known as Prussia's liberal era (*see* LIBERALISM). Reforms included the emancipation of the serfs from 1807, changes in landowning laws that opened up the sale of land to a wider social grouping than the nobility, and the establishment of limited meritocracy in the military. Stein also attempted improvements in the central government system, with plans for an elected assembly, but Frederick William found this unacceptable. However, he did successfully bring in a system of locally elected municipal councils in 1808. Stein was dismissed in 1808 at NAPOLEON's insistence, for his attempts to start a popular national rising against the French occupation (*see* NAPOLEONIC WARS). He moved to Austria and worked as an advisor to Tsar ALEXANDER I of Russia, before returning to Prussia in the wake of Napoleon's retreat from Russia. As the chief administrator of the German territories, Stein again attempted to organise a national rising that could lead to a unification of the German states. However, these plans were barred by METTERNICH as they clashed with HABSBURG policy of Austria being the dominant German state. Stein retired from national politics after the Napoleonic Wars, but remained active at the regional level in Westphalia.

Stolypin, Piotr (1862–1911) Russian politician. Stolypin entered the Russian civil service in 1884, working for the Ministry of the Interior. In 1903 he became Governor of Saratov province, which experienced significant disorders during the Revolution of 1905 (*see* RUSSIAN REVOLUTION 1905). Stolypin's repressive response here earned him a central post, as Minister of the Interior, in April 1906. In July 1906 NICHOLAS II promoted Stolypin to the post of Prime Minister. He used repressive tactics to stamp out the revolutionary movement of 1905, with large-scale summary trials and executions, and extensive press censorship. He also limited the democratic advances of the 1905 revolution by reducing the size of the electorate in 1907. Alongside this reactionary strand, Stolypin also attempted to reform the agrarian sector in order both to increase Russia's productivity, and to create a new class of small landowners. This was attempted through granting peasants the right to own land outside their village commune, with loans being provided by the Peasant Land Bank to offset the initial costs. He also ended the redemption payments that had been set up as part of the settlement of the EMANCIPATION OF THE SERFS, and encouraged peasant migration to Siberia. Stolypin's plans for more wide-ranging reforms in education, religion and social welfare were unsuccessful, and towards the end of his career he lost influence by alienating various interest groups. Stolypin was assassinated by a left-wing group in 1911, possibly with secret police assistance.

Straits Convention (1841) Multilateral agreement on access rights to the Straits, settled in London in July 1841. The Straits – the navigable waterway between the Aegean Sea and the Black Sea – had proved contentious throughout the century. Foreign military access to the Straits had been denied in 1809 by a bilateral treaty between Turkey and the UK: but this had been overturned by the treaties of ADRIANOPLE of 1829 and UNKIAR-SKELESSI of 1833, which gave Russia greater access through its protectorate of Turkey. In 1840, influenced by growing instability in the region caused by Egypt's war with the OTTOMAN EMPIRE that had started in 1839, the British and French insisted that the area should be internationally regulated, due to their interests in supporting the Ottomans and denying Russia military access to the Mediterranean, and established a convention on the issue in London in 1841. The Convention, attended by representatives from the HABSBURG empire, France, Prussia, Russia, Turkey and the UK, ruled that the Straits should be closed to non-Turkish warships when Turkey was at peace. Although this did not finally settle the issue (*see for example* CRIMEAN WAR), the 1841 Convention remained in force until the treaty of LAUSANNE of 1923.

Stresa Front Tripartite agreement against German rearmament, April 1935. In the wake of HITLER's announcement in March 1935 that Germany was rearming despite the restrictions imposed by the treaty of VERSAILLES, France, Italy and the UK convened at Stresa to discuss a response. The three powers issued a joint statement condemning German rearmament, and pledging their continued support of the treaties of Versailles and LOCARNO. The Stresa Front thus stood for a while as a potentially powerful block against German aggression. However, beyond demonstrating the increasing ineffectiveness of the LEAGUE OF NATIONS, the Stresa Front involved little real commitment from any of the signatories. The UK soon diluted it by concluding the ANGLO-GERMAN NAVAL AGREEMENT, as did France through its mutual aid agreement with the USSR. The ITALO-ABYSSINIAN WAR damaged relations between the Stresa powers. The Front was finally annulled in November 1936 by the creation of the AXIS, which put Italy into a closer relationship with Germany.

Stresemann, Gustav (1878–1929) German politician. Stresemann entered national politics in 1907 as a Deputy. He supported the FIRST WORLD WAR, and, despite his broadly liberal alignment, supported some of the right-wing attempts against the WEIMAR REPUBLIC in its early days. Leader of the People's party from 1919, he then became accommodated to the republic, but did not accept the terms of the treaty of VERSAILLES: however, he developed the strategy of negotiating changes to the settlement rather than attempting to overturn it. In August 1923 Stresemann became Chancellor of a coalition government. In this role, he helped to solve the inflation crisis through adopting a policy of austerity and by appointing SCHACHT as finance commissioner. His government collapsed in November 1923 when the left-wing parties withdrew over the use of force against communists, but Stresemann remained in office as Foreign Minister. Here, he was able to work with the victorious powers of 1918 towards a revision of the peace settlement. He helped to solve the RUHR occupation crisis, negotiated the Dawes plan on REPARATIONS, and helped Germany's international rehabilitation through the LOCARNO treaties of 1925 (for which he shared the Nobel Peace Prize with BRIAND) and by taking Germany into the LEAGUE OF NATIONS in 1926. Stresemann signed the KELLOGG-BRIAND PACT in 1928. He died in office in October 1929.

Struggle of Cultures *see KULTURKAMPF.*

Svoboda, Ludvik (1895–1979) Czechoslovakian soldier and politician. After serving in the FIRST WORLD WAR, Svoboda remained in the army throughout the inter-war period, teaching at Czechoslovakia's staff college from 1937. In the USSR from 1939, he helped to build up the Czechoslovak Army Corps in association with the Red Army, and he served in the successful advance on Prague, which ended in May 1945 (*see* SECOND WORLD WAR). After serving as Minister of Defence in the post-war government, he was targeted by STALIN in 1950, suffering dismissal and a brief period of imprisonment. After Stalin's death in 1953, Svoboda rejoined the army, and retired in 1959. In the early 1960s, KHRUSHCHEV promoted Svoboda as a national hero for his role in the Second World War, and this new prominence established him as a safe president in March 1968 to replace NOVOTNÝ. Svoboda worked with DUBČEK's reform programme (*see* PRAGUE SPRING), and made some efforts to minimise the Soviet-backed repression that followed. He stayed in office until 1975.

syndicalism Political and economic ideology. Syndicalism emerged in the late nineteenth century. Related to ANARCHISM, particularly through the influence of PROUDHON, syndicalism centred on trade unions rather than political parties as agents of revolutionary change. It aimed to achieve workers' control of industries and of political power, through strike action including general strikes. It was particularly influential before the FIRST WORLD WAR in France, through the General Confederation of Labour (CGT), although the union's failure fully to oppose the war dented its radical credibility. It was also influential in Spain from this period until the SPANISH CIVIL WAR through the National Confederation of Labour (CNT); and in Italy, where the Syndical Union (US) promoted the ideology, which subsequently influenced the economic programme of FASCISM. Syndicalism declined in influence during the inter-war period.

T

Talleyrand-Périgord, Charles de (1754–1838) French politician. After working as a priest, Talleyrand became Bishop of Autun in 1788. He attended the meeting of the Estates-General in 1789 (*see* FRENCH REVOLUTION), and quickly allied himself with the revolutionary movement. He served as a Deputy in the Constituent Assembly, where he advocated the state confiscation of church property as a way of raising revenue. Talleyrand was one of only four bishops to cooperate with the Civil Constitution of the Clergy, introduced in July 1790, for which he was excommunicated. From 1792 Talleyrand served as France's Envoy to London. Despite his willingness to promote change, he retained some royalist sympathies, and did not return to France after LOUIS XVI's execution in 1793, moving instead to the USA. He returned to France after the Directory was established in July 1795, and worked with this new government as Foreign Minister from 1797, while also plotting with NAPOLEON, who he saw as a potentially strong leader. Talleyrand helped Napoleon come to power in the BRUMAIRE coup of 1799, and kept office until 1807. In this post, he was influential in such diplomatic developments as France's 1801 Concordat with the Roman Catholic Church, the treaty of AMIENS of 1802, and the creation of the CONFEDERATION OF THE RHINE in 1806. He resigned after the treaty of TILSIT of 1807. *See* NAPOLEONIC WARS.

In 1814 Talleyrand established contacts with the allies and the Bourbon family, and was instrumental in the Senate's deposition of Napoleon. He helped to broker the restoration by getting LOUIS XVIII to agree to establish a constitution, and strengthened France's post-war position through his diplomacy, as Foreign Minister once more, at the Congress of VIENNA. Although he retired in 1815, he remained active in politics, and helped to arrange LOUIS-PHILIPPE's accession to the throne during France's 1830 revolution (*see* REVOLUTIONS OF 1830). He served as France's Ambassador to London from 1830 until his final retirement in 1834.

Tannenberg, battle of (August 1914) FIRST WORLD WAR battle. In August 1914 Russia invaded East Prussia, using two armies under generals Alexander Samsonov and Paul Rennenkampf. Russia's fast mobilisation had not been foreseen by the Germans (*see* SCHLIEFFEN PLAN), and troops earmarked for the west were quickly moved eastwards, thus diluting the attack on Paris (*see* MARNE, FIRST BATTLE OF). The German forces were developed by HINDENBURG and LUDENDORFF, who exploited the lack of contact between Samsonov and Rennenkampf and surrounded Samsonov's army at Tannenberg. The Russians were heavily defeated, and Samsonov committed suicide. The German success was consolidated in early September with the defeat of Rennenkampf's army at the Masurian Lakes: with only one more major engagement, also at the Masurian Lakes in February 1915, this represented the end of Russia's invasion of Germany. The Russians lost approximately 250,000 men in the two battles to the Germans' 20,000. The battle's popular success with the German people formed the basis of Hindenburg's and Ludendorff's subsequent political and military careers, and established it in German nationalist mythology as a key site. This status was confirmed in 1934 when Hindenburg was buried there.

Tehran Conference (November–December 1943) Inter-allied planning conference of the SECOND WORLD WAR. The conference at Tehran, called to discuss common strategy at a time when the ITALIAN CAMPAIGN and the Soviet offensive after STALINGRAD and KURSK were pushing Germany back from its territorial peak of 1942, was the first joint meeting of the leaders of the UK, the USA and the USSR, represented by Winston Churchill, Franklin Roosevelt, and STALIN respectively. The allies agreed on the broad outline of an invasion of northern France in the spring or summer of 1944 as a way of opening a major second front in Europe, which would be coordinated with a new offensive by the Red Army in the east. Stalin agreed to declare war on Japan once the AXIS was defeated in Europe, with Soviet interests in some Asian territories being recognised (*see* IMPERIALISM). The future territorial alignment of parts of Europe was considered, particularly the border between Germany and Poland (*see* ODER-NEISSE LINE) and the settlement of eastern Prussia. In this, and in Stalin's expressed interest in the Baltic republics, some of the fault lines in the alliance that were later to dominate the COLD WAR were becoming visible. The other major issue discussed at Tehran was the possibility of establishing an international organisation with the power to maintain peace as a replacement for the LEAGUE OF NATIONS, an idea that developed into the UNITED NATIONS.

Teplitz, treaty of (September 1813) *see* NAPOLEONIC WARS.

Tereul offensive (December 1937) *see* SPANISH CIVIL WAR.

Terror, the (1793–94) Period of mass killing and political suppression during the FRENCH REVOLUTION, lasting from 1793 until the Thermidor coup of July 1794, and strongly associated with the leadership of ROBESPIERRE and the work of the Committee of Public Safety, the Committee of General Security, and the Revolutionary Tribunal. The contexts for the introduction of brutal tactics included the FRENCH REVOLUTIONARY WARS, the internal factional divisions within the Convention, and provincial revolts against central regulations on conscription and taxation. The machinery of the Paris-based committees and Tribunal was supplemented elsewhere by the work of local watch committees and centrally appointed representatives-on-mission in the armed forces. These various agencies convicted and punished a large number of people, both genuine counter-revolutionaries and individuals implicated in factional disputes and regional dissent, from leading figures such as the GIRONDINS in 1793 and DANTON and his followers in 1794, to thousands of peasants and workers in the Vendée and elsewhere. Overall there were 16,594 official executions, and an estimated 20–25,000 other casualties.

Texel, battle of (October 1797) *see* FRENCH REVOLUTIONARY WARS.

Thiers, Adolphe (1797–1877) French pol -itician. A lawyer, journalist and historian, who wrote a multi-volume history of the FRENCH REVOLUTION in the 1820s, Thiers entered politics in 1830 as one of LOUIS-PHILIPPE's supporters (*see* REVOLUTIONS OF 1830). He served as Minister of the Interior in 1832 and from 1834 to 1836, and also as Prime Minister in 1836 and 1840. During this period he initiated some reforms, but also used force against protests and riots. In 1840 Thiers resigned when his foreign policy in the Middle East almost led to a war with the UK. Thiers backed Louis Napoleon (*see* NAPOLEON III) for the presidency in 1848 (*see* REVOLUTIONS OF 1848), but did not support his 1851 coup and the assumption of imperial power, for which he was briefly exiled (*see* SECOND EMPIRE). He returned to politics in 1863 as a Deputy. In February 1871, in the first elections of the THIRD REPUBLIC, Thiers' successes led to his appointment as Head of Executive Power, leading to his presidency in August 1871. In this role he made peace with Germany (*see* FRANCO-PRUSSIAN WAR), crushed the PARIS COMMUNE, and raised loans to pay off the indemnities involved in the peace terms. Thiers fell from office in 1873 when he lost the support of the predominantly monarchist Assembly.

Third Coalition *see* NAPOLEONIC WARS.

Third International Soviet-dominated organisation for communist parties, 1919–43. In March 1919 LENIN established the Communist International (Comintern, or Third International) as a counter to the re-formation of the SECOND INTERNATIONAL. Aiming to promote COMMUNISM in all countries, the International primarily called for revolutions throughout Europe, and fostered contacts between parties in different countries. Under ZINOVIEV's leadership, this policy changed in 1921 to one of subversion and infiltration, with communists encouraged to work in trade unions, political parties and other agencies, to further communism in their own countries. The International was purged by Stalin in 1927 (*see YEZHOVSHCHINA*), and promoted frequently shifting policies in the late 1920s and 1930s: from non-cooperation with anyone but communists in 1928, to the POPULAR FRONT model after 1933, to a declining hostility towards FASCISM and NAZISM after the NAZI-SOVIET PACT in 1939. In 1943, Stalin dissolved the International during the USSR's wartime alliance with the UK and the USA, although it was effectively re-established as the Communist Information Bureau (COMINFORM) in 1945.

Third Reich Name applied to Germany for the period of the Nazi party's dictatorship from 1933 to 1945, promoted by HITLER to stress the historical legitimacy of the system of government, in which the HOLY ROMAN EMPIRE was the First Reich, and the Second Reich was Germany from unification in 1871 (*see* GERMAN UNIFICATION) to the establishment of the WEIMAR REPUBLIC in 1919. Germany under this system was run as a one-party state under the personal dictatorship of Hitler. It was ideologically underpinned by NAZISM, thus combining extreme ANTI-SEMITISM with a limited welfare state on racial lines. Domestically, the government relied heavily upon terrorism, propaganda and coercion, although the administrative confusion of the period impeded much of its desired and projected efficiency. Internationally, the government of the Third Reich was committed to revision of the treaties of VERSAILLES and ST GERMAIN, which gave rise to rearmament and expansionist policies (*see ANSCHLUSS*, APPEASEMENT, MUNICH AGREEMENT, RHINELAND, REMILITARISATION, SECOND WORLD WAR). The Third Reich came to an end with Germany's collapse in 1945, after which Germany was divided into two nations on COLD WAR lines until 1990, when it was reunified. *See* GERMAN REUNIFICATION.

Third Republic France's political system from 1871 until 1940. The Third Republic developed out of the FRANCO-PRUSSIAN WAR and NAPOLEON III's collapse, and was characterised in its early years by tensions between monarchist and republican factions over the best model of government. When no restoration proved viable, the Republic was consolidated by an informal constitution in 1875. Throughout its history it remained characterised by coalition governments. Governments of the pre-FIRST WORLD WAR period introduced various changes to French political, social and economic life, while also developing international interests in IMPERIALISM and European alliances (*see* FRANCO-RUSSIAN ALLIANCE, *ENTENTE CORDIALE*); although this period also saw significant tensions in public life, particularly over religion, and the authority of successive governments and politicians was damaged by such scandals as the BOULANGER AFFAIR and the DREYFUS AFFAIR. The Third Republic survived the FIRST WORLD WAR, and stayed in place for the inter-war period. It was dissolved in July 1940 after France's defeat by Germany in the SECOND WORLD WAR.

Three Emperors' Alliance *see DREIKAISERBUND.*

Three Emperors' League *see DREIKAISERBUND.*

Tilsit, treaties of (July 1807) Treaties between France and Prussia, and France and Russia, of the NAPOLEONIC WARS. After the Prussians were defeated by the French at Jena and Auerstadt in October 1806, and the Russians at Friedland in July 1807, the treaties of Tilsit were signed to settle the conflict. The Prussian treaty dealt with the defeated power harshly. Territorial losses included all of Prussia's lands west of the Elbe, which went into the Kingdom of Westphalia, and the land taken from Poland, which went into the Grand Duchy of Warsaw. Prussia also had its army reduced in size, had to pay an indemnity to France, and was forced to join the CONTINENTAL SYSTEM against the UK. Russia was treated on more equitable terms, due to mutual advantages that could accrue from the treaty. Its territorial losses – the Ionian islands and part of the Dalmatian coast – were relatively light, and it gained Bialystock. ALEXANDER I agreed to recognise NAPOLEON's empire in northern, central and southern Europe, and took Russia into the Continental System, while Napoleon agreed that he would not allow Poland to re-emerge as an independent country (*see* IMPERIALISM). Alexander also agreed to attempt to mediate between France and the UK. However, by the secret clauses of the treaty, Napoleon committed himself to supporting Russia's territorial ambitions against Sweden and the OTTOMAN EMPIRE: in return, Alexander agreed to declare war on the UK if negotiations failed. Coming eighteen months after the treaty of PRESSBURG, Tilsit provided a great degree of security for the French empire. It was Alexander's renewal of trade with the UK in 1810, contrary to the treaty of Tilsit, that precipitated Napoleon's invasion of Russia.

Tirpitz, Alfred von (1849–1930) German sailor and politician. Tirpitz joined the Prussian navy in 1865. In 1891, he produced an influential paper on the development of a high seas fleet which would be powerful enough to deter attack from the UK, and would thus allow Germany's peaceful colonial development (*see* IMPERIALISM). Minister of Marine from 1897, Tirpitz led the development of the German fleet along these lines. Through navy laws of 1898 and 1900, the fleet was expanded, with *Dreadnought*-style battleships introduced from 1906. He also supervised improvements in the Kiel Canal to allow greater flexibility, built up a submarine fleet, and encouraged popular support for the naval programme through the German Navy League. When the FIRST WORLD WAR started, Tirpitz concentrated on submarine warfare rather than the use of the fleet. He resigned in March 1916 after the Kaiser forced the limitation of submarine attacks following the sinking of the *Lusitania*. After the war Tirpitz remained active in right-wing politics.

Tito (Josip Broz) (1892–1980) Yugoslav soldier and politician. Born in Croatia, Broz fought for the HABSBURG army in the FIRST WORLD WAR, and was taken as a prisoner of war by the Russians in April 1915. He became attracted to COMMUNISM during his imprisonment, and served in the Red Army during the RUSSIAN CIVIL WAR before returning to Croatia in 1920. Here, he was a founder of a Communist party, taking the name 'Tito' in 1922 when the party was outlawed. A THIRD INTERNATIONAL agent, he served a six-year prison sentence from 1928. He returned to his activities in 1934, working mainly from Moscow, where he was appointed as Secretary General of the Yugoslav Communist party in 1937. In 1939 Tito returned to Yugoslavia. When Germany invaded Yugoslavia in 1941 (*see* SECOND WORLD WAR), he moved south and built up a RESISTANCE movement which waged a successful guerrilla war against the occupation. In 1943, his predominance was confirmed at the Jajce conference, at which representatives of six republics agreed to a post-war federated Yugoslav republic with Tito as its first leader. After the war he duly became Prime Minister of the new republic, but he lost STALIN's support in 1948 by insisting on a non-Stalinist path of development for the Balkan region as a whole. His success in defying the USSR in the early COLD WAR won him western support. In 1953 Tito was elected as President, a post he retained through five further election victories and, from 1974, through being given the office for life. He oversaw Yugoslavia's successful reconstruction after the Second World War, with economic, welfare and social reforms, but the compromises involved in maintaining the republic became evident after his death in office in 1980. *See* YUGOSLAVIA, DISSOLUTION.

Trafalgar, battle of (October 1805) *see* NAPOLEONIC WARS.

Trianon, treaty of (June 1920) Peace treaty between the allied powers and Hungary at the end of the FIRST WORLD

WAR, one of the treaties written during the PARIS PEACE CONFERENCE. With the collapse of the Austro-Hungarian empire at the end of the war, the allies dealt with Hungary as an independent republic. The treaty imposed massive territorial losses on Hungary: in all, approximately two thirds of its pre-1914 territory, and three fifths of its population, were lost. It left Hungary as a predominantly Magyar nation state with few minorities, although it left approximately one third of the Magyar population in other countries. The territorial losses were mainly in favour of the new successor states in eastern Europe. Czechoslovakia gained Slovakia and Ruthenia, part of northern Slovakia went to the revived Poland, and Croatia-Slavonia and Vojvodina went to the new Kingdom of the Serbs, Croats and Slovenes. Other areas went to two of the victorious allies: Romania gained Transylvania and part of Banat (a gain that was larger than the remainder of Hungary after Trianon), while Italy gained Fiume. In addition, the Burgenland area on the Austro-Hungarian border went to Austria, although within this Sopron was allowed a plebiscite which, in 1921, returned it to Hungary. The treaty also imposed reparations payments on Hungary, and limited the army to 35,000 troops. The severity of the treaty remained a major political issue in inter-war Hungary.

Triple Alliance Military alliance between Austria-Hungary, Germany and Italy, signed at Vienna in May 1882. With the DUAL ALLIANCE already in place, Germany was eager to gain further allies against France. In 1882, Italy showed an interest in moving closer to Germany after French imperial actions in Tripoli (*see* IMPERIALISM). This, along with BISMARCK's fear of a Franco-Russian alliance, provided the context for the Triple Alliance, designed to work in parallel with the Dual Alliance. By the terms of the alliance, Germany would gain the backing of the other two partners if it was attacked by France and/or Russia; Italy would gain aid from the other two partners if it was attacked by France; while Italy would remain neutral in any war between Austria-Hungary and Russia. The treaty also committed Austria-Hungary and Germany to remain out of Italy, thus providing confirmation of ITALIAN UNIFICATION. The Alliance, which was renewed a number of times between 1882 and 1912, helped to cement Franco-Russian relations. Ultimately, it was never fully used, as Germany's attack on France in 1914 (*see* FIRST WORLD WAR) left Italy free not to intervene. In May 1915, Italy's signature of the treaty of LONDON led to its withdrawal from the Alliance, and thus the Alliance's termination.

Triple Entente Name popularly applied to the network of agreements between France, Russia and the UK that existed from 1907. France and Russia had been in a military alliance since 1894 (*see* FRANCO-RUSSIAN ALLIANCE), while the UK's 1904 colonial agreement with France, the *ENTENTE CORDIALE*, brought the UK into this anti-German orbit. In August 1907, Russia and the UK reached their own colonial agreement in St Petersburg, which mirrored the *Entente Cordiale* by settling long-standing disputes: most notably it involved the division of Persia into spheres of influence, and recognised British interests in Afghanistan. This agreement thus completed the network of relations between the three countries, and created a context for further cooperation and military preparations against the assumed enmity of the TRIPLE ALLIANCE. For example, in 1912, France and the UK made joint naval plans for action in the North Sea, the English Channel, the north Atlantic, and the Mediterranean. The Triple Entente effectively became a military alliance by the London declaration of September 1914, whereby the three powers agreed that none would make a separate peace with Austria-Hungary and/or Germany. This declaration formed the basis of the military alliance of the FIRST WORLD WAR, until Russian withdrawal in 1917 (*see* RUSSIAN REVOLUTIONS 1917), and the subsequent treaty of BREST-LITOVSK, destroyed the Entente.

Troppau, Congress of (October–December 1820) One of the meetings of the QUADRUPLE ALLIANCE powers plus France in the CONGRESS SYSTEM. The Congress was called by ALEXANDER I of Russia in response to the revolutions that were taking place in Portugal, Spain and the Kingdom of the Two Sicilies (*see* SPANISH RISINGS, NEAPOLITAN RISING). Alexander called for the Alliance to use military force against revolutions, but this policy was rejected by the British government on the grounds that intervention in internal affairs of other states would destroy the balance of power. The Congress assembled at Troppau in October, with the UK and France sending only observers. The HABSBURG empire and Prussia broadly agreed with the Russian anti-revolutionary attitude, and the protocol of 19 November 1820 committed members to act against a state if that state's internal affairs endangered any other state. This formed the basis for intervention in Spain, Portugal and the Two Sicilies, and confirmed the British fears about the way in which the Quadruple Alliance had developed. The Congress reconvened at LAIBACH in January 1821.

Trotsky, Leon (Lev Bronstein) **(1879–1940)** Russian and Soviet politician and theorist. A Social Democrat from 1896, Bronstein was exiled to Siberia in 1898 for his revolutionary activities. Here, he took the name of 'Trotsky'. He escaped from Siberia, and worked with LENIN in London from 1902. In the party's 1903 split, Trotsky sided with the MENSHEVIKS. He returned to Russia during the 1905 Revolution (*see* RUSSIAN REVOLUTION 1905) and set up a workers' soviet in St Petersburg. Exiled again after the revolution, he escaped and travelled in Europe and the USA. In May 1917 Trotsky returned to Russia as a BOLSHEVIK, and worked with Lenin in planning and coordinating the October revolution (*see* RUSSIAN REVOLUTIONS 1917). Trotsky led the early negotiations with Germany to end Russian involvement in the FIRST WORLD WAR, although he deliberately extended these talks that eventually led to the treaty of BREST-LITOVSK. He then concentrated on military affairs as Commissar for War, developing the Red Army to fight against counter-revolutionary forces in the RUSSIAN CIVIL WAR. A close ally of Lenin's, Trotsky's influence declined after Lenin's death as STALIN used his support network within the Communist party to confirm his own succession. In 1925 Trotsky lost his government post. Two years later he was expelled from the party, and in 1929 was deported from the USSR. He spent his exile in Europe and Mexico, writing historical and theoretical works on COMMUNISM and the Russian Revolution. He was used as the symbol of divergence and subversion by Stalin during the purges (*see* *YEZHOVSHCHINA*), when many of the victims were accused of 'Trotskyism'. In 1940 he was murdered in Mexico on Stalin's orders. Trotskyism, with an emphasis on global rather than purely national revolution, remained an influential strand in left-wing politics after Trotsky's death.

Two plus Four talks (1990) *see* GERMAN REUNIFICATION.

U

Ulbricht, Walter (1893–1973) German and East German politician. Ulbricht joined the German Communist party at its foundation in 1919 *See* COMMUNISM, and after a brief spell in the USSR, sat in Saxony's parliament from 1926 and in the Reichstag from 1928, until the party was outlawed under the THIRD REICH. Ulbricht left Germany for France and then the USSR, where he remained until the end of the SECOND WORLD WAR. In April 1945 he returned to Berlin, and with Soviet backing reconstructed the communist movement in the Soviet occupation zone of Germany. In 1946 he headed the Socialist Unity party, and in 1950 became the leader of the Communist party of the newly created German Democratic Republic (GDR). Effectively the country's leader, particularly after his appointment as Chairman of the Council of State in 1960, he imposed a rigid Stalinist policy on the GDR, and contributed to COLD WAR tensions by suppressing the rising of 1953, and by erecting the BERLIN WALL in 1961. Ulbricht retired in 1971.

United Nations (UN) International intergovernmental organisation that succeeded the LEAGUE OF NATIONS after the SECOND WORLD WAR. The idea of a new international organisation to promote collective security developed during the Second World War, formally emerging at allied foreign ministers' talks in Moscow in October 1943, and subsequently at TEHRAN, Dumbarton Oaks and YALTA. The UN was set up in June 1945 at the San Francisco conference, which drafted its charter, subsequently signed by governmental representatives from fifty-one nations. The UN held its first sessions in London, before moving to New York City. The General Assembly was established as the body's debating forum, while the Security Council was set up as the executive, consisting of five permanent members (China, France, the UK, the USA and the USSR, the latter replaced by Russia in 1991) and ten temporary members. The World Court was instituted as the UN's judiciary. The post of secretary-general was created for the head of the UN's administration. This structure has survived throughout the UN's history; and, to date, three Europeans have held the secretary-generalship: LIE, HAMMARSKJØLD and WALDHEIM. Although it has never developed its own armed forces, all member countries have been committed to providing resources for military actions when required: this key difference has set it apart from the League of Nations, as have the USA's membership and the prominent place given to collective security through the Security Council.

In its main work of promoting peace through collective security, the UN has had mixed successes in Europe. It helped to manage cease-fires in Cyprus in 1964 and 1974 (*see ENOSIS*); and provided a significant peace-keeping force for the Balkans during the violence involved in the break-up of Yugoslavia (*see* YUGOSLAVIA, DISSOLUTION) from 1992. However, each Security Council member's power of veto meant that it was unable to act in a number of COLD WAR flashpoints in which Soviet troops were involved, such as the HUNGARIAN RISING of 1956, or the PRAGUE SPRING of 1968. Moreover, the UN was effectively bypassed by NATO during early stages of the KOSOVO WAR of 1999.

As well as its role in promoting collective security, the UN sponsored and promoted a number of specialist agencies and organisations, including the United Nations Relief and Rehabilitation Administration (UNRRA, 1943–49), which it inherited from an inter-allied initiative; the United Nations Educational, Scientific and Cultural Organisation (UNESCO, established in 1946); the International Labour Organisation (ILO, inherited from the League of Nations in 1946); the Food and Agriculture Organisation (FAO, established in 1945); the International Bank for Reconstruction and Development (*see* BRETTON WOODS CONFERENCE), established in 1945; the World Health Organisation (WHO, established in 1948); and the United Nations Children's Fund (UNICEF, established in 1947). The diversity of these agencies demonstrates the UN's broadening remit.

United Nations Children's Fund (UNICEF) *see* UNITED NATIONS.

United Nations Educational, Scientific and Cultural Organisation (UNESCO) *see* UNITED NATIONS.

United Nations Relief and Rehabilitation Administration (UNRAA) *see* UNITED NATIONS.

Unkiar-Skelessi, treaty of (July 1833) Bilateral treaty between Russia and the OTTOMAN EMPIRE. Following on from Russian aid to the Ottoman empire in its war against Egypt, the treaty created a military alliance. Russia committed itself to providing military assistance in case of future attacks; while the Ottoman empire agreed to close the Straits to warships from other powers. This aspect of the treaty built on Russia's gains in the treaty of ADRIANOPLE of 1829, but was overturned in 1841 by the STRAITS CONVENTION. Beyond the Straits issue, the treaty demonstrated the Ottoman empire's declining power, and Russia's intention to maintain a presence in the eastern Balkans.

V

Valmy, battle of (September 1792) Battle in the FRENCH REVOLUTIONARY WARS. After the Prussian invasion of France, and defeats at Languy and Verdun, the Duke of Brunswick's army was set to attack Paris in order to enforce LOUIS XVI's restoration. This threat caused great instability within Paris, most evident in the mass killings of aristocrats and others in the city's prisons in September (*see* FRENCH REVOLUTION). However, on 20 September, the French army met the Prussians at Valmy. The numerically inferior Prussians attacked the French artillery, and retreated soon after this attack had been withstood. Although there were relatively few casualties – approximately 300 French and 180 Prussians were killed – the Prussians chose to withdraw back into Prussia. The French victory provided the revolutionary government and its supporters with great momentum, seen most obviously in the abolition of the monarchy in the battle's immediate aftermath.

Vendean Revolt (1793–6) *see* FRENCH REVOLUTIONARY WARS; FRENCH REVOLUTION.

Venizelos, Eleutherios (1864–1936) Greek politician. Originally from Crete, Venizelos was active in the anti-OTTOMAN movement of the late nineteenth and early twentieth centuries. As President of Crete's Assembly, he led Crete into union with Greece in 1905, before moving to Athens. In 1910 he became Prime Minister of Greece, introducing a number of reforms and strengthening Greece's international position through his work on the Balkan League. Venizelos led Greece in the BALKAN WARS of 1912 and 1913, and was credited with the country's territorial gains. He resigned in October 1915 after failing to secure Greek entry into the FIRST WORLD WAR against Germany: King CONSTANTINE I favoured neutrality. Venizelos established a provisional government in Salonika, and in 1917 was able (with overseas backing) to secure Constantine's abdication. As Prime Minister again, he declared war on Germany and Bulgaria, and duly represented Greece at the PARIS PEACE CONFERENCE, through which Greece made significant territorial gains (*see* treaty of SÈVRES). Venizelos lost the 1920 election, but held office again in 1924, from 1928 until 1932, and in 1933. He left Greece in 1935 after an unsuccessful coup attempt, and died in France the following year.

Verdun, battle of (September 1792) *see* FRENCH REVOLUTIONARY WARS.

Verdun, battle of (February–December 1916) FIRST WORLD WAR battle in northeast France. Verdun had historical significance for France, and had been developed as a strategic fortification after the FRANCO-PRUSSIAN WAR. In February 1916, German forces launched a massive attack on Verdun, aiming to carry out a sustained campaign which would bring hundreds of thousands of French troops into action. The battle started with the largest artillery bombardment of the war to date, and by the summer the Germans had captured two key forts, at Vaux and Douaumont. However, German resources were then diluted by the battle of the SOMME and, on the eastern front, by the BRUSILOV OFFENSIVE, and the French, under PÉTAIN and Robert Nivelle, regained the lost ground. The battle continued until December 1916. Although Verdun did not fall, the Germans achieved their aim of depleting French resources: approximately 362,000 French troops were killed. However, Germany lost some 337,000 in return. The allies used Verdun as the basis for further campaigns in August 1917 and September 1918.

Verona, Congress of (October–December 1822) Last major meeting of the QUADRUPLE ALLIANCE powers plus France under the CONGRESS SYSTEM. The Congress was called to discuss the revolutionary situations in Greece and Spain (*see* GREEK WAR OF INDEPENDENCE, SPANISH RISINGS). The UK continued to advocate non-intervention, and was partially backed in this by METTERNICH, but the Congress established a plan which allowed France to intervene in Spain, which it duly did in 1823. This resolution effectively ended the Congress System, as it finally stressed the different objectives of the UK and the continental powers, although informal meetings of the remaining powers continued to take place.

Versailles, treaty of (June 1919) Peace treaty between the allied powers and Germany at the end of the FIRST WORLD WAR, one of the treaties written during the PARIS PEACE CONFERENCE. Territorially, Germany lost outright Alsace and Lorraine to France; North Schleswig to Denmark; and parts of Posen and West Prussia to the restored state of Poland as the 'POLISH CORRIDOR' so that it could have access to the sea, which also divided East Prussia from the rest of Germany. A number of areas were set up for plebiscites: through these, Germany lost Eupen and Malmédy to Belgium in 1920 and part of Upper Silesia to Poland in 1921, although plebiscite areas in East Prussia and the rest of Upper Silesia were returned to Germany in 1920 and 1921 respectively. The coal-rich area of the Saar was to be run by the LEAGUE OF NATIONS for the benefit of France for fifteen years: the subsequent plebiscite of 1935 returned this area to Germany. The Memmelland was placed under allied administration to ensure that the new state of Lithuania had access to the sea; while Danzig was established as a free city under League control. As in the treaty of ST GERMAIN, *ANSCHLUSS* with Austria was forbidden. Germany also lost all of its non-European colonies, which were managed as MANDATES. The area between the Rhine and Germany's western borders was placed under allied military occupation for a projected fifteen years, while the eastern bank of the Rhine was demilitarised to a depth of fifty kilometres (*see* RHINELAND, REMILITARISATION). Germany was forcibly disarmed by the treaty: the army was reduced to 100,000 volunteers, the General Staff was abolished, and tanks were banned. The airforce was proscribed, and the navy cut in both tonnage and personnel. As well as these territorial and military clauses, the treaty established German guilt for starting the war, and established a system of compensatory REPARATIONS. The treaty proved extremely unpopular in Germany, and became a major cause for resentment and instability in the WEIMAR REPUBLIC. Its revision was consistently championed by the Nazi party (*see* NAZISM), while the lack of faith that a number of British and French politicians had in the settlement helped to inform APPEASEMENT.

Vichy Name applied to the interim government of the unoccupied part of France, July 1940–July 1944, taken from the town where its administration was based. In June 1940, after Germany's early successes in the SECOND WORLD WAR left France facing defeat, Prime Minister PÉTAIN secured a peace settlement which left three fifths of France under a German occupation, and the remainder under a French government. In July, this interim government took Vichy as its capital, with the National Assembly voting to destroy the constitution of the THIRD REPUBLIC, and Pétain assuming dictatorial powers. He worked closely with both LAVAL and DARLAN as chief ministers. The government had very little real power, and relied upon German approval for its existence: it thus developed as a focus for many reactionary strands in recent French history, promoting anti-republicanism, ANTI-SEMITISM, the Catholic Church, and corporatism. Acts that exemplified these ideologies included the use of compulsory labour from August 1942; and cooperation with the German government's anti-Jewish policies, which led Vichy to help organise the deportations of approximately 75,000 Jews from France. *See* FINAL SOLUTION.

In November 1942 the German army occupied Vichy territory as a defensive move against the possibility of an invasion from north Africa, although the French government continued to function. In July 1944, after the NORMANDY CAMPAIGN, the government was moved to Sigmaringen in Germany, where it worked as a puppet government-in-exile until May 1945. After the war, many of the leading politicians of Vichy were punished by the new French government: Laval was executed, for example, and Pétain sentenced to life imprisonment. The legacy of the collaboration involved in Vichy remained a problematic feature in post-war French politics and society.

Victor Emmanuel II (1820–78) King of Piedmont-Sardinia 1849–61, and of Italy 1861–78. The son of King Charles Albert, Victor Emmanuel succeeded in 1849 after his father's abdication during the revolution of 1848 (*see* REVOLUTIONS OF 1848). He accepted the role of a constitutional monarch, retaining control in foreign and military policy. He worked with CAVOUR and GARIBALDI towards a unified Italy under Piedmontese leadership, secretly backing the latter's Sicilian campaign of 1860 (*see* ITALIAN UNIFICATION). He led an army south to meet Garibaldi in the Papal States in 1861, subsequently taking the title of King of Italy. Victor Emmanuel added Venetia to his kingdom in 1866 after backing Prussia in the AUSTRO-PRUSSIAN WAR, and made Rome the new capital in 1870 when the French garrison left.

Victor Emmanuel III (1869–1947) King of Italy, 1900–46. Victor Emmanuel III succeeded in July 1900 when his father, Umberto, was assassinated. His political role was constitutionally limited, but he was involved in Italy's pragmatic foreign policy of the pre-FIRST WORLD WAR period, and supported the country's entry into the war in 1915 on the side of the TRIPLE ENTENTE powers. He held this policy despite Italy's commitment to the TRIPLE ALLIANCE (*see* LONDON, TREATY OF, 1915) and despite parliamentary opposition to the war. After the war, Victor Emmanuel was involved in the Fascists' rise to power (*see* FASCISM): in the face of growing unrest, he invited MUSSOLINI to form a government in October 1922, and refused to declare martial law as advised by his prime minister, FACTA (*see* MARCH ON ROME). Thereafter he became effectively a figurehead who provided the government with an air of legitimacy. He was made Emperor of Ethiopia in 1936 and King of Albania in 1939. In 1943 he dismissed Mussolini after the Fascist Grand Council had agreed to depose him (*see* SECOND WORLD WAR, ITALIAN CAMPAIGN) and appointed BADOGLIO in his place. In May 1946, with a referendum on the monarchy imminent, he abdicated and went into exile in Egypt. The Italian monarchy was abolished the following month. Victor Emmanuel died in Egypt in 1947.

Vienna, Congress of (November 1814–June 1815) International conference on European peace, established by the treaty of PARIS of May 1814. The Congress began in November 1814, under METTERNICH's management, and brought together leading representatives from all of the countries that had been involved in the twenty-three years of conflict of the FRENCH REVOLUTIONARY WARS and the NAPOLEONIC WARS. France, represented by TALLEYRAND, was included in the negotiations. The work of the Congress was interrupted in March 1815 when NAPOLEON escaped from his exile on Elba and regained power in France. The Congress led to the formation of the QUADRUPLE ALLIANCE in November 1815, and to the short-lived CONGRESS SYSTEM.

The Congress dealt with territorial issues throughout the continent and beyond. In the German states, the GERMAN CONFEDERATION of thirty-nine independent states under Austrian leadership was established, while Prussia was enlarged and strengthened through the award of the Rhineland, and parts of Pomerania, Saxony and Westphalia. The HABSBURG empire gave up its territories in the Netherlands, which were joined with Holland to form the United Kingdom of the Netherlands, but gained territories in the Italian states (including Venetia, Lombardy and Illyria), part of the Dalmatian coast, and Tyrol and Salzburg. Russia gained most of Poland, which was established as a kingdom under the Tsar, along with Finland from Sweden and Bessarabia from Turkey. The UK gained a number of strategic sea ports in Europe and beyond, including Heligoland, Malta, Ceylon and the Cape of Good Hope. Piedmont gained Genoa, while there were royal restorations in Spain and some of the Italian states. Switzerland was established as an independent state, while France made some colonial gains in the Caribbean.

The Congress had three broad aims: to restore monarchies where possible; to settle territorial issues that had arisen out of the wars; and to promote peace and stability in Europe through a 'balance of power'. These aims, which were not always mutually compatible, and the sheer number of states and thus national interests represented, meant that a number of issues were resolved only by compromise. Divisions between the victorious powers were often evident. This was clearest in the discussion over the division of Poland: Russia wanted all of Poland, including Prussian territories, and suggested that Prussia have all of Saxony in compensation. This solution was unattractive to Habsburg empire and the UK, due to the strength it would give to both Russia and Prussia, and these two powers formed a secret military alliance with France. Although this issue was settled by compromise, it indicated the fragility of the wartime partners' peacetime relationships. However, despite the many loose ends, there was no major war in Europe until the CRIMEAN WAR began in 1853; and many of the changes made at Vienna were still in place in 1914.

Vienna, treaty of (October 1864) Peace treaty that ended the SCHLESWIG WAR of 1864, between the victorious HABSBURG empire and Prussia and the defeated Denmark. Denmark agreed to give up all claims to the disputed territories of Schleswig, Holstein and Lauenberg. The duchies were given to the Habsburg empire and Prussia, to be administered jointly. This proved to be unsatisfactory in practice, with the two powers meeting at Gastein (*see* GASTEIN, CONVENTION OF) in August 1865 to agree a future model of administration. This bilateral action, taken without consultation with the GERMAN CONFEDERATION, demonstrated that body's declining influence in relation to Prussia. *See also* GERMAN UNIFICATION.

Villafranca, treaty of (July 1859) Peace treaty between France and the HABSBURG empire which ended the FRANCO-AUSTRIAN WAR of 1859. After the French victories at Magenta and Solferino in June 1859, NAPOLEON III called an armistice rather than risk an escalation of the war. The peace terms were settled, without Piedmontese representation, between Napoleon III and FRANCIS JOSEPH at Villafranca in July. By the treaty, most of Lombardy was taken by France, to be transferred in turn to Piedmont-Sardinia. The Habsburg empire kept Venetia, and the dukes of Tuscany and Modena were restored. The treaty was unpopular with many nationalists in the Italian states, as it appeared to represent the end of French support for the idea of ITALIAN UNIFICATION, and CAVOUR resigned over it. However, it did reflect the decline in Habsburg influence in the Italian states.

Vittoria, battle of (June 1813) *see* NAPOLEONIC WARS.

Vittoria Veneto, battle of (October–November 1918) *see* FIRST WORLD WAR.

W

Wagram, battle of (July 1809) *see* NAPOLEONIC WARS.

Waldheim, Kurt (born 1918) Austrian politician and diplomat. After serving in the German army during the SECOND WORLD WAR, Waldheim entered the Austrian diplomatic service. He was involved in the negotiation of the AUSTRIAN STATE TREATY of 1955. In 1968, four years after leaving the service, he became Foreign Minister, a post he held until 1970. The following year he stood unsuccessfully for election to the presidency. In 1972 he succeeded U-Thant as Secretary-General of the UNITED NATIONS, although his ten years in office were not distinguished by any great successes: despite some progress over Cyprus (*see ENOSIS*), Waldheim made few advances in various African and Middle Eastern problems. He retired in 1981. In 1986 he ran for the Austrian presidency again. His campaign presented his critics with the opportunity to publicise his war record, which had included active roles in the killing of Yugoslav partisans and the deportation of Jews (*see* FINAL SOLUTION, RESISTANCE). Waldheim denied these allegations, and won the election, but he was refused entry to a number of other countries during his term in office. He did not stand for re-election in 1982.

Walesa, Lech (born 1943) Polish trade unionist and politician. Walesa worked as an electrician in the Gdansk shipyards from 1967 until his dismissal in 1976. He re-emerged in 1979 as a strike leader in the docks, which led to his negotiating role with the Polish government in the talks that led to the establishment of SOLIDARITY, a free trade union. In August 1980 he became Solidarity's chairman. In December 1981 he was imprisoned when JARUZELSKI's government imposed martial law: he served eleven months. On his release, he returned to his role as a spokesman for Solidarity, and gained a high profile nationally and internationally: for example, he developed contacts with Pope JOHN PAUL II, and won the 1983 Nobel Peace Prize. In the late 1980s he participated in the talks that re-established Solidarity, and in Poland's revolution of 1989 (*see* REVOLUTIONS OF 1989–91). Walesa won the presidential election in 1990. His term in office was characterised by attempts at economic and social reform, a promotion of the Roman Catholic Church, and an increase of power in the hands of the presidency. He lost the 1995 election to the former communist, Alexander Kwasniewski.

Wall Street Crash (1929) *see* DEPRESSION, GREAT.

war communism Name given to the BOLSHEVIKS' domestic policies from March 1918 until March 1921, during the RUSSIAN CIVIL WAR. The Bolsheviks had envisaged a gradual take-over of the Russian economy. However, circumstances in early 1918 created an environment for a more rapid movement towards COMMUNISM. The development of the Civil War brought strains on supplies; the loss of territory at the treaty of BREST-LITOVSK removed significant agricultural and industrial producers from Russia; and the refusal of some institutions to cooperate with the Bolsheviks, notably the state bank, meant that the new government felt the need to intervene directly.

War communism had a number of strands. It included the nationalisation of virtually all industries and businesses, including banking; the conscription of large parts of the labour force; the dilution of trade union power; the banning of private commerce in agricultural goods; and the requisitioning of agricultural produce. The measures were backed up by force and terror, particularly in the countryside, where special committees were established to inform on any producers hoarding supplies: this directly increased class tensions, with 'kulaks' (the richer farmers) being vilified.

The results of war communism were disastrous, economically, socially and politically. Hyper-inflation led to the collapse of money, creating an unstable and unpredictable barter economy. Industrial production declined to approximately 20 per cent of Russia's 1913 output (although the loss of territory in 1918 must be remembered here), while urban dwellers migrated to the countryside in large numbers in the face of starvation in the cities: the population of Petrograd, for example, fell by 80 per cent between 1917 and 1920. The requisitioning policies in the countryside led many producers to hoard their produce, and to produce less: combined with the military disruption and deliberate government policies in some areas, this caused famine and epidemics that contributed significantly to the total Civil War dead of up to 10,000,000. Black markets thrived in all towns and cities. The Bolsheviks began to turn away from war communism in early 1921 in the light of the discontent it was causing, with the naval mutiny at Kronstadt coming as a decisive factor. It was replaced by the partial free market of LENIN'S NEW ECONOMIC POLICY in March 1921.

Warsaw Pact Military alliance. After the establishment of NATO in 1949 as a US-backed military alliance for western and southern Europe, the USSR did not immediately respond with a similar alliance. However, it took this option under KHRUSHCHEV in May 1955 at a crucial stage in the COLD WAR, following anti-communist demonstrations in the German Democratic Republic (GDR) in 1953, the Federal Republic of Germany's (FRG) membership of NATO in 1954, and the impending end of the allied occupation of Austria (*see* AUSTRIAN STATE

TREATY). In this context, the Treaty of Friendship, Cooperation and Mutual Alliance signed at Warsaw in May 1955 established the Warsaw Pact as a military alliance based on mutual aid between signatories in case of aggression, an integrated command, and the basing of Soviet forces in signatories' territories. The founder members were Albania, Bulgaria, Czechoslovakia, the GDR, Hungary, Poland, Romania and the USSR, although Soviet domination was inherent not just through its basing of troops in the other countries, but also through the relative size of its contribution, the structure of the high command, and the alliance being based in Moscow. Finland declined an invitation to join in 1955.

In 1956, troops based in Hungary under the Pact were involved in suppression the HUNGARIAN RISING, a move which showed that part of the Pact's agenda was the maintenance of Soviet domination through eastern Europe (*see* IMPERIALISM). This was shown again in 1968, when Warsaw Pact forces invaded Czechoslovakia to suppress the PRAGUE SPRING. Albania withdrew from the pact in 1968. During the REVOLUTIONS OF 1989–91, the USSR's refusal to re-invoke the BREZHNEV doctrine meant that one of the Warsaw Pact's purposes had gone; while it lost the GDR in 1990 through GERMAN REUNIFICATION. The pact was formally dissolved in April 1991, and a number of former members moved closer to NATO in the general realignment of alliances that characterised the end of the COLD WAR in Europe. In May 1999 the Czech Republic, Hungary and Poland became the first former Warsaw Pact members to join NATO.

Warsaw Treaty Organisation *see* WARSAW PACT.

Washington Naval Agreement (February 1922) Multilateral agreement on naval disarmament. In November 1921, Belgium China, France, Italy, Japan, the Netherlands, Portugal, the UK and the USA met in Washington, primarily to discuss their interests in the Far East. However, the conference also produced a naval agreement which had implications for European disarmament. By this agreement, France, Italy, Japan, the UK and the USA agreed to limit their navies in relation to each other (on a ratio of 1.75: 1.75: 3.15: 5.25: 5.25), and agreed to place a moratorium on all new capital ship construction for ten years. This agreement was renewed by Japan, the UK and the USA at London in 1930.

Waterloo, battle of (18 June 1815) Ultimate battle of the 'Hundred Days' phase of the NAPOLEONIC WARS, fought by France against an alliance of the Netherlands, Prussia and the UK. After NAPOLEON's escape from Elba, and his reacquisition of power in Paris, the victorious powers of 1814 remobilised against France. The British and Dutch built up a combined army in the Netherlands under the Duke of Wellington, with the Prussians under Gebhard von Blücher aiming to join them. Napoleon marched into the Netherlands to take on these forces, aiming to prevent their combination, and to remove them from Europe before the HABSBURG empire and Russia could fully mobilise. On 16 June 1815, the French beat the Prussians at Ligny, and fought an indecisive battle with the Dutch army at Quatre Bras. The French then advanced on Brussels, but they were stopped at Waterloo by the Anglo-Dutch force on 18 June. For much of the day the French seemed to be gaining ground, with repeated attacks of the Anglo-Dutch army causing many casualties, but by the early evening the French began to show their exhaustion, and the battle turned against them when the Prussians arrived, and when a final attack by Napoleon's elite Imperial Guard on the centre of the Anglo-Dutch lines was shattered by a rifle volley and a bayonet charge. The French army broke up, and Napoleon fled. French losses totalled approximately 60,000, including prisoners and deserters, while the British, Dutch, and Prussian armies suffered around 55,000 casualties. Waterloo proved decisive: Napoleon gave up his aims of rebuilding France's power, and abdicated for the second time. The battle was followed by the treaty of PARIS of 1815, which was less lenient than the treaty of 1814.

Weimar Republic The name applied to Germany's republican political system which lasted from November 1918 until March 1933. The republic was formed in November 1918 in the face of Germany's defeat in the FIRST WORLD WAR. Various pressures coalesced to encourage Kaiser WILLIAM II to abdicate and for the politicians to reconstruct the empire into a republic: revolutionary pressure from communists; the loss of popular support for the government at the end of the war; and politicians' perceptions that the victorious powers would establish a relatively sympathetic peace if they were dealing with a new republic rather than the imperial regime of 1914, all influenced this major shift in German politics. After a transitional government ruled from late November, elections held in January 1919 created an assembly, which met at Weimar in February 1919 to produce the constitution. This constitution, published in July 1919, featured numerous extremely democratic aspects, including adult suffrage, proportional representation, the provision for plebiscites on specific issues, and a president as head of state, elected separately from the bicameral legislature. However, it also contained a number of centralising features, including a dilution of local and regional power, and a system for presidential decrees which could be used in emergency to over-ride the legislature. Moreover, key areas in public and political life, including the judiciary, the military and parts of the civil service, were not thoroughly reformed on the democratic principles of the constitution. The government returned to Berlin in 1920.

The first years of Weimar were extremely volatile, as Germany attempted to adapt to both peace and the new democracy: this, combined with popular outrage at the peace terms of VERSAILLES and the economic impact of both REPARATIONS and post-war inflation, led to a number of revolutionary coup attempts from both left and right. The former included the socialist republic in Bavaria, which lasted from November 1918 until it was dissolved with force in April 1919, and the Spartakist rising in Berlin in January 1919, led by Karl Liebknecht and Rosa LUXEMBURG. From the right, new nationalist parties combined with demobilised soldiers in such abortive coups as the Kapp putsch in Berlin of March 1919 and the Nazi party's Beer Hall putsch in Munich in November 1923 (*see* NAZISM, HITLER). The country became relatively stabilised from 1924, when the Dawes plan reduced reparations: in this period Germany gained some international rehabilitation through the LOCARNO treaties and admission to the LEAGUE OF NATIONS. However, even through this period the electoral system worked against continuity in government. The republic was badly damaged by the DEPRESSION after 1929, as foreign investment ended and loans were recalled: by mid-1932, 6,000,000 people were unemployed. In this climate extremist parties gained ground, notably the Nazis and the Communists, while President HINDENBURG used decree powers excessively to force through legislation. The republican experiment ended in March 1933 when the new chancellor, Hitler, ensured emergency powers for the government by securing the ENABLING ACT.

Western European Union (WEU) Defence alliance involving European nations. When the proposals to form the EUROPEAN DEFENCE COMMUNITY (EDC) failed, the signatories of the 1948 BRUSSELS TREATY developed the WEU as an alternative model for a mutual defence organisation. Belgium, France, Luxembourg, the Netherlands and the UK negotiated with Italy and the Federal Republic of Germany (FRG) for a joint body in 1954, and the WEU was duly established in May 1955. Its greatest significance at the time was its inclusion of the FRG only ten years after the end of the SECOND WORLD WAR, although limitations on German military capacity were insisted upon. The WEU was run by an Executive Council of ministers from member states, with discussions and debates taking place in an Assembly. Unlike NATO, the WEU did not develop its own military force, but used contributions from member states. The WEU had little real significance in the COLD WAR, due to the domination of Europe by NATO and the WARSAW PACT, but it developed a new role in the 1980s in conjunction with the EUROPEAN COMMUNITY: it was, for example, mentioned in the treay of MAASTRICHT of 1992 as the EUROPEAN UNION's prospective military wing. Moreover, it enlarged in this period, with Spain and Portugal joining in 1989, and Greece in 1994.

William I (1797–1888) King of Prussia 1861–88, and Emperor of Germany 1871–88. William became regent of Prussia in 1858 due to his brother FREDERICK WILLIAM IV's health problems, and succeeded as king in 1861 on Frederick William's death. Although he did not sympathise with LIBERALISM, he accepted the 1850 constitution and generally worked with it, but his main interests were military and diplomatic. He attempted to strengthen Prussia's army, in particular in relation to that of the HABSBURG empire: but when, in 1862, the laws for this were refused by the Diet, he appointed BISMARCK as Minister-President and managed to get the legislation through. He worked closely with Bismarck thereafter, and kept a high profile in Prussia's wars of the 1860s, which were instrumental in Prussia's growth as the dominant German state. He personally commanded the army in the AUSTRO-PRUSSIAN WAR of 1866, and helped to engineer the start of the FRANCO-PRUSSIAN WAR of 1870, in which he took command of the army for the battle of Sedan. At Versailles in 1871, William was declared Emperor of the newly unified Germany (*see* GERMAN UNIFICATION). He reigned until his death in 1888, giving support to Germany's INDUSTRIALISATION and diplomatic initiatives that made it one of the most powerful continental states by the end of the century. William survived an assassination attempt in 1878: during his recovery his son Frederick ruled briefly as regent. Frederick succeeded William in 1888 as Frederick III, but died in the same year.

William II (1859–1941) Emperor of Germany and King of Prussia, 1888–1918. William succeeded his father Frederick III in June 1888, and quickly moved to a 'new course' in German policy by prioritising an imperial role rather than a merely European one (*see* IMPERIALISM). In the course of making this shift, he dismissed his grandfather WILLIAM I's chancellor, BISMARCK, in 1890, and worked more closely with military advisors, such as CAPRIVI, Alfred von Schlieffen (*see* SCHLIEFFEN PLAN), TIRPITZ and Alfred von Waldersee. His attempts at a direct style of rule on such issues as SOCIALISM and trade union activities brought him into confrontations with the Reichstag. He also undermined some of Bismarck's diplomatic achievements, particularly by neglecting Germany's relationship with Russia, and by alienating both France and the UK over colonial issues (*see* MOROCCAN CRISES). William's political influence declined after 1908, and while he favoured a Balkan war in 1914, he had only a limited role in its prosecution. During the FIRST WORLD WAR his influence declined further, with Germany being run effectively as a military dictatorship from 1916 by HINDENBURG and LUDENDORFF. William abdicated in November 1918 before the armistice, on the assumption that Germany would get more favourable peace terms if he was no longer head of state. He moved to the Netherlands, where the royal family protected him from some allied calls for his trial after the war. He died there in 1941.

Witte, Sergei (1849–1915) Russian politician. After a career in railway administration, Witte took office under ALEXANDER III in 1892 as Finance Minister, a post he retained under Alexander's successor NICHOLAS II. In this role, Witte attempted to modernise Russia through INDUSTRIALISATION. Through heavy foreign loans (particularly from France and the UK) and new taxes, he promoted development in iron and steel, coal and railways, and was largely responsible for planning the Trans-Siberian railway. In 1897 he reformed the currency and placed Russia on the GOLD STANDARD to encourage foreign investment. Although these policies brought some successes, they also produced foreign debts, and worsened conditions in the countryside. In 1903 Witte was dismissed, but Nicholas recalled him in September 1905 to negotiate the peace treaty with Japan. During the 1905 Revolution (*see* RUSSIAN REVOLUTION 1905), Witte advised Nicholas on the

October Manifesto, and the following month Nicholas appointed him as Prime Minister, primarily in order to gain a new loan from France. He was dismissed in May 1906, as his ideas for constitutional reform were no longer welcome at the time of Nicholas' Fundamental Laws. He never held office again, although he remained a critic of the Tsar and, in particular, of Russia's entry into the FIRST WORLD WAR.

World Bank *see* BRETTON WOODS CONFERENCE.

World Health Organisation (WHO) *see* UNITED NATIONS.

Y

Yalta Conference (February 1945) Inter-allied planning conference of the SECOND WORLD WAR. The conference was called to allow the three main allied representatives, Winston Churchill, Franklin Roosevelt and STALIN, to look forward to the end of the European war and develop strategies for peacetime. The three agreed to divide Austria from Germany (*see ANSCHLUSS*), and temporarily to split each country into zones of occupation under American, British, French and Soviet control. The territorial settlement of Poland was further discussed, developing ideas from the previous year's TEHRAN conference: it was agreed that Poland would be shifted to the west, with the CURZON LINE being established as the Polish-Soviet border (which would regain for the USSR territories lost to Poland during the RUSSIAN CIVIL WAR), and a new western border being established between Poland and Germany (*see* ODER-NEISSE LINE, POLISH CORRIDOR). The three also published their declaration on liberated Europe, which envisaged democratic governments being developed in all areas taken from Germany. Specifically, this obliged Stalin to agree to a representative provisional government and to elections in Poland: his failure to fulfil this subsequently caused major tensions in the early COLD WAR. The USSR built on its Tehran commitment to the Far East by agreeing to join the war against Japan within three months of victory in Europe: in return, Soviet territorial demands in the Far East were recognised (*see* IMPERIALISM). The three powers also committed themselves to the nascent UNITED NATIONS. Yalta was the final meeting of the three major allies during the European war: they next met at POTSDAM after the defeat of Germany.

Yeltsin, Boris (born 1931) Soviet and Russian politician. An engineer, Yeltsin joined the Communist party in 1961. He was elected to the Supreme Soviet in 1976, and quickly made an impact under GORBACHEV's leadership, on both the party's Central Committee, which he chaired from 1985, and on the Moscow party structure. In June 1990 he resigned from the party and outlined a radical plan for converting Russia to a free market economy in under two years. Having called for Gorbachev's resignation in February 1991, Yeltsin raised his own profile by resisting the anti-Gorbachev coup. In June 1991, he was overwhelmingly elected as President of Russia, from which position he led the dissolution of the USSR into the Commonwealth of Independent States (*see* REVOLUTIONS OF 1989–91). As President of newly independent Russia, he introduced radical economic reforms, and used military force against the parliament when it failed to act quickly enough in November 1993. Gaining greater powers with the December 1993 constitution, Yeltsin became more erratic, and lost a lot of support through his aggressive intervention in Chechnya in 1996. However, despite notoriously poor health, he was re-elected in 1996. His approach became increasingly erratic and dictatorial, particularly evident in his dismissal of his governments in 1997 and 1999, and in his frequent clashes with parliament.

Yezhovshchina Umbrella term for purges in the USSR under STALIN, taking its name from Nicholas Yezhov, Commissar for Internal Affairs from 1936 to 1938. The process of ridding the Soviet government and Communist party of Stalin's real and imagined enemies and rivals began in 1934 after KIROV was murdered. Leading figures ZINOVIEV and KAMENEV were charged with planning Kirov's death and plotting to kill Stalin. After a major show trial in 1936, the leaders of this alleged conspiracy were executed. This was followed by two other show trials, which led to the deaths of BUKHARIN and others. In all some seventy people were tried, in formulaic events in which the accused confessed after torture. However, most of those targeted during the purges were tried secretly or not at all. Between 1936 and 1938, the height of the purges, a number of groups were attacked, including the party itself, the armed forces, the Young Communist League, and foreign communists living in the USSR. Charges included maintaining contacts with TROTSKY, and conspiracy with foreign governments. Industrial managers and workers were targeted for alleged failings and sabotage in the FIVE YEAR PLANS. The excessive use of state terrorism created a climate of fear in the USSR, which itself contributed to a culture of denunciation. The purges were scaled down after 1938, when Yezhov himself fell victim to the process, but the state retained its use of arbitrary arrest and selective purging of suspect groups (including Jews, Germans and doctors) throughout the rest of the Stalinist period. From 1956, Stalin's successor KHRUSHCHEV publicised some of the excesses of the purges in his policy of destalinisation; while a number of leading victims were rehabilitated under GORBACHEV's *GLASNOST* policies in the 1980s. The numbers involved are impossible to quantify exactly, although estimates of 10,000,000 arrests and 3,000,000 executions are generally recognised. In addition to the executions, millions were also imprisoned during the purges, many of whom died as a result of poor conditions in prisons and in forced labour camps.

Young Plan *see* REPARATIONS, GERMAN.

Young Turks Liberal and nationalist political grouping in the OTTOMAN EMPIRE. Pressure for reform in the empire began to emerge in the late nineteenth century, as army officers influenced by LIBERALISM and NATIONALISM (who came to be known as 'Young Turks') began to press for a return to the constitutional reforms of 1876 (*see* BALKAN REBELLIONS), upon which Sultan Abdul Hamid II had reneged. In 1889 an informal reformist grouping emerged as the Association for the Union of Ottomans, which formed the focus for discussion of constitutional reform and the maintenance of the empire. In 1908, as the Committee for Union and Progress, Young Turk officers organised a rebellion, which forced the Sultan to accommodate some of their demands, including the reconstitution of parliament and freedom of the press. The leadership gained significant political influence. The following year Abdul Hamid II planned a military rising against the Young Turks, which they met with a counter-coup in which the Sultan was deposed. Despite some splits within the movement, particularly over liberal and nationalist goals, the Young Turks worked with the new Sultan, Mohammad V, who operated as a constitutional monarch. This period saw the introduction of liberal reforms in education and religious life, but military failures and territorial losses in the BALKAN WARS and then the FIRST WORLD WAR showed that the Young Turks' imperial agenda was not viable. The movement remained a factor in Ottoman politics throughout the First World War, and can be seen to have prepared some of the liberal ground for the new republic which was formed in 1922. *See* ATATÜRK, GREEK-TURKISH WAR.

Ypres, battle of (October–November 1914) *see* FIRST WORLD WAR.

Yser, battle of (October 1914) *see* FIRST WORLD WAR.

Yugoslavia, dissolution (1990–95) Process by which the Socialist Federal Republic of Yugoslavia disintegrated. The republic was constituted in November 1945 on the basis of TITO's wartime diplomacy within the former kingdom of Yugoslavia. This structure, with some federal devolution to the republics (Bosnia-Herzegovina, Croatia, Macedonia, Montenegro, Serbia (with Kosovo and Vojvodina as autonomous areas) and Slovenia), remained in place until after Tito's death. It began to come under strain from nationalist and inter-ethnic tensions in the mid-1980s, helped by the widening of political debates under the influence of *GLASNOST*, and by the significant economic differences that existed between the republics. The tensions were highlighted by nationalist demonstrations in Serbia (*see* NATIONALISM), by Serbia's effective annexation of Kosovo in 1989, and by the central government's resignation over the budget in December 1988. In this climate, the influence of COMMUNISM declined in some republics (notably Slovenia and Croatia) while remaining strong in Serbia under MILOSEVIC's presidency, as each republic took more control of its own affairs. *See* REVOLUTIONS OF 1989–91.

In June 1991, Croatia and Slovenia declared their independence from the federation. After a week of fighting in Slovenia, and six months in Croatia, their secession from Yugoslavia was fully established with UNITED NATIONS' assistance. Macedonia withdrew from the federation peacefully between September 1991 and April 1992, although its independence raised tensions with Greece over territorial and ethnic issues. In April 1992, Montenegro and Serbia reconstituted the federation as the Federal Republic of Yugoslavia. In March 1992 Bosnia-Herzegovina, under a predominantly Muslim government, declared its independence. This gave rise to a civil war, as the secession was opposed by Bosnian Serbs, who wished to remain linked to Serbia. The war developed along ethnic and religious lines, with Serbia supporting the minority rebels. Despite pressure from the UN, the EUROPEAN UNION and NATO for economic sanctions, the Bosnian Serbs gained territory and, through terrorist tactics against civilian populations, established a wave of migration in the interests of what they labelled 'ethnic cleansing', an attempt to clear Croats and Muslims from areas they wished to colonise. In 1994, NATO forces were used (for the first time since the alliance's creation) against the Bosnian Serbs. This increase of pressure against the Serb cause led to the Dayton Agreement in November 1995, a settlement that reconstituted the republic as the Confederation of Bosnia-Herzegovina, divided into two regions along ethnic lines: the Serb Republic and the Croat-Muslim Federation. The settlement was supported by the presence of NATO forces. The excesses of the war, which included civilian massacres and the use of concentration camps by the Bosnian Serbs, came under the scrutiny of the UN's International Criminal Tribunal for the former Yugoslavia, formed in May 1993. In 1999 further territorial changes in the post-1992 Yugoslavia, involving Serbian persecution of ethnic Albanians in Kosovo, initiated renewed international involvement. *See* KOSOVO WAR.

Z

zemstva (Russian: 'provincial councils') Provincial and district councils established in rural areas of Russia in 1864. Following the EMANCIPATION OF THE SERFS, ALEXANDER II introduced a number of political and social reforms. The *zemstva* system was part of this. Individual *zemstvo* were set up on an elected basis, funded by central government and through local taxation, with the brief to manage certain local affairs. Such issues as health provision, education, road-building and the management of agriculture came into their remit. The *zemstva* were limited in a number of ways: for example, the electoral system ensured that the bulk of power in each *zemstvo* remained with nobles and landowners; while *zemstva*'s need to work with central government on policing and taxation limited their opportunities for radicalism. However, they did produce significant levels of local political involvement, and established traditions and practices of local government. In many areas, they remained active and effective until the revolution of 1917 (*see* RUSSIAN REVOLUTIONS 1917), when they were replaced by soviets.

Zhukov, Georgi (1896–1974) Soviet soldier and politician. A conscript in the FIRST WORLD WAR, Zhukov joined the Red Army in 1918 and the Communist party in 1919. He fought in the RUSSIAN CIVIL WAR, and stayed in the army afterwards, gaining promotions through the 1930s. In January 1941 he became Chief of General Staff. After a brief decline in influence at the start of Operation BARBAROSSA in June 1941, Zhukov fought at Leningrad and Moscow before launching a successful counter-offensive in December 1941 which pushed the German army back from Moscow. Deputy Supreme Commander after STALIN from August 1942, Zhukov led the defeat of the Germans at STALINGRAD and KURSK in 1943, and the relief of Leningrad in 1944, before leading the Red Army to Berlin. In May 1945 Zhukov accepted the German surrender (*see* SECOND WORLD WAR). He remained in Germany as Commander of the USSR's zone until 1947, when Stalin demoted him as a potential rival. He returned to prominence after Stalin's death in 1953, helping KHRUSHCHEV's leadership struggle, and he served as Defence Minister from 1955 until 1957. He was then dismissed by Khrushchev.

Zinoviev, Grigori (Radomyslsky Apfelbaum) (1883–1936) Soviet politician. Zinoviev joined the Social Democrats in 1901, moving into the BOLSHEVIK faction in 1903. In 1907 he left Russia to work with the exiled LENIN. He returned to Petrograd with Lenin in April 1917, and became the chairman of the Petrograd Soviet (*see* RUSSIAN REVOLUTIONS 1917). He did not support the October Revolution, preferring instead a more gradual move towards COMMUNISM, but he subsequently took a leading role in the THIRD INTERNATIONAL, with particular duties for links with foreign communist movements. A member of the POLITBURO from 1921, he worked with STALIN and KAMENEV against TROTSKY after Lenin's death in 1924. In 1926, however, he turned against Stalin and was dismissed from his post, and expelled from the party in 1927. After readmission, re-expulsion, and a second readmission in 1933, Zinoviev was arrested in 1935 and sentenced to ten years imprisonment for his alleged role in KIROV's murder. In August 1936 he was retried with Kamenev in the first major show trial of the *YEZHOVSHCHINA*. Convicted of treason and of conspiring with Trotsky, he was executed immediately.

zionism Jewish nationalist movement. During the late nineteenth century, ANTI-SEMITISM in a number of European countries encouraged some European Jews to advocate the establishment of a Jewish nation state in Palestine: as such, it was related to other forms of nineteenth-century NATIONALISM. Taking Mount Zion as its symbol, from ancient Jewish history, zionism became organised in 1897 through HERZL's World Zionist Organisation (WZO), formed at a congress in Basle. The WZO acted as a pressure group, while also encouraging and financing emigration. The British government supported the idea from 1917, although during its tenure of Palestine as a mandate (*see* MANDATES) from the OTTOMAN EMPIRE it was unable to settle the territorial disputes between Arabs and Jews. Zionism gained a great deal of liberal support during the renewed anti-semitism of the THIRD REICH: and the FINAL SOLUTION confirmed much international opinion in favour of a Jewish nation state. Israel was accordingly established in 1948, with anti-Arab and anti-British terrorism being used during the final phases of negotiation. After 1948, once the basic nationalist cause had been met, zionism became strongly associated not only with supporting continued Jewish migration (particularly from the USSR and eastern Europe), but also with anti-Arab attitudes, for which it was condemned as racist by the UNITED NATIONS in 1975.

Zog (Ahmed Bey Zogu) (1895–1961) Albanian politician; King of Albania, 1928–39. A rich Moslem landowner, Zogu was involved in the Albanian nationalist movement against the Italians during the FIRST WORLD WAR. Emerging as one of the country's most powerful figures in 1920, when Albania was admitted to the LEAGUE OF NATIONS, Zogu became Prime Minister in 1923 and, after a revolt and a brief exile in 1924, President in 1925 with Yugoslavian backing. In 1928 Zogu forced through a new constitution which replaced the republic with a monarchy, and he assumed the crown as King Zog. He reigned until 1939, during which time

Albania became effectively an Italian dependency. When Italy invaded Albania in April 1939, Zog was deposed, and MUSSOLINI named the Italian monarch VICTOR EMMANUEL III as King of Albania. The monarchy was abolished in 1946. Zogu died in exile in 1961.

Zogu, Ahmed Bey *see* ZOG.

Zollverein (German: 'customs union') Customs union of the German states, established in 1833. After Prussia had removed its internal trade barriers shortly after the NAPOLEONIC WARS, discussions within the GERMAN CONFEDERATION began on the possibility of a wider free trade area. The *Zollverein* was duly established with eighteen members in 1833, to come into effect in 1834. The union abolished internal tariffs, and set up uniform import duties for goods from non-member states. Prussian models and rates were adopted for the union as a whole, and Prussia was empowered to lead talks with other countries over mutually beneficial trading arrangements, which helped to ensure that Prussia gained the leading role in this economic development. The bulk of the German states joined the union through the 1840s and 1850s, while its continental position was secured through agreements with, among others, Belgium, France and Piedmont-Sardinia. The *Zollverein* helped to facilitate INDUSTRIALISATION and commercial developments in the German states, and facilitated an economic foundation for subsequent political unification. *See* GERMAN UNIFICATION.

Appendix

European monarchs, 1789–1999

This appendix provides summary information on the geopolitical status of Europe's monarchies in the period 1789–1999. It covers empires, kingdoms, and the major principalities, grand duchies and duchies, although it excludes the satellite kingdoms (Etruria, Holland, Italy) and grand duchy (Warsaw) created by Napoleon during the Napoleonic Wars. The names and dates in brackets after each state's name are those of the royal houses in power for the given periods, starting with those in power in 1789. The summary paragraph for each state describes that state's extant geopolitical status in 1789, and outlines the major changes thereafter. The lists provide the names and regnal dates of the monarchs.

Albania (Zogu, 1928–44)

The kingdom of Albania was established in 1928. From 1939 until 1944 it was ruled by the King of Italy. A republic was restored in 1944.

1928–44	Zog (in exile, 1939–44)
1939–44	Victor Emmanuel III (also King of Italy)

Austria (Habsburg, 1276–1918)

Austria was a duchy at the heart of the Habsburg and Holy Roman empires from the thirteenth century. In 1867 a dual monarchy was established with Hungary, making the ruling monarch the Emperor of Hungary. Austria and Hungary became separate republics in 1918.

1780–90	Joseph II (also Holy Roman Emperor)
1790–92	Leopold II (also Holy Roman Emperor)
1792–1835	Francis (also Holy Roman Emperor, 1792–1804)
1835–48	Ferdinand
1848–1916	Francis Joseph (also Emperor of Hungary, 1867–1916)
1916–18	Charles (also Emperor of Hungary)

Baden (Zahringen, *c.* 1100–1918)

The margraviate of Baden was established in the twelfth century. It became a grand duchy in 1806. In 1871 it joined the new German empire, retaining its own monarchy until 1918, when Germany became a republic.

1738–1811	Charles Frederick
1811–18	Charles
1818–30	Ludwig I
1830–52	Leopold
1852–58	Ludwig II
1858–1907	Frederick I
1907–18	Frederick II

Bavaria (Wittelsbach, 1623–1918)

The electorate of Bavaria was established in 1623. It became a kingdom in 1806. In 1871 it joined the new German empire, retaining its own monarchy until 1918, when Germany became a republic.

1777–99	Charles Theodore
1799–1825	Maximilian IV (King Maximilian I from 1806)
1825–48	Ludwig I
1848–64	Maximilian II
1864–86	Ludwig II
1886–1913	Otto
1913–18	Ludwig III

Belgium (Saxe-Coburg since 1831)

The kingdom of Belgium was established in 1830.

1831–65	Leopold I
1865–1909	Leopold II
1909–34	Albert I
1934–50	Leopold III (imprisoned 1940–45)
1944–50	Regency
1950	Leopold III (restored)
1950	Regency
1951–93	Baudouin
1993–	Albert II

Brunswick (Welf 1735–1806; Bonaparte, 1807–13; Welf, 1813–84)

The duchy of Brunswick was established in 1735. In 1871 it joined the new German empire, retaining its own monarchy until 1884.

1780–1806	Charles II
1807–13	Jerome Bonaparte

1813–15	Frederick-William
1815–30	Charles III
1830–84	William

Bulgaria (Battenburg, 1879–86; Saxe-Coburg-Gotha, 1887–1946)

Bulgaria became an autonomous principality within the Ottoman empire in 1879, and an independent kingdom in 1908. In 1946 it became a republic.

1879–86	Alexander
1886	Regency
1887–1918	Ferdinand
1918–43	Boris III
1943–46	Simeon II

Denmark (Oldenburg since 1448)

The kingdom of Denmark was established in the tenth century. From 1523 until 1814 its rulers were also kings of Norway.

1766–1808	Christian VII
1784–1808	Regency
1808–39	Frederick VI
1839–48	Christian VIII
1848–63	Frederick VII
1863–1906	Christian IX
1906–12	Frederick VIII
1912–47	Christian X
1947–72	Frederick IX
1972–	Margaret II

France (Bourbon, 1589–92; Bonaparte, 1804–14; Bourbon, 1814–30; Orléans, 1830–48; Bonaparte, 1852–70)

The kingdom of France was established in the ninth century. It became a republic in 1792, and, under Napoleon, an empire in 1804. The monarchy was restored in 1814, lasting until 1848, when a new republic was established. Between 1852 and 1870, France was again an empire, becoming a republic at the end of Napoleon III's reign.

1774–92	Louis XVI
1804–14	Napoleon I
1814–24	Louis XVIII
1824–30	Charles X
1830–48	Louis-Philippe
1852–70	Napoleon III

Germany (Hohenzollern, 1871–1918)

The German empire was formed in 1871, with the reigning king of Prussia becoming emperor. It became a republic in 1918.

1871–88	William I (King of Prussia since 1861)
1888	Frederick (also Frederick III of Prussia)
1888–1918	William II (also William II of Prussia)

Greece (Wittelsbach, 1832–62; Glücksburg, 1863–1974)

The kingdom of Greece was established in 1832. It became a republic in 1924. In 1935, the monarchy was restored. This lasted until 1974, when a new republic was declared, although the country was governed by a military grouping from 1967 until 1973.

1832–62	Otho
1863–1913	George I
1913–17	Constantine I
1917–20	Alexander
1920–22	Constantine I (restored)
1922–23	George II
1923–24	Regency
1935	Regency
1935–47	George II (restored)
1947–64	Paul
1964–74	Constantine II

Hanover (Welf, 1692–1866)

The electorate of Hanover was established in 1692. In 1814 it became a kingdom. From 1714 until 1837 its monarchs were also those of Great Britain (United Kingdom of Great Britain and Ireland (UK) from 1801). In 1866 it was annexed by Prussia.

1760–1820	George III (also King of Great Britain 1760–1801, and the UK 1801–20)
1811–20	Regency
1820–30	George IV (also King of the UK)
1830–37	William III (also King of the UK)
1837–51	Ernest Augustus
1851–66	George V

Hesse (Hesse, 1567–1918)

The landgraviate of Hesse-Darmstadt was formed in 1567. In 1806 it was reconstituted as the grand duchy of Hesse. In 1871 it joined the new German empire, retaining its own monarchy until 1918, when Germany became a republic.

1768–90	Ludwig IX
1790–1830	Ludwig X (Grand Duke Ludwig I of Hesse from 1806)
1830–48	Ludwig II
1848–77	Ludwig III
1877–92	Ludwig IV
1892–1918	Ernest-Ludwig

Holy Roman Empire (various dynasties: predominantly Habsburg)

The Holy Roman Empire was established in the tenth century. It dissolved in 1806.

1765–90	Joseph II (also Emperor of Austria, 1780–90)
1790–92	Leopold II (also Emperor of Austria)
1792–1806	Francis II (also Emperor of Austria 1792–1835)

Hungary (Habsburg, 1867–1918, 1920–44 [nominally])

Hungary was established as a partner in the dual monarchy with Austria in 1867, with the Austrian emperor becoming Emperor of Hungary. Austria and Hungary became separate republics in 1918. In 1920, Miklós Horthy re-established Hungary as a monarchy under Charles IV, with himself as regent in Charles' absence. Hungary became a republic again in 1945.

1867–1916	Francis Joseph (also Emperor of Austria, 1848–1916)
1916–18	Charles IV (also Charles, Emperor of Austria)
1920–44	Regency

Italy (Savoy, 1861–1946)

The kingdom of Italy was established in 1861, which eventually covered the whole of the peninsula. Italy became a republic in 1946.

1861–78	Victor Emmanuel II (formerly King of Piedmont–Sardinia)
1878–1900	Umberto I
1900–46	Victor Emmanuel III
1946	Umberto II

Liechtenstein (Liechtenstein since 1719)

The principality of Liechtenstein was established in 1719.

1781–1805	Alois I
1805–07	John I
1807–13	Charles
1813–36	John I (restored)
1836–58	Alois II
1858–1929	John II

1929–38	Francis
1938–89	Francis Joseph II
1989–	Hans Adam II

Luxembourg (Nassau-Wilberg, 1816–66; Nassau since 1890)

The duchy of Luxembourg was established in 1816. There was no duke between 1866 and 1890, when Luxembourg was re-established as a grand duchy.

1816–39	William
1839–66	Adolf
1890–1905	Adolf (restored)
1905–12	William IV
1912–19	Marie-Adelaide
1919–64	Charlotte (exiled, 1940–44)
1964–	John

Mecklenburg-Schwerin (Mecklenburg, 1611–1918)

The duchy of Mecklenburg-Schwerin was established in 1611. It was re-established as a grand duchy in 1815. In 1871 it joined the new German empire, retaining its own monarchy until 1918, when Germany became a republic.

1785–1837	Frederick-Francis I
1837–42	Paul
1842–83	Frederick-Francis II
1883–97	Frederick-Francis III
1897–1918	Frederick Francis IV

Mecklenburg-Strelitz (Mecklenburg, 1701–1918)

The duchy of Mecklenburg-Strelitz was established in 1701. It was re-established as a grand duchy in 1815. In 1871 it joined the new German empire, retaining its own monarchy until 1918, when Germany became a republic.

1752–94	Adolf-Frederick IV
1794–1816	Charles
1816–60	George
1860–1904	Frederick-William
1904–14	Adolf-Frederick V
1914–18	Adolf-Frederick VI

Modena (Este, 1597–1797; Habsburg, 1814–59)

The duchy of Modena was formed in 1597. From 1797 until 1814 it was under French control as part of the Cisalpine republic and its successors, the Italian republic and the Bonapartist kingdom of Italy. The duchy was restored, under the Habsburgs, in 1814. In 1859 it was dissolved on its accession to the new Kingdom of Italy.

1780–97	Ercole III
1814–46	Francis IV
1846–59	Francis V

Monaco (Grimaldi since 1297)

The principality of Monaco was established in 1612. From 1793 until 1814 it was part of the French empire.

1733–93	Honoré III
1814–19	Honoré IV
1819–41	Honoré V
1841–56	Florestan
1856–89	Charles III
1889–1922	Albert
1922–49	Louis II
1949–	Rainier III

Montenegro (Petrovich, 1696–1918)

Montenegro was an autonomous part of the Ottoman empire from the late seventeenth century onwards. It was ruled by hereditary prince bishops until 1851, and thereafter run as a principality. In 1910 it became a kingdom which, in 1918, joined the new Kingdom of the Serbs, Croats and Slovenes (subsequently Yugoslavia).

1782–1830	Peter I
1830–51	Peter II
1851–60	Danilo II
1860–1918	Nicholas

Netherlands (Orange, 1572–1795, since 1813)

The United Provinces of the Netherlands were constituted under a *staatholder* in 1572, with the post being held by the Orange dynasty. This state was dissolved in 1795. The Netherlands was formed as a kingdom in 1813.

1751–95	William V
1813–40	William I
1840–49	William II
1849–90	William III
1898–1898	Regency (Emma)
1898–1948	Wilhelmina

1948–80	Juliana
1980–	Beatrix

Norway (Oldenburg since 1905)

The kingdom of Norway was established in 1905.

1905–57	Haakon VII
1957–91	Olaf V
1991–	Harald V

Oldenburg (Holstein-Gottorp, 1777–1806, 1815–1918)

The duchy of Oldenburg was established in 1777. From 1806 until 1813 it was controlled by France, with the duchy being restored in 1815. In 1871 it joined the new German empire, retaining its own monarchy until 1918, when Germany became a republic.

1785–1823	William
1823–29	Peter I
1829–53	August
1853–1900	Peter II
1900–18	Frederick-August II

Ottoman Empire (Ottoman)

The Ottoman empire was formed in the late thirteenth century, under a hereditary sultan. It dissolved in 1922.

1774–89	Abdul Hamid I
1789–1807	Selim III
1807–08	Mustafa IV
1808–39	Mahmud III
1839–61	Abdul Mejid
1861–76	Abdul Aziz
1876	Murad V
1876–1909	Abdul Hamid II
1909–18	Mohammed V
1918–22	Mohammed VI

Palatinate of the Rhine (Wittelsbach, 1214–1799)

The electorate of the Palatinate of the Rhine was formed in 1356. In 1799 it became part of Bavaria.

1742–99	Charles Theodore

Parma (Bourbon-Parma, 1731–99; Bourbon, 1814–59)

The duchy of Parma was formed in 1545. From 1799 until 1814 it was under French control, formally being annexed in 1805. The duchy was restored in 1814. In 1859 it was dissolved on its accession to the new kingdom of Italy.

1765–99	Frederick
1814–47	Marie-Louise
1847–49	Charles II
1849–54	Charles III
1854–59	Robert

Piedmont–Sardinia (Savoy, 1720–1861)

The kingdom of Piedmont–Sardinia was formed in 1720. In 1861 it became the leading state in the new kingdom of Italy, with its kings becoming kings of Italy.

1773–96	Victor Amadeus III
1796–1802	Charles Emmanuel IV
1802–21	Victor Emmanuel I
1821–24	Charles Felix I
1824–49	Charles Albert
1849–61	Victor Emmanuel II (subsequently King of Italy, 1861–78)

Poland (elected kings)

The kingdom of Poland was formed in 1320. It was dissolved in 1795.

1764–95	Stanislas Augustus

Portugal (Bragança, 1640–1910)

The kingdom of Portugal was formed in 1095. In 1910 it became a republic.

1777–86	Pedro III and Maria I
1786–1816	Maria I
1816–26	John VI
1826	Pedro IV
1826–28	Maria II
1828–34	Miguel
1834–53	Maria II (restored)
1853–61	Pedro V
1861–89	Luis
1889–1908	Carlos
1908–10	Manuel II

Romania (Cuza, 1859–66; Hohenzollern-Sigmaringen, 1866–1947)

The principality of Romania was formed in 1859. It became a kingdom in 1879, and a republic in 1947.

1859–66	Alexendru Cuza
1866–1914	Carol I
1914–27	Ferdinand
1927–30	Michael
1930–40	Carol II
1940–47	Michael (restored)

Saxony (Wettin, 1423–1918)

The electorate of Saxony was formed in 1423. In 1806 it became a kingdom. In 1871 it joined the new German empire, retaining its own monarchy until 1918, when Germany became a republic.

1763–1827	Frederick-August III (King Frederick-August I from 1806)
1827–36	Anton
1836–54	Frederick-August II
1854–73	John
1873–1902	Albrecht
1902–04	George
1914–18	Frederick-August III

Serbia (Obrenovich, 1817–42; Karageorgevich, 1842–58; Obrenovich, 1858–1903; Karageorgevich, 1903–18)

Serbia was made an autonomous principality of the Ottoman empire in 1817. It became an independent principality in 1878, then an independent kingdom in 1882. In 1918 it formed the core of the new Kingdom of the Serbs, Croats and Slovenes (subsequently Yugoslavia), with the Serbian monarch becoming monarch of the new kingdom.

1817–39	Milosh Obrenovich
1839	Milan I
1839–42	Michael
1842–58	Alexander Karageorge
1858–60	Milosh Obrenovich (restored)
1860–68	Michael (restored)
1868–89	Milan II
1889–1903	Alexander II
1903–18	Peter (subsequently Peter I, King of the Kingdom of Serbs, Croats and Slovenes)

Serbs, Croats and Slovenes

See Yugoslavia.

Sicilies, Two (Bourbon, 1734–1806; Bonaparte, 1806–15; Bourbon, 1815–60)

The kingdom of the Two Sicilies (Naples and Sicily) was formed in 1516 under the Spanish crown. It had its own king from 1759. It dissolved in 1860 on its accession to the new kingdom of Italy.

1759–1806	Ferdinand I
1806–08	Joseph Bonaparte
1808–15	Joachim I Bonaparte
1815–25	Ferdinand I (restored)
1825–30	Francis I
1830–59	Ferdinand II
1859–60	Francis II

Spain (Bourbon 1700–1808; Bonaparte, 1808–14; Bourbon, 1814–68; Savoy, 1870–73; Bourbon, 1874–1931, and since 1975)

The kingdom of Spain was formed in 1516. It was a republic from 1868 until 1870, and again from 1931 until 1939. Between 1939 and 1975 it was ruled by Francisco Franco as a one-party state, with a restoration of the monarchy planned to take place on his death. This occurred in 1975.

1788–1808	Charles IV
1808	Ferdinand VII
1808–14	Joseph Bonaparte
1814–33	Ferdinand VII (restored)
1833–68	Isabella II
1870–73	Amadeo
1874–85	Alfonso XII
1886–1931	Alfonso XIII
1975–	Juan Carlos

Sweden (Holstein-Gottorp 1751–1818; Bernadotte since 1814)

The kingdom of Sweden was formed in 1523.

1771–92	Gustavus III (also King of Norway)
1792–1809	Gustavus IV Adolphus (also King of Norway)
1809–18	Charles XIII (also King of Norway)
1818–44	Charles XIV John (also King of Norway)
1844–59	Oscar I (also King of Norway)
1859–72	Charles XV (also King of Norway)
1872–1907	Oscar II (also King of Norway until 1905)
1907–50	Gustavus V
1950–73	Gustavus VI

1973–	Charles XVI

Tuscany (Habsburg-Lorraine, 1737–1801, 1814–59)

The grand duchy of Tuscany was formed in 1569, and taken over by the Habsburgs in 1737. It was under French control from 1801 until 1814, established as the satellite kingdom of Etruria in 1801. The grand duchy was re-established in 1814. It was dissolved in 1859 on its accession to the new Kingdom of Italy.

1765–90	Leopold I
1790–1801	Ferdinand III
1814–24	Ferdinand III (restored)
1824–59	Leopold II

United Provinces

See Netherlands.

Württemburg (Württemburg, 1495–1918)

Württemburg was established as a duchy in 1495, and as a kingdom in 1806. In 1871 it joined the new German empire, retaining its own monarchy until 1918, when Germany became a republic.

1737–93	Charles-Eugene
1793–95	Ludwig-Eugene
1795–97	Frederick-Eugene
1797–1816	Frederick I
1816–64	William I
1864–91	Charles
1891–1918	William II

Yugoslavia (Karageorgevich, 1918–45)

The Kingdom of the Serbs, Croats and Slovenes was formed in 1918, changing its name to Yugoslavia in 1929. Yugoslavia became a republic in 1945.

1918–21	Peter I (formerly King of Serbia, 1903–18)
1918–21	Regency (Alexander)
1921–34	Alexander I
1934–41	Regency (Paul)
1941–45	Peter II (in exile, 1941–45)

Index

This index lists all of the entries in the text, arranged thematically under the following headings:

1 International relations, treaties and conferences
2 Non-state organisations, movements, political parties and ideologies
3 People
4 Revolutions and rebellions
5 Social and economic issues
6 Wars, battles and military campaigns

These thematic headings are followed by entries relating to internal events within individual countries. Some items appear in more than one category.

International relations, treaties and conferences

Non-state organisations, movements, political parties and ideologies

People

Revolutions and rebellions

Social and economic issues

Wars, battles and campaigns

Individual countries: internal events

Austria

Cyprus

Czechoslovakia

France

German states (see also Germany, Prussia)

Germany (see also German states)

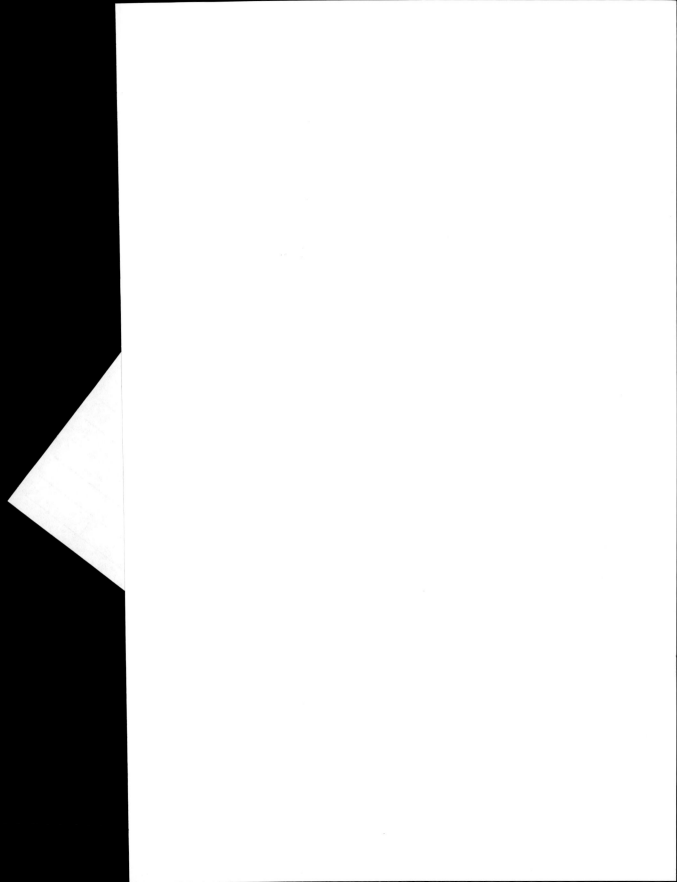

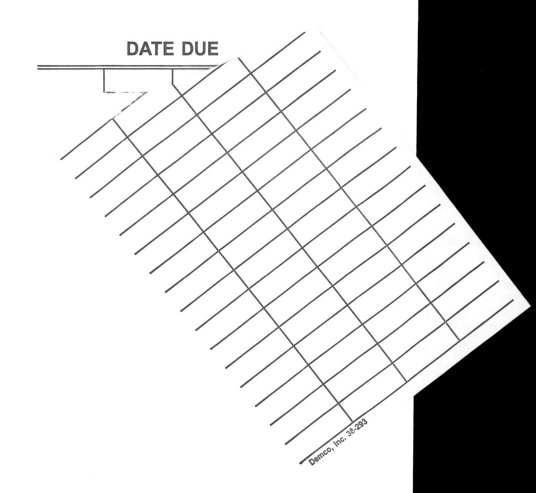